"This remarkable compendium of Jane Jacobs's writing covers a period that begins long before the publication of *The Death and Life of Great American Cities* and ends long after. We see how, piece by piece, she expanded her range into the next ring of connected ideas, periodically consolidating them in a book or an article, edging ever closer to a kind of unified theory linking ecology, economy, ethics, and social mores and their manifestations in real places. Like her fundamental observation about the city itself, her work was never finished."

—KEN GREENBERG, urban designer
and author of *Walking Home*

"Reading Jane Jacobs's short works again tells us what a visionary and creative thinker she was. Her words are as fresh today as when she wrote them and speak to us by telling compelling stories. There is, yesterday, today, and tomorrow, 'no virtue in meek conformity.' This collection is a treasure for us all."

—JANICE GROSS STEIN, professor, Munk School
of Global Affairs, University of Toronto

"*Vital Little Plans* is an immensely important retrospective of Jane Jacobs's articles and speeches. Her belief in the power of residents to make cities economically, environmentally, and socially successful shines through, as does her disdain for those who would build cities for cars, not people."

—DAVID MILLER, president and CEO of
WWF-Canada and former mayor of Toronto

"This indispensable anthology is a delight. Through older works and new writings, the urgency of Jane Jacobs's message continues to ring clear. This book further exposes us to Jacobs's unconventional, process-oriented thinking, and positions us to take action to transform our cities. There is a better world around us, if we are willing to see it. *Vital Little Plans* is simply superb."

—JENNIFER KEESMAAT, chief planner,
City of Toronto

"A book to get your blood running and ideas soaring!"
—MINDY THOMPSON FULLILOVE,
author of *Urban Alchemy*

"We seem to be facing a perfect storm. The population of cities will double to 7 billion in just thirty-five years, while we endure climate change, traffic congestion, a public health crisis, and an aging population. These are challenges, but we can also see them as opportunities. The world clearly needs more Jane Jacobs. In *Vital Little Plans*, she provides vision and action to create cities for people, especially those most vulnerable: children, older adults, and the poor."
—GUILLERMO (GIL) PEÑALOSA, founder and chair of
8 80 Cities and chair of World Urban Parks

"We know Jane Jacobs wrote brilliant books, and it would a crime to let her equally brilliant smaller writings, speeches, and interviews be lost. This collection is more than the sum of its parts, and is a great book to have at your fingertips."
—BRENT TODERIAN, city planner and urbanist, TODERIAN
UrbanWORKS, and former chief planner of Vancouver

"Don't cheat yourself of the pleasure that lies between these covers."
—JEFF SPECK, author of *Walkable City*

"An essential read for those wanting to understand the contradiction and chaos of a woman whose legacy is that we must all think for ourselves. The editors have brilliantly selected and sequenced Jacobs's writing so that we can plainly see how she wrestles with, and problem-solves around, messy and complex systems. Many of us have only scratched the surface with Jacobs, ending our love affair with her work at a time when she'd just begun to connect the dots. Reading through the entire pilgrimage makes the calls to action more vivid and more urgent than ever before."
—DENISE PINTO, executive director, Jane's Walk

VITAL LITTLE PLANS

VITAL LITTLE PLANS

—

THE SHORT WORKS OF

JANE JACOBS

—

EDITED BY

Samuel Zipp and Nathan Storring

RANDOM HOUSE

NEW YORK

Published in the United States by Random House,
an imprint and division of Penguin Random House LLC, New York.

RANDOM HOUSE and the HOUSE colophon are registered
trademarks of Penguin Random House LLC.

Most of the essays in this work have been previously published.
Original publication information is included with each essay. Credits and
permissions are on page 467.

LIBRARY OF CONGRESS CATALOGING-IN-PUBLICATION DATA
NAMES: Jacobs, Jane, 1916–2006, author. |
Zipp, Samuel, editor. | Storring, Nathan, editor.
TITLE: Vital little plans : the short works of Jane Jacobs / edited by
Samuel Zipp and Nathan Storring.
DESCRIPTION: New York : Random House, [2016] | Includes bibliographical
references and index.
IDENTIFIERS: LCCN 2016014099| ISBN 9780399589607 |
ISBN 9780399589614 (ebook)
SUBJECTS: LCSH: City planning—United States. | City planning. |
Sociology, Urban—United States. | Sociology, Urban. | Urban policy—
United States. | Urban policy. | Jacobs, Jane, 1916–2006.
CLASSIFICATION: LCC HT167 .J324 2016 | DDC 307.1/2160973—dc23
LC record available at lccn.loc.gov/2016014099

Printed in the United States of America on acid-free paper

randomhousebooks.com

9 8 7 6 5 4 3 2 1

First Edition

Title page portrait by Ruth Orkin
Book design by Barbara M. Bachman

TO NEW YORK AND TORONTO,
TWO GREAT NORTH AMERICAN CITIES

Contents

———

Jane Jacobs lost in thought as she reads The Decline and Fall of the Roman Empire *in the living room of her house at 555 Hudson Street, New York City, circa 1956.*

Introduction

—

Samuel Zipp and Nathan Storring

"More Jane Jacobs, less Marc Jacobs" reads the bold-faced sign peering out from behind age-rippled glass along a side street in New York's Greenwich Village. This minor protest, which popped up several years ago in the windows of the neighborhood's few remaining unprimped townhouses and non-chain stores, pits urbanist icon against fashion designer in a proxy war between locality and luxury. A small, clever note trilling in a familiar sorrow song, it's a discordant flutter disturbing an otherwise triumphant era of urban symphony. We live in a golden age for city life, we're told again and again these days. In the rich parts of the world, despite deepening inequality (probably because of it, the sorrow song objects) the streets are teeming with cyclists and new condos and artisans and pop-up parklets. But cities, it seems, are somehow also dying. Or, at the very least, a certain idea of the city is under threat. Some cherished sense of what it means to be urban feels as if it might be losing its footing, staggering, and going down.

Most city lovers have an intimate sense of what this loss might entail, even if they don't know exactly how to describe what they are losing. The sign's maker, Mike Joyce, said that most people got the point even if they didn't quite follow the joke. Anyone could see that there was suddenly a surplus of Marc Jacobs–like chain boutiques popping up around the neighborhood. But who, they often asked, is this Jane Jacobs? It's a tragic irony: Marc Jacobs, a self-described native son and lover of New York, unwittingly drives out the urban virtues that Jane Jacobs taught the world to see, even as her name begins to fade from popular memory.[1]

What is at stake here, it seems, is the "intricate sidewalk ballet" that Jane Jacobs famously witnessed on Hudson Street in Greenwich Village and described in her most celebrated book, *The Death and Life of Great American Cities* (1961). The performance Jacobs recounted, with its daily circulation of motley players—schoolkids and shopkeepers, longshoremen and office workers, slaughterhouse hands and beatniks on motor scooters, drunks with hats unapproved by the "Hat Council," and "beautiful girls" getting out of snappy British sports cars—is increasingly imperiled for all but the latterday descendants of those beautiful girls. In the very neighborhood where Jacobs discovered the self-organizing drama of healthy urban order, the chance for just anyone to play a part in the city dance, to enjoy the perennial promise of a local life lived close to the grain of the streets, stoops, and stores, seems to be slipping away or already departed.

So what else is new? "The Village" was lost as soon as it was found. Gentrification panic is perennial, too, going back years before Jacobs made her name there in the 1950s and '60s. People still flock to Greenwich Village to shop and eat, to stroll around and gawk at everyone else shopping and eating and strolling around. People still go just to be there—these pleasures are part of the dance, too. So the Village endures, but as a bright and blurry clone of a past self. With astronomic rents came chain stores, fashion boutiques, luxury condo conversions in glass and steel. They have crowded out hardware stores, bodegas, diners, bookstores, small manufacturing shops, the unpredictable and the odd. Real estate speculation, long a New York obsession, has finally chased out most everything else but rarefied shopping and eating and looking. The diverse mixture of people with plans both humble and grand that Jacobs celebrated can find little purchase in this meager city soil.

So it goes in Toronto, too, Jane Jacobs's second home. In the Annex, the neighborhood where she lived until her death in 2006, the commercial vitality she often celebrated feels under threat. Rents are on the rise, neighborhood businesses fold and are replaced by replicas of the most profitable uses on the street, mostly high-traffic restaurants, college bars, and bank branches. Even a Bloor Street icon like Honest Ed's isn't safe. A vast neon-fronted discount emporium where generations of immigrants, working-class shoppers, bargain lovers, and in-the-know ironists foraged among the shelves is soon to be leveled and replaced with a cluster of glassy condos and retail boxes. Everywhere like this, the familiar lament goes, in London, San Francisco, Boston, Paris, and other urban magnets across the Global North where money and people cluster, the city is turning on itself, its very success becoming its undoing.[2]

There's no doubt, then, that this is just the right time for "more Jane Jacobs." Whether it's a Golden Age or a Dark Age, it is just the right time for more of her incomparable writings about cities and the worlds they create, just the right time to retrieve her bracing, obstinate voice for readers who've forgotten it or never knew it in the first place. And yet one of the chief reasons to return to Jacobs now, and to this collection of shorter works spanning her entire career as a writer, is to help us reimagine Jacobs herself as something more than a symbol of urban sorrow or urban triumph. Always idiosyncratic and unorthodox, often surprising, often willing to risk being wrong if it means reorienting stale conventional wisdom, she pushes beyond the familiar alarms to see urban transformation as a source of radical possibility and opportunity, not nostalgia and loss. More than a tribune of the ideal neighborhood, Jacobs was perhaps our greatest theorist of the city not as a modern machine for living but as a living human system, geared for solving its own problems.

Learn to look as Jacobs did at cities, as well as the other themes she considered over the course of her long writing life—economies, morality, politics, and history—and things may come to seem more complex and interconnected than we first expect, and even perhaps less dire. Cities are not only quaint stage sets imperiled by gentrification but also the medium of our collective public and economic life, the forum in which we can learn to harness change to resolve our shared problems and to produce shared opportunity. Even in an era in which our society seems ever more stagnant, marked by both the fattening of the rich and the multiplying of the poor, reading Jacobs anew suggests that the way out lies not only in rearguard actions to protect what we cherish but in reinvigorating the creative, chaotic, improvisational economies of cities.

This book offers readers a chance to see Jane Jacobs whole for the first time. Over the years she has been called many things: an urban visionary, an anti-planner, an amateur economist, a geographer, a community activist, and a radical centrist. Each label captures some facet of her work, but in hemming her in with one category or another, each fails to encompass the range, variety, and provocative power of her ideas and pursuits, not to mention the way she was able to cross and blur the lines between disciplines, often outflanking one school of thought with another. The essays, speeches, interviews, and one long-forgotten poem collected here show her first and foremost as she herself hoped to be understood: as a thinker and writer with one of the most distinctive literary voices of the last century.

Vital Little Plans is organized chronologically, following the long arc of Jacobs's writing career. But even as she added new work to her old work (as she might have put it) she returned to older ideas with fresh insights. Each part of the book builds on the last as she embellishes her lifelong interest in cities, economies, and morality. Whenever possible we have presented her words unaltered and unabridged. We have also included notes to identify unfamiliar references and to point out some useful connections among the ecology of her ideas.

The selections begin with her first pieces of magazine and newspaper reportage from Depression-era New York and culminate with the big ideas about humanity's past and future that she wrestled with at the end of her life. Parts One and Two, "A City Naturalist" and "City Building," follow her first thirty years in New York, from the 1930s to the 1960s, as she learns the journalism trade and discovers the city. Many readers will be most familiar with Part Two, where we find Jacobs rehearsing the critique of city planning for which she would become famous in *Death and Life*. Perhaps surprisingly, however, the pieces collected here show us that early on in her career, as she rose to become an editor at *Architectural Forum* and an expert on contemporary architecture, she was a supporter of modern city planning and rebuilding. They reveal how she turned on those orthodoxies as she discovered that the new highways, slum clearance projects, and "tower-in-the-park" complexes were uprooting old neighborhoods, scattering community life, deepening racial segregation, and trampling the rough and ready city she had come to love. Her famed showdowns with New York's urban renewal bureaucracy and her jousts with the "master builder" Robert Moses are here, as are her celebrations of the pleasures and necessities of everyday city life, the very "chaos" that modern planning looked to weed out of the cityscape.[3]

Readers tend to cherish Jacobs for a series of scenes from this period: *Death and Life*'s opening "attack on current city planning and rebuilding"; the "eyes on the street" that make cities safe; her four "generators of city diversity" (density, mixed uses, short blocks, and cheap old buildings); and of course the much-beloved "sidewalk ballet." But this volume shows that the episodes and ideas for which she is still best remembered are the prelude to a much greater body of work. She spent the rest of her long life, in six other books, dramatically expanding the ideas she had debuted in *Death and Life*. In the process she forged a unique take on the interrelated life of cities, economies, and morality, one that readers can watch evolve in the pages of *Vital Little Plans*.

Much of that work was jumpstarted by another of her unique observations, one that is sometimes overlooked. What planners viewed as chaos she had come to see as a "complex and highly developed form of order." The city, she surmised at the close of *Death and Life,* was an always-unfolding problem in handling this "organized complexity." Rather than a simple two-variable problem as in the physical sciences or a million-variable problem of statistics, Jacobs saw the city as something akin to an ecosystem with many moving parts, each with its own relationship to the others. This idea would become a touchstone of her later work, informing all her investigations of economic and social life, but it had its roots in her earliest interests in the workings of cities at the micro scale.

In fact, readers of *Vital Little Plans* will discover that she had been on the trail of this idea from the very beginning of her career. Her earliest writings for *Vogue* and other magazines, collected in Part One, may appear insubstantial at first, but linger a bit and they shed the guise of conventional magazine reportage to come alive as limpid little gems of close noticing. In "Caution, Men Working," for instance, she investigates the manhole landscape of Manhattan, uncovering the vast networks of underground "spaghetti" beneath the city streets. The essay gives us the indelible image of Jacobs, "the city naturalist," standing at Fourteenth Street and Fourth Avenue feeling the mail shunting by in pneumatic tubes under her feet at thirty miles an hour. Like the other 1930s pieces collected here—on the diamond trade and the flower market—it reveals her setting out to find clues to the way individual elements of her surroundings are linked by larger processes hiding in plain sight.

What we are seeing in these pieces is the original spark for her trademark inductive method and her discovery of the city's "organized complexity." She follows anecdotes and observations up from the street, scale by scale, to discover the systems that make them go. Later she would call such bits and pieces of data "fractals," renditions of a broader pattern in miniature. At the center of these stories are the relationships within particular industries; each florist and jewel merchant is a node in the self-inventing, self-organizing network of the city. It's a first glimpse of what, two decades later, in her celebrated essay "Downtown Is for People" (included here) she'd call "the small specialized enterprise," strung in a web of interdependencies with other diverse yet complementary undertakings. Imagine Joseph Mitchell, the legendary *New Yorker* city reporter, turned loose in the city to find odd occupations rather than odd characters. Where Mitchell discovered solemn urban nocturnes and disappearing ways of life, Jacobs found interlinked economic niches, messy meshes of city work and trade giving rise to cosmopolitan verve and bustle.

Jacobs's long-standing curiosities were brought to a head in the decades after the publication of *Death and Life,* when, like so many others, she wondered why cities and nations in the West were in decline. She had shown that modern planning schemes were misguided attempts to revive city life. But she felt that something deeper, something more pervasive and odious, was afoot in these years. What had gone wrong? In true Jacobs fashion, she flipped the question on its head. The quandary was not why cities stagnated but why they grew in the first place. Poverty has no causes, she believed; only prosperity has causes. Figure out how economic growth worked, and the causes of the era's problems would become clear.

Her essays and speeches from the 1960s to the 1980s see her returning to the scenes and concepts that informed *Death and Life*—she was often asked to "play the hits"—but always with an eye to asking the broader questions she pursued in her two major works of the period: *The Economy of Cities* (1969) and *Cit-*

ies and the Wealth of Nations (1984). Across Parts Three and Four of this volume, "How New Work Begins" and "The Ecology of Cities," readers will find Jacobs distilling the chief lessons of her years spent thinking about city economies. She considered these ideas the most important of her career, and near the end of her life she returned to them in *Uncovering the Economy,* a book she hoped would fully explain her vision. She never finished it, but the opening section of that book, published here for the first time (in Part Five) reveals her final understanding of how economic growth unfolds. In short, Jacobs argues that healthy cities are where new work springs up. Their dense fabric of interdependencies incubates economic expansion and innovation at large. Cultivating vibrant urban centers with small, diverse commercial and industrial enterprises is the linchpin of any meaningful strategy to combat decline.

But how to actually do this on the ground, in existing cities? Little seemed to be working. Like many of the so-called free market advocates, those devotees of Friedrich Hayek or Milton Friedman who rose to public prominence in the wake of the economic downturn of the 1970s, Jacobs believed in the self-organizing capacities of economic life. "Organized complexity" could produce order without orders from above. She was also dubious about the forms of aid offered by various national or international plans for economic development—the War on Poverty, World Bank lending programs, massive federal spending on the defense industry—seeing them as just more prescriptive dictates unleashed from on high, sure to deaden urban economies. But unlike the "neoliberals" whose market fundamentalism has, until recently, dominated public life in the United States, she understood how these strategies tended to plow subsidies to already entrenched interests. In that sense, she saw a more active role for government as what she called a "third force" in the market, ready to protect young enterprises from established players. Instead of obsessing over stabilizing the business cycle, she advocated for policies that would enable self-organizing networks of small producers to solve problems in new ways and overturn the socioeconomic status quo (see "The Real Problem of Cities," included in Part Three).

Jacobs's ideas went largely unheeded in the halls of power, but they led her to think more deeply about the classic tussle between commerce and government. Cities, she told an audience of Amsterdammers in 1984, lived or died by the "web of trust" between people in their everyday working lives (see "The Responsibilities of Cities" in Part Four). In order to preserve the open-ended possibility inherent in vital cities, societies had to recognize that this trust depended on a system of morality—she came to call it the "commercial moral syndrome"—and carefully delineate its relations with government and other watchdogs, which were guided by a different, opposed set of morals, the "guardian syndrome." As she says in her 1992 book *Systems of Survival* (and here in "Two Ways to Live"), guardians value loyalty, tradition, and the right to use deception and force, while those who work under the "commercial syndrome" prize honesty, novelty, and collaboration with "strangers and aliens." These syndromes, Jacobs argues, govern society at every level, from public policy to individual decision-making. Not all businesspeople are honest, nor are all police officers loyal, but to violate these tenets—or worse yet, mix them in a "moral hybrid"—is to court disaster.

While she thought government should intervene in the market as a nimble regulator, she also believed it was perverse for it to engage in commerce and industry itself.[4] Given that much public policy by the 1980s and '90s—particularly in cities—was carried out by way of public-private partnership, it's no surprise that she found the prospects for vibrant city growth in these years wanting. What was lacking, she argued, was a proper vision of the "symbiotic" relations between the two "moral syndromes." They had to remain separate but mutually beneficial. To her, that balancing act was the very "art of civilization" that we all negotiate in our everyday public lives.*

Beyond the lifelong quandaries she pursued in her books, *Vital Little Plans* reveals that Jacobs had a host of incisive things to say about issues she's not often remembered for. In "Metropolitan Government" she delivers one of the first popular exposés of the "cross-purpose jackstraw heap of local sovereignties" that continue to hamstring cities today. "The Sparrow Principle" sees her thinking aloud about the linked histories of imperialism and globalization. Elsewhere in this volume she takes on any number of topics that still resonate: civil disobedience and the dynamics of social movements, the perennial predicament in public finance of ample "money for building things" and little "money for running things," the future of suburbs and skyscrapers, the politics of cycling in the city, the coming boom in urban agriculture, the trouble with zoning, and many more besides, including feminism, environmentalism, and immigration,

---

* See Jane Jacobs, "Systems of Economic Ethics, Part 2," *Ethics in Making a Living: The Jane Jacobs Conference,* 1989, p. 269.

Jane Jacobs sits in a jail cell next to Susan Sontag after being arrested during an anti-Vietnam War demonstration at an armed forces induction center in New York, 1967. They were arrested alongside more than 250 others, including Dr. Benjamin Spock and poet Allen Ginsberg.

not to mention the gentrification troubles so vexing to city lovers today.

THERE IS A MUCH-LOVED photograph of Jane Jacobs sitting in jail, awaiting booking. She is side by side with the writer Susan Sontag, who looks characteristically defiant. Jacobs appears calmer, and a bit world-weary, as if she were barely enduring the regular idiocy of bureaucratic authority. They ended up there, along with more than 250 other demonstrators, after an antiwar protest at New York's Whitehall draft induction center in December of 1967. The picture puts her at the heart of her times—it's a snapshot from our collective idea of "the Sixties." And it's all the more poignant when we know what is on the horizon: A year later the Vietnam War would bring to a boiling point the frustrations Jacobs first felt at the onslaught of modern planning a decade before and push her family to flee the United States for Canada.

Death and Life remains a great predictor of the era's upheaval, one of the first in that remarkable early Sixties run of seismic books—Paul Goodman's *Growing Up Absurd,* Frantz Fanon's *The Wretched of the Earth,* Rachel Carson's *Silent Spring,* Betty Friedan's *The Feminine Mystique,* Michael Harrington's *The Other America,* James Baldwin's *The Fire Next Time,* Herbert Marcuse's *One-Dimensional Man*—that would start to rearrange the minds of a whole generation. Like so many writers and thinkers in those years, she made her name skewering received wisdoms. By the end of the decade, when she found herself sitting with Sontag in central booking, her distress with New York and America had reached a tipping point. In 1970 she would find herself, in "The Real Problem of Cities," endorsing battles against urban freeway construction with that trusty Sixties slogan, "Power to the People!"

But look again and the overall picture becomes murkier. For all her disgust with the abuse of power, incandescently apparent in "On Civil Disobedience" in Part Three, her intellectual work sits uneasily next to the radical thinkers of the moment like

Sontag and Fanon or Baldwin and Marcuse or Norman Mailer or Shulamith Firestone or Michel Foucault. While others were exposing hierarchies and celebrating the seditious rush of excess, making strange the normal and questioning the given order of things, Jacobs set her sights on revealing the beauty and necessity of underlying norms. Her work is cousin to critical theory and social history and the other radical visions of the era, but Jacobs was ultimately working to reinvent the principles by which we understand urban and economic life. She was not afraid to shatter settled thought, but she was set on fitting the shards back together, too, with ideas some of those other Sixties icons would have found altogether bourgeois.[5]

Her politics, like her urbanism, tended toward the pragmatic. She distrusted most visions of utopia. For her, the rallying cry of the 1968 Paris general strikes—"Under the paving stones, the beach!"—wasn't likely to inspire. Beneath the city streets, she might have retorted, was nothing more than the dirt to which we will all return. Another world isn't possible, certainly not if it's some eden of plenty and ease, reachable only by revolution or the utopian imagination. A better world is here already, in the streets themselves, waiting to be discovered and brought forth by all of us, not just a radical vanguard.

Jacobs looked askance at any situation in which people were spoken for, rather than allowed to speak for themselves. Like many who came of age during the Depression, World War II, and the Cold War, she had watched the authoritarian drift of the Soviet Union with dismay and feared that orders, violence, and censorship from on high were endemic to utopian plans of that sort. She was even wary about the social movements she joined and led and for which she is now often remembered and revered. In "The Responsibilities of Cities," she worries that too often, popular movements "have to claim that they speak for people who, in fact, have never given them a mandate to do so." Protest was a necessary hassle—and she always resented the way campaigns to stop what she called "absurd" plans disrupted her writing life—but the very need for demonstrations, she thought, was a symptom of institutional bankruptcy.

The truth is that Jacobs offers little comfort to established political traditions, whether radical or conservative, or to official scholarly pursuits. She inspires and frustrates in equal measure. The left loves her community rabble-rousing and her democratic spirit but distrusts her faith in the private sector; the right thinks her a closeted ally, keen to promote privatization, but ignores her concessions to government. Mainstream economists have assimilated her account of the added benefits of competitive, diverse clusters of industries to economic productivity—"Jacobs externalities," they call them—but they also fault her for her willingness to flout (some say misinterpret) long-established economic principles and practices, like supply and demand or statistics-driven analysis. Architects and planners have taken her critiques to heart but sometimes feel that she threw the baby of planning out with the bathwater of modernist city building. Historians and sociologists appreciate her close attention to the details of everyday city life, but fault her for a failure to understand the way that the social power of race, class, and gender has shaped both public policy and private markets. Stratified social relations, they argue, will always undermine the self-organizing networks Jacobs hoped to uncover and nurture.

Jacobs delighted in irking all the specialists and ideologues, from planners and sociologists to libertarians and Marxists. She was wary of traditions of political thought and suspicious of rigid modes of disciplinary academic knowledge production. Despite her interest in the systems by which life organizes itself, she nevertheless kept systems of organized thought at arm's length. As a result her work often feels sui generis, crafted from her various enthusiasms, her eye for details and processes, and her wide-ranging, unstructured reading in history, philosophy, economics, science, and literature. One thing, however, underpinned all her work: a basic faith that the market is not inherently exploitative. Inequality and economic crises are problems to be solved. They are bugs, not features, of capitalism.

In fact, reading Jacobs, some may feel that the last three hundred years never quite happened. Where, some might ask, in her world of streets and sidewalks and plucky small firms, is the rise of capitalism and its twin products, great wealth and great inequality? Where is industrialization, with its steam engines and railroads and smokestacks plunging the day into sooty dark? Where is the rise and fall of slavery, the formation of the working class, the commodification of human labor, the power of race to immiserate whole classes of people due to the color of their skin? Where are finance and credit as instruments of accumulation or the political and legal fabrication of the corporation as an entity akin to a person? Where is the great consolidating sweep of modernity, rushing ahead to forge an economy of great power and violence, an economy in which, just as Jacobs was coming of age, industrial unions were facing off against bosses over the conditions of work in the great assembly-line factories? And what about the world-altering forces that shaped the troubled cities she surveyed during her own career: deindustrialization and the mobility of capital, globalization, and out-sourcing?

Of course, many of these great processes were present in her work. She had read Karl Marx and Adam Smith; she wrote about Henry Ford, the Dodge brothers, General Motors, and the rise of Detroit. She told the story of Eastman Kodak and Xerox in the making and unmaking of industrial Rochester; she analyzed the way new technologies could devastate whole regions and "make people redundant." But these case studies never quite formed up on the page in any of the usual historical narratives of industrial growth or inequality in the modern age. In fact, Jacobs favored an ahistorical take on economies, looking for principles that stretched across all of human history. Many of her models, for instance, were drawn from antiquity or the Middle Ages. As sources of telling patterns she favored the digs at prehistoric Çatal Hüyük in what is today Turkey, or the story of ancient Rome, or the rise of the medieval trading towns scattered along the rim of the emerging Atlantic world. And when it came to the big factory cities of the past two centuries she looked for inspiration in what she called the "unaverage clues" offered by places where small firms rather than giant assembly plants predominated: Birmingham not Manchester, New York not Detroit.

Jacobs tended to look at history the way she did a cityscape. She scouted around for promising examples of individual phenomena, situations in which city or economic life seemed to have been working, and then sought to understand the processes that organized these data into constructive systems. Large, amorphous categories, particularly those that carried with them guarantees about how people would behave, left her cold. Class, capitalism, the division of labor—in Jacobs's view these have descriptive but not explanatory power. They are neither the driving forces of history nor the fundamental conundrums of human life. And for her they risk shackling us to preformed narratives that restrict our ability to understand how actual people make and remake the market in everyday life.

At its core, one might say, Jacobs's vision is one of markets without capitalism. It's a theory not of historical development but of always existing possibility.[6] Markets are a source not only of alienation but of exchange and contact, not simply building blocks of national productivity but wellsprings of new ideas and self-making in concert with others. She rested her conception of human social life not on the struggle between workers and capitalists or the laws of supply and demand but on the struggle of humans to forge new work from old in a society that favors established interests. Small, young enterprises and their employees, particularly those engaged in unglamorous work producing necessary goods and services that solve everyday problems behind the scenes—industrial adhesives, for instance, or a new kind of window frame—need protection from corrosive concentrations of bureaucratic power, whether corporate or governmental, private or public. And not only the "innovators" we fetishize today. While innovation often solves our pressing problems, Jacobs argues, all kinds of new local work drive our economy. Creative imitation, not innovation, in her words, is the major driver of economic expansion. This, in a way, was as close as she came to utopia, her vision of "power to the people." The just city and nation is a place where anyone's creative impulses to "dicker" and improvise and reinvent them-

selves would be unleashed, where everyone would have the opportunity to make their own "vital little plans."

BY THE END OF HER LIFE, Jacobs had begun to think toward
her own, unique account of the great transformations of the
past several centuries. She even ventured some glimpses of possible futures. "The End of the Plantation Age," in Part Five, sees
Jacobs developing a theory of human history, one she did not
have the chance to complete. A companion piece to *Dark Age
Ahead* (2004), the speech finds her leavening the gloom of that
book's dire worries with the prospect of a profound, forward-
looking transformation.

The "Plantation Age" of her title is a long era of human history from which she believes we are only now emerging. For
centuries, she says, human effort was organized on the top-
down "plantation" model. The term invokes the horrors of
slavery and forced labor, of course, but it also includes industrialization, with its armies of workers enduring routinized, "sci-
entifically managed" tasks. Unlike other thinkers, whether
radical, centrist, or conservative, she did not see the Industrial
Revolution as a fundamental disjuncture in history. To her, the
factory was little more than a machine-made plantation, as
much an icon of the age as urban renewal, mass suburbs, or the
twin towers of the World Trade Center. This era may have produced great wealth—culminating in the relatively shared prosperity of the mid-twentieth-century boom—but it was always
a "monoculture" inevitably tending toward stagnation and
waste. The plantation mentality used economies of scale and
planned results to turn workers into little more than peons—

each a potential "trader" betrayed and wasted. It was a form of production for production's sake that eclipsed the far more vibrant worlds of exchange and everyday innovation found in cities enlivened by trade, with their small enterprises, diverse peoples, and mixtures of face-to-face uses.

But now, she says, that era might be receding. What's on the horizon? Jacobs never relished the role of prophet, but at the end of her life she hazarded two related but opposite guesses. One path was what she called, in *Dark Age Ahead,* "cultural collapse." Jacobs found evidence of imminent decline in the erosion of family, community, science, education, governance, and professional integrity in North America. She even identified the danger of the housing bubble, just as it was inflating in the early years of the millennium. More than a decade later it's hard not to remain dismayed. In a time of renewed inequality and recalcitrant structural racism, with lead staining the water of Flint, Michigan, the grim and ongoing exposure of police brutality, and the craven exploits of financial capitalism fresh in so many people's minds, the "symbiosis" between "guardians" and "traders" Jacobs hoped for appears considerably out of whack. The guardians are asleep, inept, vicious, or on the take, the traders simply gone feral.

More orthodox thinkers, on the left or right, might consider these outcomes endemic to their usual targets: capitalism or big government or privatization or the welfare state. Jacobs, however, offered a different story, a possible path out of the morass. In that last speech she spied signs of not a Dark Age coming but an "age of human capital." Elsewhere, in notes for the book she hoped to write—tentatively titled "A Short Biography of the Human Race"—she called it the "second creative age." Those notes suggest that racism and other plantation-age "concepts of industrial, spatial, and political order" linger as "hangovers" or "anachronisms," but she also foresaw an emerging possibility that humans might find a way to return, by way of their creative impulses, to an era of revivified people power, when a new-found symbiosis between traders and guardians would push cities back into the business of producing "new work."

Jacobs never finished her own new work, and she was, until the end, quite mindful of the possibility that any innovative tendencies could be betrayed by the lure of plantation-style bigness. It's fitting, though, that in her final speech she would not accept that the future was foreclosed. Her radical pragmatism, in this as in all things, led her to look for the ways people might live in the flow of their own time and, in making do with what they have, also make their world anew.

Whatever one thinks of her diagnoses and prognostications —and they certainly rely on a robust faith in the essential goodness and industriousness of people—the promise of even a bit "more Jane Jacobs" is surely welcome. Beset as we are by any number of trials, whether it's the threat of climate change, the dovetailing of globalization and automation, persistent poverty and inequality, the twin perils of terrorism and nationalism, or just misguided urban projects and the creep of gentrification, longtime followers of Jacobs will relish returning to her for fresh problem-solving inspiration. And if a new generation of readers find it galvanizing to discover her bracing, plainspoken talent for revealing the interwoven problems of cities, economies, and morals, we can all take heart knowing that even in her last years she was still pushing on, offering us a new vision of death and life.

NOTES

1.   See "More Jane, Less Marc," *Jeremiah's Vanishing New York*, October 16, 2009, vanishingnewyork.blogspot.com/2009/10/more-jane-less-marc .html. Accessed March 7, 2016. Jane Jacobs's memory, however, received a boost that very same summer when the stretch of Hudson Street where she lived was renamed Jane Jacobs Way.

2.   Jacobs's vision of the city has sometimes been blamed for the gentrification of neighborhoods like the Village or the Annex. In *Death and Life*, however, before the term "gentrification" had even been invented, she herself saw that too much neighborhood success resulted in the "self-destruction of diversity," and offered potential policy solutions, too. In this volume, see "Reason, Emotion, Pressure" and "Time and Change as Neighborhood Allies" for some of her ideas about forestalling gentrification.

3.   For more on Jacobs's early history and the formation of the ideas that would go into *Death and Life*, see Peter L. Laurence, *Becoming Jane Jacobs* (Philadelphia: University of Pennsylvania Press, 2016).

4.   She did make two significant exceptions to her disapproval of government service provision. She saw healthcare and education as guardian functions and therefore fair game for an active government role. See "Efficiency and the Commons" in Part Five.

5.   See Timothy Mennel, "Jane Jacobs, Andy Warhol, and the Kind of Problem a Community Is," in Max Page and Timothy Mennel, *Reconsidering Jane Jacobs* (Chicago: Planners Press, 2011), 119–28, for further thoughts on Jacobs, the Sixties, and norms.

6.   For an elaboration of this idea, see the work of the philosopher Manuel De Landa, who likens Jacobs to historians like Fernand Braudel who have written about the "meshwork" of early market economies. De Landa, *A Thousand Years of Nonlinear History* (Brooklyn, N.Y.: Zone Books, 1997), 25–99.

Timeline

————

LIFE EVENTS	YEAR	WRITING
MAY 4: Jane Jacobs (née Butzner) is born in Scranton, Pennsylvania	1916	
Attends stenography course at Powell School of Business	1933	
Works at the *Scranton Republican* newspaper		
Visits aunt Martha for four months in isolated Higgins, North Carolina, laying foundation of thinking about economic stagnation	1934	
Moves to Brooklyn, New York, to live with sister		PART ONE: *A City Naturalist*
Moves to Greenwich Village in New York City	1935	"While Arranging Verses for a Book"
	1936	"Diamonds in the Tough"
	1937	"Flowers Come to Town"
Is given manuscript of memoir by great-aunt Hannah Breece published fifty years later as *A Schoolteacher in Old Alaska*		
Father, John Decker Butzner, dies		
Enrolls in University Extension program at Columbia University	1938	

Daughter, Burgin (née Mary) Hyde Jacobs, is born	1955	"Philadelphia's Redevelopment: A Progress Report"
Takes first tour of East Harlem with William Kirk of Union Settlement House, who teaches her about social capital		
Begins career as Greenwich Village activist by signing petition to stop highway construction through Washington Square Park		
Begins covering urban renewal for *Forum*		
Speaks at Harvard conference on urban design, gaining notoriety among architects and critics	1956	"Pavement Pounders and Olympians"
		"The Missing Link in City Redevelopment"
	1957	"Our 'Surplus' Land"
		"Reason, Emotion, Pressure: There Is No Other Recipe"
		"Metropolitan Government"
Works with Joint Emergency Committee to Close Washington Square Park to Traffic to secure trial closure	1958	"Downtown Is for People"
		"A Living Network of Relationships"
Takes leave from *Forum* to write *Death and Life*		
Washington Square Park closed to car traffic for good	1959	
Leads fight to save sidewalks along Hudson Street from removal	1960	
Leads Save the West Village Committee against plans to raze and rebuild part of neighborhood	1961	*The Death and Life of Great American Cities*

NYC Planning Commission removes slum designation on West Village, preventing any redevelopment	1962	
Design work begins on West Village Houses infill project, facing much resistance and delays		
Leaves *Architectural Forum* for good to become a full-time author		
Joins on-again, off-again fight against Robert Moses's Lower Manhattan Expressway (LOMEX), seemingly saving Soho from the wrecking ball by the end of 1962		
	1964	"A Great Unbalance"
Mayor Wagner announces plans to revive LOMEX but Mayor John Lindsay wins election in 1966, promising to kill project	1965	"The Decline of Function"
		PART THREE: *How New Work Begins*
Participates with family in march on Pentagon to protest Vietnam War	1967	"The Self-Generating Growth of Cities"
		"On Civil Disobedience"
Arrested in NYC Vietnam War protest		
Mayor Lindsay revives LOMEX for third time	1968	
Arrested, accused of inciting riot at community meeting		
Secretly moves with family to Toronto, Canada, to avoid sons being arrested as draft dodgers		
Mayor Lindsay declares LOMEX dead for good	1969	*The Economy of Cities*
		"Strategies for Helping Cities"
Joins Stop Spadina Save Our City Coordinating Committee (SSSOCCC) to protest construction of Spadina Expressway		"A City Getting Hooked on the Expressway Drug"

	1990	*The Girl on the Hat*
	1992	"Foreword to the Modern Library Edition" of *The Death and Life of Great American Cities*
		Systems of Survival
	1993	"Two Ways to Live"
Co-founds Consumer Policy Institute, an initiative of Energy Probe Research Foundation	1994	"First Letter to the Consumer Policy Institute"
		"Women as Natural Entrepreneurs"
Donates papers to Burns Library at Boston College	1995	"Market Nurturing Run Amok"
Second Quebec sovereignty referendum fails by a margin of one percent		*A Schoolteacher in Old Alaska*
Awarded Order of Canada	1996	
Husband, Bob Jacobs, dies		
Joins Citizens for Local Democracy (C4LD) opposing province's plans to amalgamate Toronto with its suburbs		
Leaves board of Energy Probe	1997	"Against Amalgamation"
In nonbinding referendum, Metro Toronto citizens oppose amalgamation by a three-to-one ratio		
"Self-organizing" festival, "Jane Jacobs: Ideas That Matter," held in Toronto		
Joins board of Ecotrust, an environmental NGO in Portland, Oregon, encouraging it to consider urban issues		

Government of Ontario amalga-mates Toronto with its suburbs	1998	
Government of Ontario privatizes its public electric utility, Ontario Hydro, following Energy Probe recommendations		
Breaks her hip, severely limiting mobility of someone who consid-ers walking both a pastime and a tool of her trade	2000	PART FIVE: *Some Patterns of Future Development*
		The Nature of Economies
		"Time and Change as Neighborhood Allies"
Co-founds C5, coalition of Canada's biggest cities demanding devolution of powers	2001	"Canada's Hub Cities"
		"Efficiency and the Commons"
	2002	"The Sparrow Principle"
C5 disbands	2003	
Jacobs supports SSSOCCC veterans Allan Sparrow and David Crombie in successful opposition to expansion of Toronto Island Airport		
	2004	*Dark Age Ahead*
		"The End of the Plantation Age"
	2005	*Uncovering the Economy*
April 25: Jane Jacobs dies at age eighty-nine, survived by her children, Jim, Ned, and Burgin, and two unfinished books	2006	

Jane and Bob Jacobs and their son Jim undertake a renovation of their home at 555 Hudson Street in Greenwich Village, circa 1950.

PART ONE

A CITY NATURALIST

1934–1952

JANE JACOBS WAS FORTY-FIVE YEARS OLD WHEN SHE PUB-lished *The Death and Life of Great American Cities*. By the time she sat down to write her best-known book in the late 1950s, she'd already spent half her life as a journalist, student of economic geography, wartime propagandist, and expert in modern archi-tecture. Although she became a public figure in the 1960s, the story of her writing life begins in the depths of the Great De-pression.

Jane Jacobs (née Butzner) arrived in New York City in 1934 as an "obstreperous" eighteen-year-old writer and sometime poet, intent on seeking her fortune.[1] Although the city offered better prospects than her hometown, the declining mining cen-ter of Scranton, Pennsylvania, she spent the next four years scrounging for work, taking on odd jobs at factories and offices, and trying to scare up writing gigs wherever she could.

Her early freelance articles show Jacobs trying on a host of writerly flourishes she would later use to great effect. Quirky, detailed lists, unusually hyphenated words, liberal use of alliteration—all are in full force here. More important, they give us an early glimpse of her future incarnation as an urban and economic thinker. For a series of articles in *Vogue* magazine, Jacobs painted four literary portraits of the working districts of New York City, which she had discovered during her never-ending job hunt. Fur, leather, diamonds, and flowers may have been the preferred luxuries of *Vogue* readers, but in her articles (two of which are included here) Jacobs shows them to be much else besides: animators of street scenes, mediums for diverse city livelihoods, the threads that connect makers and distributors and sellers in an economic network. What makes these pieces particularly remarkable is how, even during the lean times of the Depression, she discovered vibrant, small-scale city economies clipping along on their own energies, scenes so different from our shared vision of the 1930s.

This Depression-era work finds Jacobs inventing a new intellectual vocation, too. The "city naturalist" attentively observes the minute details that make places tick, like the marvelous mess of wires, tunnels, and tubes that rush people, information, electricity, water, and waste around New York. However, she also notices evidence of how things stop ticking. Describing Matinicus Island off the coast of Maine in "Islands the Boats Pass By," included here, she captures a way of life in mysterious decline. Although the piece is more portrait than analysis, she might have already had an inkling of what was afoot. In the months before her arrival in New York, Jacobs had visited a missionary aunt in Higgins, North Carolina, a tiny impoverished hamlet tucked in the Appalachian Mountains.[2] There, much like in Matinicus, as the generations wore on, the residents had begun to lose the traditions and skills that were not connected to their bare-bones subsistence economy. Not only had they forgotten these practices, Jacobs would later argue, but, as if in a miniature Dark Age, they had forgotten what they had forgotten. The suggestion that the inhabitants should build their new church out of masonry, a skill their colonial ancestors had arrived with, was met with incredulity: How would the stacked stones not fall over? According to Jacobs, it took the services of a mason from a nearby city to revive their belief in stone construction. Jacobs's depiction of Matinicus suggests a community at the beginnings of the same trajectory—unless the enlivening forces of an urban economy intervene, that is.

After Jacobs settled into her life in New York, she took classes in Columbia University's Extension program (renamed the School of General Studies in 1947). Between 1938 and 1940 she fed her omnivorous mind with studies in geography, history, law, philosophy, and the physical and natural sciences. It was here that she would first read the writings of historian Henri Pirenne, whose account of the rise of urban culture in medieval Europe would become one of the greatest influences on Jacobs's ideas about cities, economies, and the possibility of another Dark Ages. Meanwhile, her classes in law gave her the opportunity to write her first book. Published when she was just twenty-five, *Constitutional Chaff* reveals an early glimpse of her unorthodox mind: The book interprets the U.S. Constitution by compiling the failed alternative proposals made for each and every line of the document at the Constitutional Convention of 1787. Unfortunately, due to a bureaucratic foible, the university forced Jacobs out of the Extension program and attempted to reclassify her as a student at Barnard College. When her poor high school grades led the women's college to reject her "application," she realized that she had effectively been expelled. This bitter moment planted the seeds of a deep skepticism toward academia and the faulty correlation between credentials and genuine education. In fact, she would go on to refuse every honorary degree presented to her throughout her successful career and write at length about the failures of academia over sixty years later in her final book, *Dark Age Ahead*.

If Jacobs's greatest joys can be detected in her explorations of human life at street level, she made the bulk of her living in this period writing about issues of national concern. When she took a position as a secretary at a metals industry trade journal called *The Iron Age* in 1941, World War II was already in full swing in Europe, and the Japanese attack on Pearl Harbor was on the immediate horizon, even if nobody knew it. Quickly rising from secretary to associate editor, she found herself with some leeway to take on stories of interest. In 1943, she embarked on an investigation into the failure of the national War Production Board to establish factories in Scranton despite shortages of labor and housing elsewhere (see "30,000 Unemployed and 7,000 Empty Houses in Scranton, Neglected City"). The article was the culmination of what was likely Jacobs's first community organizing effort, a letter-writing campaign that successfully secured war work for Scranton, and the un-bylined story was picked up by more than three hundred newspapers around the country.[3] But most of what she wrote was dry reporting for a highly technical audience, and her editor resisted her attempts to broaden the appeal of her articles. By the end of 1943, she was at odds with her boss and out of a job.

Luckily for Jacobs, the war was hungry for writers. Between 1943 and 1952, she found work in the U.S. government's propaganda mills, first for the Office of War Information, targeting nonaligned nations during World War II, and later for the State Department, where she contributed to a publication called *Amerika* directed at the people of the Soviet Union. In both positions, her primary task was to communicate American values through tales of the nation's history, government, geography, economy, and people. By all accounts Jacobs excelled at her job and believed in the work, but her eccentric, rabble-rousing personality and her growing knowledge of the Soviet Union got her in trouble with the FBI. In 1948, in the midst of the second Red Scare, the bureau opened an investigation into Jacobs and her ostensible communist ties. When interrogated she defended herself eloquently, writing that there is "no virtue in conforming meekly" to the majority beliefs of the day, but government surveillance only ended in 1952, when Jacobs left her post at the State Department.

As Jacobs herself told the State Department's loyalty board, her lifelong skepticism toward convention and authority was exactly what made her a patriotic American and not a Soviet sympathizer. Her early writing may reveal little of that native skepticism, but her ongoing encounters with the federal government and other callous bureaucracies in the Cold War years—from McCarthyism to urban renewal to the Vietnam War—would eventually lead her to turn her skeptical eye upon America itself.

NOTES

1.   For more on Jacobs's childhood as "an obstreperous young girl," see *Genius of Common Sense* (Boston: David R. Godine, 2009), an illustrated biography for youth by Glenna Lang and Marjory Wunsch. Although Jacobs wrote poetry regularly in high school and continued to dabble for years afterward, she found her calling as a journalist and nonfiction writer soon after moving to New York.

2.   Jacobs provides a full account of the town under the pseudonym Henry—as in Henry Higgins of *My Fair Lady*—in *Cities and the Wealth of*

Nations, 124–29. Jacobs argues that such "passive economies," if they aren't bypassed altogether, are shaped by one of five powerful forces of urban economies: markets for goods and services; jobs that attract people to the city; transplants of factories or other city work into outlying areas; technology, especially the kind that increases rural productivity; and capital in the form of aid or investment.

3.   This campaign seems out of character for Jacobs, both in her deference to the powers that be and in her apparent belief that the plants could revive Scranton's economy. In *Becoming Jane Jacobs,* Peter L. Laurence argues that she must have already known that Scranton could not be saved this way, considering that her move to New York coincided with a wave of out-migration from the city. Whether she knew already or learned as much through this very experience, by the time she wrote *The Economy of Cities,* she was criticizing exactly the kind of industrial transplants she fought for here.

While Arranging Verses for a Book

—

NEW YORK HERALD TRIBUNE,
JANUARY 22, 1935

I should approach these sheets with reverent eye,
Thinking, with mental halo, how I sought
The perfect word to clothe the perfect thought,
The phrase to bring a tear, a smile, a sigh.
Or, failing that, I think at least I ought
To sweat again on seeing fragile verse
I brought into the world with groan and curse,
Whose every rippling foot was ripped and fought,
Or think of how it should have been, and moan,
And wish for the effects I seem to miss,
But all the things I'd think I'd think are flat,
The words and sheets have memories of their own:
I ate brown sugar while I thought of this,
And my nose tickled when I worked on that.

Diamonds in the Tough

———

VOGUE, OCTOBER 15, 1936

"EVERYTHING COMES TO THE BOWERY, IF YOU WAIT LONG enough," say the dealers in the diamond center between Hester and Canal Streets, one of the largest and strangest jewel exchanges in the world. There, seventy percent of the unredeemed jewelry pawned in the country is bought and sold. Through this single block of shops, a glittering island in the most squalid section of New York City, has passed every sort of quaint and lavish jewelry, the most extraordinary pieces in the world—crown jewels of royalty, seal-rings of lords, love-tokens of courtiers, and unsophisticated lockets of children.

No one seems to know why this location was chosen or why the district continues here. Twenty-five years ago, the first of the merchants settled in this incongruous setting for no reason now remembered. It is adjacent to no allied centers; it exists by itself, across the street from the entrance to the Manhattan Bridge, surrounded by the almost legendary Bowery life.

None of the dealers rents a whole shop. Each has a counter in a store with a dozen or so other dealers. The more affluent ones also rent little partitioned spaces in the show-windows and put up such signs as ALL ARTICLES HERE MAY BE PURCHASED ONLY AT THIRD COUNTER TO LEFT.

No effort is made for artistic or dramatic displays, but some bizarre effects are unwittingly obtained by festooning quantities of jewelry haphazardly over little statuettes that seem to bear no relation to the other merchandise. A plaster goat, probably of bock-beer ancestry, has several rings suspended from one horn, a necklace rakishly wrapped around the other, a watch over his tail, and assorted trinkets along his back. King Arthur, already burdened with his armor, supports several necklaces about his shoulders, a wristwatch around his waist and a lavaliere from his visor.

In the showcases, there is no black velvet, no particular gem placed to catch the eye, but row on row of gleaming diamonds and shining gold, or sometimes just a jumble of rings and watches and bracelets. Frequently bold, definite-looking prices are marked on the jewels, but these represent chiefly a starting-point for dickering.

The specialty of the district is diamonds, of course, but every other sort of jewelry and precious metal work is also traded in. Probably the most magnificent article now in the district is a samovar, said to have been made about three hundred years ago for the Czar of Russia. Seventy-six pounds of solid silver, finer than sterling, with an intricate gold inlay pattern! It was bought from a pawn shop where it had been left by gypsies. No one knows where the gypsies got it.

Some of the jewelry sold in the Bowery is new, but most of it comes through the three large auction houses on the block between Hester and Canal Streets. It is sent there by pawnbrokers after the twelve months stipulated by law—and one month of grace—have elapsed from the time it was pawned.

Except in the summer, sales are held nearly every day. The jewelry to be sold is put on display for the dealers to examine and to make notations of its value. These notations are all in codes of a primitive sort, letters representing numbers, and each dealer keeps his a secret. The notes are to remind the dealer in the excitement of the sale what, in a cooler moment, he considered paying.

The auction proceedings are baffling to an outsider. They are completely silent. All the dealers able to touch the auctioneer crowd around him, and the rest sit on two benches facing him. The auctioneer indicates a figure to begin the bidding, and the dealers raise it silently. Those near the auctioneer squeeze his arm, nudge his ribs, or press his foot, and those on the benches wink, hold up their fingers, rub their elbows, or make any other noticeable gesture. With half their minds, they seem to be making bids, and, with the other half, they are figuring out their neighbors' bids. It is all done quickly; in a moment the jewel is awarded to the highest bidder, and everyone seems satisfied. It looks extremely haphazard, a cross between hocus-pocus and mind reading.*

Some of the gems that reach the Bowery are reset there, particularly those with settings that are more valuable for bullion than for their workmanship. One dealer has used forty-eight rubies, once belonging to the Romanoffs, to make a bracelet, a

---

* Jacobs would continue to be fascinated by the strange rituals and superstitions that various professions use to foster a sense of trust. Her *Systems of Survival*, which explores the systems of ethics that keep working life viable, presents many other colorful practices, like British barristers wearing payment pouches only on the backs of their robes (to preserve their dignity) or hunting tribes deciding where to hunt by throwing sticks onto the ground willy-nilly.

small diamond between each ruby. In the center is a diamond-studded plaque that snaps open to reveal a tiny watch.

One of the oldest articles is not really a jewel at all, but a fifteenth-century etching-plate made in Vienna, a portrait of the Pope. In addition to its antiquity, it has a peculiarity. The eyeballs seem to move, not merely to follow the observer as they do in many pictures, but actually to shift from side to side.

An example of early American metal work is a stiff little silver statuette of an Indian holding an eagle. In position and general appearance, he is a miniature cigar-store Indian.

From time to time, a "poison ring," with a secret cavity and sometimes a sharp little prong to give a lethal prick, reaches the Bowery. These are usually melted down because, although people like to look at them, they don't buy them.

Initial rings, however, are not often melted. Eventually someone with similar initials finds the ring irresistible.

All sorts of wedding rings reach the dealers. One early French engagement ring has no gems, but is a cluster of gold lovers' knots that shake with a sweet jingle.

One of the few pieces whose complete history is known is a watch, made in England and bought one hundred and forty-four years ago by a Vermont college professor. The face is so clear and so beautiful and the engraving on the edges so artful that at first there seems to be no crystal covering it. The professor used it only a few years and then put it in a vault to be kept for his son. Somehow, it was forgotten until long after the son had died, and it has never been used since.

A graceful little French clock, one hundred years old, rests on two Ionic pillars, and on a rail at the base of the pillars sits a laughing ivory cupid. A bracelet made about the same time in

France has six sections, each with a peasant figure in exquisite mosaic of brilliant colors.

On a large cameo necklace is the profile of a lady with an identical cameo on her necklace, and on that cameo, microscopic but clear, another necklace with a cameo. Is it a likeness of the lady who wore it so that she could complete the sequence of ladies with their portraits on their necklace?

With how much fantasy and imagination were these jewels made, with how much love were they given, and with how much sentiment were they treasured? Maybe there was bitterness, too. At any rate, loved or hated, here they all are on the Bowery, waiting to be sold, to begin another cycle that will doubtless return them once more to the Bowery.

Many of the jewels have come back again and again. The most frequent repeater is a man's enameled fob-watch, which is intricately designed and valuable, but it is also massive and pink in color, and seems to be the first thing its owners pawn.

The dealers say it is hardly possible for jewels to stay in a family more than a few generations. Estates must be settled, or money is needed, or the old jewels are traded for more modern ones. Nearly every day, the gems of royal and of famous people pass through the exchange and are sold for their intrinsic worth, with little regard for sentiment. The only jewels with associations that seemed to have impressed the blasé dealers in recent years were those of Rudolph Valentino and Texas Guinan.*

---

*   Rudolph Valentino (1895–1926) and Mary Louise Cecilia "Texas" Guinan (1884–1933) were both American actors of the silent film era. Valentino was an Italian immigrant who became known as a sex icon for his dancing and his "exotic" look. Guinan was an actress of stage and screen known as "The Queen of the West" for her pioneering role as a movie cowgirl. She also owned and emceed the 300 Club, a Prohibition-era speakeasy in New York City.

Occasionally, someone, usually a lady, attempts to redeem an article just after it has gone to the auction rooms. It is traced to the dealer who almost invariably has sold it, for the turnover in the exchange is fast. Sometimes, it must be traced through several subsequent buyers before the woman retrieves it.

THERE HAS NEVER BEEN a robbery in the center, probably because of the precautions taken. No jewels are left in the show windows overnight, or even in the showcases inside the stores.

Upstairs, in small light rooms over the stores, diamonds are cut and polished and set or reset, and silver is buffed. The doors and vestibules to the rooms are barred, and there is no superfluous furniture, just the tools and tables where the workmen sit with hammocks to catch the chips and dust of diamonds and metal.

Silver is polished against a cloth-covered revolving wheel. There is a pleasant acrid odor of burning cloth, caused by the friction, and infinitesimal bits of metal are sent like dust through the room.

All the sweepings are carefully saved to be refined, and the silver recovered. The walls and ceiling are brushed, and the old oilcloth coverings and work clothes of the men are burned to extract the silver dust. Even the water in which the workmen wash their hands is saved. A small room where silver is polished may yield to a refiner hundreds of dollars' worth of metal a year.

Outside on the Bowery, the lusty, tumultuous life of the Lower East Side converges. The "El" roars, trucks rumble, Chinamen from Mott Street mince by, snatches from foreign tongues are caught and lost in a reek of exotic and forbidding odors. Absorbed in the raucous chaos, the visitor forgets the cool diamonds and the metal until, a few blocks away, he sees the glittering gold-leaf roof of the new building at Foley Square.*

---

* The "new building at Foley Square" is the United States Courthouse, now named for Supreme Court Justice Thurgood Marshall. Completed in 1936, it was designed by Cass Gilbert, the architect of the nearby Woolworth Building, and his son. Lewis Mumford, who would later be both supporter and critic of Jacobs, called it "the supreme example of pretentiousness, mediocrity, bad design and fake grandeur." As the *AIA Guide to New York City* notes, times change; it is now a well-known landmark.

Flowers Come to Town

———

Vogue, FEBRUARY 15, 1937

ALL THE INGREDIENTS OF A LAVENDER-AND-OLD-LACE STORY, with a rip-roaring, contrasting background, are in New York's wholesale flower district, centered around Twenty-Eighth Street and Sixth Avenue. Under the melodramatic roar of the "El," encircled by hash-houses and Turkish baths, are the shops of hard-boiled, stalwart men, who shyly admit that they are dottles for love, sentiment, and romance.

Apprentices, dodging among the hand-carts that are forever rushing to or from the fur and garment districts, dream of the time when they will have their own commission houses. Greeks and Koreans, confessing that they have the hearts of children, build little Japanese gardens. Greenhouse owners declare that they would not sell—at any price—the flowers which grow in their own backyards. A dealer plans how to improve the business that grandfather started. And orchids in milk-bottles nod at field-flowers in buckets.

Early in the morning, the market opens. From five o'clock on, boxes and hampers of flowers are brought into the district and unloaded. Most of them, from Long Island, Connecticut, and New Jersey, arrive in the city via truck, but those from

Florida, California, and Canada come by fast express, and those from South America and Holland by ship. Occasionally, a shipment of gardenias is flown from California by airplane.

For most of the morning, hundreds and hundreds of thousands of cut flowers and blossoming shrubs fill the shops and overflow onto the sidewalk. Their damp, sweet perfume, blowing across the pavement, filters from hampers and crates piled beside doorways.

By noon, most of the flowers have been taken away by retail florists or peddlers, and, in the early afternoon, the rest are put in storage or sent to other markets. Then the cool, sweet-smelling shops have an empty, leisurely air. A few buckets of peonies and lilacs splash against the dark walls, and the proprietors and workers, sitting on the high, metal-topped tables, their feet dangling, smoke and talk.

The wholesale market started about fifty-five years ago, well within the memory of the older dealers. At that time, most of the growers lived on Long Island and brought their flowers over in market-baskets every morning. They were met by the retail florists at the ferry landing at Thirty-Fourth Street and the East River.

As competition sharpened, the growers appeared earlier and earlier in the morning, and—in order to get the choicest flowers—the florists also appeared earlier and earlier, until the first sales were made in the middle of the night!

Near the docks was a place called Dann's Restaurant, run by a horse-car conductor and kept open all night for the patronage of other conductors. Flower buyers and sellers began to drift in there to conclude their dickering, until finally they used it to house a fairly well-organized market. The first rule adopted was that no one could take the cover off his basket until a gong rang at six o'clock.*

In a few years, some of the growers started a competing market at Twenty-Third Street. Then, both groups leased a building at Twenty-Sixth Street and Sixth Avenue. The New York Cut Flower Association was formed and located on the second floor of the building. Other growers took the third floor.

Before the growers brought their flowers to Thirty-Fourth Street, retail florists had to go to the country themselves—to buy, if they could, what their customers wanted. Sometimes they didn't succeed and had to substitute sentiment. One early florist, commissioned to get nineteen pink roses for a girl's birthday, could find among all the near-by growers only eighteen blossoms and one very tight little bud. So, with this bouquet, he sent a card: "For eighteen happy years and one to come."

Two actresses and an actor—Lotta Crabtree, Clara Morris, and Lester Wallack—financed what is now the oldest floral house in Manhattan and established it in the lobby of the old Wallack Theatre in the Bowery, where it became the favorite flower shop of a generation of theatrical people. At first, its most popular flowers, and sometimes the only ones in stock, were pond-lilies, picked by Mr. Le Moult, the proprietor, in Washington Heights and Westchester. This shop (like, perhaps,

---

* It's hard not to see these careful depictions of everyday commerce as Jacobs's primal scene, the original inspiration for much later work. The comings and goings of the sellers throughout the day foreshadow the famous "intricate sidewalk ballet" outside her front door on Hudson Street from *Death and Life* (50–54), while the relationships between florists, restaurants, actors, basket makers, and others are an early version of what, in *Cities and the Wealth of Nations,* she would call "symbiotic nests of suppliers and producers" (119).

a third of the wholesale houses) is managed by the grandson of the founder. Most of the other dealers are former employees or sons of employees of these first flower merchants and played among the roses and cornflowers and daffodils before they were old enough to help.

Occasionally, an overzealous heir brings on catastrophe. One boy, home from college, thought he would help by sprinkling the orchids—he ruined three thousand dollars' worth before he realized he was giving them the treatment for gardenias.

Behind the brownstone fronts on Twenty-Eighth Street are basket factories, most of which are owned by Greeks, Italians, or Orientals. Reeds, wooden disks, and scraps of wicker are piled haphazardly in halls and on stairways and in the old, high ceilinged rooms. The baskets are sold in the florist accessories shops, which share the district with the wholesale flower houses and supply ribbons, pottery, terrariums, and even artificial flowers.

The wholesale dealers' business is done entirely on commission. They, the middlemen for the growers and retailers, sell to established florists and to sidewalk vendors and peddlers. During Easter week, approximately twelve thousand boxes of daffodils, ten dozen in a box, were sold to peddlers alone.

A phenomenon of the last year or two is the successful chain of subway flower vendors. They buy cheaper flowers in quantity, have very little overhead, and, on a good weekend, they make as much as thirty thousand dollars.

New Yorkers buy tremendous amounts of cut flowers and foliage. Each year, they purchase about two hundred million ferns. One firm keeps one hundred and twenty thousand ferns on hand at all times. And, in season, one grower sends in twenty thousand dozen iris a day; and another, one hundred and fifty thousand roses. All the large passenger liners are supplied from the New York market, and, on her eastward trips, the *Hindenburg,* too, carries flowers from Twenty-Eighth Street.*

Growers devote a good deal of time to breeding new varieties and are able to protect their creations with patents. They also attempt to produce flowers out of season. Last year, several growers competed with early chrysanthemums from California by fooling their plants into thinking autumn had come. Every day, for a few hours, they shut out the sun with heavy black canopies. It worked!

The whole flower business is based on supply and demand, with no set prices, and the supply must start far, far ahead of the demand. Occasionally, among all the hundreds of varieties, it is impossible to find a fairly commonplace flower, and a florist may hunt in vain for a dozen white roses or yellow snapdragon.

---

* Unfortunately, the *Hindenburg* was itself not long for the world. Just a few months after this piece appeared, on May 6, 1937, the airship caught fire as it came in to its port at Lakeland, New Jersey, killing thirty-six people and bringing the era of passenger travel by zeppelin to an abrupt end.

Caution, Men Working

———

CUE, MAY 18, 1940

THE LIGHTS OF NEW YORK ARE THE CITY'S JEWELS, BUT her buttons and hooks and eyes are the squares and circles of metal that dot asphalt and sidewalks. Nobody knows how many manhole and service box covers there are in the city. Nobody even knows how many varieties there are. Companies long out of business or swallowed in mergers still have initials and devices on the lowly iron waffles.

Probably the oldest of the covers on the streets are those of the Croton Water Company, now part of the city water supply, whose system ran down Amsterdam Avenue from 173rd Street to the reservoir at 93rd. The covers, with their elaborate iron center pattern—two stars, and "Croton Water" in block letters—date from Civil War days. One of the few series of covers to bear dates also runs along Amsterdam Avenue: a design of interrupted spokes carrying the legend, "DPW Sewers 1874."

The covers never are stolen, never disappear, and rarely break. Slowly they do wear smooth or begin to rattle in their sockets. Probably not more than a few hundred, all told, are replaced in Manhattan each year, but as the city grows and the underground "spaghetti"—the name used for the maze of pipes and cables by those who design and install them—becomes more complicated, new covers with new and varying designs and letters are added to the accumulation of nearly a century. During President Hoover's administration, a National Conference for Standardization of Manholes was held, but nothing came of it.

Despite the almost hopeless variety, the city naturalist, keeping an eye on the letters of the covers, can tell whether he is following the course of one of the great underground rivers, whether he is on the trail of a main stream of electricity, or gas, or one of the tributaries, whether brine to chill the produce markets or steam to heat the skyscrapers is running under his feet. Or, if he stands on the right corner—southwest corner of Fourth Avenue and Fourteenth Street for instance—he can feel beneath his feet the shudder of five hundred letters in a pneumatic tube, clipping along at thirty miles an hour on their way to an uptown post office.*

The lights of New York are the city's jewels, but her buttons and hooks and eyes are the squares and circles of metal that dot asphalt and sidewalks.

New York City's engineers are the world's leading research workers and experimenters on manhole covers, and other cities usually follow their lead in weight and design specifications.

---

* The U.S. Post Office's pneumatic tube network was one of many such systems built in New York and other cities around the world. First installed in 1897 and run by private companies, the NYC mail tube system by the early twentieth century featured twenty-seven miles of pipe connecting twenty-three post offices. The tubes sat four to six feet below the street, and each canister held up to five hundred letters. A run from Bowling Green, at the southern tip of the island, to Manhattanville at the northern end of the system took about half an hour. Automobile delivery chipped away at tube service, but the tubes survived until 1953, when the final canister went whooshing beneath the street. Since then, most if not all of the system has been dug up and lost during routine infrastructure repairs.

For the past three years the city has been experimenting on silent manhole covers, non-clankers. Clanking is responsible for most of the replacements. On corners where buses stop or the main stream of traffic turns, the whirling wheels, catching the manhole off center, give it a twist and eventually it becomes a clanker with possibilities of becoming a tiddly-wink.

Up Washington Street, as far north as King, is a row of manhole covers set about six hundred feet apart, marked "USTD." Underneath them is the pneumatic tube system of the United States Treasury Department, carrying papers from the Customs House at Bowling Green to the Appraisers' Stores on Varick Street. Like most of the conduits on the periphery of the island, the lower Washington Street system is under tidewater. When this part of the Treasury tubes was built, it could be worked on only at low tide, for three hours a day.

The covers saying "W-U-TEL CO" mark another pneumatic tube system of downtown Manhattan.* That one is easy to guess, but how about "NYM&NT," "ECSCOLTD," "CT&ES CO," "HPFS," "MRC," and "BPM"?

The New York Mail and Newspaper Tube Company manholes, one to every three or four blocks, string for fifty-two miles along the city streets, from 125th Street down to the tip of the island and over to Brooklyn, linking the main post office to

---

* Well known to Jacobs's readers in 1937 as a way to communicate person to person, the Western Union Telegraph Company survives today largely as a way to send money. Almost as fantastic as the idea of vast subterranean mazes of pneumatic tubes crisscrossing Manhattan is the idea that Western Union operators once tapped messages out on the "Victorian Internet" and sent them out along a great network of telegraph wires to stations far and wide, from which they were printed and delivered to their intended recipients by horse, bicycle, car, truck, and pneumatic tube.

the branch stations. Spaced between the manholes, to facilitate the spotting of leaks, are service boxes with six-inch square metal covers from which the NYM&NT initials are soon worn. The mail tube covers are replaced at the rate of only about one a year, but once during a skyscraper construction job, a heavy truckload of steel broke every cover on its route and had to be trailed by a mail tube truck with a load of new manhole tops.

HPFS for High Pressure Fire Service can be seen only south of 34th Street, where the Department of Water Supply provides pumping stations and additional pressure to be used in case of fire. The very large manhole covers with an unequivocal "FIRE" are part of the Fire Department's alarm system.

Those little rectangles, marked BPM, set in the corner of the sidewalk, are under the jurisdiction of the Borough President of Manhattan, and cover the city's sunken surveying monuments.

The ubiquitous CT&ES CO castings, Consolidated Telegraph and Electrical Subway Company, mark the course of electric wires. Their abundance is astonishing, evocative of the city's probable appearance if the wires they cover were all strung up on poles. About six years ago, when Edison's conviction that the wires should be put underground was hooted at, he countered with the suggestion that the water and sewage pipes be carried overhead on crossers too. Among the first wires to go underground were those of Maiden Lane. During a few hours of the installation, the moist earth of the street conducted a current, mildly electrifying the horses that passed by.

Some of the early electric company manhole covers were square, but now, like most of the other manhole covers of the city, almost all the CT&ES CO covers are round; they're easier to cast and they can't slip edgewise through their holes. The electricity manhole covers, designed to carry a twenty-ton truck, weigh 475 pounds.

Manhattan's share of the city's 10,000,000 miles of telephone wire is harbored in the ducts of the Empire City Subway Company, so 10,000 square and round covers marked with a cryptic ECSCOLTD mean "telephone." When the lead-covered cables are installed, they are inched along their underground duct banks with pushers and pullers, and are spliced where they emerge at the manholes.

The Gas Company has no manholes proper, but it has a multiplicity of doors to the underground—12,091 drip boxes, 5,443 main valve boxes, and 150,000 service valve boxes in Manhattan, the Bronx, and Queens. Those little iron-bound concrete squares, imprinted with a "G," that dot the sidewalks are the surface indications of a gas tributary. If, in an emergency, a building's gas supply must be cut off, the concrete cover is smashed and a valve turned with a four-foot-long key. Iron covers might corrode and stick at harrowing times.

The only system to bolt down all of its manhole covers is the Steam Company, not for fear of geysers but because most of the covers are out near the center of the street where high-speed traffic would rock and wear them. The 3,000 manholes, marked NYS CO or NYS CORP, are all in Manhattan, from the Battery to 96th Street, and First to Ninth Avenues. In this area there are also 20,000 square valve boxes, marked NYS. The steam main encasements are square, with a twelve-inch pipe entered in three feet of asbestos insulation, tile, and concrete. Even so, on cold or rainy days, dank little clouds of water vapor float from the edges of the metal covers. The Steam Company has used manholes only since 1925; before that time they dug whenever they wanted to get at their conduits.

To chill the refrigerators of the great wholesale produce and meat markets, cold brine travels underground, 0°F on its way from the cooling plant, 5°F on its way back. East of Hudson Street, from Fourteenth on the north to Horatio on the south, the heart of the meat distribution center, are the manholes of the Manhattan Refrigerating Co., bearing the initials MR CO on their covers. In the vegetable district, especially on Greenwich Street, between Franklin and Duane, the pavement is spotted with MRC irons, covers of the Merchants Refrigerating Company.

The city's new sewer manhole covers will say "BPM," meaning "Borough President, Manhattan." For the past thirty-four years they have said "DPW Manhattan." The Star Heads, those openwork drainage covers starred in the center, used to say "Dept. of Public Works, Borough of Manhattan," but the new ones will be streamlined, without the star and with "BPM" on the back. Some of the oldest sewer covers merely say "S," some "BS." The southernmost manhole cover on the island in Battery Park bears simply an "S."

The city's enormous water supply tunnels are as much as 850 feet below the surface, and these torrents through Manhattan rock are not punctured from the street. But the mains that tap the underground rivers, and the mains that tap the mains that tap the mains that tap the rivers are given access to the surface by 24,827 manholes. Except for the covers antedating the city water supply department, most of these are labeled "DWS."

Of course the most familiar initials are on the transit line manhole covers, giving access to the lines feeding the power cables of the underground trains. "BMT," "IRT," "NYRT," they all follow the route of the subways and branch off to the power houses, far to the east and west side of town.* Even the vanishing streetcars have their manholes; the Third Avenue Railway system lines are riddled with covers so that their contact rail may be cleaned.

Like everything else in the world that has been made by man or nature in more than one design, manhole covers have their collectors. At the Municipal Building they speak with awe of a caller who had, as a hobby, made elaborate full-sized tracings of scores of the iron squares and circles. Even so, his collection was not yet complete; he had only made a beginning.

---

* Before the New York subway system was consolidated, a host of independent companies operated various lines in the city. These acronyms were the commonly used handles for three of the companies in existence during the mid-1930s: the Brooklyn-Manhattan Transit Corporation (BMT), Interborough Rapid Transit (IRT), and New York Rapid Transit (NYRT). All three of these lines would be taken over in 1940 by the city's Board of Transportation, which already operated the Independent Subway System (IND). In 1953 New York State created the New York City Transit Authority to run the entire system.

30,000 Unemployed and 7,000 Empty Houses in Scranton, Neglected City

THE IRON AGE, MARCH 25, 1943

WHILE MANPOWER AND HOUSING SHORTAGES CAUSE PROB-
lems in war production centers, there exist in the U.S. 82 para-
doxical industrial areas of unemployment and empty houses.
These areas of surplus men and homes include some of the best
established industrial cities of the country, with trained labor,
transportation, and economically sound locations.

The strange neglect of these areas appears even stranger and
more tragic upon examination of their World War II case histories. As an example, the case of Scranton, Pennsylvania, is presented here. In many ways its experience in attempting to get
war work and the frustration it has encountered parallel that of
other depressed areas. It is, however, atypical in that it is believed to have made the hardest fight to channel its idle labor
into war production.

In Scranton men are now applying for women's jobs.* In the
greater Scranton area, with a population of 300,000, there are

---

* It appears that Jacobs means that because of the shortage of industrial work, men are
seeking positions that in a traditional patriarchal sense would have been considered women's
jobs, like secretarial or teaching jobs. As she implies, this was the reverse of many other parts
of the country where women took on industrial positions usually reserved for men.

more than 30,000 unemployed and 7,000 empty homes. More than 20,000 men have entered the armed forces, one of the highest per capita rates in the country. Another 20,000 or more men and women have left for Bridgeport, Baltimore and other already crowded war boom cities. They send back to their families in Scranton more than half a million dollars a month.

Heightening this paradox, the War Department, in awarding about 25 percent of its contracts for camouflage nets to Scranton plants, called the city one of the best locations in the country for war production, well protected in the mountains, near points of embarkation, with good transportation, good fuel and good labor. "Economically," said the War Department spokesman, "there are few like it."

The veins of anthracite coal in Lackawanna County, of which Scranton is the seat, are running out. During the last decade 25,000 miners' jobs have disappeared, leaving only 12,000 employed in coal mining. The manufacturing plants already in existence in the area are working nearly at capacity, but the great need of Scranton and its idle labor is new plants. This was the conclusion reached by the Federal Anthracite Coal Commission, appointed in January 1942, by the President.* The Commission commented as follows:

> This investigation has shown that the anthracite area has substantial possibilities for industrial expansion. At a time when most manufacturing areas of the nation are driving desperately to meet shortages of manpower and

---

*   The "President" was, of course, Franklin Delano Roosevelt, then in the middle of his unprecedented third term as president of the United States.

to build new housing and other community facilities, it is in the national interest that the industrial resources of the anthracite area be utilized. It is strongly recommended that the war agencies of the Federal Government give careful consideration to the suitability of the area for the location of necessary war plants, particularly those for the production of aluminum, zinc, synthetic ammonia, explosives, castings, forgings, armor plate, machine parts, aircraft parts, tank parts and ammunition.

In April this report was sent to the Army, Navy and WPB by the President, together with a letter urging that they act on the Commission's findings.* In June another Presidential letter was sent to Secretaries Stimson and Knox and to Donald Nelson, WPB chief, asking what had been done and urging action.

To date, the only concrete result has been the location of a piston ring factory, employing 400 on a shift, obtained over opposition that provides a strange tale.

The director of the Scranton Chamber of Commerce and the editor of its morning newspaper, hearing that the Air Corps had requested greater piston ring production from the U.S. Hammered Piston Ring Co. of Sterling, New Jersey, persuaded the company to build the necessary new plant in Scranton. After much battling with the WPB Plant Facilities section, which wanted to locate the plant in Baltimore as a part of American

---

* Established by President Roosevelt in January of 1942, the War Production Board supervised the production of weapons and supplies for the U.S. war effort in World War II. It oversaw the conversion of peacetime industry to war-related production, regulated and directed the manufacture of munitions and equipment, and enforced rationing of materials and commodities needed for the war effort.

Hammered Piston Ring Co., the Scranton site was finally approved. Approval proved to be only tentative, however; the company was abruptly asked for a stiff production guarantee which it felt unable to meet and the plant building was canceled. This created so much protest that the plant was relocated in Scranton, under management of the Silkening Mfg. Co. of Philadelphia. It will be ready for operation in June.

After many months of cajoling the WPB's Plant Facilities section and its aluminum and magnesium branch, Scranton was promised, in June of last year, an aluminum extrusion plant to employ 2,000 on a shift. It was to have been located at Harding, between Scranton and Wilkes-Barre. This approval again proved to be only tentative. WPB reported that engineers who drilled at the proposed site said the ground would be unable to stand the pounding of the machinery because of quicksand between the rock strata.

Scranton hired Dr. Arthur Casagrande, soil mechanics expert of Harvard University, to make drillings and a survey. He reported no quicksand to be present and reported that he found no reason why the site was unsuitable. When this report was submitted to WPB, it replied that new arrangements had already been made for the plant. The plant was assigned to Erie, one of the cities of acute housing shortage (though the government has built several housing projects there).

In the meantime, the city has pushed its case by other means. Late in 1941, the Greater Scranton Foundation Fund was formed with $25,000, to bring work to Scranton. The fund has $9,000 not yet spent. It has succeeded in bringing to the city the Standard Piezo Co., a radio parts plant which by the end of the year will employ about 1,000, mostly women, and two tobacco companies and four clothing companies, representing a total of 5,000 jobs. Through the Smaller War Plants division of WPB and the Army, the city has obtained camouflage net work employing 1,000 people.

The newspaper editor and the Chamber of Commerce director have made weekly trips to Washington for the past 15 months in an effort to get war plants for the city, and recently a permanent Washington representative for the city was hired.

Since the first of the year, letters have been written to 400 officials of the Army, Navy and WPB, setting forth in detail, in many instances with charts and figures, what Scranton has in surplus electric power, labor, sites, transportation, etc. More than 300 answers have been received and have been examined by a member of *The Iron Age* staff. They provide a post-graduate course in the runaround.

Since the letters on Scranton emphasized the city's surplus of labor and housing and its need of new plants, the reply from the WPB Plant Facility section's assistant director, J.O. Lanham, Jr., is something of a classic. It reads, "We have analyzed the contents of your letter and it is our opinion that your chief asset is the possession of buildings and potential employees. Basically you lack the machine tools which are most important to the war program. Because of this, it is doubtful whether you will be successful in obtaining prime contracts under your present conditions and plans." It was to this division that most of the other government replies referred the Scranton representative.

The reasons for all this strange frustration appear to be veiled in mystery. The ostensible reasons, when any have been given at all, have been implausible.

A member of *The Iron Age* staff, seeking an explanation, recently spoke with R.H. Bailey, Jr., secretary to Senator Joseph F. Guffey, of Pennsylvania. Mr. Bailey, queried on why he believed the recommendations of the Anthracite Commission had not been followed, said: "I think the real reason is very simple and plain. Just about the time, very soon after, the report was submitted the construction of plants was curtailed."

When it was pointed out to him that even now new plant sites are chosen and that the lists are published, he replied, "Is that so?"

Mr. Bailey, after mentioning the piston ring plant as evidence that Scranton was not doing so badly, disavowed any knowledge of the opposition to its location. He finally said, "Anyway those anthracite regions, that area around Scranton, why they've been going back for years. What if they did get some war plants? It wouldn't help."*

It was pointed out to him that this viewpoint was at odds with the one expressed in the report of the Federal Anthracite Coal Commission, which Senator Guffey had signed. Mr. Bailey's reply to this was a query as to whether his questioner wanted information or an argument.

---

* In later years, ironically, Jacobs would come to agree with Bailey's judgment. See "Strategies for Helping Cities" in this volume, and chapters 7 and 12 of *Cities and the Wealth of Nations,* "Transplant Regions" and "Transactions of Decline," respectively, for more on the failure of industries "transplanted" into declining regions and war work to spark economic development.

Islands the Boats Pass By

EXCERPT FROM *HARPER'S BAZAAR,*

JULY 1947

SOME LOOK LIKE NEATLY CUT CHRISTMAS COOKIES. SOME ARE like drop cakes that spattered too much, and some are old-fashioned, golden cornmeal sticks. They are dotted all along our Atlantic coast—the green and brown islands which are the fringes of a continent.

A few are familiar to mainlanders as summer resorts. But many—like Matinicus off Maine, the Elizabeths off Massachusetts, Tangier in the Chesapeake, Ocracoke off North Carolina—are Never-Never lands where life follows its own eccentric course, unnoticed and little disturbed by the rest of the world.

To live happily, as well as comfortably, on their few square miles, the natives of these islands have developed special talents for self-sufficiency and gregariousness. Silently, patiently, and by the hour, island children watch the ways of men and boats, then copy the adult skills with precision and delight. In the idle late afternoons on the wharfs, they are tireless listeners, and assured narrators of their own small adventures in crossing a cow pasture or making an off-island visit. It is no accident that so many good yarns are tales of islands and islanders.

Matinicus Island, at the mouth of Penobscot Bay, is, except

for one lighthouse rock, the last outpost between Maine and Spain. Summer visitors are few and the island has never had a hotel or boarding house. Even in summer, the mailboat from Rockland reaches it only three times a week. But the occasional visitor always finds, after some searching and inquiring, that islanders are willing to take him in and treat him well.

It is no accident that so many good yarns are tales of islands and islanders.

The men of Matinicus are tall and hardy. During the bitter Maine winter their sturdy boats beat through the icy waters to haul lobster. They take their bearings by landmarks called Whaleback, Two Bush, Rum Guzzle, the Barrel, the Hogshead, Tenpound, and Wooden Ball. In the snug workshops along the waterfront, they still build most of their own boats, endlessly whittle buoys, and fashion lobster pots. Questions are answered slowly and obliquely, leaving it to the listener to supply the conclusion. "What time am I putting out tomorrow? Well, we go by Boston almanac, but Boston's a hundred and thirty-five miles by water, two hundred miles Rockland way. Sun's up here twenty minutes before Boston."

No capricious fortune has touched Matinicus, but something strange and a little sad is happening on this island. Its inhabitants speak wistfully of the days when they used to have a band and there were dances in the lodge hall. Men and women in their forties like to remember the vanished spelling and wood-chopping bees of their childhood, the croquet tournaments and the hanging of May baskets, the bonfires on Hallowe'en. Other people remember when everyone used to turn out for town meetings, and elections for selectmen were fiercely contested. In those days, there were four stores on the island, and the stove and cracker barrel sessions lasted far into the night.*

The parents of today's fourteen school children had thirty or forty classmates. Their grandparents had seventy or eighty. Since 1880, the population of Matinicus has dwindled to little more than a third. Over the same period, lobster fishing has become so profitable that the Matinicans have given up farming. They are more prosperous than ever before.

Just why these changes should have been accompanied by a virtual disappearance of community life, the islanders do not know. Today the one store closes at five o'clock in the afternoon, the public library has vanished, the lodge hall is boarded up, and town meetings are conducted by rote. "The old American stock is dying out, and not just in population," says one old-timer thoughtfully. "Well, what other ways?" "Oh, knowing about how to have fun together, cooperating."

But Matinicus still has a gently exuberant flavor and an extraordinary natural beauty. The fields, where hay and potatoes were once raised, have the feeling of remote hilltop pastures, quiet and close to the sun. Roads and paths wind along the mossy, hummocky floors of spruce and fir forests so deep and

Today the one store closes at five o'clock in the afternoon, the public library has vanished, the lodge hall is boarded up, and town meetings are conducted by rote.

---

* In chapter 9 of *Cities and the Wealth of Nations,* "Bypassed Places," Jacobs diagnoses the loss of such practices as a result of prolonged isolation from dynamic urban economies. This theory of cultural forgetfulness through economic stagnation also underpins her final book, *Dark Age Ahead.*

dark they seem unending, then emerge suddenly among tumbled granite boulders at the sea.

The burying ground at Matinicus is small, but its gravestones span almost two centuries. The newer ones, surrounded by trimmed turf and planted flowers, bear only names and dates. The older ones, the ones that lean crazily into a tangle of blueberry bushes and long, ragged grass, say bravely again and again, "Gone But Not Forgotten." You need scratch away only a little of the lichen to read it.

No Virtue in Meek Conformity

FOREWORD TO STATE DEPARTMENT LOYALTY SECURITY
BOARD INTERROGATORY, MARCH 25, 1952

UPON FIRST READING THE QUESTIONS SUBMITTED TO ME, I was under the impression that possibly I was to be charged with belonging to the UPWA union and to registering in the American Labor Party.* But since neither of these has been declared illegal for government workers, I concluded, upon further thought, that I am probably suspected of being either a secret

---

* The United Public Workers of America was a union for government workers affiliated with the Congress of Industrial Organizations, or CIO. Jacobs was a member between 1943 and 1945, when she worked for the Office of War Information (OWI), and again between 1947 and 1951, when she worked for the State Department. Called the United Federal Workers of America when Jacobs joined during the war, it was a militant union, active in progressive and civil rights politics, particularly in New York. Some of the union's leaders and members were Communists, which attracted the attention of the FBI and congressional Cold Warriors in the late 1940s and led to its expulsion from the CIO in 1950.

The American Labor Party was a political party, founded by socialist union leaders, which briefly flourished in the 1930s and '40s in New York. Riven by internal battles between socialists and Communists, the ALP began a slow collapse in the late '40s. Just as she believed in the fundamental role of unions in the workplace, Jacobs liked third parties for their "valuable function in needling popular opinion." She had registered with the ALP in the 1940s but began to grow disillusioned with both party and union when they followed the Communist Party line on domestic and foreign policy issues. She stayed in both organizations as a matter of principle, convictions she defended when her memberships made her a target of the FBI and State Department's Cold War campaigns to expose Communists. For Jacobs's full response to the Loyalty Security Board's "interrogatory," see *Ideas That Matter* (pp. 169–79).

Communist sympathizer or a person susceptible to Communist influence. I then realized that it is probably at least as difficult for you to put me and my answers in context, so to speak, as it is for me to put the questions in context. Therefore, I am including this foreword to "put myself in context" as best I can. I shall try not to waste your time by repeating material which is in my answers.

It still shocks me, although we should all be used to it by this time, to realize that Americans can be officially questioned on their union membership, political beliefs, reading matter and the like. I do not like this, and I like still less the fear that arises from it. But I understand the necessity for such questions in the case of government workers in sensitive departments. And I understand that you must examine carefully where there appear to be inconsistencies or deviations. For my part, I am interested, as a citizen deeply concerned in the preservation of traditional American liberties, in presenting my viewpoint as fully and as plainly as possible. I am not answering the enclosed questions in a spirit of sparring with you or trying to get away with anything. I want you to know how I feel.

I was brought up to believe that there is no virtue in conforming meekly to the dominant opinion of the moment.

First of all, I was brought up to believe that there is no virtue in conforming meekly to the dominant opinion of the moment. I was encouraged to believe that simple conformity results in stagnation for a society, and that American progress has been largely owing to the opportunity for experimentation, the leeway given initiative, and to a gusto and a freedom for chewing over odd ideas. I was taught that the American's right to be a free individual, not at the mercy of the state, was hard-won and that its price was eternal vigilance, and that I too would have to be vigilant. I was made to feel that it would be a disgrace to me, as an individual, if I should not value or should give up rights that were dearly bought. I am grateful for that upbringing. My grandfather, on my mother's side, was a lifelong enthusiast of third-party movements in the agrarian and populist tradition. On at least one occasion, in 1872, he ran for Congress on the Greenback-Labor ticket, and a scrapbook of that campaign has come down to me through the family.* I am pleased to see how many of that party's planks, "outlandish" at the time, have since become respectable law and opinion, and I am proud that my grandfather stuck his neck out for them. I am proud of my country that he could do this and also be a respected and successful lawyer. Some members on my father's side of the family, in Virginia, did not believe in secession or slavery, and opposed their state's participation in the Civil War. They too were respected for their beliefs, even in the heat of war and of divided family. After the War, they became Republicans, in further assertion of their beliefs, a tradition which passed down to my father and his brother. I am proud of that also, and of a remoter relative, a Quaker, who, believing in women's rights and women's brains, set up her own little printing press to publish her own works without a masculine *nom de*

---

* The Greenback-Labor Party was a late-nineteenth-century third party that united rural farmers and urban workers. Formed in 1876 as the Greenback Party, its main goal was to push for the increased availability of paper money not backed by gold—"greenbacks"—in order to make it easier for farmers and workers to pay off their debts. The party elected a number of congressmen in 1878 but faded away in the 1880s. The goal of loosening the money supply and ending the gold standard did not fade, however, and was taken up by the Populists and eventually the Democrats, thereby earning Jacobs's admiration for the party's role in pushing new, untested ideas.

plume. Perhaps it is partly because of such personal tradition that I feel our American tradition of freedom to deviate from the accepted viewpoint is not a cliché or of secondary value.

I believe that there are today two great threats to the security of the American tradition. One is the power of the Soviet Union and its satellites.

Elsewhere in this interrogatory I say what I think of the Soviet government.* I believe that our military preparations are necessary for countering the power of the Soviet Union and for halting further aggressive war. But I do not think military readiness, in itself, will defeat Communism. I do not think we can consider the job finished with that. I think it buys us time to do the bigger job. We must demonstrate that it is possible to overcome poverty, misery and decay by democratic means, and we must ourselves believe, and must show others, that our American tradition of the dignity and liberty of the individual is not a luxury for easy times but is the basic source of the strength and security of a successful society.

The other threat to the security of our tradition, I believe,

---

*   The Loyalty Security Board asked Jacobs about her "attitude toward the Communist Party, the Soviet system of government, and the aims and policies of the Soviet Union." She answered that insofar as it could be proved that the Communist Party in the United States was "an apparatus for espionage or sabotage, I believe it is dangerous and that such activities must be rooted out, hampered and so far as possible destroyed, for the sake of our national security." However, she did not think the Communist Party dangerous as a political force because it "never has convinced more than a relative handful of Americans. . . . Ideas and ideologies will become a domestic menace only if we fall into the trap of believing that each of us must think like all the others." As for the Soviet Union, she said, "I fear and despise the whole concept of a government which takes as its mission the molding of people into a specific 'kind of man,' i.e. 'Soviet Man'; that practices and extols a conception of the state as 'control from above and support from below' (I believe in control from below and support from above)." The Communist Party in Russia, she said, was "a ruthless device for maintaining power, an apparatus for political tyranny." See *Ideas That Matter* (pp. 178–79).

lies at home. It is the current fear of radical ideas and of people who propound them. I do not agree with extremists of either the left or the right, but I think they should be allowed to speak and to publish, both because they themselves have, and ought to have, rights, and because once their rights are gone, the rights of the rest of us are hardly safe. Extremists typically want to squash not only those who disagree with them diametrically, but those who disagree with them at all. It seems to me that in every country where extremists of the left have gotten sufficiently in the saddle to squash the extremists of the right, they have ridden on to squash the center or terrorize it also. And the same goes for extremists of the right. I do not want to see that happen in our country.

I do not agree with extremists of either the left or the right, but I think they should be allowed to speak and to publish, both because they themselves have, and ought to have, rights, and because once their rights are gone, the rights of the rest of us are hardly safe.

In the case of the first threat I mentioned, the international threat of Communist systems of government, I have been able to do something practical through my work in the State Department. In the case of the second threat, that of McCarthy—or of the frame of mind of which McCarthy is an apt symbol—there is little practical that I could do other than take a stand in assertion of my own rights.*

I believe I should tell you where I draw my lines. I believe in

---

* This is a reference, of course, to Senator Joseph McCarthy of Wisconsin (1908–57; in office 1947–57), whose zealous, self-aggrandizing, and ultimately self-defeating pursuit of waning Communist influence in America in the early 1950s gave the popular name "McCarthyism" to the entire period of the Second Red Scare of the 1940s and '50s.

the right of Communists, or anyone else, to speak and publish and promulgate ideas in the United States. I believe they or anyone else definitely does not have any right to spy or to sabotage, and should be prosecuted for these acts.

In my personal behavior, I believe I have the right to criticize my government and my Congress. I make these criticisms within the framework of our own system and tradition. I would not aid another country instead of the United States or do any act which would be against the national or international interests of our country and for the interests of the Soviet Union or its satellites.

I would not personally ostracize anyone on account of their political beliefs, but I do not and would not disclose or talk about any material entrusted to me by the government.

Among the public figures who are making known their views today, I would say that the point of view of Justice William O. Douglas most closely coincides with my own.*

This is how I stand. I realize you too must draw lines. I am deeply concerned, not only for my own personal welfare, but as a citizen, in where you draw your lines.

Perhaps people with my point of view are in a minority today. But the fact of being in a minority does not, in itself, trouble me, nor do I see anything un-American about being in a minority position. Quite the contrary. The minority views of one day are frequently the majority views of another, and in the possibility of this being so rests all our potentiality for progress. Perhaps hindsight will show me to have been right, perhaps

---

* Supreme Court Justice William O. Douglas (1898–1980) sat on the high court for over thirty-five years (1939–75), the longest tenure of any justice in American history, and was particularly known for his defense of individual rights and personal liberty.

wrong. But we cannot run our lives by hindsight. These are hard times for any American to steer a course. The only guide which I feel that I can follow is not the fluctuating dicta of those who are victors in the battle for popularity at a given moment, but my own understanding of the American tradition in which I was brought up.

Jane Jacobs speaking at an anti–urban renewal rally in 1966, protesting the construction of a new library for New York University.

PART TWO

CITY BUILDING

1952–1965

JANE JACOBS BEGAN WORK AT *ARCHITECTURAL FORUM* IN May 1952. Published by Time-Life, *Forum* was one of the leading design magazines of its day and a champion of modernism in architecture and city planning. Douglas Haskell, the magazine's editor-in-chief, initially offered Jacobs a position covering the design of schools and hospitals. Over time she would become his most trusted editor and writer on architectural and urban planning issues of all sorts, lending her observant eye and skeptical wit to accounts of housing, shopping centers, suburbanization and sprawl, metropolitan governance, and urban renewal.

Jacobs had written about architecture and urbanism at *Amerika,* and she learned much from her husband, Robert Jacobs, a practicing architect whom she had married in 1944. But in her writing at *Forum* she developed a particular interest in the way a building *worked,* rather than simply how it looked. How did the architect organize the building's complicated mix of uses in space? How did he or she solve practical problems or save money in novel ways? How did the building's users experience it day to day? What did the building do differently than others of its kind that came before? She shared with the modern architects and planners she covered a wholehearted belief in the primacy of function in design, and in the potential for putting science to work in improving human life.

She and her colleagues also saw that American cities in the postwar era faced grave problems: People were fleeing to the suburbs, factories and offices followed hard on their heels, and swaths of so-called "slums" and "blight" spread in the neighborhoods left behind near downtown. Unlike their "decentrist" peers who favored building at the fringes of cities as the solution to urban ills, *Forum*'s editors believed in cities, so when the federal government authorized subsidies for public housing programs and privately backed urban renewal projects, the magazine applauded. Federal money and power would be used to acquire "blighted" land through eminent domain, clear the "slums," and build new apartment complexes, hospitals, universities, and other projects, all of which would be designed in the latest modern styles. Over the course of the 1950s, the number of redevelopment projects around the country boomed, more than doubling between 1954 and 1958. As Haskell summed it up in a 1956 editorial, "A new order of architecture and building is not only coming, it is here already: city architecture, city building and rebuilding." However, personal experience would soon shake Jacobs's belief in the conceits of modern architecture, if not the functionalist foundations on which it rested. In fact, she would soon find herself at the heart of a series of debates about city life that would drastically alter her understanding of the modernist credo "form ever follows function."

In 1955, Haskell tasked Jacobs with covering the urban renewal beat, and under the heading "City Building" Jacobs favorably reviewed projects in Philadelphia, Cleveland, Washington, Fort Worth, and Baltimore. Although she found praiseworthy elements in every plan, beneath the surface she began to have doubts about the true impact of this emerging urbanism. One moment particularly gnawed at her. As she toured Philadelphia with planning officials, they tried to demonstrate the contrast between a "bad, old street" and a "good, new street" for her. As Jacobs recalled nearly fifty years later, the "bad" street was "just crammed with people, mostly black people, walking on the sidewalks and sitting on the stoops and leaning out of the windows," while the "good" one, a recent patient of urban renewal, sat empty except for a lone little boy, idly kicking a tire in the gutter.[1] She admired Ed Bacon and Louis Kahn, the masterminds behind Philadelphia's renewal, describing them as the kind of "pavement pounding" planners she valued. But something wasn't working.

Over the next year, it became clear to Jacobs that to design and build on the scale of a city demanded an understanding of the *functions* of the city itself that modern rebuilders had not yet grasped. Another encounter helped her see this. In 1956, Jacobs met William Kirk and Ellen Lurie, workers at Union Settlement House in New York's East Harlem, where the city had been putting up chunk after chunk of public housing. Eager to demonstrate to *Architectural Forum* the deleterious effects of modern rebuilding, they took Jacobs on several walks around East Harlem, showing her how the "bad, old streets" really worked. They pointed out that the dense, intricate mixture of storefronts, residences, and workplaces gave rise to what Jacobs would later call "a living network of relationships" between neighbors that provided them with friendship, trust, safety, and the ability to collaborate when under threat. In short, they taught her about the city's role in building what she would later call "social capital." No amount of policing, planning, or subsidized services, she argued, could replace this indispensable, self-organizing asset of urban life.

Later that year, Jacobs got a chance to publicly express her growing concerns. Extending Kirk and Lurie's observations about East Harlem to a general principle, Jacobs delivered a speech at a Harvard design conference criticizing how modern architects—her very audience—excised storefronts from the streetscape at the expense of social capital. Their supposedly functionalist projects had betrayed that great function of the city. "The Missing Link in City Redevelopment," as it was called when it appeared in *Architectural Forum* (and in this volume), was a hit and set Jacobs on her path to notoriety.

Jacobs's contrarian views were starting to be known among the architecture and planning cognoscenti. But she wouldn't find a national audience for them until 1958, when she got a chance to launch a full takedown of city planning orthodoxy in the pages of *Fortune, Forum*'s older sibling in the Time-Life family. "Downtown Is for People," which summed up everything she was learning in East Harlem, Philadelphia, and other neighborhoods undergoing renewal, appeared in editor William H. Whyte's influential series of articles on urban problems, later published as a book called *The Exploding Metropolis*. The stir "Downtown" kicked up attracted the attention of the Rockefeller Foundation, which agreed to support Jacobs as she set out to research and write the book that would become *The Death and Life of Great American Cities*.

Death and Life was an instant sensation upon its publication in 1961, and Jacobs soon found herself giving talks all over the country, including at the White House. Today the book is considered a great turning point in the art of understanding cities. Although it began with the well-known words "This book is an attack on current city planning and rebuilding," in truth *Death and Life* took modernist planners and architects to task *on their own terms.* In her decade at *Architectural Forum,* Jacobs had become disillusioned with modern city building in practice, but its purported principles and goals still resonated with her. While postmodern critics like Charles Jencks and Robert Venturi would later denounce the aesthetics of modern architecture—a poverty of ornament, meaning, and historical or popular reference—Jacobs sought instead the lost promise of modernism in the city itself—the squandered possibility of true scientific understanding, functionalism, and progress. Instead of relying on abstract reasoning and statistics, though, she called for students of the city to observe its economic and social processes firsthand. Instead of embracing a narrow, discipline-driven interpretation of functionalism, she demanded that architects and planners better express those broader economic and social functions in their design. And to improve the lives of city dwellers, she proposed that reformers start with the already existing assets of neighborhoods, rather than violently ordaining a clean slate.

Jacobs's reformist take on modern city building was spurred not only by her discoveries of the abuses of urban renewal, or the intricacies of East Harlem street life, but also by an appreciation for the textures of life in her own Greenwich Village, where she had lived for two decades. Jacobs, her husband, and their three children occupied a hundred-year-old storefront building on Hudson Street that she and Robert were renovating in their spare time. So when she heard, in 1955, that New York's public works czar Robert Moses wanted to run a roadway through the neighborhood's chief amenity, Washington Square Park, she resolved to do all she could to help stop it. Jacobs was only a rank-and-file member of the successful campaign to stop the road—the effort had started years before she even knew Moses had proposed it—but it would not be her last run-in with the city planning establishment she attacked in *Death and Life*. Between early 1961, just months before the book's publication, and her departure from New York in 1968, she led successful campaigns against an urban renewal project for the Village and a freeway across Lower Manhattan, experiences that further fueled both her ire at the forces of modernization from above and her ambition to understand what it was that truly makes cities work.

NOTES

1.   Interview with Eleanor Wachtel, *Writers & Company*, CBC Radio, August 6, 2002.

Philadelphia's Redevelopment: A Progress Report

ARCHITECTURAL FORUM,

JULY 1955

ONCE UPON A TIME THE GENERAL PROBLEM OF THE CITY Chaotic looked so simple.

Boulevards and civic monuments were going to create the City Beautiful. After that proved insufficient, regional plans were to create the City Sensible. These proved unacceptable and now we are struggling, sometimes it seems at the expense of everything else, to improvise the City Traversible.

And still the deserts of the city have grown and still they are growing, the awful endless blocks, the endless miles of drabness and chaos. A good way to see the problem of the city is to take a bus or streetcar ride, a long ride, through a city you do not know. For in this objective frame of mind, you may stop thinking about the ugliness long enough to think of the work that went into this mess. As a sheer manifestation of energy it is awesome. It says as much about the power and doggedness of life as the leaves of the forest say in spring. All else can only be oases in the desert. Hundreds of thousands of people with hundreds of thousands of plans and purposes built the city and only they will rebuild the city.

Philadelphia is a city, perhaps the only U.S. city thus far, that has looked at this appalling fact and begun to deal with it.

In Philadelphia, a redevelopment area is not a tract slated only—or necessarily primarily—for spec-

Hundreds of thousands of people with hundreds of thousands of plans and purposes built the city and only they will rebuild the city.

tacular replacements. In short, it is not simply to be an oasis. Most certified areas include a great deal of acreage that never will have a magic wand waved suddenly over it. Some of Philadelphia's redevelopment money is to be spent thinly and very, very shrewdly in interstices of these areas to bring out the good that already exists there or play up potentialities.*

The Philadelphia approach also means a busybody concern with what private developers will be up to next: a jump ahead. To keep the desert from spreading interminably, plans and persuasion for thinly settled outer reaches have already been marshaled. Downtown, Penn Center is an example of this approach. By the time the Pennsy decided to remove its tracks and old Broad St. Station, the planning commission was ready with a

---

* Urban renewal in Philadelphia, pioneered by City Planning Commission director Edmund Bacon (1910–2005), sought to avoid the excesses of the "bulldozer approach" to slum clearance and rebuilding by designating smaller renewal areas, trying to minimize evictions, holding community meetings early in the process, preserving local institutions, employing innovative architects, and incorporating local history into plans. Jacobs found herself both inspired and provoked by Bacon, but if nothing else, she approved of his attempt to use renewal as a catalyst for rejuvenation. At the 1958 conference where Jacobs made her public debut as a critic of urban renewal, Bacon described city neighborhoods as "dynamic organisms which have within themselves the seeds of self-regeneration." Jacobs would echo this idea in the closing moments of *Death and Life*: "Lively, diverse, intense cities contain the seeds of their own regeneration, with energy enough to carry over for problems and needs outside themselves" (p. 448).

suggested scheme and through thick and thin it has never let the essentials of the scheme get lost.* It has not been easy, but the gain to the city—and the developers—is incalculable.

Whether a new oasis is public or private, Philadelphia's planners look at it not simply as an improvement, but as a catalyst.

Little good can happen to people or to buildings when a sense of neighborhood is missing. Philadelphia's inexpensive devices toward the enormous gain of restoring the neighborhood to the desert may be its greatest contribution to city planning. As part of this aim, the city's public housers are not rearing alien institutions unrelated to the surrounding murk, nor are they using public housing as social and economic wall-building to dam off portions of the city. Instead, the projects are being sunk into their neighborhoods, to help rehabilitate, not eviscerate, them.

In this atmosphere of hope for the city, the initiative of private citizens seems to be thriving in the little and the large. The new food distribution center will not only be a huge improvement in its own right and serve as a two-way catalyst (removing blight from several parts of the city, instituting improvement in another), but it is an unprecedented display of public-spirited, private building.†

What is happening in Philadelphia is of such scope and involves so many people there is no neat and easy explanation for what started it or why. Physical rejuvenation of the city seems to be related to a booming hinterland, dissatisfaction with long

---

* "Pennsy" was contemporary vernacular for the Pennsylvania Railroad. Founded in 1846, it went on to become the biggest railroad in the United States and one of the largest corporations in the world. Its passenger lines were folded into the new Amtrak system in the 1970s.

† See part 4 of this article, "Finest Food Distribution Center in the World."

do-nothing, a surge of municipal reform and citizen activity, the jolt of the war years.

There is something else you cannot help seeing as you walk about the city or listen to its planners, its architects and business-men. Philadelphia's abrupt embrace of the new, after long years of apathy, has by some miracle not meant the usual rejection of whatever is old. When a city can carry on a love affair with its old and its new at once, it has terrific vitality.

When a city can carry on a love affair with its old and its new at once, it has terrific vitality.

I.

TEN THOUSAND ACRES OF CHANGE

When Philadelphians talk about a program to transform their city, they mean just that, as a glance at the map shows. Philadel-phia, first city to take advantage of the redevelopment law, has now certified a total of 10,524 acres (16 sq. mi.) for redevelop-ment in 18 major planning tracts. Fourteen of the tracts, with about half the total acreage, form almost one continuous swatch covering the mid city and pushing out to north and west. The mid city "hole" is the well-kept Rittenhouse Square area and part of the main business district.* There is no intention that the

---

* Rittenhouse Square, originally called Southwest Square, was one of the five original parks that William Penn designed for the central district of Philadelphia in the seventeenth century. It was renamed after the clockmaker David Rittenhouse in 1825. In *Death and Life,* Jacobs would say that the Square and its siblings provided "almost a controlled experiment" on the successful ingredients of a city park. While others, more isolated from their surround-ings, had grown stagnant, she praises Rittenhouse Square for its success as a much-beloved and -used park, which benefited from the diverse and intricate uses of the neighborhood around it and enriched that diversity in turn.

bulldozers can, or should if they could, run loose through these great tracts; rehabilitation and catalyst improvements are a very important part of the program.

Expressways (connecting on east and west with the New Jersey and Pennsylvania turnpikes) will have two cross-city extensions; the long-term plan is to line these with parking. Mass surface transit is to connect these extensions with the center of town, thus keeping the city from strangling in its traffic.

Public housing projects, which formerly averaged about 630 units to a project, average about 270 in work under construction or recently completed. In the future many projects will be only 20 to 100 units, with even smaller groups of only a few houses in nearby blocks. Idea: to clear out pockets and edges of blight in larger stable areas, to give leadership in areas with good rehabilitation potential, and to avoid total clearance projects so costly that extremely high densities must result. Philadelphia housers prefer putting only small families in elevator buildings, aim at placing three- to five-bedroom families in two- and three-story row houses with individual yards. This means about one-third of units high-rise.

2.

PENN CENTER'S FIRST
BUILDING GOES UP

This is Philadelphia's first new office building in more than twenty years. Long after the ephemeral advantage of being the most-up-to-date is gone, this building and its future twin will have something that sets them apart: their wonderful seats on the Penn Center promenade.*

Arrangements are now being worked out with Philadelphia's museums for sculpture pieces on loan, and everyone concerned seems agreed not to do the thing timidly.

Uris Brothers, owners of the building, have an unusual deal with Pennsylvania Railroad, owners of the land, who have agreed not to permit a competing structure until whatever Uris has is 85 percent rented. But no matter how fast the first building rents, Uris has until next summer to get first crack at the second office site. Uris leases back to the railroad the underground portions of its structure.

The missing ingredient is something out of the ordinary **happening,** *if only the splash of water.*

What the general Penn Center plans still lack, and badly need, is some sort of enterprise not strictly workaday. The promenade is a help, but once the office workers are gone, it will sleep. The missing ingredient is something out of the ordinary *happening,* if only the splash of water, but better yet some focus of entertainment or sport.

3 ·

HISTORY WITH A FUTURE

The new Independence malls (being done with state and federal participation) are disengaging Independence Hall and a group of other fine historic buildings from the clutter that has con-

---

* Jacobs would later turn on Penn Center and particularly the "promenade" she praises here. Ed Bacon designed it as a superblock featuring office towers and a pedestrian walk, but he placed all the shops and commerce in the development underground. In "Downtown Is for People," Jacobs criticizes it and other big office redevelopments for shoving "its liveliest activities and brightest lights underground."

gealed around them over the years. Among the side effects of this improvement: it is already stimulating private rehabilitation of the rundown but fundamentally lovely old areas nearby; it is building back into the district its prestige as an office center; it ties the district visually to the Delaware River bridge, a main entrance to the city; it is a counterweight to Penn Center, which by itself would likely accelerate the movement of business westward, leaving a trail of more blight. These side effects were no accident; the malls were conceived and placed to propel this whole seedy district out of the gloom.

The state mall has been criticized as out of scale, embalming Independence Hall in its grand distances like a fly in amber. However, mall or no mall, the Hall is a fly in amber—whole, stimulating to the sense of wonder, but infinitely, infinitely remote. The quaintsy lamps, urns and pedestals that irritate the mall's edges are a pathetic try at concealing the joints between then-and-now, but the design that counts is the long tree-lined bits which acknowledge the Hall is an exhibit that most people first view at 35 mph. Happily for those who stop, the existing park behind and the building-dotted federal mall lend a congenial urban scale.

The problem of harmonizing then-and-now without going phony is also posed by the new office buildings that will focus on the malls. The first has already created quite a hassle. A statement adopted by the Philadelphia AIA sensibly recommends candid contemporary design, tallness with rigid adherence to setback on the mall side, sensitive study of the neighbors and plentiful planting.*

---

* A reference to the Philadelphia chapter of the American Institute of Architects, the major professional organization for architects in the United States.

4 ·
"FINEST FOOD DISTRIBUTION
CENTER IN THE WORLD"

That is what Department of Agriculture's marketing experts call this 400-acre, $35 million project which is to start building within six months and will serve not only the city and a 90-mile radius but will likely make Philadelphia the major food distribution point on the middle Atlantic Coast.

It will unify and vastly enlarge wholesale facilities now scattered in half a dozen places—most of them crowded, dirty, festering sources of blight and bottlenecking, put them at a transportation hub, provide enough parking and loading so the city's 5,000 independent retailers can shop speedily, competitively and oftener, so suppliers can function in an eight-hour day and so working conditions will attract high-grade labor. Motel, hostel, eating places, 23 acres of planted area, go with it.

Because of what it will do for the old market districts, what it will do for its site (burning dumps and squatters' shacks) and what it will do for the city's economy, this is Philadelphia's most important single improvement.

Why should a step like this be so rare? For one thing, slum markets are like slum housing; there are big profits in them for some people, at the expense of all people.* It takes ability to

---

* Jacobs is using the conventional mid-twentieth-century term for the mixed residential, commercial, and industrial districts surrounding the downtowns of big cities. Despite its wide use as shorthand for "bad neighborhood," the term *slum* was, like the closely related term *blight*, far from an objective description. Although the two terms were often used interchangeably in everyday usage, they had slightly different connotations. In the early twentieth century *slum* initially meant that a city district suffered from a range of physical and social

overcome a kicking, scratching opposition, ability to line up wholesalers' support, ability to think big and to finance big.

How Philadelphia got this project is as remarkable as the project itself. It is the baby of the Greater Philadelphia Movement, a small, very high-powered group of nongovernmental Philadelphia leaders, mostly businessmen and bankers. These men applied themselves to study and action on food wholesaling with the fervor their business ancestors applied to building the railroads or cornering wheat. But observe a startling difference in motives: these new tycoons expect their nonprofit corporation, the Greater Philadelphia Food Distribution Center, to lower distributing costs for the consumer and at the same time pay for itself. And when capital costs are paid off, the whole development will be converted to the ownership of the city of Philadelphia which will then pocket the profits. In the meantime, the city should receive about $1 million a year in property tax and the school district $800,000. The sponsor's share seems to be the bang they get out of doing something big, and satisfaction in helping the city.

---

problems—from high incidences of crime, disease, and fires to overcrowding and physical dilapidation of older housing stock—while *blight* tended to refer to districts that were economically fallow, largely because they were not returning their highest values in terms of tax dollars to city coffers. Thus the major difference: overcrowded neighborhoods tended to be seen as "slums," areas with vacancies and abandoned buildings as "blight." In popular usage the two terms tended to merge as conjoined judgments about the social, physical, and economic viability of whole swaths of the city. They were used, despite their vague and capacious natures, as official justifications in policy for slum clearance plans.

5 ·

HOW TO PUT THE NEIGHBORHOOD
BACK INTO THE CITY

Mill Creek redevelopment area is a chunk of typical city desert. Building coverage runs as high as 74 percent, dwelling density as high as 50 units per acre. Nothing gives the whole amorphous mass backbone; block after block is more of the dreary same.

The city planning commission's Mill Creek redevelopment plan, with Louis I. Kahn as consulting architect, contains some wonderfully clever and practical devices for jacking up the district, almost by its own bootstraps.*

As Kahn studied the area, he noticed that a good proportion of its few institutions—churches, school, a playground—occurred along one street, although the fact was hardly noticeable, they were so underplayed.

The plan reinforces these institutions with a few additional, and gives them a new kind of Main St., primarily for pedestrians, closed off to vehicles where it runs through new housing, widened and side-planted in other places, joining subsidiary spurs. "It brings out, instead of burying, the things built by unselfish effort," says Kahn.

Looking at the old housing, he concluded the worst thing about it was the gridiron streets "which were not nearly so bad in the more peaceful days of the horse when these houses were

---

* The architect Louis Kahn (1901– 74) not only designed Mill Creek, he also served as the "chief planner-architect" for Philadelphia's entire redevelopment program. He would become one of the most celebrated modern architects of his generation. As with Ed Bacon, Jacobs found herself inspired by Kahn's respect for the city fabric, although in the long run she became dismayed by the impact of his plans on the city. Mill Creek was demolished in 2002 and replaced by a low-rise, single-family development called the Lucien E. Blackwell Homes.

built." Where cross-streets were sufficiently wide, he has turned the gridiron into loops by inserting a trail of little connected parks and decorative pavings. Within the street loops, he has added parking across from the parks. Both this device and the new greenway or pedestrian main street have been approved, are to be tried.

New housing, mostly in the southeast corner, combines public low-cost and private middle-income projects. Tall buildings are ingeniously sited so they do not confront each other. Circles, some containing sand, some grass, some paving, are the basic landscaping unit and path-determiners. "It puts shortcuts into the paths in the first place."

Mill Creek's new housing, particularly its mixture of high, low and differing-income projects and its tall-building siting, have already influenced planning in other cities, notably in Detroit.

Pavement Pounders and Olympians

ARCHITECTURAL FORUM,

MAY 1956

EDGARDO CONTINI, ONE OF THE AUTHORS OF THE SPLENDID Gruen plan for Fort Worth, had it in mind one Saturday morning a few weeks ago in Fort Worth to buy himself a new pair of walking shoes.* When a visitor from *Forum* turned up, however, he agreed to postpone his shopping and talk about the city instead.

Talking about the city, it quickly developed over a cup of coffee, also meant walking about the city, and over the next few hours the visitor began to understand why Contini's walking shoes needed replacing. He knew that square mile of downtown, on foot, the way most people know their own block. Between side excursions into backyards, prowls into alleys, sallies

---

* Jacobs wrote frequently about the work of architect Victor Gruen (1903–80), particularly his plan for Fort Worth, Texas. An émigré from Vienna, Gruen gained fame as the architect of the first enclosed, climate-controlled, regional shopping mall, Southdale Center in Edina, Minnesota (1956), and many subsequent malls. Jacobs admired his love for city life and his attempts to concentrate city-like uses in his designs. His Fort Worth plan turned what he'd learned designing malls back on the downtown, combining genuine urban liveliness with the theatricality and traffic engineering of a suburban shopping mall. For other examples of Jacobs's analysis of Gruen's work, see "Downtown Is for People" and "Do Not Segregate Pedestrians and Automobiles" in this volume and chapter 18 of *Death and Life,* "Erosion of Cities or Attrition of Automobiles."

into the middle of the street (future domain of the pedestrian) and plunges up stairs (for a different angle of vision), he enthusiastically detailed the history of this store, the activities on that block, the qualities of the restaurant yonder, the potentialities of around-the-corner.

Contini belongs to a breed which seems to be on the increase—the pavement-pounding city planner. Edmund Bacon, Philadelphia's executive director of planning, is another representative. Bacon delights in having figured out, by trial and error, a zigzag route across Philadelphia, from river to river, that never subjects the walker to a dull vista or uninteresting street. The same passion for intimate examination of the city extends right through his staff. A visitor gets the impression that any one of them chooses his lunchtime restaurant more for the quality of the walk to it (generally long) than the food at the goal. Out in Cleveland, a supposed tour by car with Planning Officials Ernest Bohn and James Lister actually amounts to a series of short automobile hops and long exploratory stops. San Francisco has the tirelessly ambulant and observant Paul Oppermann as director of planning; Carl Feiss will walk anyone's legs off at home in Washington or wherever he happens to be, and there are happily others like them.

We had reason to be especially appreciative of the pavement pounders after a recent talk with a representative of another type of planner—the Olympian. In a city which shall be nameless, this planning official and his colleagues had conscientiously studied, from Olympian heights, their maps, their density patterns, their social statistics, their traffic patterns—then waved their clearance wands. And they were in process of committing economic, aesthetic and social outrages on the adjoining neighborhoods because they lacked awareness of such simple things as the distinction between convenience "neighborhood" shops and widely patronized "district" shopping. And on being told there were some good and well-kept streets embedded in a statistical slump area under discussion, the Olympian exclaimed in genuine surprise, "Where?" Bacon and Lister would not only know where, they would know why.

The pavement pounders are coming up with by far the best planning these days, but we doubt the relationship is simple cause-and-effect, salutary as first-hand knowledge is. More likely, the walking and the good planning are two sides of the same attitude, two sides of the pavement pounder's fascination, on an intimate level, with all details of city life and city relationships, of his consuming curiosity about the way the city develops and changes, of his endless preoccupation with the *living* city, and—at the bottom of it all—of his affection for the city.

The pavement pounders are a new breed: they are the men who want to change and rebuild the city not out of fundamental disgust with it, but out of fascination with it and love for it.

Affection for the city, curiously enough, has not always been an attribute of city planners in the past. The City Beautiful men valued a minute part of the city as a grand showplace, but pretty well ignored and despised "the antheap."* Twenty years ago,

---

* One of Jacobs's many derisive references to the City Beautiful movement, an influential city planning movement from the turn of the twentieth century that hoped to rescue the city from the effects of rampant industrialization by laying out great boulevards, ceremonial squares, civic centers, greenbelts, and parks, and then studding these new open spaces with statuary and monumental buildings. The movement is most often associated with planner Daniel Burnham (1846–1912), he of the famous maxim "Make no little plans." It was respon-

the most stimulating planners were putting their most stimulating thinking into schemes for decentralizing the city, not rebuilding it. Implicit was a rather hopeless feeling about the city itself. The pavement pounders are a new breed: they are the men who want to change and rebuild the city not out of fundamental disgust with it, but out of fascination with it and love for it. Equally hopeful for the city's future: their ranks are being joined, gradually, by real estate men and financiers and promoters—who are also capable of feeling, influencing and acting either as pavement pounders or Olympians.

We wish Contini and all his kind a long succession of the most comfortable shoes, well worn.

---

sible for a host of city plans in the early years of the century that drew inspiration from Burnham's 1893 World's Fair in Chicago and the cityscape of imperial Paris. Most were only implemented piecemeal—remnants can be seen in Boston, Chicago, Washington, D.C., San Francisco, and in lone monuments like Grand Army Plaza in Brooklyn, New York.

The Missing Link in
City Redevelopment

ARCHITECTURAL FORUM,

JUNE 1956

SOMETIMES YOU LEARN MORE ABOUT A PHENOMENON WHEN it isn't there, like water when the well runs dry—or like the neighborhood stores which are not being built in our redeveloped city areas. In New York's East Harlem, for instance, 1,110 stores have already vanished in the course of rehousing 50,000 people.

Planners and architects are apt to think, in an orderly way, of stores as a straightforward matter of supplies and services. Commercial space.

But stores in city neighborhoods are much more complicated creatures which have evolved a much more complicated function. Although they are mere holes in the wall, they help make an urban neighborhood a community instead of a mere dormitory.

A store is also a storekeeper. One supermarket can replace 30 neighborhood delicatessens, fruit stands, groceries and butchers, as a Housing Authority planner explains. But it cannot replace 30 storekeepers or even one. The manager of a housing project in East Harlem says he spends three-fourths of his time on extraneous matters; he says: "I'm forced into trying to take the place of 40 storekeepers." He is no better trained to handle this than a storekeeper and not as good at it because he does it grudgingly instead of out of pleasure of being a neighborhood hub and busybody. Also it happens that most of the tenants heartily dislike him, but he is the best they have in the way of a public character in that super-block and they try to make him do.

The stores themselves are social centers—especially the bars, candy stores and diners.

A store is also often an empty store *front*. Into these fronts go all manner of churches, clubs and mutual uplift societies. These storefront activities are enormously valuable. They are the institutions that people create, themselves. Sometimes they end up famous. Many real ornaments to the city have started this way. The little struggling ones are even more important in the aggregate.

Most political clubs are in storefronts. When an old area is leveled, it is often a great joke that Wardheeler so-and-so has lost his organization. This is not really hilarious. If you are a nobody, and you don't know anybody who isn't a nobody, the only way you can make yourself heard in a large city is through certain well defined channels. These channels all begin in holes in the wall. They start in Mike's barbershop or the hole-in-the-wall office of a man called Judge, and they go on to the Thomas Jefferson Democratic Club where Councilman Favini holds court, and now you are started on up. It all takes an incredible

If you are a nobody, and you don't know anybody who isn't a nobody, the only way you can make yourself heard in a large city is through certain well defined channels.

number of confabs. The physical provisions for this kind of process cannot conceivably be formalized.

When the holes in the wall disappear, several different things can happen. Stuyvesant Town in New York City clearly demonstrates one result. That development is now surrounded by an unplanned, chaotic, prosperous belt of stores, the camp followers around the Stuyvesant barracks. A good planner could handle that belt. Tucked in here are the hand-to-mouth cooperative nursery schools, the ballet classes, the do-it-yourself workshops, the little exotic stores which are among the great charms of a city. This same process happens whether the population is middle income like Stuyvesant Town or predominately low income like East Harlem.

Do you see what this means? Some very important sides of city life, much of the charm, the creative social activity and the vitality shift over to the old vestigial areas because there is literally no place for them in the new scheme of things. This is a ludicrous situation, and it ought to give planners the shivers.*

When rebuilding happens wholesale, sometimes there is almost no convenient vestigial area left. In one project, in this fix, in East Harlem, the people are very much at loose ends. There is a "community center" but it is a children's center. Some settle-

---

* Jacobs claimed that some architects had latched on to her observations in this speech very superficially as a dogmatic slogan: "We must leave room for the corner grocery store!" In *Death and Life,* she writes, "At first I thought this must be a figure of speech, the part standing for the whole. But soon I began to receive in the mail plans and drawings for projects and renewal areas in which, literally, room had been left here and there at great intervals for a corner grocery store. These schemes were accompanied by letters that said, 'See, we have taken to heart what you said.' This corner-grocery gimmick is a thin, patronizing conception of city diversity, possibly suited to a village of the last century, but hardly to a vital city district of today" (p. 191). Jacobs despised dogma in all its forms, including when her own ideas came back at her in unthinking regurgitations.

ment house workers fine-tooth-combed that development of 2,000 people to find where they could make easy-going contact with adults. Absolutely the only place that showed signs of working as an adult social area was the laundry. We wonder if the planner of that project had any idea its heart would be in the basement. And we wonder if the architect had any idea what he was designing when he did that laundry. We wonder if it occurred to either of them that this represents one kind of social poverty beyond anything the slums ever knew.

Even in the projects a decade old the inhabitants do a lot of visiting in old neighborhoods but relatively few visitors come to the new. Nothing to do.

There are degrees to which all this can be better or worse. Putting in shopping centers, defining neighborhood units in proper geographic and population scale, mixing income groups and types of housing, and being very sensitive about just where the bulldozers go are all basic. There is already thinking, if not much action, about these matters.

Here are four added suggestions:

- First, look at some lively old parts of the city. Notice the tenement with the stoop and sidewalk and how that stoop and sidewalk belong to the people there. A living room is not a substitute; this is a different facility. Notice the stores and the converted store fronts. Notice the taxpayers and up above, the bowling alley, the union local, the place where you learn the guitar. We do not suggest these units be copied, but that you think about these examples of the plaza, the market place and the forum, all very ugly

and makeshift but very much belonging to the inhabitants, very intimate and informal.

- Second, planners must become much more socially
astute about the zoning of stores and the spotting of
stores. Fortunately, in retail business economic and
social astuteness can make fine allies if given a
chance.

- Third, architects must make the most out of such
fortuitous social facilities as laundries, mailbox con-
glomerations and the adult hangouts at playgrounds.
Much can be done to play up instead of play down
the gregarious side of these seemingly trivial conve-
niences.

- Fourth, we need far more care with outdoor space.
It is not enough that it lets in light and air. It is not
enough that unallocated space serve as a sort of easel
against which to display the fine art of the buildings.
In most urban development plans, the unbuilt space
is a giant bore. The Gratiot plan for Detroit by
Stonorov, Gruen and Yamasaki, which is not to be
built, the Southwest Washington plan by I. M. Pei
and some of the Philadelphia work such as Louis
Kahn's Mill Creek, are unusual exceptions. The outdoor space should be *at least* as vital as the slum sidewalk.

There is the problem of what to do with activities that go
into empty stores and basements. True, nobody planned for
these among the old tenements and brownstones, but physically
there were places to insinuate them. There is no such flexibility

in rebuilt neighborhoods. The answer is *not* in providing multi-purpose public rooms for them. They will die on the vine. The essence of these enterprises is that they have a place indisputably their own. Unless and until some solution for them can be found, the least we can do is to respect—in the deepest sense—strips of chaos that have a weird wisdom of their own not yet encompassed in our concept of urban order.

The city has its own peculiar virtues and we will do it no service by trying to beat it into some inadequate imitation of the noncity.

We are greatly misled by talk about bringing the suburb into the city. The city has its own peculiar virtues and we will do it no service by trying to beat it into some inadequate imitation of the noncity. The starting point must be study of whatever is workable, whatever has charm, in *city* life, and these are the first qualities that must find a place in the architecture of the rebuilt city.

Our "Surplus" Land

ARCHITECTURAL FORUM,

MARCH 1957

EVERY SO OFTEN, THINGS "EVERYBODY KNOWS" NEED TO BE reexamined. For instance everybody, including City Hall, knows the place to look for plentiful building land is not in the asphalt and brick burdened city. Everybody knows the place to look for land is out in the country.

Is that so?

About five years from now, when we look back at the good old fifties, one of the things that may look good about them is the troublesome crop surpluses. It seems unbelievable (after all, the 1958 budget sets a record for farm subsidies), but at the rate construction is now gobbling countryside, population and tillable land will come into delicate balance in the early sixties. From that point on, the problem will be to hold on to enough farmland to feed an ever-growing population, and eventually the problem may be how to increase farmland at the expense of buildings and pavement. It is not farfetched to imagine today's school children struggling in their maturity with legislation, subsidies and bids on rural development, so they can eat.[*]

[*]   Population and total farmland did not come into delicate balance in the 1960s. Total amounts of actively used farmland have, in fact, dipped from 1.2 million acres in 1949 to 0.9

If this calendar for change sounds abrupt, remember the Sioux who only 85 years ago plucked their dinners at will from horizon-filling herds of buffalo "innumerable as the stars of the heavens"—then saw the herds reduced to virtual extinction in less than a decade, thanks to the railroad. Things can change fast in this country, especially, it seems, when wheels carry the change.

The scale at which open land is now vanishing, thanks to the automobile, compares in scale with the vast buffalo slaughter of the 1870s. Each year 1.1 million acres by present estimates go out of crop use and into suburbs, industrial sites, airports, highways and the like. The bite promises to grow bigger year by year, not smaller. For instance, the new federal highway program alone will put pavement over 1 million acres in the next decade. Representative Clair Engel of California— a state where the unequal contest between the artichoke and the bulldozer is especially vivid—has delved into the land-holdings of the military and come up with the report that its present holdings would constitute a strip fourteen and a half miles wide from San Francisco to New York. "If they got everything they are asking for now," he says, "that strip would be increased to eighteen and a half miles wide."

Everybody is using land and more land, as if the reservoir of open land were inexhaustible. When the day of reckoning with our stomachs arrives, we shall have to cast about for some new reservoir of building sites. It is already waiting, in the place

---

million in 2002, especially in metropolitan areas. However, consolidation, specialization, and industrialization of farms have simultaneously made every acre more productive (and more environmentally destructive).

where it is "self evident" that land is the one thing in short supply—in the cities.*

Even in inner city cores, supposedly the most intensively used areas on the map, pools of surplus and underused land abound.

Very few cities have made inventory of their land reservoirs. The few that have demonstrate that the slums are a drop in the bucket, for much of the urban land reservoir is not residential at all. Much is cast off and semi-abandoned industrial; much is underused commercial; much is interstitial land which never was developed or which now stands derelict and empty. Even in inner city cores, supposedly the most intensively used areas on the map, pools of surplus and underused land abound. In replacing the one-square-mile downtown of Fort Worth, architect Victor Gruen found the underused or derelict reservoir was large enough to provide space for a belt highway, parking garages for 60,000 cars, green belts, a 300 percent increase in retail area, 60 percent increase in office space, 80 percent in hotel space, and new civic, cultural and convention centers. Fort Worth is not a special case. Architects Garber, Tweddell & Wheeler, as consultants to the Cincinnati City Planning Commission, have surveyed Cin-

* Increasingly, many places have embraced the idea that every inch of the city has to work hard, often performing a double duty, to justify the high cost of building and living. In Boston, Massachusetts, capping sunken highways and rails has provided space for new buildings. In New York City, a recent green infrastructure program addresses stormwater management while creating new recreational opportunities by adding natural spaces to the cityscape. In 2015, the City of Toronto even announced a new park under the elevated Gardiner Expressway. As Marc Ryan, the architect of the latter project, told *The Globe and Mail,* "We realize we're not going to find new public realm in the conventional places. . . . There are no more Central Parks to be built." See Alex Bozikovic, "$25-Million Project Reimagines Area Under Gardiner with Paths, Cultural Spaces," *The Globe and Mail,* November 16, 2015.

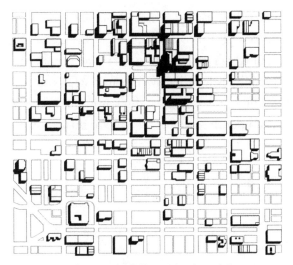

Map by Garber, Tweddell & Wheeler of downtown
Cincinnati, revealing the abundance of unbuilt space.

cinnati's core, and left its underused or derelict portions blank
on the map above. This is not a map of downtown outskirts;
this is *downtown*.

Hints of the relative plentifulness of city land can already be
read in prices and in ratio of land costs to total costs. Land costs
are now running less than 17 percent of total cost for building
on the most coveted sites in midtown New York—compared
with an average of 20 percent for suburban residential building.

City Halls which have been thinking of renewal problems
and opportunities only in terms of slum clearance and residential development should wake up to the fact that they have
unrealized quantities of a most basic commodity which is inexorably going to be in short supply elsewhere, and they should
begin to do some hard and creative thinking about it.

The half-trillion dollars which will be spent on construction in the next ten years needs land, and as much of it as possible must be land which will do our future food supplies and recreational possibilities least harm. The first step is to realize that unlimited land is not where we think it is, but that a wealth of it lies almost unnoticed where we think it isn't.

Reason, Emotion, Pressure:
There Is No Other Recipe

THE VILLAGE VOICE,

MAY 22, 1957

I WOULD LIKE TO REMIND YOU OF A STORY YOU HAVE PROBABLY all heard—the one about the man who caught a bad cold in February weather and went to his doctor in hopes of a cure. "We can't do much for you," said the doctor. "It has to run its course." "But I want to be *cured,*" said the patient.

"All right," the doctor told him. "Go home, put up the window, lie down with your pajamas open, and let the wind run through." "But doctor," said the man, "I might get pneumonia!" "Exactly," said the doctor, glancing at his aureomycin: "We know how to cure that!"

This is very much like the case of Greenwich Village. Here is the Village, conferring with Drs. Wiley and Moses. "I tell you what," says Dr. Wiley, "Go home, lay down your park, open it up and let the traffic rush through." "But doctor," says the Village, "I might get Blight!" "Exactly," chimes in Dr. Moses, glancing at his bulldozer: "We know how to cure that!"*

---

*   Drs. Wiley and Moses are T. T. Wiley (1908–99) and, of course, Robert Moses (1888–1981). Wiley served as New York City's first traffic commissioner between 1949 and 1961. Moses has figured in many stories of Jacobs's life as her bête noire. Variously head of slum clearance, parks, construction, and planning projects of all sorts in both New York City and

LIKE A CANCER

Medical analogies were first introduced at meetings back in March, when Mr. Brooks of the Committee for Slum Clearance very kindly explained to us that a slum is like a cancer. In the traffic for Washington Square, we see how neatly a cancer can be planted. Unfortunately, these doctors seem to be confusing their guinea pigs with their patients.

The outrageous plan for Washington Square is a vital issue in itself. But it is important for another reason. It shows us so clearly something we must understand and face: This city either is not interested, or does not know how, to preserve and improve healthy neighborhoods.

This is a curious situation. On the one hand, the city fathers worry because formerly stable neighborhoods deteriorate, because middle-income families move out, because Manhattan is rapidly becoming a place of only the very rich, the very poor, and the transient. Their solution is redevelopment.

LESSER EVIL

The best you can say for redevelopment is that, in certain cases, it is the lesser evil. As practiced in New York, it is very painful. It causes catastrophic dislocation and hardship to tens of thousands of citizens. There is growing evidence that it shoots up juvenile-delinquency figures and spreads or intensifies slums in

New York State over the course of his long career, he was probably best known for his role as head of the Triborough Bridge and Tunnel Authority. The "outrageous plan" mentioned here was to extend Fifth Avenue south through Washington Square Park, encircling its iconic arch in a traffic circle.

the areas taking the dislocation impact. It destroys, more surely than floods or tornados, immense numbers of small businesses. It is expensive to the taxpayers, federal and local. It is not fulfilling the hope that it would boost the city's tax returns. Quite the contrary.

The great virtue of the city, the thing that helps make up for all its disadvantages, is that it is interesting.

Furthermore, the results of all this expense and travail look dull and are dull. The great virtue of the city, the thing that helps make up for all its disadvantages, is that it is interesting. It isn't easy to make a chunk of New York boring, but redevelopment does it.

ALL BY ITSELF

On the other hand, here is the Village—an area of the city with power to attract and hold a real cross-section of the population, including a lot of middle-income families. An area with a demonstrated potential for extending and upgrading its fringes. An area that pays more in taxes than it gets back in services. An area that grows theaters all by itself, without arguments between Mr. Moses and Mr. Albert Cole.* All this without benefit of

---

* As Jacobs prepared these comments, Robert Moses was involved in a closely covered feud with Albert Cole, the federal Housing and Home Finance Agency administrator responsible for approving federal funds for urban renewal projects. Jacobs and her audience would have been reading about it in a series of *New York Times* articles that year. Cole, upset by revelations of scandal in New York's urban renewal projects, was withholding funds from the Lincoln Square project that included Lincoln Center for the Performing Arts. He didn't like the way that Moses preselected the developers for urban renewal projects without competitive bidding, and he was spooked by rising clamor over the social costs of relocation on urban renewal sites. Moses still enjoyed much support, however, and by August, a behind-the-scenes campaign by Lincoln Square's many supporters, from the Rockefeller family to a host

bulldozers, wholesale write downs of land cost, or tax exemptions.

Wouldn't you think the city fathers would want to understand what makes our area successful and learn from it? Or failing such creative curiosity, that they would at least cherish it?

Obviously they do not.

However, *so long as we recognize this,* there is no reason to despair of our future. The Village will deteriorate only if we let City Hall take care of things with one short-sighted expediency after another, and await the sure sequel to that: the surgery of Dr. Moses.

POTENTIAL ALLIES

In our efforts to forestall the wrong things happening and to win the right things, it would be useful if we had the help of two potential allies who perhaps do not understand how much stake they have in the stability of the Village. One is the owners of the new apartment houses which have been spurting up. In March, Daniel Rose, the builder of some of them, spoke here and told us the Village was fated to become largely an area of high-rent apartments with a transient population. This of course is one of the classic steps toward deterioration. You can see the sad, final stages of this process in several parts of the city. Mr. Rose paid tribute to the magnetism of Washington Square, but said the Village is so popular with tenants because of convenient transportation. Nonsense. If transportation were the governing factor, East

---

of union heads, business executives, religious leaders, bankers, and city officials, forced Cole to relent. For more on Lincoln Square, see Samuel Zipp's *Manhattan Projects* (pp. 157–249).

Harlem, 12 minutes from the Grand Central Area and with great bargains in land, would be burgeoning with new private construction. It hasn't had one stick since 1942. Chelsea would be booming. No. The fact is, we have a better mousetrap down here. The new apartment-house owners would do well to realize they are in on a good thing, and see to it that the environment in which their tenants like to bathe does not go down the drain.

PRETTY COY

The other potential ally is New York University, which is part and parcel of the Village but apt to be pretty coy about it when anything "controversial" like the highway through the Square comes up. NYU ought to take a good look at the horrible problems of institutions in some other parts of the city, whose neighborhoods have rotted around them. It ought to be every bit as sensitive to danger signs, of which there are now a number, and every bit as eager to foster our wondrous combination of variety and stability, as the Greenwich Village Association or the Washington Square Association. Purely for its own self-interest. NYU can ask Columbia—which is now bitterly discovering that redevelopment leaves a lot unsolved—or the Manhattan School of Music, or City College, whether an intimate concern for its neighborhood is worthwhile.

The chief means of preserving the Village and improving it consist of:

First, zoning to retain our scale, our variety, and the wonderful flexibility which make the Village so successful an incubator of the arts and business;

Second, traffic control to keep us from being destroyed by traffic plans gone completely antisocial;

Third, judicious rebuilding to mend the wear and tear of time and use;

Fourth, careful siting and design of public facilities to make most sense for the community.

Constructive, creative use of zoning, as suggested by Albert Mayer at the first of these meetings, and traffic control are more important to our future than everything else put together.*

These are the means, but the citizens of the Village, with or without the two allies I have mentioned, are going to have to think how to put these means to work for our good. Nobody else will. Councilman Stanley Isaacs, speaking to the Inter-School committee of this area, gave the recipe: Agree on what you want, and use every pressure, rational and emotional, to get it. There is no other recipe.†

---

* Albert Mayer (1897–1981) was a planner and architect, well known for his interest in modern housing and his master planning efforts at Chandigarh, a new town in India eventually designed by Le Corbusier. Mayer was an unorthodox modernist. He and Jacobs probably met in East Harlem, where they both assisted the social workers of Union Settlement House in their efforts to assuage the impact of public housing on the neighborhood. Zipp, *Manhattan Projects* (324–50).

† Stanley Isaacs (1882–1962) was a New York City politician and a longtime member of the City Council. An outspoken advocate on housing issues, in 1951 he joined Councilman Earl Brown in drafting and passing a bill making discrimination in publicly assisted housing a crime in New York. In 1957, his Sharkey-Brown-Isaacs bill also outlawed discrimination in private housing. In the mid-1950s, he was one of the first politicians to distance himself from Robert Moses and publicize the trauma suffered by those relocated from clearance sites.

Metropolitan Government

ARCHITECTURAL FORUM,

AUGUST 1957

IN SPITE OF A POTENT GRASS-ROOTS-AND-TOWN-MEETING folklore, the U.S. has become a nation of metropoli; very peculiar metropoli with problems that are something new—at least in degree—under the sun. Sprawling over municipal lines, township lines, school district lines, county lines, even state lines, our 174 metropolitan areas are a weird mélange of 16,210 separate units of government. The Chicago metropolitan area, one of the prize examples of fragmentation, has about a thousand contiguous or overlapping local government units. But the problem is similar everywhere: how does the metropolitan area (which lacks governmental entity) contend with urgent and massive problems of a metropolitan nature, armed with a cross-purpose jackstraw heap of local sovereignties representing genuinely clashing interests?*

The metropolitan problems—monstrous traffic, missing or

---

*   Jacobs returns to this question in chapter 21 of *Death and Life,* "Governing and Planning Districts." However, there she comes to different conclusions: "Workable metropolitan administration has to be learned and used, first, within big cities, where no fixed political boundaries prevent its use" (p. 427). In other words, before cities can govern and plan effectively at a regional level, they must solve these problems at the neighborhood level.

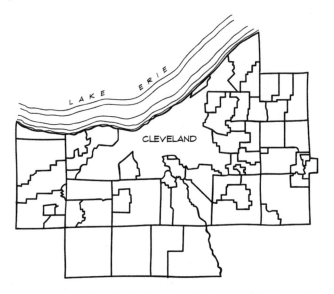

Jigsaw government: The Cleveland metropolitan area, with sixty-odd municipalities, cannot plan its waterfront rationally, nor can it distribute the cost of its services fairly. This typically fragmented metropolis is now merging into two other metropolitan areas, also jigsaw puzzles.

bankrupt transit, incompatible land uses, unbalanced land uses with their sequel of unbalanced tax structures, transformation of old core cities into racial and economic ghettos, pollution of air and water, and a host of others—are not new in kind. But they have become abruptly massive and urgent during the past ten years because we have had a phenomenal growth of metropolitan population and this has coincided with the phenomenal scatteration made possible by the automobile. These problems will become still more massive as the present metropolitan area populations of about 96 million increase by an estimated 54 million in the next eighteen years.

Cumulatively, the number, size, and complexity of the metropolitan problems add up to a metropolitan crisis, as set forth in last month's *Forum*.* Looked at another way, they also add up to one of the greatest adventures in inventive self-government that any people has ever had a chance at.

Governmentally, we have never really come to full grips with the fact of cities, and this is a root of our trouble. Our governmental structure is based on static units of territory, rather than on dynamic units of populations. Our states, divided into their revealingly named *counties,* are an organizational heritage from feudal territorial war lords who fitted the city into their scheme of things as a special, chartered "exception." It is still an "exception" theoretically, although the ancient legal form of the city and its phys-

Governmentally, we have never really come to full grips with the fact of cities, and this is a root of our trouble.

ical reality began to part company half a century ago, when the early suburbanites hop-skipped along the railroad lines out in the county.

But it would be folly to jump to the conclusion that the states, and the cities' positions within them, represent a troublesome archaism necessarily. The American political genius has consisted in the ability to take the instruments at hand and evolve them to new purposes as needed. It is quite possible that the salvation of our fragmented metropoli will be found in the existing states, rather than in the creation of new layers of "supercity" metropolitan government, an idea now intellectually fashionable.

In any event, the first thing to understand about metropoli-

*   See "The Hundred Billion Dollar Question," *Architectural Forum,* July 1957.

tan government is that it is going to be dealt with not by abstract logic or elegance of structure, but in a combination of approaches by trial, error and immense experimentation in a context of expediency and conflicting interests. Whatever we arrive at, we shall feel our way there.

THE APPROACHES

In broad terms, there are three possible approaches to metropolitan government and one impossible approach.

The possible approaches are: 1) much greater extension and evolution of present *ad hoc* devices such as special districts, authorities, compacts, contracts, and taxation ingenuities; 2) greater dependence on the federal government for the required money and hence for the required decisions and authority; and 3) federation of governmental units within metropolitan areas; such a joint government might be a council, or it might be a decentralized agency of the state, and the local units would surrender sovereignty over certain problems.

The impossible approach is consolidation of municipalities within metropolitan areas, making the metropolitan area one big city, at least within state lines.* It is well to deal with this

---

* Before the early twentieth century the problem Jacobs identifies here—American cities finding themselves at the center of a "jackstraw heap" of competing municipalities—was comparatively rare. During the long industrial boom that began in the nineteenth century, outlying municipalities or unincorporated areas offset costs of infrastructure improvements by allowing themselves to be annexed by swelling cities. Only a very few exclusive residential districts risked rebuffing annexation bids. By the 1910s and '20s, however, as cities got larger and more expensive to run, more and more outlying areas began to resist annexation or tried to incorporate to control their own destinies. By the middle of the twentieth century many small industrial cities, suburbs, or towns at the fringe of a great city were far more likely to go it on their own and hold themselves out as an escape from the increasingly crowded city,

idea first and at some length because it shows, in sharpest relief, many of the limitations and complexities that apply to the other approaches too.

CONSOLIDATION: IMPOSSIBLE

Consolidation is impossible, first, as a pragmatic fact, because the citizenry of most of the units concerned strongly oppose it. Annexation, for example, has very lean pickings nowadays. Last year no cities other than Houston, Mobile, Dallas and El Paso annexed so much as 10 sq.mi. Among annexations by 348 other municipalities having a population of 10,000 or more, the average was three-fifths of a square mile. And these figures, so pathetic against immense urban scatteration, are the best since the war.

The bigger the metropolis, as a rule, the more ardently its outliers will defend themselves against being "swallowed." This fear, while possibly selfish and shortsighted, is not imaginary, as one illustration of a common situation shows. In Philadelphia, the city government has to contend with the problem of "the suburbs in the city," areas within the city of low density housing which the city needs to intersperse with higher density zoning because of population pressures and costs of services. Although the citizenry in the "suburbs" involved has been vociferous and politically active in its opposition, it has consistently been defeated because it is a minority voice in the city as

with its relatively high taxes, expensive and aging infrastructure, and tension between classes and races. With this resistance came the classic social shape of the divided metropolis of the mid-twentieth century—a city with a declining office and commercial downtown surrounded by industrial neighborhoods undergoing racial transition and a few prestigious white neighborhoods, all encircled by booming wealthy, middle-class, and working-class white suburbs.

a whole. Conflict of precisely this nature, in many different guises, is the hard core of the whole metropolitan government problem.

Political scientist Edward C. Banfield comments: "The problem is not, as many seem to think, merely one of creating organization for effective planning and administration. It is also—and perhaps primarily—one of creating or of maintaining organization for the effective management of conflict, especially of conflict arising from the growing cleavage of race and class. These needs may be incompatible to some extent. . . . Indeed it may be that area-wide planning and administration would of necessity heighten conflicts by raising questions which can only be settled by bitter struggle. Conflict is not something to be avoided at all costs. It may be well, nevertheless, to consider whether there are not decisive advantages in organizational arrangements . . . which, although handicapping or entirely frustrating some important undertakings, nevertheless serve to insulate opposed interests and to protect them from each other."*

---

* One of the leading conservative political scientists of his generation, Edward Banfield (1916–99) was well known, particularly after the publication of *The Unheavenly City* in 1970, for his critiques of liberal social welfare policies. He blamed crime and social disorder on the inherent "culture" of the lower class, which he said disavowed future-oriented thought and indulged in instant gratification. Government largesse would only encourage this tendency and so could only deepen the "urban crisis." His ideas fed many of the conservative social policy initiatives of the 1970s, '80s, and '90s—particularly the "broken windows" theory—that sought to criminalize low-level disruptions of order and heighten policing of the behavior and movement of the urban poor. Here Jacobs seems to agree with Banfield's argument that regional solutions to metropolitan fragmentation are impractical because they are likely to run up against the closely defended lines of race and class that divide metropoli, a judgment that later critics of metropolitan fragmentation would contest, however much it may have reflected experience on the ground and the difficulty of solving the problem. Not surprisingly, metropolitan fragmentation remains one of the great problems besetting cities today.

Aside from being politically impossible—and in the Banfield view perhaps politically undesirable—consolidation may also be illusory as a planning solution for the following reasons, which have their influence on all schemes of metropolitan government. It presupposes more or less neat and manageable arrangements of core cities surrounded by satellites. However, there are now eighteen growing "urban regions" in America where two or more standard metropolitan areas overlap or adjoin. Where we had wheel or star-shaped urban structures, we are now getting amorphous masses. In even the largest of these regions, the core-city-satellite concept still does have validity for many purposes, especially the journey to work, but it has little validity in solving other problems such as general traffic, air pollution, water supply. The logical "jurisdictions" of such problems do not even necessarily coincide with each other, nor is the territory involved today likely to be the same in twenty years or even five years.

THEN THERE IS THE entire problem of size, workable size for a specific governmental function. The problem of the school district too small for efficiency, or of the suburb with its tax base and child population wildly out of whack, is well known. On the other hand, the huge New York City Board of Education, with more than 900,000 children to provide for, tries hard to plan but also has poor success with it, probably because it is just too big. Decisions on sites and buildings, for instance, are necessarily made so remotely from the "communities" intimately involved, and with such an absence of natural give-and-take and explanation, that the result is a system of ukases from above, countered by frenzied pressures from below, with planning lost in the shuffle. Execution of planning, generally, suffers many defeats by dealing in units of great size, as well as by being confined in units too small. In a unit of very large population, departments and bureaus, each an empire in miniature, require increasing layers of coordination and mayoral assistants constantly engaged in attempting, often vainly, to pull things together.

Size also involves the entire problem of local responsibility and the principle, probably inseparable from vigorous self-government, that any division of government should be kept as close to the people as function permits.

In short, consolidation does not answer the situation: if the metropolitan problems themselves are a fearsome snarl, the problem entailed in going at them make a fearful snarl too.

AD HOC DEVICES

How much promise is there in such *ad hoc* devices as special districts, authorities, compacts, contracts, and taxation ingenuities? (This we have called the first of the "possible" approaches.) A great deal of invention is now being spent on unraveling the metropolitan snarl one knot at a time. For instance, "special districts" created to deal with problems that cross governmental lines are by far the most rapidly growing category of governmental unit. Since 1942, 6,124 new special districts have been created. California, with 330 municipalities (and 1,841 school districts), has 1,652 special districts. Illinois has 1,785. Not all special districts are metropolitan, but most are. Their ancestor was the Boston metropolitan sewage district created in 1889.

Many are authorities with independent borrowing power, modeled after the Port of New York Authority, which was created in 1921.

Among dozens of other inventions for attacking this facet or that of fiscal or physical disability are ungraduated city income taxes (applying to suburbanites too), county home rule (for metropolitan areas within a county), state taboos on new incorporations in the sphere of a core city, and planning powers for the core city extending a few miles beyond its boundaries.

One of the strangest inventions is the Lakewood Plan, named for a Los Angeles suburb of 75,000, which in 1954 incorporated and contracted with Los Angeles County for almost all its services. This scheme, hugely popular, has triggered 11 incorporations in the county since, and detailed price lists have been worked out for buying services, such as $3.63 for each health call; $7 a day for women in jail, $3.50 for men; $73,000 per year for one around-the-clock police patrol car. These communities even contract with the county for technical services in tax assessment and collection, planning and zoning and civil service administration. They have made headway in solving the problem of duplicated governmental overhead and inefficiency, but these communities still retain their autonomy, set their own policy—notably zoning—a point to keep in mind.

Looking at current devices as a pattern, two rather alarming motifs stand out. The first is the effect of the "special district" approach. "The great disadvantage of special districts and authorities lies in the cumulative effect of their use," comments political scientist Victor Jones. "One special district may be of no import, but ultimately their use will lead to functional disintegration. This is a problem of politics, of control as well as of administration, and will force us to reorder our values or start all over again to build a community from functional fragments."

The second motif is the apparent inability of any of the inventions to come to grips with land planning policy. Many existing arrangements do pretty well with things that flow and fly: with water supply, sewage, smoke control, pest control and, to a degree, even with traffic and transit. If things that fly and flow were all that need be considered, we might expect the metropolitan problems to come under reasonable control in time, with existing devices.

THE FIXED ANARCHY

But something very fixed is involved: the land. And land planning remains in complete anarchy. This anarchy touches everything. It is the road which in the city is zoned to serve as a fast-moving arterial feeder, but at the city line becomes a stop-and-go road town.* It is Suburb A zoning for heavy industry against the residential district of Suburb B. It is School District C, divided so swiftly into builders' developments that, before anyone realizes, it has no way of getting money to support the schools it needs. It is the suddenly vanished open land that had given the city relief and recreation. It is the new bridge approach, tearing out the heart of an old community or cutting off school from students. It is the ever greater segregation of low income and minority populations in the core city, daily increasing the cleavages and conflicts with which Banfield is so

---

* "Road town" was a catchphrase Jacobs adopted from her editor Douglas Haskell at *Architectural Forum* to describe the effects of sprawl on the American metropolis.

concerned. It is an ever longer journey to work. It is shopping centers, whose inpouring of traffic and lack of buffer territory cast blight.

Anarchy in land planning makes new metropolitan problems faster than they can be solved. And it is the untouchable among metropolitan problems. Perhaps the best example of dealing with it thus far is Nashville, and there only the negative step can be taken of county veto on proposed zoning changes. Even Miami and its environs, which have just voted in a form of federated metropolitan government for Dade County, have left zoning and planning to local municipal control. Schemes like the Lakewood Plan, referred to above, are devised mainly to keep land policy thoroughly local because land planning policy also involves who your neighbor shall be, or in what way you can make money from your holdings and how much.

Regional or metropolitan planning in the land area is always set up as a voluntary or advisory arrangement because everyone recognizes that anything else would be politically impossible. But, as Planning Director Henry Fagin of the Regional Plan Association in New York points out, the advisory regional planning board with no metropolitan governing officials to give advice to is a "floating" body, by definition politically irresponsible—and it acts politically irresponsible. "It does not need to come to grips with the real conflicts, as effective decision makers do," says Fagin. "Too often the 'lesson' it teaches is that planning is futile or undesirable." At best, Fagin thinks, the floating planning board can indicate realistically what it thinks is going to happen anyway, which is useful information. This is mainly the role played by those regional advisory boards, such as Detroit's, which have managed to earn respect.

Law Professor Charles M. Haar, analyzing the statutes by which 22 states authorize regional planning activity, notes how boldly they prescribe research, studies and the drafting of a master plan, and how vague they leave the question of what is to be done with it.* "Even the process of preparation is not drawn up so as to elicit public support nor to be illuminating either to the general citizenry or to the planning staffs and boards. Certainly the procedures for adoption are not devised with the thought of . . . having the final acceptance of the plan, which after all sets basic goals that affect the lives of the citizens in many intimate ways, a matter of public concern. Without clarification, there is small hope for a reconciliation of divergent interests, without which planning becomes simply a pleasant intellectual hobby." He notes that 90 major planning surveys have been made of metropolitan areas, of which only three can lay any possible claim to having had any effect. But hope springs eternal. In June, Chicago civic groups finally succeeded in getting a metropolitan planning commission past the legislature. It will be advisory—because nothing else is politically possible.

FEDERAL SOLUTIONS?†

This missing link—lack of means for adopting genuinely effective metropolitan land planning policy—is important to keep in

---

* Charles M. Haar (1920–2012) was a specialist in land-use law at Harvard Law School who advocated for federal and state laws that would help cities and metropolitan regions create land-use regulations intended to alleviate the environmental and planning problems of metropolitan fragmentation.

† Jacobs returns to the question of federal involvement in municipalities and metropolitan areas more comprehensively in "Strategies for Helping Cities" in this volume.

mind when considering the second "possible approach" toward metropolitan government: the use of federal cooperation, aid and authority. The main point in this approach is that the federal government has highly effective ways of getting tax money out of localities and, in returning it as expenditure, can use the powers of decision that accompany powers of money disbursal. The hope that federal means will succeed, where the means available to cities and states cannot, is implied in current bills for establishment of a cabinet rank Department of Urban Affairs and proposals for a White House conference on urban problems.*

The federal government does already have an enormous influence on metropolitan land planning. For instance, Federal Housing Administration and Public Housing Administration policies, between them, have probably had more to do with the progressive ghettoizing of core cities, the class segregation of the suburbs and the form of metropolitan scatteration, than any other factors. These results have not been deliberate, however; the two agencies have been unable to formulate policies that take cognizance of each other, let alone take cognizance of the metropolitan situation as a whole. The great federal highway program now getting started will influence metropolitan land use for good or ill more than all the metropolitan land planning ventures of our time put together, but there is no sign that this is understood by those who wrote the legislation or those who will administer it. While these great forces blunder about blindly, doing "planning" on true metropolitan area scale, the

---

* In 1965 Congress passed the Department of Housing and Urban Development Act, making HUD a cabinet-level agency in the executive branch.

Urban Renewal Administration applies its little poultices and encourages municipalities to produce plans—on a municipal scale.

Most proposals for a Department of Urban Affairs recognize this unhappy situation; they list among the Department's proposed functions investigation of the impact of federal programs on cities and coordination of such programs.

Is such coordination actually possible? With all its money and authority, can the federal government succeed in producing rationality where the cities and states have not? First, there is the difficulty of federal programs coordinating among themselves. "No community ever approaches its government problem *in toto,* for it never exists that way historically," notes sociologist Albert J. Reiss Jr. This is spectacularly true of the federal government, as witness the current misidentification of urban rebuilding with the depression-fighting theory out of which it was born, or the inability of the HHFA coordinator to coordinate the historically separate FHA and PHA.*

Second, there is the difficulty of coordinating federal programs with the local situation. "Planning by its nature looks to the coordination and integration of governmental functions," points out lawyer Jerome J. Shestack. "There is an overall and continuing aspect to planning that requires involvement of all the community resources." At the most optimistic, even assum-

---

* These acronyms stand for, respectively, the Housing and Home Finance Agency, the Federal Housing Administration, and the Public Housing Administration. Jacobs's comment suggests the "two-tier" nature of housing finance after the New Deal. Public housing suffered in a system in which unequal revenue streams flowed into private housing programs (FHA) and public housing programs (PHA). The two systems were left at odds with one another, in competition for dollars, and difficult to administer for the organization charged with overseeing the overall finance of housing (HHFA).

ing that the federal government could miraculously coordinate its own parts with respect to their impacts on the metropolis, it is impossible to imagine Washington filling a planning role satisfactorily for the metropolitan area. "All of the community resources" means many with which the federal government cannot possibly be concerned or be aware of. On the contrary, if and when we do get effective metropolitan governments, one of their most pressing tasks will certainly be to bend, educate and influence federal aid and controls as they apply to specific metropolitan areas.

THE FEDERATED CITY

Most students of metropolitan government are now agreed that the most logical aim is the third "possible approach": some form of federation of governmental units within a metropolitan area, with the units surrendering some of their sovereignty to a metropolitan government.

This is by no means a "simple" approach. There is nothing simple about such relationships, as the entire history of our federal-state partnership attests. The only metropolitan federation in operation thus far in North America—the federation of Toronto and 12 suburban satellites (all in one county, with some planning powers overlapping two other counties)—is a little too simple, in fact.* So much power resides in the metropolitan

---

*   In this context, a federation consists of multiple municipalities brought together under a common regional governance structure. Much like states or provinces under a federal government, powers and responsibilities can be divided between the two levels of government in a variety of ways. *Satellites* refer to the less populous communities surrounding the urban core of a metropolitan area. Coincidentally, Jacobs would move to Toronto in 1968 and encounter firsthand the difficult art of being simple when it comes to metropolitan government. In her

council, and especially in its chairman, that, for U.S. consumption, it embodies many of the objections that apply to consolidation.

The nearest approach in the U.S. is the Miami plan (again involving one core city and its satellites in one county) which the voters have just accepted. The Miami scheme does not provide for unified planning as such, but it does give unified powers over slum clearance, traffic, and parking drainage, for instance—activities which in practice determine many great questions of land planning policy.

Powers of this type are probably the great opportunity for achieving metropolitan government. For they are the handle, several authorities believe, by which we can best grasp hold of reasonably unified planning and administration.

Jones suggests, for example, that the way out of the impasse of having single-minded authorities or special districts is to form their governing boards from elected officials of the municipalities and counties concerned, as the San Francisco Bay Area Air Pollution Control Board is organized. The next step would be for the *same* local officials to serve on new special boards as they are created. This collection of boards with the same elected officials on them could evolve into a metropolitan district with many general powers of government, an integrated view of the many different but related problems and, eventually, a popularly elected chief executive.

1997 speech "Against Amalgamation" in this volume, Jacobs would say of Toronto's federation of municipalities, "Whatever Metro's virtues were at the start, it now behaves like a dysfunctional family. Its members are suspicious of one another, they gang up on each other. The wrangles concern activities that are already amalgamated. The few Metro coordinating services really necessary are now geographically irrelevant."

Haar suggests that the state is the logical instrument of federation—or at least federated planning—because its role is already so large in many matters affecting metropolitan and regional development: flood control, highways, schools, for example. The state judiciaries, he argues, are already "plunged into the vacuum of [planning] power," with intercommunity disputes about land use increasingly thrust on them.

Fagin suggests that a practical first step would be to abandon the idea of the floating regional planning board, but by no means abandon metropolitan and regional planning. Instead the regional planning staff should be attached *as a working instrument* to a regional agency which has decision-making powers over key aspects of regional and metropolitan development. This could be a federated metropolitan council or it could be a regional agency of the state. To govern properly, many states have already decentralized the administration of parks, roads and health into districts. Such districts could be redrawn and pulled together to permit them to deal with their functions on a metropolitan level. To them could be added powers over pollution or over transit, over almost anything which the states now delegate to special districts or authorities. The point would be that these powers would be exercised consciously in the context of a broad area plan, and that the plan, for its part, would be formed in the context of genuine decision making.

Like Jones, Fagin thinks the agency of federation should be composed of elected local officials, but Fagin would add elected officials of the state, including some from the areas involved. After experimentation with the process of delegating some powers of the state "downward" to a region, and some of the powers of the local communities "upward," the scheme might be regularized. The states, long the declining stars of our national firmament, might well become more important in their role as senior partners in state-city federations than in their role as junior partners in the nation-state federation.

This or any other federated scheme would work, Fagin thinks, only if the metropolitan or regional body were firmly confined, probably by a "constitution type" statute, to matters of regional import. This would not preclude a joint underwriting of certain minimum standards throughout the area, with option by the communities to better the standards locally, a concept already familiar in many types of state aid. It would preclude centralization of all real decision making and the degeneration of local units into janitorial government. For example, how the suburb of Bronxville, N.Y., wants to zone the commercial district around its railroad station, or what internal street pattern a builder chooses to put in his housing development, would be of no regional import. But whether New York puts public housing or port facilities on its waterfront, or where a parkway runs and what borders it, likely would be. Litigation would draw the effective lines between what is regional and what is local—a process already under way, as Haar has shown, but with no planning framework or theory at present to assist the judges.

There are several persuasive reasons for the states to take over the new function of metropolitan government. Metropolitan areas are dynamic, not fixed, and a state regional body (even one made up of local officials) could have a matching flexibility of jurisdiction, difficult to build into a distinctly new layer of supercity government. Where metropolitan areas cross state lines, state governments are the logical units for making pacts and setting up joint bodies or programs. Most important, the states have a strong and well-understood tradition of popular government and of give-and-take with localities, something that has to be worked into, slowly and chancily, with new managerial layers of government.

There is a further reason, little noted yet, but vital. In California, where the future seems to happen faster than anywhere else, two of the "Lakewood Plan" incorporations in Los Angeles County happen to be rural dairy-farm districts which incorporated to protect themselves from urban encroachment. Agricultural conservation is going to become deeply enmeshed, in many places, with the metropolitan problem.* Thus the very "rural mindedness" of the state legislatures, long a burden to the development of the cities, could be a valuable pressure on the metropoli of the future. Certainly no scheme of federation which overlooks the problem of agricultural conservation—or is set up to deal with it strictly from an urban viewpoint—will be suited to making planning policy for our monstrously growing metropoli.

If the problems of achieving metropolitan government seem formidable, and even the thinking about means to achieve it maddeningly tentative, it is well to remember that nobody has been trying very long. Most planners and many theorists were unaware of the metropolitan government idea until Jones's *Metropolitan Government* was published in 1942. Most government officials have learned of the idea only within the past three or four years. Some have not yet grasped its importance to them. Predecessors of current state governors showed no public

---

*   See "Our 'Surplus' Land" in this volume.

awareness of the concept, but several present governors have, notably Ribicoff of Connecticut and Williams of Michigan.* It is, in fact, encouraging that the era of experiment and of investigation (much of it with foundation money, as in Cleveland and St. Louis) should have begun so quickly and should be enlisting so many lively and practical minds.

And for those who despair that it can ever be worked out with neatness and certitude, it is well to remember architect Henry Churchill's wise words: "Within the broadest possible framework of the general good, disorder must be allowed for, lest the people perish. Any form of initiative is disordering of the status quo and so needs encouragement, not suppression, if democracy is to retain vitality."

---

* Abraham Ribicoff (1910–98) was governor of Connecticut and a U.S. senator as well as secretary of Health, Education, and Human Welfare under President John F. Kennedy. G. Mennen "Soapy" Williams (1911–88) was governor of Michigan and a State Department official. Both were big supporters of liberal urban policy to aid cities at the federal and state levels, and key backers of President Lyndon B. Johnson's Great Society and War on Poverty programs in the 1960s.

Downtown Is for People

FORTUNE, APRIL 1958

THIS YEAR IS GOING TO BE A CRITICAL ONE FOR THE FUTURE of the city. All over the country civic leaders and planners are preparing a series of redevelopment projects that will set the character of the center of our cities for generations to come. Great tracts, many blocks wide, are being razed; only a few cities have their new downtown projects already under construction; but almost every big city is getting ready to build, and the plans will soon be set.

What will the projects look like? They will be spacious, parklike, and uncrowded. They will feature long green vistas. They will be stable and symmetrical and orderly. They will be clean, impressive, and monumental. They will have all the attributes of a well-kept, dignified cemetery. And each project will look very much like the next one: the Golden Gateway office and apartment center planned for San Francisco; the Civic Center for New Orleans; the Lower Hill auditorium and apartment project for Pittsburgh; the Convention Center for Cleveland; the Quality Hill offices and apartments for Kansas City; the downtown scheme for Little Rock; the Capitol Hill project for Nashville. From city to city the architects' sketches conjure up the same dreary scene; here is no hint of individuality or whim or surprise, no hint that here is a city with a tradition and flavor all its own.

These projects will not revitalize downtown; they will deaden it. For they work at cross-purposes to the city. They banish the street. They banish its function. They banish its variety. There is one notable exception, the Gruen plan for Fort Worth; ironically, the main point of it has been missed by the many cities that plan to imitate it. Almost without exception the projects have one standard solution for every need: commerce, medicine, culture, government—whatever the activity, they take a part of the city's life, abstract it from the hustle and bustle of downtown, and set it, like a self-sufficient island, in majestic isolation.

Consider what makes a city center magnetic, what can inject the gaiety, the wonder, the cheerful hurly-burly that make people want to come into the city and to linger there.

There are, certainly, ample reasons for redoing downtown— falling retail sales, tax bases in jeopardy, stagnant real-estate values, impossible traffic and parking conditions, failing mass transit, encirclement by slums. But with no intent to minimize these serious matters, it is more to the point to consider what makes a city center magnetic, what can inject the gaiety, the wonder, the cheerful hurly-burly that make people want to come into the city and to linger there. For magnetism is the crux of the problem. All downtown's values are its byproducts. To create in it an atmosphere of urbanity and exuberance is not a frivolous aim.

We are becoming too solemn about downtown. The architects, planners—and businessmen—are seized with dreams of order, and they have become fascinated with scale models and bird's-eye views. This is a vicarious way to deal with reality, and it is, unhappily, symptomatic of a design philosophy now dominant: buildings come first, for the goal is to remake the city to fit an abstract concept of what, logically, it should be. But whose logic? The logic of the projects is the logic of egocentric children, playing with pretty blocks and shouting "See what I made!"—a viewpoint much cultivated in our schools of architecture and design. And citizens who should know better are so fascinated by the sheer process of rebuilding that the end results are secondary to them.

With such an approach, the end results will be about as helpful to the city as the dated relics of the City Beautiful movement, which in the early years of this century was going to rejuvenate the city by making it parklike, spacious, and monumental. For the underlying intricacy, and the life that makes downtown worth fixing at all, can never be fostered synthetically. No one can find what will work for our cities by looking at the boulevards of Paris, as the City Beautiful people did; and they can't find it by looking at suburban garden cities, manipulating scale models, or inventing dream cities.

You've got to get out and walk. Walk, and you will see that many of the assumptions on which the projects depend are visibly wrong. You will see, for example, that a worthy and well-kept institutional center does not necessarily upgrade its surroundings. (Look at the blight-engulfed urban universities, or the petered-out environs of such ambitious landmarks as the civic auditorium in St. Louis and the downtown mall in Cleveland.) You will see that suburban amenity is not what people seek downtown. (Look at Pittsburghers by the thousands climbing forty-two steps to enter the very urban Mellon Square, but balking at crossing the street into the ersatz suburb of Gateway Center.)

You will see that it is not the nature of downtown to decentralize. Notice how astonishingly small a place it is; how abruptly it gives way, outside the small, high-powered core, to underused area. Its tendency is not to fly apart but to become denser, more compact. Nor is this tendency some leftover from the past; the number of people working within the cores has been on the increase, and given the long-term growth in white-collar work it will continue so. The tendency to become denser is a fundamental quality of downtown and it persists for good and sensible reasons.

If you get out and walk, you see all sorts of other clues. Why is the hub of downtown such a mixture of things? Why do office workers on New York's handsome Park Avenue turn off to Lexington or Madison Avenue at the first corner they reach? Why is a good steak house usually in an old building? Why are short blocks apt to be busier than long ones?

It is the premise of this article that the best way to plan for downtown is to see how people use it today; to look for its strengths and to exploit and reinforce them. There is no logic that can be superimposed on the city; people make it, and it is to them, not buildings, that we must fit our plans. This does not mean accepting the present; downtown does need an overhaul, it is dirty, it is congested. But there are things that are right about it too, and by simple old-fashioned observation we can see what they are. We can see what people like.

HOW HARD CAN A
STREET WORK?

The best place to look at first is the street. One had better look quickly too; not only are the projects making away with the noisy automobile traffic of the street, they are making away with the street itself. In its stead will be open spaces with long vistas and lots and lots of elbow room.

But the street works harder than any other part of downtown. It is the nervous system; it communicates the flavor, the feel, the sights. It is the major point of transaction and communication. Users of downtown know very well that downtown needs not fewer streets, but more, especially for pedestrians. They are constantly making new, extra paths for themselves, through mid-block lobbies of buildings, block-through stores and banks, even parking lots and alleys. Some of the builders of downtown know this too, and rent space along their hidden streets.

Rockefeller Center, frequently cited to prove that projects are good for downtown, differs in a very fundamental way from the projects being designed today. It respects the street. Rockefeller Center knits tightly into every street that intersects it. One of its most brilliant features is the full-fledged extra street with which it cuts across blocks that elsewhere are too long. Its open spaces are eddies of the streets, small and sharp and lively, not large, empty, and boring. Most important, it is so dense and concentrated that the uniformity it does possess is a relatively small episode in the area.

As one result of its extreme density, Rockefeller Center had to put the overflow of its street activity underground, and as is so often the case with successful projects, planners have drawn the wrong moral: to keep the ground level more open, they are sending the people into underground streets although the theoretical purpose of the open space is to endow people with more air and sky, not less. It would be hard to think of a more expeditious way to dampen downtown than to shove its liveliest activities and brightest lights underground, yet this is what Philadelphia's Penn Center and Pittsburgh's Gateway Center do. Any department-store management that followed such a policy with its vital ground-floor space, instead of using it as a village of streets, would go out of business.

THE ANIMATED ALLEY

The real potential is in the street, and there are far more opportunities for exploiting it than are realized. Consider, for example, Maiden Lane, an odd two-block-long, narrow, backdoor alley in San Francisco. Starting with nothing more remarkable than the dirty, neglected back sides of department stores and nondescript buildings, a group of merchants made this alley into one of the finest shopping streets in America. Maiden Lane has trees along its sidewalks, redwood benches to invite the sightseer or window shopper or buyer to linger, sidewalks of colored paving, sidewalk umbrellas when the sun gets hot. All the merchants do things differently: some put out tables with their wares, some hang out window boxes and grow vines. All the buildings, old and new, look individual; the most celebrated is an expanse of tan brick with a curved doorway, by architect Frank Lloyd Wright. The pedestrian's welfare is supreme; during the rush of the day, he has the street. Maiden Lane is an oasis

with an irresistible sense of intimacy, cheerfulness, and sponta-
neity. It is one of San Francisco's most powerful downtown
magnets.

Downtown can't be remade into a bunch of Maiden Lanes;
and it would be insufferably quaint if it were. But the potential
illustrated can be realized by any city and in its own particular
way. The plan by Victor Gruen Associates for Fort Worth is an
outstanding example. It has been publicized chiefly for its arrangements to provide enormous perimeter parking garages and
convert the downtown into a pedestrian island, but its main
purpose is to enliven the streets with variety and detail. This is
a point being overlooked by most of the eighty-odd cities that,
at last count, were seriously considering emulation of the Gruen
plan's traffic principles.

There is no magic in simply removing cars from downtown,
and certainly none in stressing peace, quiet, and dead space. The
removal of the cars is important only because of the great opportunities it opens to make the streets work harder and to keep
downtown activities compact and concentrated. To these ends,
the excellent Gruen plan includes, in its street treatment, sidewalk arcades, poster columns, flags, vending kiosks, display
stands, outdoor cafes, bandstands, flower beds, and special lighting effects. Street concerts, dances, and exhibits are to be fostered.
The whole point is to make the streets more surprising, more
compact, more variegated, and busier than before—not less so.

One of the beauties of the Fort Worth plan is that it works
with existing buildings, and this is a positive virtue not just a
cost-saving expedient. Think of any city street that people
enjoy and you will see that characteristically it has old buildings mixed with the new. This mixture is one of downtown's

greatest advantages, for downtown streets need high-yield, middling-yield, low-yield, and no-yield enterprises. The intimate restaurant or good steak house, the art store, the university club, the fine tailor, even the bookstores and antique stores—it is these kinds of enterprises for which old buildings are so congenial. Downtown streets should play up their mixture of buildings with all its unspoken—but well understood— implications of choice.

THE SMALLNESS OF BIG CITIES

It is not only for amenity but for economics that choice is so vital. Without a mixture on the streets, our downtowns would be superficially standardized, and functionally standardized as well. New construction is necessary, but it is not an unmixed blessing: Its inexorable economy is fatal to hundreds of enterprises able to make out successfully in old buildings. Notice that when a new building goes up, the kind of ground-floor tenants it gets are usually the chain store and the chain restaurant. Lack of variety in age and overhead is an unavoidable defect in large new shopping centers and is one reason why even the most successful cannot incubate the unusual—a point overlooked by planners of downtown shopping-center projects.

We are apt to think of big cities as equaling big enterprises, little towns as equaling little enterprises. Nothing could be less true. Big enterprises do locate in big cities, but they find small towns as congenial. Big enterprises have great self-sufficiency, are capable of maintaining most of the specialized skills and equipment they need, and they have no trouble reaching a broad market.

But for the small, specialized enterprise, everything is reversed; it must draw on supplies and skills outside itself; its market is so selective it needs exposure to hundreds of thousands of people. Without the centralized city it could not exist; the larger the city, the greater not only the number, but the proportion, of small enterprises. A metropolitan center comes across to people as a center largely by virtue of its enormous collection of small elements, where people can see them, at street level.

THE PEDESTRIAN'S LEVEL

Let's look for a moment at the physical dimensions of the street. The user of downtown is mostly on foot, and to enjoy himself he needs to see plenty of contrast on the streets. He needs assurance that the street is neither interminable nor boring, so he does not get weary just looking down it. Thus streets that have an end in sight are often pleasing; so are streets that have the punctuation of contrast at frequent intervals. Gÿorgy Kepes and Kevin Lynch, two faculty members of M.I.T., have made a study of what walkers in downtown Boston notice.* While the feature that drew the most comment was the proportion of open space, the walkers showed a great interest in punctuations of all kinds appearing a little way ahead of them—spaces, or greenery, or windows set forward, or churches, or clocks. Anything really different, whether large or a detail, interested them.

---

* Gÿorgy Kepes (1906–2001) and Kevin Lynch (1918–84) collaborated on a study of "urban aesthetics" that resulted in Lynch's famous work *The Image of the City* (1960)—a huge influence on Jacobs for its attention to the way that city dwellers actually used and understood urban space. Their work, like that of Jacobs, was supported by the Rockefeller Foundation's urban research initiative.

Narrow streets, if they are not too narrow (like many of Boston's) and are not choked with cars, can also cheer a walker by giving him a continual choice of this side of the street or that, and twice as much to see. The differences are something anyone can try out for himself by walking a selection of downtown streets.

This does not mean all downtown streets should be narrow and short. Variety is wanted in this respect too. But it does mean that narrow streets or reasonably wide alleys have a unique value that revitalizers of downtown ought to use to the hilt instead of wasting. It also means that if pedestrian and automobile traffic is separated out on different streets, planners would do better to choose the narrower streets for pedestrians, rather than the most wide and impressive. Where monotonously wide and long streets are turned over to exclusive pedestrian use, they are going to be a problem. They will come much more alive and persuasive if they are broken into varying parts. The Gruen plan, for example, will interrupt the long, wide gridiron vistas of Fort Worth by narrowing them at some points, widening them into plazas at others. It is also the best possible showmanship to play up the streets' variety, contrast, and activity by means of display windows, street furniture, imagination, and paint, and it is excellent drama to exploit the contrast between the street's small elements and its big banks, big stores, big lobbies, or solid walls.

Most redevelopment projects cannot do this. They are designed as blocks: self-contained, separate elements in the city. The streets that border them are conceived of as just that—borders, and relatively unimportant in their own right. Look at the bird's-eye views published of forthcoming projects: if they bother to indicate the surrounding streets, all too likely an airbrush has softened the streets into an innocuous blur.

MAPS AND REALITY

But the street, not the block, is the significant unit. When a merchant takes a lease he ponders what is across and up and down the street, rather than what is on the other side of the block. When blight or improvement spreads, it comes along the street. Entire complexes of city life take their names, not from blocks, but from streets—Wall Street, Fifth Avenue, State Street, Canal Street, Beacon Street.

Why do planners fix on the block and ignore the street? The answer lies in a shortcut in their analytical techniques. After planners have mapped building conditions, uses, vacancies, and assessed valuations, block by block, they combine the data for each block, because this is the simplest way to summarize it, and characterize the block by appropriate legends. No matter how individual the street, the data for each side of the street in each block is combined with data for the other three sides of its block. The street is statistically sunk without a trace. The planner has a graphic picture of downtown that tells him little of significance and much that is misleading.

Believing their block maps instead of their eyes, developers think of downtown streets as dividers of areas, not as the unifiers they are. Weighty decisions about redevelopment are made on the basis of what is a "good" or "poor" block, and this leads to worse incongruities than the most unenlightened laissez faire.

The Lincoln Center for the Performing Arts in New York is

a case in point.* This cultural superblock is intended to be very grand and the focus of the whole music and dance world of New York. But its streets will be able to give it no support whatever. Its eastern street is a major trucking artery where the cargo trailers, on their way to the industrial districts and tunnels, roar so loudly that sidewalk conversation must be shouted. To the north, the street will be shared with a huge, and grim, high school. To the south will be another superblock institution, a campus for Fordham.

And what of the new Metropolitan Opera, to be the crowning glory of the project? The old opera has long suffered from the fact that it has been out of context amid the garment district streets, with their overpowering loft buildings and huge cafeterias. There was a lesson here for the project planners. If the published plans are followed, however, the opera will again have neighbor trouble. Its back will be its effective entrance; for this is the only place where the building will be convenient to the street and here is where opera-goers will disembark from taxis and cars. Lining the other side of the street are the towers of one of New York's bleakest public-housing projects. Out of the frying pan into the fire.

If redevelopers of downtown must depend so heavily on maps instead of simple observation, they should draw a map that looks like a network, and then analyze their data strand by strand of the net, not by the holes in the net. This would give a picture of downtown that would show Fifth Avenue or State Street or Skid Row quite clearly. In the rare cases where a downtown

---

* For a more in-depth analysis of Lincoln Center, see "A Living Network of Relationships" in this volume.

street actually is a divider, this can be shown too, but there is no way to find this out except by walking and looking.

THE CUSTOMER IS RIGHT

In this dependence on maps as some sort of higher reality, project planners and urban designers assume they can create a promenade simply by mapping one in where they want it, then having it built. But a promenade needs promenaders. People have very concrete reasons for where they walk downtown, and whoever would beguile them had better provide those reasons.

The handsome, glittering stretch of newly rebuilt Park Avenue in New York is an illustration of this stubborn point. People simply do not walk there in the crowds they should to justify this elegant asset to the city with its extraordinary crown jewels, Lever House and the new bronze Seagram Building. The office workers and visitors who pour from these buildings turn off, far more often than not, to Lexington Avenue on the east or Madison Avenue on the west. Assuming that the customer is right, an assumption that must be *Project planners and urban designers assume they can create a promenade simply by mapping one in where they want it, then having it built. But a promenade needs promenaders.* made about the users of downtown, it is obvious that Lexington and Madison have something that Park doesn't.

The already cleared site for the postponed Astor Plaza building offers a great opportunity to provide the missing come-on and make Park Avenue a genuine promenade for many blocks. Instead of being aloof and formal, the ground level of this site ought to have the most commercially astute and urbane collection possible of one- and two-story shops, terraced restaurants, bars, fountains, and nooks. The Seagram tower and Lever House with their plazas, far from being disparaged, would then harvest their full value of glory and individuality; they would have a foil.

The deliberately planned promenade minus promenaders can be seen in the first of the "greenway" streets developed in Philadelphia. Here are the trees, broad sidewalks, and planned vistas—and there are no strollers. Parallel, just a few hundred feet away, is a messy street bordered with stores and activities— jammed with people.* This paradox has not been lost on Philadelphia's planners: along the next greenways they intend to include at least a few commercial establishments.

Fortunately, Philadelphia's planners and civic leaders are great walkers, and one result is their unusually strong interest in trying to reinforce the natural attractions of the city's streets. "We ought to do it a street at a time," says Harry Batten, chairman of the board of N.W. Ayer & Son and a leading figure in the Greater Philadelphia Movement. "Take Chestnut, which is a fine shopping street; we ought to get rid of everything that hurts it, like parking-lot holes. Find merchants who ought to be there and sell them on the idea of relocating." At the other end of the pole is Market Street opposite Penn Center: cheap stores, magic shops, movie houses, and garish signs—exactly the kind of street most cities see as a blight. Batten, who thinks a city is made up of all kinds of people, is against making Market Street

---

* In a 2002 interview with Eleanor Wachtel on the CBC Radio program *Writers & Company,* Jacobs describes seeing the contrast between the planned promenades and the nearby streets in Philadelphia as a "moment of awakening," regarding the bankruptcy of modern city planning and rebuilding. Ironically, she may have encountered this scene on a tour with city planner Edmund Bacon or Louis Kahn in 1955 while researching a favorable review of the city's efforts. See "Philadelphia's Redevelopment" in this volume.

more prim. "It should be made more like a carnival," he says, "more lights, more color."

FOCUS

No matter how interesting, raffish, or elegant downtown's streets may be, something else is needed: focal points. A focal point can be a fountain, or a square, or a building—whatever its form, the focal point is a landmark, and if it is surprising and delightful, a whole district will get a magic spillover.

All the truly great downtown focal points carry a surprise that does not stale.

All the truly great downtown focal points carry a surprise that does not stale. No matter how many times you see Times Square, with its illuminated soda-pop waterfalls, animated facial tissues, and steaming neon coffee cups, alive with its crowds, it always makes your eyes pop. No matter how many times you look along Boston's Newbury Street, the steeple of the Arlington Street Church always comes as a delight to the eye.

Focal points are too often lacking where they would count most, at places where crowds and activities converge. Chicago, for instance, lacks any focal point within the Loop. In other cities perfectly placed points in the midst of great pedestrian traffic have too little made of them—Cleveland's drab public square, for example, so full of possibilities, or the neglected old Diamond Market in Pittsburgh, which, with just a little showmanship, could be a fine threshold to Gateway Center.

Unfortunately, most of the focal points that are being planned seem foredoomed to failure. Those ponderous collections of government architecture, known as civic centers, are the prime example. San Francisco's, built some twenty years ago, should have been a warning, but Detroit and New Orleans are now building centers similarly pretentious and dull, and many other cities are planning to do the same. Without exception, the new civic centers squander space; they spread out the concrete, lay miles of walk—indeed, planners want so much acreage for civic centers now that the thing to do is to move them out of downtown altogether, as New Orleans is doing. In other words, the people supposedly need so much space it must be moved away from the people.

But city halls never have needed much grounds, if any, a fact that our ancestors—who knew why they wanted courthouse squares—grasped very well. Newspapermen who make it their business to know politicians soon discover their own city has a kind of political Venturi—one spot where politicians gather, one stretch of sidewalk where, if you stand there at noon, you will see "everybody in town."* Even in the largest metropolitan centers you will find the political Venturi easy to spot; it is here that lawyers, officeholders, office seekers, various types of insiders and would-be insiders, cluster and thrive, for information is their staff of life. This vital trading post is never marked on the official city map; nor have the city's architects found space or color for it in their diagrams of Tomorrow's City. In fact, if you ask some of them about it, all you get is a blank look, perhaps a bit of scorn.

---

* Jacobs here appropriates the "Venturi effect"—a principle of fluid dynamics named after the Italian physicist Giovanni Battista Venturi (1746–1822) in which a fluid flowing through a constriction point increases in velocity and decreases in pressure. Her "political Venturi" is a point of concentration where all the flowing people are likely to converge.

Big open spaces are not functional for this kind of civic activity; the prestige and attractiveness of a sidewalk garden, such as that of the new Federal Reserve Bank in Jacksonville, or a side garden, such as that of the Federal Reserve in Philadelphia, would be about right for city halls and city-county offices and would enable them to stay where they belong, near the lawyers, pressure groups, and others who must deal with the local government.

THE ECHO

Backers of the project approach often argue that giant super-block projects are the only feasible means of rebuilding downtown. Projects, they point out, can get government redevelopment funds to help pay for land and the high cost of clearing it. Projects afford a means of getting open spaces in the city with no direct charge on the municipal budget for buying or maintaining them. Projects are preferred by big developers, as more profitable to put up than single buildings. Projects are liked by the lending departments of insurance companies, because a big loan requires less investigation and fewer decisions than a collection of small loans; the larger the project and the more separated from its environs, moreover, the less the lender thinks he need worry about contamination from the rest of the city. And projects can tap the public powers of eminent domain; they don't have to be huge for this tool to be used, but they can be, and so they are.

Architects, similarly, lament that they have little influence over the appearance and arrangement of projects. They point out that redevelopment laws, administrative rulings, and economics resulting from the laws do their designing for them. This is particularly true in residential projects, where stipulations about densities, ground coverage, rent ranges, and the like in effect not only dictate the number, size and placement of buildings, but greatly influence the design of them as well (including such items as doorways and balconies). Nonresidential projects are less regulated, but they are cast in much the same mold, and many an office-building project is all but indistinguishable from an apartment-building project.

The developers and architects have a point. They have a point because government officials, planners—and developers and architects—first envisioned the spectacular project, and little else, as the solution to rebuilding the city. Redevelopment legislation and the economics resulting from it were born of this thinking and tailored for prototype project designs much like those being constructed today. The image was built into the machinery; now the machinery reproduces the image.

WHERE IS THIS PLACE?

The project approach thus adds nothing to the individuality of a city; quite the opposite—most of the projects reflect a positive mania for obliterating a city's individuality. They obliterate it even when great gifts of nature are involved. For example, Cleveland, wishing to do something impressive on the shore of Lake Erie, is planning to build an isolated convention center, and the whole thing is to be put on and under a vast, level concrete platform. You will never know you are on a lake shore, except for the distant view of water.

But every downtown can capitalize on its own peculiar combinations of past and present, climate and topography, or accidents of growth. Pittsburgh is on the right track at Mellon Square (an ideally located focal point), where the sidewalk gives way to tall stairways, animated by a cascade. This is a fine dramatization of Pittsburgh's hilliness, and it is used naturally where the street slopes steeply.

Waterfronts are a great asset, but few cities are doing anything with them. Of the dozens of our cities that have riverfronts downtown, only one, San Antonio, has made of this feature a unique amenity. Go to New Orleans and you find that the only way to discover the Mississippi is through an uninviting, enclosed runway leading to a ferry. The view is worth the trip, yet there is not a restaurant on the river frontage, nor tiny rooftop restaurants from which to view the steamers, no place from which to see the bananas unloaded or watch the drilling rigs and dredges operating. New Orleans found a character in the charming past of the Vieux Carre, but the character of the past is not enough for any city, even New Orleans.

A sense of place is built up, in the end, from many little things too, some so small people take them for granted, and yet the lack of them takes the flavor out of the city.

A sense of place is built up, in the end, from many little things too, some so small people take them for granted, and yet the lack of them takes the flavor out of the city: irregularities in level, so often bulldozed away; different kinds of paving, signs and fireplugs and street lights, white marble stoops.

THE TWO-SHIFT CITY

It should be unnecessary to observe that the parts of downtown we have been discussing make up a whole. Unfortunately, it is necessary; the project approach that now dominates most thinking assumes that it is desirable to single out activities and redistribute them in an orderly fashion—a civic center here, a cultural center there.

But this notion of order is irreconcilably opposed to the way in which a downtown actually works; what makes it lively is the way so many different kinds of activity tend to support each other. We are accustomed to thinking of downtowns as divided into functional districts—financial, shopping, theater—and so they are, but only to a degree. As soon as an area gets too exclusively devoted to one type of activity and its direct convenience services, it gets into trouble; it loses its appeal to the users of downtown and it is in danger of becoming a has-been. In New York the area with the most luxuriant mixture of basic activities, Midtown, has demonstrated an overwhelmingly greater attractive power for new building than Lower Manhattan, even for managerial headquarters, which, in Lower Manhattan, would be close to all the big financial houses and law firms— and far away from almost everything else.

Where you find the liveliest downtown you will find one with the basic activities to support two shifts of foot traffic.* By

---

* Later, in *Death and Life,* Jacobs would observe the ability of a functional street to attract numerous "shifts" of foot traffic, not just two. The complex interplay between the roles, entrances, and exits of these shifts prompted her to compare them to a ballet—as seen in one of her most famous phrases, "the ballet of the good city sidewalk" (p. 50).

night it is just as busy as it is by day. New York's Fifty-seventh Street is a good example: it works by night because of the apartments and residential hotels nearby; because of Carnegie Hall; because of the music, dance, and drama studios and special motion-picture theaters that have been generated by Carnegie Hall. It works by day because of small office buildings on the street and very large office buildings to the east and west. A two-shift operation like this is very stimulating to restaurants, because they get both lunch and dinner trade. But it also encourages every kind of shop or service that is specialized, and needs a clientele sifted from all sorts of populations.

It is folly for a downtown to frustrate two-shift operation, as Pittsburgh, for one, is about to do. Pittsburgh is a one-shift downtown but theoretically this could be partly remedied by its new civic auditorium project, to which, later, a symphony hall and apartments are to be added. The site immediately adjoins Pittsburgh's downtown, and the new facilities could have been tied into the older downtown streets. Open space of urban—not suburban—dimensions could have created a focal point or pleasure grounds, a close, magnetic juncture between the old and the new, not a barrier. However, Pittsburgh's plans miss the whole point. Every conceivable device—arterial highways, a wide belt of park, parking lots—separates the new project from downtown. The only thing missing is an unscalable wall.

The project will make an impressive sight from the downtown office towers, but for all it can do to revitalize downtown it might as well be miles away. The mistake has been made before, and the results are predictable; for example, the St. Louis auditorium and opera house, isolated by grounds and institutional buildings from downtown, has generated no surrounding activity in its twenty-four years of existence!

WANTED: CAREFUL SEEDING

When it comes to locating cultural activities, planners could learn a lesson from the New York Public Library; it chooses locations as any good merchant would. It is no accident that its main building sits on one of the best corners in New York, Forty-second Street and Fifth Avenue, a noble focal point. Back in 1895, the newly formed library committee debated what sort of institution it should form. Deciding to serve as many people as possible, it chose what looked like the central spot in the northward-growing city, asked for and got it.

Today the library locates branches by tentatively picking a spot where foot traffic is heavy. It tries out the spot with a parked bookmobile, and if results are up to expectations it may rent a store for a temporary trial library. Only after it is sure it has the right place to reach the most customers does it build. Recently the library has put up a fine new main circulation branch right off Fifth Avenue on Fifty-third Street, in the heart of the most active office-building area, and increased its daily circulations by 5,000 at one crack.

The point, to repeat, is to work with the city. Bedraggled and abused as they are, our downtowns do work. They need help, not wholesale razing. Boston is an example of a downtown with excellent fundamentals of compactness, variety, contrast, surprise, character, good open spaces, and a mixture of basic activities. When Boston's leaders get going on urban re-

newal, Philadelphia and Pittsburgh can show them how to organize, Fort Worth can suggest how to handle traffic, and
Boston will have one of the finest downtowns extant.

THE CITIZEN

The remarkable intricacy and liveliness of downtown can never
be created by the abstract logic of a few men. Downtown has
had the capability of providing something for everybody only
because it has been created by everybody.

So it should be in the future; planners and architects have a vital contribution to make, but the citizen has a more vital one. It is his city, after all; his job is not merely to sell plans made by others, it is to get into the thick of the planning job himself.

Downtown has had the capability of providing something for everybody only because it has been created by everybody.

He does not have to be a planner or an
architect, or arrogate their functions, to ask the right questions:

- How can new buildings or projects capitalize on the
  city's unique qualities? Does the city have a waterfront that could be exploited? An unusual topography?
- How can the city tie in its old buildings with its new
  ones, so that each complements the other and reinforces the quality of continuity the city should have?
- Can the new projects be tied into downtown streets?
  The best available sites may be outside downtown—
  but how far outside of downtown? Does the choice
  of site anticipate normal growth, or is the site so far

away that it will gain no support from downtown, and give it none?

- Does new building exploit the strong qualities of the street—or virtually obliterate the street?
- Will the new project mix all kinds of activities together, or does it mistakenly segregate them?

In short, will the city be any fun? The citizen can be the ultimate expert on this; what is needed is an observant eye, curiosity about people, and a willingness to walk. He should walk not only the streets of his own city, but those of every city he visits.

When he has the chance, he should insist on an hour's walk in the loveliest park, the finest public square in town, and where there is a handy bench he should sit and watch the people for a while. He will understand his own city the better—and, perhaps, steal a few ideas.

Designing a dream city is easy; rebuilding a living one takes imagination.

Let the citizens decide what end results they want, and they can adapt the rebuilding machinery to suit them. If new laws are needed, they can agitate to get them. The citizens of Fort Worth, for example, are doing this now; indeed, citizens in every big city planning hefty redevelopment have had to push for special legislation.

What a wonderful challenge there is! Rarely before has the citizen had such a chance to reshape the city, and to make it the kind of city that he likes and that others will too. If this means leaving room for the incongruous, or the vulgar or the strange, that is part of the challenge, not the problem.

Designing a dream city is easy; rebuilding a living one takes imagination.

A Living Network of Relationships

———

SPEECH AT THE NEW SCHOOL
FOR SOCIAL RESEARCH,
NEW YORK, APRIL 20, 1958

THE PROGRAM SAYS WE ARE TO TAKE A LOOK INTO NEW YORK'S future. Back in high school I had to write the class prophecy. That experience finished me off as a prophet so I am not going to take any daring leaps across time tonight.* Instead I am going to assume that we are shaping the future right now, and that the best way to find out what New York is going to be in ten, twenty or more years is to take a hard look at what is happening in the city today. And perhaps if we look hard enough at this emerging New York of the future, and do not like what we see, the future will take on a different shape.

Let us look at the city of the future which is taking shape from our official projects. I do not like it because it ignores the single greatest fact about our city: that New York consists of an intricate, living network of relationships—made up of an enormously rich variety of people and activities. Look at the 2,000 pages of

---

* Jacobs carried her disdain for prophecy to the end of her life. As she puts it succinctly in *Dark Age Ahead,* "Life is full of surprises. . . . Prophecy is for people too ignorant of history to be aware of that, or for charlatans" (pp. 25–26). Likewise, see chapter 7 of *The Nature of Economies,* "Unpredictability," or her comments regarding the future in "The End of the Plantation Age" in this volume.

the Manhattan Redbook for example, and consider what this alone tells us of the thousands upon thousands of pieces, most of them quite small, which make our city.* Consider the interdependence, the constant adjustment, and the mutual support of every kind which must work, and work well, in a city like ours.

This criss-cross of supporting relationships means, for instance, that a Russian tearoom and last year's minks and a place to rent English sports cars bloom well near Carnegie Hall, or that on the same block the Advanced Metaphysicians and the Dynamic Speakers and the Associates of Camp Moonbeam have all discovered they can fit sympathetically into the studios that do well for music too. It means that the Puerto Rican Orientation Club of East Harlem finds a place it can actually afford in a beat-up tenement basement—an unprepossessing place but a place of its own, beholden to no one, and thus it can flourish. This criss-cross network means that the textile companies of Worth Street move uptown from a quiet, uncrowded place into the maelstrom of the garment district because they see a higher logic in being closer to their customers. It means that tourists and the transients who stay in the city four or five years can continue enjoying the flighty bohemia of Greenwich Village, but only because the Village still has enough solid, rooted Italian families and sober-sided middle-class parents to battle year, after year, after year Mr. Moses's schemes for making it like everywhere else.[†]

* The Manhattan Redbook or "Red Book" was a guide to the city's street addresses, residences, public and private amenities, and principal points of interest published in various versions over the course of the twentieth century.

† The scheme in question is Robert Moses's attempts to run a roadway through Washington Square Park in the Village, a plan he pursued, futilely and against much opposition, across the 1950s. See "Reason, Emotion, Pressure" in this volume for more on Washington Square Park and Moses.

All that we have in New York of magnetism, of opportunities to earn a living, of leadership, of the arts, of glamor, of convenience, of power to fulfill and assimilate our immigrants, of ability to repair our wounds and right our evils, depends on our great and wonderful criss-cross of relationships. In fact, so primitive a matter as whether our very lives are safe from each other depends on maintaining intricate community networks, for no quantity of policemen can enforce civilization where the informal means of community self-policing fall to pieces.

All that we have in New York of magnetism, of opportunities to earn a living, of leadership, of the arts, of glamor, of convenience, of power to fulfill and assimilate our immigrants, of ability to repair our wounds and right our evils, depends on our great and wonderful criss-cross of relationships.

This is all so obvious it should be unnecessary to mention. But it is necessary, for our slum clearers, housing officials, highway planners and semi-public developers have been treating the city as if it were only a bunch of physical raw materials—land, space, roads, utilities. They are destroying New York's variety and disorganizing its economic and social relationships just as swiftly and efficiently as rebuilding money can destroy them.

The most direct destruction is, of course, associated with clearance, and this is a painful aspect of slum elimination of which we are all becoming aware. It was described well by Harrison Salisbury, in his *New York Times* series on delinquency.* "When slum clearance enters an area," says Salisbury, "it does

---

* Harrison Salisbury (1908–93) wrote a much-followed series of articles about kids in the city, a common theme at a time in which "juvenile delinquency" was seen as a new social problem. The series became an influential book in 1958, called *The Shook-Up Generation*.

not merely rip out slatternly houses. It uproots the people. It tears out the churches. It destroys the local businessman. It sends the neighborhood lawyer to new offices downtown and it mangles the tight skein of community friendships and group relationships beyond repair."

Salisbury says "beyond repair" and he is right, and this is much the most serious part of the problem. Our rebuilders have no idea what they are destroying, and they have no idea of repairing the damage—or making it possible for anyone else to do so. The entire theory of urban rebuilding rests on the premise that subsidized improvements will catalyze further spontaneous improvement. It is not working that way in New York. Living communities, portions of living commercial districts, are so ruthlessly and haphazardly amputated that the remnants, far from improving, get galloping gangrene.

Furthermore, the newly built projects themselves stifle the growth of relationships. We are now conscious that this is true of the huge public housing projects. What we may not be so aware of is that this stifling of variety and of economic and social relationships is inherent in the massive project approach itself, whether public or private housing or anything else.

Take the Lincoln Center for the Performing Arts for example. It is planned entirely on the assumption that the logical neighbor of a hall is another hall. Nonsense. Who goes straight from the Metropolitan Opera to the Philharmonic concert and thence to the ballet? The logical neighbors of a hall are bars, florist shops, non-institutionalized restaurants, studios, all the kind of thing you find on West Fifty-seventh Street or along Times Square or generated by the off-Broadway theaters down here in the Village. True, halls and theatres are desirable to each other as nearby neighbors to the extent that their joint support is needed to generate this kind of urbanity and variety. But Lincoln Center is so planned and so bounded that there is no possible place for variety, convenience and urbanity to work itself in or alongside. The city's unique stock-in-trade is destroyed for these halls in advance, and for keeps, so long as the Center lives. It is a piece of built-in rigor mortis.

This project will also be harmful to Midtown, because it segregates and removes from the working and shopping areas a whole group of activities which generate evening and weekend use. When you get daytime and evening, workaday and leisure activities mixed intimately together in a city, you get a wonderful generating capacity for restaurants and every sort of unique, big-city variety. The city's magnetism depends on this sort of thing. There are parts of Midtown which need this help.*

In the past many cities have made the mistake of segregating and buffering culture; Pittsburgh, Cleveland, St. Louis, Detroit and Philadelphia for example. Every one of them has an impressive, dull center with no urbanizing to it, just as Lincoln Center will be, and in every one of those cities the downtown suffers demonstrably because of what has been removed. It is a very old-fashioned mistake.

Lincoln Center shows a brutal disregard for still another type of urban relationship. It will have a catastrophic effect on Amsterdam Houses, a ten-year-old, 800-family public housing

---

* In chapter 8 of *Death and Life*, "The Need for Primary Mixed Uses," Jacobs calls those uses with a strong ability to attract users, such as residences, workplaces, and leisure destinations, "primary diversity," and the additional uses they support, such as restaurants, "secondary diversity." She also observes that municipalities can treat their civic uses as "cultural chessmen," using different pieces in concert. For instance, an opera house could be placed in an area without enough nighttime uses (pp. 167–68).

project. Amsterdam Houses is now bordered by factories, railroad tracks, garages and institutions except on its eastern side. On that one side, fortunately, it faces, across the street, fortyeight lively neighborhood stores, part of a non-project, ordinary community. The stores and the non-project community will be cleared out to make way for Lincoln Center. The tenants of Amsterdam Houses will therefore no longer have neighborhood stores or any contact with non-project community life, which they desperately need. Instead they will have the Metropolitan Opera. This project will be utterly shut off to itself and isolated. I should think its people would explode. What kind of irresponsibility is this that deliberately, and at great expense, makes intimate neighbors of public housing and the Opera, depriving each of the neighbors it needs?

All over the city public and semi-public projects are going forward with just as cruel a disregard of people's needs and of the city's unique assets. Subsidies are being used to escape not only the pressure of economics, but the pressure of ordinary common sense.

Notice the advertisements for our rebuilt city. One currently appearing, for example, is for Park West Village, the former Manhattantown, one of the many middle-income clearance projects which have turned high-income along the way. The Park West advertisement depicts three apartment towers set upon a vast meadow. The scene is more rural than anything within twenty miles of New York, let alone Ninety-seventh Street and Amsterdam Avenue. "Your own world in the heart of Manhattan," says the ad. This advertisement, objectively a lie, is unfortunately subjectively true. It is an honest picture of the fundamental rejection of the city which is part and parcel of New York's slum clearance and rebuilding program.

None of us can have our own world in the heart of Manhattan. What happens for good or evil to the relationships on those streets which the artist has so blandly airbrushed away, what happens in Central Park—which is no exurbanite meadow—is going to affect Park West Village. It is going to affect us all.

If Lincoln Center, and Corlears Hook and Morningside Gardens and Park West Village and Washington Square Village and Peter Cooper Village and Stuyvesant Town and Fort Greene Houses and Red Hook Houses and Taft Houses and Grant Houses and Washington Houses and Jefferson Houses and Madison Houses and Franklin Houses and Carver Houses and Kingsview Houses and Bellevue Houses and Typographers Houses and Meatcutters Houses and Amalgamated Houses and their like are, in truth, the forecast of New York of the future, you do not need to be a prophet to see what we are going to have.* We are going to have an urban monster that never was—a pseudo-city composed of economically segregated islands, with dreadful and endless social consequences; composed of large, repetitive, separated, monotonous buildings, with dreadful economic consequences. For the New York of the future

---

* This roll call of projects underway or completed in New York by the late 1950s includes both urban renewal and public housing projects, which includes those built by both private developers using federal funds available through renewal laws—including nonprofits, universities, hospitals, insurance companies, real estate developers, and unions—as well as public agencies, primarily the New York City Housing Authority. Here Jacobs is concerned about their impact on the physical shape of the city, but the way she lumps public and private projects together suggests as well that she objects to the fact that both public and private projects are enabled by top-down sources of what she would later call "cataclysmic money."

will have less and less capacity to accommodate change, less and less room for initiative by anybody but officially anointed builder barons, less and less relationship of anything to anything outside itself.

But will the whole city of the future have to undergo the clearance treatment? Yes, almost all of it, for our rebuilders are going about their work of economic destruction and social disintegration with greater efficiency than you might suppose. There are ways of softening up areas so that clearance must finally follow. One way is to designate the area for future slum clearance; this automatically discourages private and public maintenance and improvement, and even though the area was not a slum insures that it will become so.

Another way is to disorganize or blight the very heart of the community, a mortally vulnerable spot if you know how to get at it. Look at Greenwich Village for example, since we are in it. Its mortally vulnerable core is the Washington Square area. If this core is to be drastically changed for the worse, the repercussions will be felt throughout all the Village.

Now Greenwich Village, although it has its serious problems, is probably the most successful community within New York, and certainly the most popular and attractive to visitors. It even has the power of spontaneously expanding and upgrading its edges, a power which is becoming almost unique in our city. Planners who respected the city and its potentialities would not only attempt to learn from the Village—and there is much to learn from it—but they would certainly protect such an asset to the city from needless blight.

But instead we find that Mr. Moses the Commissioner of Parks, Mr. Moses the Slum Clearance Chairman, Mr. Moses the

City Coordinator of Construction, and Mr. Wiley the Commissioner of Traffic are all four in cahoots, determined that the heart of this community, Washington Square Park, shall be made a parkway so it can carry an arterial stream of through traffic between widened West Broadway and, ultimately and inevitably, through a widened lower Fifth Avenue. They have made no traffic study to determine what useful purpose this will serve or what alternatives make better sense. The scheme is just as haphazard and whimsical as the juxtaposition of the Metropolitan Opera with public housing. It is oblivious to all values—even traffic and transportation values. The one thing it will surely do is blight a successful community. The classic misuse of raw material is the attempt to make a silk purse out of a sow's ear. Our builders are more remarkable. They are determined to make a sow's ear out of a silk purse.

Because Greenwich Village is still an effective, functioning community, we are going to defeat this attempt at vandalism and get Washington Square Park closed to all but emergency traffic. We have to. For this is a chips-down test of the whole question of whether human values and indeed urban values, can survive in this city.

For you see, the bulldozer is not the only portent of our future. Something else is shaping the future of our city too, something which is even more important than the form of the monotonous, inhuman pseudo-city which is visibly emerging. This other shaper of the future is invisible; it is what is going on in people's heads. Judgment, sense of values and ideas are real things too, that forecast the future, and because this is true I think the ruthless, raw-material approach to New York will soon be obsolete.

What will we have in its place? Now I will go out on a limb and make some predictions, based on what is beginning to happen in other cities, and on what seems to be happening inside some of the heads I encounter.

In place of bulldozer unplanning, we will have urban renewal planning, much more sensitive to exactly what is cleared out of an area, what is left in, what is put back and why. The West Side Urban Renewal study of the City Planning Commission, which is to be released this Wednesday, is our first small portent of this approach.*

We will also begin to examine and to care about what is good about the city, instead of concentrating only on what is wrong about the city as we have in past rebuilding. I think we will find much wisdom practically embedded in city features we have considered beneath notice or have been willing to toss away because they are bedraggled. For instance, as we find out more about the ways a great city, full of strangers, polices itself, I think we shall find the old city was not so stupid in orienting all its eyes and activities toward the street. As we find that a neighborhood has to do with the numbers of people, not geo-

---

* In the margins next to this paragraph of the original manuscript Jacobs scrawled "Haw!" We can't be sure, but this was likely a retrospective touch on her part, signifying how much she'd changed her mind about this revision of urban renewal. The West Side Urban Renewal Study was heralded as a revision of Moses-style urban renewal in the Philadelphia vein, with more attention to local context and less clearance. Mayor Robert Wagner ordered the study as a response to protests over Moses's methods. Jacobs, as she says here, hoped that what she called "spot renewal" would end the abuses of modern clearance and rebuilding. A few years later, though, just as she was finishing *Death and Life,* a renewal project guided by these principles was announced for Greenwich Village, and seeing the effect it would have on her own neighborhood she lost all faith in this piecemeal revision of urban renewal. See box 19, folder 3 of the Jacobs Papers at the Burns Library, Boston College.

graphic size, we may find that our drugstore owners were not so stupid in the frequency of their locations. As we learn more about big-city magnetism we will discover something that Mr. Dowling has known all along, that our commercial theater owners were not so stupid in their instinct to mix in where it is lively and make it livelier.*

We will begin to think of traffic as part of the whole problem of land use, and as part of the total problem of transportation of people. We will stop thinking of it in terms of nasty little destructive piecemeal expediencies, and use it as a positive constructive framework in ways which Victor Gruen has brilliantly shown us are possible.

We will recognize that any community within New York needs all kinds of activities and people mixed up in it to make it work. We will especially avoid fostering communities composed only of the transient, either rich or poor transients. We will recognize that public housing should have outgrown the theories of the 1930s, something Charlie Abrams has been trying to tell us for years.† I think we are at last ready to listen, and to plan for the publicly housed to be part of the normal community.

---

*   Robert Dowling (1895–1973) was a real estate investor and patron of New York City's theater scene.

†   Charles Abrams (1901–70) was an urbanist, author, and housing expert. He was one of the first—in the 1940s—to draw attention to the way racial discrimination in housing created a stratified metropolis and to protest federal subsidies for private redevelopment, which he labeled the "business welfare state" (Zipp, *Manhattan Projects* [101–13]). He held a number of stations over the years, from first counsel for the New York City Housing Authority to chairman of the New York State Commission Against Discrimination. He was also a resident of the Village and a commercial landlord on Eighth Street, one of the neighborhood's major business strips. In *Death and Life,* Jacobs praises his attempts to preserve the strip's commercial diversity after the street's success resulted in a growing restaurant monoculture (pp. 244–45).

We will discover that we can get parks and space for light and air, and sound planning, in rebuilt areas by the simple expedient of taking direct responsibility for these matters, instead of going all around Robin Hood's barn to do this. At present we have to find a developer big enough and then see that he has a territory big enough and buildings repetitive enough and write-down subsidy enough so that he can afford to throw in the parks and also pay himself for five years of life spent in the negotiations.

We will find economic means of rehabilitating structurally sound buildings without booting out an old, well-rooted population in the process. At present rehabilitation of buildings and upgrading of neighborhoods is usually nothing but pure misfortune to our middle-income families with children, people the city needs. If we can figure out a way to pay public subsidies for new apartments that rent at $70 a room,* as we have, surely we will find a way to save such families for the city even though their habitations need new heating plants or bathrooms. It only depends on what we want.

We will be locating our public facilities—schools, health centers, welfare offices, and the like, much more astutely to strengthen our communities. At present, I know of only one public body, the circulation division of the Public Libraries, which studies the networks of the community, the people and their paths and activities, to determine just where to locate.† We will get smarter about the importance of this; when our schools learn it, we will take a big jump ahead.

---

* This would have been considered a high rental cost at the time, at least for the "well-rooted population," equivalent to roughly $574 per room in 2016.

† For more on how the New York Public Library located its branches, see "Downtown Is for People" in this volume.

Many years ago, when I came to New York to seek my fortune,* I found a job in a very big clock company where I was put to work typing numbers and places on pink pieces of paper. Nobody told me what the pink papers were and I still don't know. But I could see very well what they represented—dozens and dozens and grosses and grosses of clocks, going everywhere. This made me very happy. "Why, we are supplying the whole world with clocks," I thought. And from morning to night I typed just as hard and as fast as I could, to help reach the day when we would have the whole world supplied with clocks, and we could wind up that job and get on with something else.

But after about a week, it suddenly dawned on me that this job was never going to be finished. Clocks would wear out, and new people would come along wanting clocks, and there was no end to it. This made me sad. I could no longer care about the pink papers, and the next day I quit to find a job where a person could get something *done,* for heaven's sake.

As you can see, I was very young and very impatient.

Now, I think most of us are apt to retain something of that feeling when we think of the job of repairing and rebuilding the city. It is very tempting to want to fix it in such a way that things will get finished and stay put and that's that, and whatever we didn't think of or was too much trouble or might not pay, can be written off as undesirable confusion. But New York is like the clock business; it is never going to get finished. This should not really be discouraging to anybody over the age of eighteen.

---

*   In a touching play on this phrase, Jacobs dedicated *Death and Life* "to New York City where I came to seek my fortune and found it by finding Bob, Jimmy, Ned and Mary," her husband and children.

In fact, it is pretty exciting to think of repairing and rebuilding the city in such a way that its people will continue to have freedom and opportunity to make thousands of intricate, big and little adjustments; to repair it in such a way that new needs, as they come along, new uses, new opportunities, new relationships, new immigrants' orientation clubs, new New Schools will find scope to grow and turn around in, instead of a massive set of masterminded straitjackets. It is pretty nice to think of people coming along in the future, who will have opinions and notions and plans and problems of their own, very big problems no doubt, but will take it for granted that the most alive, exciting, interesting, challenging, various place in the world is New York City.

That is what we inherited and we ought to pass it along even more so. Whether we can will depend on how much more bad rebuilding and community destruction we are stuck with, and how fast and well we can get to work at doing the job better.

A Great Unbalance

———

SPEECH AT THE FIFTH MONTHLY WOMEN DOERS LUNCHEON, SPONSORED BY MRS. LYNDON B. JOHNSON, THE WHITE HOUSE, WASHINGTON, D.C., JUNE 16, 1964

THIS IS AN AGE WHEN WE TALK MORE AND MORE ABOUT CITY amenity and produce it less and less. Many outrages are committed in its name. Poor people, Negroes and businesses on which many livelihoods depend are tossed out of their neighborhoods in the name of somebody's idea of amenity. Here and there our cities are given a slick, artificial mask. But neither that aberration, nor the drabness, dirt, and dispiritedness in other places answers the profound need we have for character, convenience, visual pleasure and vitality—all those things we lump together as amenity and cherish in cities.

The attractiveness of cities . . . builds up from lots and lots of different bits and details, lots of different bits of money, lots of different notions, all coming out of the concern, the affection, and the ideas of lots and lots of different people.

The attractiveness of cities is not gotten by subtraction. It builds up from lots and lots of different bits and details, lots of different bits of money, lots of different notions, all coming out of the concern, the affection, and the ideas of lots and lots of different people. The amenity of cities cannot possibly be planned or bought wholesale. It is so much more complicated and quicksilver than a choice between wall-to-wall pavement and wall-to-wall grass.

Almost unnoticed and unremarked, a great unbalance has developed in cities between money for building things and money for running things. Let me give a current example from my own neighborhood. For years we have been begging for repair and restoration of our park. For years the park has been running down. Last month the city offered to destroy the park and build a new one. Why not use that money, the citizens asked, to restore and maintain the park, and several others besides? The parks commissioner candidly explained that his department is starved for maintenance funds but is relatively well off for capital funds. He has money to build an unwanted new park for $750,000 but is hard put to find money for repairing benches, planting flowers, and picking up papers.

Almost unnoticed and unremarked, a great unbalance has developed in cities between money for building things and money for running things.

The consequences of such unbalance go far beyond dirt and disrepair. The certainty of not having enough money to run things automatically rules out wide ranges of potential recreation in cities, and many forms of potential beauty—not so much because of what these cost to develop but because they take more than routine care. Even the devastating ugliness of parking lots is insured when the hospital director or housing manager or auditorium chairman knows in advance that his budget cannot possibly support maintenance of more than hot, unrelieved asphalt and chain link fence. And how can we make headway combating private devastation of this kind when everyone can plainly see that the public standards are as low or lower?

Variety and character in parks and in the total city scene will steadily become less and less possible, no matter how lavish our lip service to amenity, unless we get many, many more cleanup people, repair people, painters, gardeners—and soon—working for the public. Many of these jobs, incidentally, require little training.

The wild unbalance between capital funds and running expenses is typical of many municipal services, and of all cities. This unbalance is compounded by the present forms of subsidies for highways, institutions, public housing, most instances of urban renewal, and by the devices of public authorities with their own borrowing power. Most of these cases of aid to cities, especially nowadays the grants for highways, remove great territories from the local tax rolls, while they simultaneously increase welfare, policing and social work burdens. Yet the subsidies themselves provide only for construction. They do not provide the equivalent of tax funds, nor even funds for the public share of their own subsequent maintenance costs. The cities' matching grants to projects can be in the form of capital improvements; this provision frequently stimulates capital expenditures that are unnecessary and even inane. The local borrowing power can be called on to finance these, but the interest comes out of the same pot as running expenses.

Theoretically, all these forms of aid are supposed either to cut running costs or bolster the local tax base; but they are not working out that way at all. The unbalance automatically feeds on itself and increases, because the harder it is to get maintenance funds, the greater the scramble for capital funds instead. Already, it has become easier for cities to let things disintegrate awaiting a big capital expenditure of some kind, and at that point sweep away the good with the bad, the beautiful with the ugly, and the productive with the unproductive. We see the paradox of cities actually impoverishing themselves by capital improvements.

The Decline of Function

—

PUBLISHED AS "DO NOT SEGREGATE
PEDESTRIANS AND AUTOMOBILES" IN
ARCHITECTS' YEAR BOOK 11, 1965

SOLICITUDE FOR CITY PEDESTRIANS SLIPS EASILY AND NATU-rally into preoccupation with the problems of traffic-separation. From this preoccupation, it is only a step to infatuation with *tour de forces* of gadgetry on a grandiose city-center scale. The pedestrians, having somewhere along the line become meta-morphosed from whole and various human beings into abstract "pedestrian traffic," become an excuse for a showy but fake, in-flexible and limited pretense at city environment.

This shift in emphasis, and its deplorable outcome, can be seen not only in the drift of ambitious pedestrian and town-center schemes as a whole, but can be followed even in the work of specific planning groups or firms. As an example, note the 1956 pedestrian scheme proposed by Victor Gruen Associates for Fort Worth, Texas; then compare it with the same firm's scheme, five years later, for East Island, a proposed development for an underused piece of land in New York's East River.* The initial conditions for the two schemes greatly differed, of

---

* The East Island project was proposed for what is now known as Roosevelt Island. Ulti-mately, Gruen's project never came to fruition, and redevelopment followed a 1969 plan by architects Philip Johnson and John Burgee.

course; East Island presented a virtual clean slate, and more freedom for the designer.

The Fort Worth scheme, for all its huge garaging and traffic service arrangements, subordinated these devices to the city center as an intricate, pluralistic, flexible collection of enterprises and establishments. The object was, quite literally, that the pedestrian was to inherit a busy bit of the earth (paved and unpaved) and it was to be a relatively various, adaptable and free piece of the earth at that.

In the East Island scheme, the gadgetry of circulation and of precinct separation has become an end in itself. Not only the pedestrian, but all of life is subordinated to it. The bit of earth under the sky which the pedestrian inherits as his purest precinct is a cold and dreary platform, little different from the monotonous promenades without promenaders that have become all too familiar in existing housing projects. The putative ingredients of a town center, along with the schools, are underground where they may be served by transportation in arrangements of endless ingenuity and perfect lifelessness. Nor is this a unique aberration. Much the same philosophy governs the long-range planning goals of center Philadelphia, for example, or the Golden Triangle center in Pittsburgh. The idea is to put underground as much as possible of what pedestrians use, and this is called providing the pedestrians with more light and air (where they will not be). In Philadelphia such an ideal must be compromised because of what exists already; and here we may venture a law about elaborate city pedestrian schemes: the more flexibility permitted the designer, the more inflexible the product.

There are other means than the tunnel of arriving at similar impasses in the name of the pedestrian. Among the most cele-brated and unworkable were Le Corbusier's mid-floor shops and roof playground in the Marseilles apartments.* Other means are to cut the whole city into series of unrelated islands. The Fort Worth scheme depended on the island approach, but ex-cusably, because all of this settlement which operates at all like a city was contained in the one island. This is the approach much used in town-center schemes, but for cities of big size it is most unpromising and artificial. The most extreme subordinations of all other functions of the city to the gadgetry of traffic and pre-cinct separation are probably the theoretical studies by Louis Kahn, which are enormously influential in U.S. schools of de-sign today.†

This drift from humanism to gimmickry reflects a difficulty that afflicts architectural design as a whole today: the decline of respect for function, and consequently lack of interest in it. Per-haps it is not surprising that urban design should share this seri-ous flaw, for the two fields of architecture and urban design draw on the same reservoir of unconscious assumptions and conscious ideas, and often on the same practitioners.

---

* A reference to Le Corbusier's first Unité d'Habitation building, the Cité Radieuse in Marseilles, France, built between 1947 and 1952. As Jacobs suggests here, Unité was intended as a "city within a city," bringing together housing with many other daily uses into one self-sufficient, comprehensively planned whole.

† Jacobs learned about Kahn's traffic philosophy while writing "Philadelphia's Redevelop-ment," which is included in this volume. In short, he based his theory of "the city travers-able," as Jacobs calls it, on the analogy of a city's roads and parking as the rivers and docks of a water system. Jacobs would directly criticize such analogies in chapter 18 of *Death and Life*, "Erosion of Cities or Attrition of Automobiles," pointing out that if planners remove a street in a city, traffic—unlike water—does not simply flow around the obstruction. It disappears. She discovered this phenomenon of urban complexity during Washington Square Park's trial closure to traffic, which she advocates for in "Reason, Emotion, Pressure," also included in this volume.

Almost unnoticed, the word "function," and the idea of function, have taken on a different sense from that understood in the formative years of modern architecture. Function, which form was to follow, then meant primarily the uses for which a building was needed. The structural methods and building materials were to abet and express these uses, free them in a sense, rather than warp or conceal them. Various building types were analyzed and understood in those terms, and some were revolutionized, such as the elementary school and the single-family house. Architecture is still living off this inheritance of analysis of function, but it is a very incomplete inheritance and, except in the case of hospital design, remarkably little has been added to it for a generation.*

Architecture with a capital A has become more and more interested in itself, and less and less interested in the world that uses it.

Instead, in the meantime, "function" has come to mean, not use of the building, but use of its structure and materials. It is possible now to write about form following function and confine oneself entirely to discussion of structure and materials; indeed it has been done. Architecture with a capital A has become more and more interested in itself, and less and less interested in the world that uses it. (Hence we get a term with connotations of functionalism, like "universal space," meaning great undifferentiated areas that are an excuse for using dramatic trusses; such space, far from approaching universality of use,

---

*   As editor of schools and hospitals for *Architectural Forum,* Jacobs was intimately familiar with the functional innovations that modern architecture brought to elementary schools and hospitals, like classrooms reorganized to reflect the new thinking in teaching and learning of the day. Reports from her husband, Robert Jacobs, an architect of hospitals, may also have influenced her view that hospital design had successfully continued to stay up to date compared to other sub-fields of design.

works out badly for almost any kind of use other than big auditoriums, and is less adaptable to a variety of needs than a row of old brownstone houses!*) When architecture concentrates ever more narrowly on its own devices, and gets farther away from interest in the world that uses it, it becomes narcissistic and that shows. Like all things that get far from the truth, it has to begin saying sensational things—about itself, because it has nothing else to talk about.

In a very similar way, the more elaborate and ambitious pedestrian and town-center schemes inform us insistently about themselves and their own novelty and cleverness. But they do not inform us about the variety and vitality and intricacy and opportunity and adaptability of prospering cities. They ignore—and even warp and thwart—the means by which cities generate the diversity that we call urbanity. Insofar as most of these schemes do draw upon the world outside themselves, they depend heavily on assumptions drawn from two very limited themes: suburban shopping centers and parks. There is a great hollowness where there should be a rich store of understanding about the complex functioning of cities and their streets.

I suggest that the way out is, first, to admit that we are not yet ready for grandiose or very radical schemes for rescuing city pedestrians. We have not done our homework. To do it, and simultaneously accomplish something, we should start quite humbly. We should start simply by giving direct, very functional and obvious consideration to pedestrians. And this should

---

* The philosophy of "universal space" was coined by the influential modern architect Ludwig Mies van der Rohe (1886–1969). An example of the philosophy in practice can be seen in his twenty low-lying buildings for the Illinois Institute of Technology, including the well-known Crown Hall (1956).

be done in precisely the places where pedestrians already appear in large numbers in spite of the inconveniences they meet and the impositions to which they are subjected. Some of these humble improvements which immediately suggest themselves are: more frequent places to cross the streets; widened sidewalks (i.e., bigger share of the road bed); more sidewalk trees; niches for standing outside the line of foot-traffic. To be sure, all such immediate, direct, functional aids to city pedestrians compete with convenience for automobiles. This is one of many truths about cities which have been too long evaded, but it cannot be evaded. Nor is it so terrifying a truth, even from the point of view of the automobile, when we realize that automobiles themselves are victimized direly by their own redundancy and that this redundancy feeds on the very palliatives conventionally intended to accommodate and relieve it.

As for visual help to the pedestrian, the most direct and sensible guidance of which I know comes from Gordon Cullen's book, *Townscape.** As Cullen demonstrates to the respectful mind, the most interesting visual ideas are suggested out of the unique reality that already exists, but needs pointing up. The Cullen approach is the very opposite of design narcissism, because the loved object is the place already existing and the purpose is to enhance its nature. The variety of vi-

The variety and intricacy of [the] real city is endless, and the means for clarifying and celebrating it are infinite.

---

*   Jacobs and her colleagues at *Architectural Forum* were influenced by the work of Gordon Cullen, J. H. Richards, and Ian Nairn at *The Architectural Review,* a British magazine that launched some of the earliest critiques of slum clearance, sprawl, and modern architecture and planning in the 1950s. This relationship culminated in "Downtown Is for People," included in this volume. Cullen contributed illustrations to the original piece in *Fortune* magazine.

sual observations and ideas in Cullen's book is astounding, and yet even this is only a beginning of the possibilities, because the variety and intricacy of [the] real city is endless, and the means for clarifying and celebrating it are infinite. Conscious attempts at this could not possibly look like the tiresomely repeated shopping-mall cliché nor like scenery for *The War of the Worlds*. And wouldn't that be a boon.

A photo taken for use on posters to promote meetings of CO72, a group aiming to secure a reform city council in Toronto's 1972 election. Jacobs, who endorsed a number of reform candidates, is believed to be holding the Y in "city."

PART THREE

HOW NEW WORK BEGINS

1965–1984

THE DEATH AND LIFE OF GREAT AMERICAN CITIES SET IN MO-
tion a new chapter in the life of Jane Jacobs. Her observations of
streets and parks had launched her into an "unexpected treasure
hunt" that would structure the rest of her life's work.[1] "It became evident to me while I was doing *Death and Life of Great
American Cities* that if the city's economy declines, that's the end
of it," she would later tell an interviewer. "It doesn't matter
what else cities have, what grand temples they have, what beautiful scenery, wonderful people, anything else—if their economy doesn't work."[2] Looking to explain how city economies
work, Jacobs left her decade-long post at *Architectural Forum* in
1962 to pursue a career as a full-time author, and started work
on her second book, *The Economy of Cities* (1969).

On a certain level, even *Death and Life* was all about economics. While taking extension classes at Columbia University in
the late 1930s Jacobs had become fascinated by an unsolved mystery: the sporadic and explosive growth pattern of cities. As she
would later write in her unfinished economics primer, *Uncovering the Economy* (see Part Five), none of her professors seemed
remotely interested in discussing or pursuing it. Over the years
she would continue to collect evidence on the subject, eventually amassing a box full of leads. While working at *Architectural
Forum* she had begun to believe that many modern planning
practices were in fact flawed attempts to rein in the chaotic effects of this growth (a dilemma captured well by the title of the

first anthology to publish Jacobs's writing, *The Exploding Metropolis*). It overwhelmed infrastructure, drove up costs, attracted unexpected migrants, increased inequality, and made predicting the future near impossible. However, given what Jacobs had observed firsthand in her time at *Architectural Forum,* she suspected that this erratic self-generating growth of cities was part and parcel of prosperity, innovation, and even "the ballet of the sidewalk" she celebrated in *Death and Life.*

Other than her box of odds and ends, however, Jacobs had little to back up her suspicions, so one day in the early 1960s as she considered her second book, she sent her teenage son Jim on a scouting mission to the public library. Tasked with proving definitively whether this explosive pattern of city growth existed at all, he delved into census data from America's metropolitan areas. Indeed, he found that while the national population tended to grow relatively steadily, individual cities grew in sporadic, unsynchronized bursts, suggesting corresponding bursts of economic activity. With this confirmation, Jacobs set out to discover what caused this growth and how the disciplines of city planning, economics, and governance could embrace it, instead of trying to control or smother it.

As she reported in *The Economy of Cities* and in an essay included here, "The Self-Generating Growth of Cities," Jacobs discovered that the source of these explosive growth episodes was the new kinds of work vital urban economies produce as people strive to solve everyday problems. However, that new work also threatens established economic and political interests, which use their considerable powers to nip incipient interests in the bud. Given the barriers such resistance poses to solving difficult social and environmental problems, Jacobs dedicated most of her speech at the inaugural Earth Week teach-in, "The Real Problem of Cities," to this subject.

Because of this conflict, Jacobs saw an important role for government in the market: a "third force" protecting new work from old.[3] Though as she explains in "Strategies for Helping Cities," included in this section, prevailing government strategies tended to have the opposite effect, preventing investment in diverse, young, and unusual enterprises and plowing benefits to incumbent interests. Only a better understanding of the dynamics of new work and its urban habitat, she argues, will clarify government's potential role in helping cities and the economy at large.

Meanwhile, interruptions to Jacobs's writing arrived in the form of "absurd" threats to her neighborhood, to her sons, and to her way of life.[4] By 1965, her biggest wins as a community organizer were behind her. Instead, she increasingly faced fights that seemed intractable, like the troubled construction of the community-driven West Village Houses she describes in "The Real Problem of Cities." Similarly, in late 1964, New York revived the Lower Manhattan Expressway (LOMEX), which Jacobs had helped defeat only two years earlier. The scheme failed again in 1965, only to return for a third time as a tunnel in 1968. Eventually the expressway would be killed for good in 1969 and the West Village Houses would open their doors in 1975, but Jacobs never got to see these victories in her time as a New Yorker.

The final straw for Jacobs turned out to be the Vietnam War. She and her family demonstrated against the war in New York and at the famous March on the Pentagon in October 1967, when gas-masked soldiers and U.S. marshals roughed up largely peaceful demonstrators. Vietnam compounded the dismay brought on by her interminable battles back in New York and prompted the bitter disgust with immoral authority recorded in "On Civil Disobedience" in this volume. It also uprooted her life in America for good. When her two draft-age sons told their parents that they would sooner go to jail than go to war, the Jacobs family decided to leave New York—the city to which she had dedicated *Death and Life* only seven years earlier—for the safety of Canada. Once, Jacobs would have considered herself patriotic. But after being marched on by her nation's own soldiers, she told a reporter in 1993, "I fell out of love with my country. It sounds ridiculous, but I didn't feel a part of America anymore."[5]

In her new home of Toronto, however, she found "the most hopeful and healthy city in North America, still unmangled, still with options." In sharp contrast to the United States, Canada in 1968 was brimming with optimism. The nation had adopted a new national flag in 1965; hosted a record-setting World's Fair, Expo 67 in Montreal; and elected the irreverent and eloquent Pierre Trudeau as prime minister in April 1968.

It didn't take long for Jacobs to become the unofficial bard of Toronto's beauties and battles, much as she had been in New York. She lent her forceful voice and her experience fighting LOMEX to a campaign against the proposed Spadina Expressway, which would have bisected downtown Toronto and run right over her family's first apartment in the city (see "A City Getting Hooked on the Expressway Drug"). But she also took pride in the efforts of the city's reform city council, which swept to power under Mayor David Crombie in 1972. Appreciation for Toronto's innovative, sensitive approaches to planning, urban renewal, and governance—which were often inspired by Jacobs's own ideas from *Death and Life*—peppers the final two speeches in Part Three and continues to pop up for the rest of her career.

Jacobs struggled with her next major book, *Cities and the Wealth of Nations* (1984). It took her years to sort out its focus: a study of how the urban economies she had explored in *The Economy of Cities* shape the economies of nations and drive macroeconomics in general. What first appeared to be another distraction from writing—a series of short radio lectures on Canada's fraught relationship with the province of Quebec, published as *The Question of Separatism* in 1980—became an inspiration. Although she was already thinking about the complex relationships connecting nations, regions, and cities, Quebec's burgeoning sovereignty movement helped her see how empires must alternately placate and suppress their colonies in order to hold themselves together. The conflict also alerted Jacobs to the difficulties that national currencies had in reflecting the varied local economic conditions of sprawling countries cobbled together through imperial expansion. *Cities and the Wealth of Nations* combined these still-disparate observations with her prior theories of urban economics into an ambitious synthesis that reveals cities—not nations—as the natural units of economic study and the rightful heirs to political power, long monopolized by nations.

NOTES

1.   See "Foreword to the Modern Library Edition" of *Death and Life*, in this volume.

2.   See Roberta Brandes Gratz, "Jacobs Tape," Jacobs Papers, 22:5.

3.   For more on the role of government as a "third force," see *The Economy of Cities*, 249.

4.   When asked whether she would ever return to New York City in an interview with Clark Whelton ("Won't You Come Home Jane Jacobs?" *The Village Voice*, July 6, 1972), Jacobs responded in the negative, explaining, "It's absurd to make your life absurd in response to absurd governments."

5.   See Mark Feeney, "City Sage," *Boston Globe,* November 14, 1993.

The Self-Generating
Growth of Cities

SPEECH AT THE ROYAL INSTITUTE OF
BRITISH ARCHITECTS, LONDON,
FEBRUARY 7, 1967

IT IS REALLY RIDICULOUS: WE LITERALLY KNOW MORE ABOUT the processes that go on in the sun than we do about the processes that go on in our cities. Mankind has lived in them for thousands upon thousands of years and we do not really know much about how they work.

It is really ridiculous: we literally know more about the processes that go on in the sun than we do about the processes that go on in our cities.

A few years ago, I became curious about why some cities stagnate economically (which means they stagnate in every other way too), and why some cities go on for extraordinarily long times without stagnating. I became interested in this because in America the stagnating cities, such as Pittsburgh, Detroit and many smaller cities, are a terrible problem. Their problems pile up faster than they can be dealt with.

London I very much admire. In fact, I am practically awe-struck by London, not only for the obvious reasons but because in historic (and probably prehistoric) times London has had a longer period of uninterrupted, self-generating, economic growth than any other city in the world. It has gone on longer without stagnation than Rome or Paris. Study of it, and of how it has generated new economic activities, would pay, not just for Englishmen but for all mankind.

When I got into this question, I did not know where to begin. I knew that there was a question here, but the customary answers to it are superficial. If you compare them, you find there is no pattern; the answers are not known. I made a hypothesis that a city that is not stagnating economically is a city that is continually casting forth new kinds of economic activity. And it does not matter whether the enterprises are privately owned or publicly owned; it is more fundamental than the arrangement of who controls things and who supplies the money.

The question arises, why do some cities produce these new things? Why are some cities creative only for a time, and then halt? If you think about these things in the abstract, you get nowhere, or else kid yourself. I decided that perhaps the best way to get a little light on the problem was to read the histories of successful businesses by early historians, especially those that were innovations at the time, in the hope that some pattern of what was important would emerge.

I found out that there *were* patterns, and they were completely surprising to me. The dominant pattern that began to emerge was something I had never remotely anticipated. These business histories became awfully tiresome; it was like reading the same three historical novels over and over and over again. The characters wore different clothing and had different accoutrements around them, at different periods, but they were the same old three stories. As these were American business histories, I wondered if this was quite special to us, and decided to try a different place and time. What better place than London, in medieval times? Luckily for me, I read the wonderful account, written at the turn of the century by George Unwin, of the guilds and companies of economic importance in Tudor and Stuart times.* There, sure enough, were the same three plots. I looked further afield; Japan, Russia and China seemed to have the same three plots. I have not yet found a fourth. It may very well be there, but I have not found it.

The strange pattern that I did not expect was that new economic activities come out of the internal economies of cities. Cities are not just great lumps of chaos. They are a form of very intricate, very wonderful order, and they seem like chaos mainly because we do not understand this order nor the processes by which it works. A city has an export economy, by which I mean not the things that it sells across national boundaries, but anything that it sells outside what we in the U.S. call a metropolitan area. If the exports of the city drop off, with an exception which I will come to later, its imports will drop off. If the exports increase, they will increase. There can be ways of evading this for a time (as in Pittsburgh, where exports dropped off so rapidly that even an out-migration of its people and welfare help from the rest of the country could not balance the loss of exports) but they are relatively immaterial. Over the long run, the city's exports are an iron determinant of the value of its imports. Quite a few of the imports go directly and immediately into making its exports—they are pre-empted imports. In Pittsburgh, im-

---

* George Unwin (1870–1925) was a British economic historian. Jacobs is referring to *Industrial Organisation in the Sixteenth and Seventeenth Centuries* (1904), which rested its account of the period's development on the division between traders and industrialists, not the conflict between workers and capitalists.

ported coal and ore go straight into steel, its big export, and form a large proportion of its imports.

The internal economy of a well-developed city is very large in comparison with its export and import economy, and it is divided into two parts—the population economy and the feeder economy.* We are all familiar with the population economy: i.e., the barbers, the policemen, schools, retail stores—all the things that serve people of the city directly. We may not be so familiar with the feeder economy, which consists of enterprises that provide repairs, parts, goods and services for the export and the population economy. They also serve each other in long chains; the feeder economy is a tremendously important part of any city's structure.

In a city's early days self-generating growth depends almost entirely upon the feeder economy. The population economy at that time is very small and very similar to that of other places. Its feeder economy may be unusual. What happens is that something in either the feeder economy or the population economy becomes an export. For example, Carnaby Street clothing, which was in the population economy of London, is now an export of London. You export to my children, for instance. This is the simplest type of something from the internal economy going into the export economy. I call it "slippage."† Some-

---

* In *The Economy of Cities,* Jacobs refers to these two parts more often as "consumers' goods and services" and "producers' goods and services," respectively.

† Although similar concepts regarding how local enterprises become exports appear in *The Economy of Cities,* the terms *slippage, mutation,* and *floating* do not. Jacobs does, however, use mutants as a kind of shorthand in *The Question of Separatism* to avoid the lengthy explanation included here. In short, she says, "Mutants are the most important form of division in economic life. . . . Existing enterprises are often open to new ideas, but most innovations take place in small, new companies" (68).

thing that was produced for a market within the city has just slipped into supplying people outside. This is a very old historical thing. When scribes in Athens copied treatises to send to the Library in Alexandria, or the engineers of Rome worked out an aqueduct for some city in Iberia, this was a slippage from the internal economy into the export economy. Most of what we call the spread of civilization amounts to slippages from internal economies of cities into their export economies.

I call the second way in which this movement from the internal economy to the export economy occurs "mutation," which is a sudden variation. A tiny firm called Lesney Products that started in London after the war was in the feeder economy, making dyes for other London firms that produced lighting fixtures. When they produced a product of their own, the first of the Matchbox toys, they were not producing just for London. The parent work in the feeder economy had a sudden variation added to it, and this went into export. Unwin tells of exactly the same kind of thing happening in the fourteenth and fifteenth centuries, when people in London making brass parts for London merchants began making brass bells for priories outside London. A mutation begins in the internal economy, and adds to itself a very logical other activity which is sold both outside the city and inside it. It arises out of that internal economy.

The third way that this happens is by "floating," which starts in the export economy, but only because the city has already developed enough feeders to do this division of labor. A spectacular example is the Ford Motor Company. When Henry Ford began producing motor-cars in Detroit, the only thing he did at first was assembly. Every single, solitary thing was done by feeders in the Detroit internal economy. If they had not existed, the Ford Motor Company could not have started. As time went on, he replaced the things that were manufactured for him by things he manufactured himself.

Slippage, I believe, is the most important, although mutation has often produced innovations that could not come in any other way. Floating is usually an imitative process. But fundamentally they are all the same in their effect.

Take a great United States company called National Packaging. How did it arise? It came out of a company that made paper milk bottle tops in Chicago, and was a feeder to the population economy. It added packaging for meat, which was logical, for Chicago is a meat packaging center. Then it sold its packages to people outside Chicago. It moved from the feeder economy into the export economy. As a result the city had a bigger export economy. The import economy of the city grows automatically, and some of its imports have to be pre-empted by the new plant. What is not pre-empted goes into the internal economy, which grows.* Something has been removed from it, in effect, and yet it is bigger than it was before. The chances that this same thing will happen again are not only as great as before, but are increased.

This, if I am correct, is a very fundamental process of self-generating growth. This is how cities keep producing new reasons for being, right out of their own internal economies. It is like a wonderful reservoir—in effect, two reservoirs. One keeps pumping things into the other but it never diminishes itself by

---

* What Jacobs omits from this early account of the economic processes of cities is her concept of "import replacement," in which cities replace former imports with improvised local production. A description of the process is described briefly in "Strategies for Helping Cities," in this volume.

doing it. Instead of diminishing itself, by the very act of pumping, it grows larger, and there is more of the reservoir to go into the other. The larger a city gets and the more various the things in its internal economy get to be, the more rapidly and the more various are the things coming and going round and round. . . .

Every kind of problem comes to a head in cities. The problem of disease: that was just the same in the country as in cities in one way but it came to a head in cities because there epidemics could affect so many people, travel so swiftly and so on, so that is where it had so urgently to be solved. Air and water pollution, transportation, or even any of our social problems, are not as difficult to solve as those that were solved in overcoming epidemics in cities. If we look at problems in this way, we can see that they are opportunities for cities. A city that begins actually solving, not evading, the air pollution problem, will begin to export devices for controlling air pollution in other cities that have not managed to solve this for their own internal economy.

What we call faults of cities are really bringing problems to a head where they can be solved.

So far from our denigrating cities because of the problems they create, we should recognize that these problems are opportunities. What we call faults of cities are really bringing problems to a head where they can be solved. The only terrible thing is when cities fall down on the job that only cities can do, and stop solving these problems within their own internal economies and then exporting their solutions to other places. A great deal of the notion that is so current in planning, that large numbers of people collecting in one place are unwholesome, should be discouraged. The countries that have these great cities have made the most progress at many times. Countries that are mainly villages have not. Life keeps casting up new problems, and the cities have been, and certainly will continue to be, the places where they can be solved.*

---

* Jacobs's argument for viewing cities as the vanguards of both problems and problem-solving forms a bridge between *Death and Life* and *The Economy of Cities,* appearing in both the final chapter of the former, "The Kind of Problem a City Is," and chapter 3 of the latter, "The Valuable Inefficiencies and Impracticalities of Cities."

On Civil Disobedience

―

CORRESPONDENCE WITH
THE NEW YORK TIMES MAGAZINE,
NOVEMBER 1, 1967, UNPUBLISHED

AN ACT OF CIVIL DISOBEDIENCE IS JUSTIFIED—IN FACT BECOMES necessary—when an individual makes the following judgments: his government is behaving wickedly or stupidly beyond the bounds of what he perceives as tolerable; dissent, having been earnestly tried, has proved of no avail; selective resistance to the law is preferable to various slyer or more violent alternatives.

These are subjective judgments, as all decisions based on conscience must be subjective. If war is an extension of diplomacy, civil disobedience is an extension of self-government.*

Vietnam demands disobedience. However plausible or implausible our presence there may have been, however rational or irrational for us to have tried to "fight Communism" there, the fact is that we lost. We defeated neither the Viet Cong nor, subsequently, Hanoi, sufficiently rapidly and with sufficient Vietnamese support to permit us to proceed with effective political and economic programs; our chances of doing so are gone.

---

* With this phrase, Jacobs references Carl von Clausewitz (1780–1831), a Prussian general and writer on military matters. Known for his realist bent, his contention in the posthumously published *On War* (1832) that war is the continuation of politics by other means is his most famous contribution to the theory of warfare.

Having lost the war, we have proceeded for the past two and a half years to engage instead in an enterprise sicker and uglier than war itself: an enterprise of slaughtering, starving, destroying and uprooting, to no purpose except to postpone acknowledging failure. This is now the only point of our presence in Vietnam. Dissent has clearly been useless in deterring this monstrous exercise.

Because the whole enterprise feeds directly and insatiably upon the bodies of our own young men, as well as upon Vietnamese, it is directly vulnerable to acts of resistance against the draft. The burden of resistance by disobedience thus falls disproportionately upon young men for a wholly practical reason. But practical disobedience is not limited to draft law resistance; we have yet to see what its limits are: they will be determined only by the ingenuity with which people discover ways to interfere concretely in the schemes of the authorities.

To be sure, not all civil disobedience consists of practical obstruction. Some is symbolic. Practical acts like draft resistance begin as symbolic acts of resistance; there is overlapping. The uttermost limit of symbolic resistance to the law is death, as in the cases of Buddhist monks and others who have set themselves afire or as in some instances of fasting.*

Merely by happening, civil disobedience affirms that outside

---

* In June 1963 in Saigon, South Vietnam, a Buddhist monk, Quang Duc, burned himself to death to protest the American-backed government of Ngo Dinh Diem, which persecuted Buddhists. Over the next few months several other monks in South Vietnam followed suit. In the coming years a handful of Americans would immolate themselves to protest U.S. involvement in Vietnam, most famously a Quaker named Norman Morrison, who in 1965 set himself afire outside the Pentagon just under the office window of Secretary of Defense Robert McNamara. The tactic lives on in our time, too, as in the case of Mohamed Bouazizi, the Tunisian street vendor whose self-immolation in late 2010 was widely heralded as having touched off the Arab Spring.

the corridors of power are men and women who make judgments, possess courage, form intentions, captain their souls, and act on their own. To those who habitually (often unconsciously) regard most other people as objects to be manipulated or ignored, the evidence of self-propelling integrity out there seems to translate to anarchy, hence is appalling. That, I think, is precisely why innocuous acts of symbolic disobedience— crossing a line at the Pentagon, say—are described as loathsome and why the perpetrators of acts so innocuous are beaten so brutally.*

Merely by happening, civil disobedience affirms that outside the corridors of power are men and women who make judgments, possess courage, form intentions, captain their souls, and act on their own.

* This was the famous March on the Pentagon on October 21, 1967. Jacobs was arrested, along with 650 others.

Strategies for Helping Cities

———

THE AMERICAN ECONOMIC REVIEW,
SEPTEMBER 1969 [*]

AMERICANS, AT PRESENT, USE TWO NATIONAL STRATEGIES THAT are presumed to help cities. One, which is impartial, is to dispense federal grants to them, either directly or through the states, for specified physical and social programs. The other is to award war and space contracts to enterprises in this or that locality, frequently a city; while this is a byproduct of other purposes, the contracts are regarded in recipient cities as aids to their economies and are highly valued for just this reason. I propose to question, from the point of view of cities' growth mechanisms, both these approaches and to suggest another strategy.

The overwhelming fact about cities is that if they do not maintain self-generating economies, they will ultimately stagnate and decline. This is not true of rural areas or towns. New export work is often be-

> *If [cities] do not maintain self-generating economies, they will ultimately stagnate and decline.*

[*] In the long run, economists embraced aspects of Jacobs's economic theories, particularly her ideas about the clustering of diverse industries and "human capital," while other ideas were largely ignored. For an overview of Jacobs's reception as an economist, see David Nowlan's article "Jane Jacobs Among the Economists" in *Ideas That Matter.*

stowed upon towns by enterprises that have transplanted their work out of cities. Rural areas prosper when their products are directly drawn upon by growing city markets and their productivity increased by city-created products and technologies. But, as for cities—even when a city receives a transplanted factory or office, the spin-off is from another city and has been "earned" by the growth of the receiving city's market or its array of input items, usually both. Rural technologies do not provide answers to unsolved practical problems in cities, nor does any city prosper and grow because of the markets provided by rural hinterlands. Cities, individually, must generate their own economic bases; and cities, taken collectively, must generate the innovations that make developing economies possible.

A city employs two major growth and development mechanisms, each of which builds upon the other: it generates exports and replaces imports. Simply to maintain an export base, a city must continually find new exports because, among other things, the city must compensate for production transplanted out to towns and countryside, and for exports lost because they are produced eventually in former customer cities. Of course, many of a city's older exports become obsolete in the course of time. A city's stream of new exporting organizations emerges directly from, and upon, production of goods and services first undertaken for the city's own market. The other major mechanism, import replacing, operates—for obvious reasons—mainly through replacements of imports from other cities, but also on occasion (e.g., artificial refrigeration in place of natural ice) from rural areas. When a city replaces imports, it shifts its purchases to other, often newer, imports from other cities as well as to larger quantities of rural goods. Replacing imports creates a large multiplier and thus, from the vantage point of that city, also creates a greatly enlarged and diversified reservoir of potential export goods and services.* Quite apart from the great problem-solving innovations that arise in cities in the course of these events, the processes themselves, considered as sheer mechanisms, are vital to city economic expansion and to dynamic inter-city trade.

The defect of the national grant strategy, as far as these vital mechanisms are concerned, is precisely that it is national. The grant program ensures that many different cities concentrate on exactly the same collections of problems and approach them in similar ways. Once a grant program has been devised, much standardization of goods and services in its cause automatically follows. One does not build a city highway on federal funds without meeting standard specifications, some of which are gratuitous but most of which are inherent in the prescription itself. Furthermore, since grants must be policed against corruption and egregious mistakes (e.g., housing with inadequate heating plants, hospital nursing units too small) or else their purpose is vitiated, it follows that most "correct" responses must be routinized; the policing, in any case a mammoth job, is impractical otherwise. What all this means, in sum, is that each city participating in a given grant program must respond with goods and services, whether imported or locally produced, very similar to

---

* As Jacobs writes in *The Economy of Cities,* in common economics usage a "multiplier" refers to the idea that "when the exports of a settlement increase, the local economy of the city grows too." These additional local jobs provide producers' goods and services for use in the export work, as well as consumers' goods and services for the workers in the export economy. Jacobs is suggesting here that replacing imports produces a similar multiplier effect. A further explanation of the complex mechanisms of the import-replacement multiplier effect can be found in *The Economy of Cities* (159–66).

those of all other cities participating. The very stuff of differential creation and dynamic city export generating and import replacing is being discouraged. This defect is more serious than the size of the grants alone would suggest. Since the grants are directed to glaring practical problems, they are automatically directed to activities, e.g. housing, transportation, health care, that have already become backward; these are precisely the problems, along with their associated economic activities, that most require development work, not premature prescriptions with their accompanying standardizations.

Not all countries, of course, have numerous cities as the United States does. Some have only one important metropolis. Denmark, Cuba, and Austria are typical instances of one-metropolis countries. Hong Kong is another, although an unusual case. In a one-metropolis country, national grant programs do not carry the defect of standardization to an extreme, simply because, in a one-metropolis country, the central government's writ does not run to the other metropolitan areas with which its own city trades most heavily.* This suggests that a strategy which can work constructively in Denmark is inherently destructive in Britain. The same kind of distinction can be drawn between Hong Kong or Malaya and multi-city India or China; and between Cuba and multi-city Brazil or the Soviet Union. The point is that in a multi-city country, a national grant strategy per se must be at cross-purposes to the mechanisms of city

---

*   In chapter 11 of *Cities and the Wealth of Nations,* "Faulty Feedback to Cities," Jacobs argues that multi-metropolis nations inevitably become one-metropolis nations because of the poor feedback provided by national currencies. In short, the value of such a nation's currency is most influenced by the city that does the most international trade, yet other cities that do little international trade receive the same feedback. Thus, New York City may be well served by feedback from the U.S. dollar, while Oklahoma City is not.

economic growth and development, no matter what the specific content and quality of the programs may be.

In the United States, the high point of faith in the grant strategy may well have been reached at the time the War on Poverty was launching its Great Leap Forward in 1965, and now may be on the wane. I base this supposition on the observation that, until the past few years, constructive criticisms of the national grants were almost wholly concerned with tactics—that is, were directed to details of administration, sizes of appropriations, emphases or omissions of the programs, and the like. But interest is growing in federal tax sharing with cities, either as an alternative or a supplement to grant programs. This speaks, if only by implication, of growing skepticism concerning the grant strategy itself.

The other American national strategy for helping cities, the war contracts for which there is so much jockeying, also works at cross-purposes to the processes of city growth and development although probably more gradually and cumulatively. From the point of view of a modern city, the war goods produced are export items. Thus they increase, often enormously and abruptly, the city's export economy. The trouble arises because war goods and services are not imported by cities. All sections of the country are paying for them but are not receiving imports in return and this import deprivation inexorably affects their economic mechanisms.

A city develops and builds its economy upon its imports as surely as upon its exports; it does so most importantly during its periodic episodes of explosive economic growth when it is replacing many former imports rapidly, in a chain reaction, and shifting its imports rapidly to other kinds of goods and services.

If import deprivation is temporary only, postponement of import replacing seems to be of no great moment. A dramatic example is afforded by Los Angeles at the end of World War II.* This probably means that a country which only intermittently engages in heavy war production, as was the case in the United States until the time of the Korean War, reaps the stimulating effect without incurring any long-range depressing effects on its cities' economies.

However, prolonged, heavy production for war is a different matter; it means that one after another, city after city is either being obstructed from replacing imports or the process is critically weakened, simply because, over a prolonged period, such large quantities of goods and services for which their people and enterprises have been paying have not reached the cities as imports.† The effect must be a cumulative inhibition on new city exports too, because cities that are not replacing and shifting imports vigorously are not serving as rapidly growing markets for new kinds of exports from other cities; nor are they, themselves, building up in their own local economies their own great potential reservoirs of new kinds of exports. The cities'

---

* In *The Economy of Cities,* Jacobs argues that Los Angeles underwent an episode of new work and import replacing–fueled growth after World War II (151–54). See "Uncovering the Economy" in this volume for a summary of that episode.

† Military goods and services act as "sterile" imports, imports that cities cannot replace, for two reasons. First, many of the imports are weapons or other military gear with strong government restrictions that prevent their participation in open-ended, symbiotic local economies. In the language of *Systems of Survival,* they are "guardian" products, not commercial products, and are thus governed by the guardian moral system, which forbids trade. Second, many military goods and services end their journeys in war zones or military bases, areas without creative urban economies capable of replacing any remaining unrestricted imports. For more on this and other national programs, see chapter 12 of *Cities and the Wealth of Nations,* "Transactions of Decline."

dwindling capacities for creating exports (and hence dwindling capacities for earning imports from other cities) reinforce the import deprivation caused directly by war production. This further undermines capacities to replace imports. In short, city economic mechanisms that ought to be building constructively upon one another are, at such a stage, converting to mechanisms of decline. A country does not have unlimited time to play games with its cities' economies.

If my reasoning is correct, it would follow that any other heavy and prolonged subsidy falling upon a nation's cities (e.g., very heavy and prolonged foreign aid consisting of goods from the donor country; heavy and prolonged exports of capital at the expense of city imports of goods and services) would also have the same effect. But so would diversion of the subsidies back into the cities themselves if they could not be used there to fuel revived and dynamic inter-city trade in many new kinds of goods and services. We are back at the standardization defect of the grant strategy again, and this time I am pointing out the fallacy of supposing that cities will necessarily prosper if subsidies for war are simply replaced by equivalent subsidies for city grant programs.

Perhaps the society of the United States is already too distraught to be capable of instituting in an orderly and constructive way a different strategy for helping cities. The common values, the sense of joint purpose, and the trust necessary to great, orderly re-reforms and their adjustments may already have been irretrievably lost. But if reform is still available to the United States, this is the course I would suggest:

First, the grant strategy should be abandoned in favor of federal tax sharing with localities. The cities' returned taxes (or as an alternative tactic, the reallocated taxing powers) would have to be given to the cities themselves, not the states, because so many states contain two or more metropolitan areas, as well as smaller, and in many cases long stagnant, cities. Thus state-administered standards or contingencies attached to the funds or powers would duplicate, on a smaller scale to be sure, the inherent defect of grant programs; and if no standards or contingencies were attached to the sharing, there would be no point in using states as conduits. The usual objection, that the cities cannot be trusted with these funds or powers because their governments are too corrupt or because racial discrimination runs too deep in them, may be true; and if so, this is merely another way of saying that reform is no longer available to the United States, but only further city stagnation and decay, or revolution and counter-revolution. Supposing things not to be so hopeless yet, the funds swiftly released to cities in lieu of specific grants should be augmented by tax money withdrawn from military spending. We might expect, considering the ingenuity of American corporations when their well-being is at stake, and the experience after earlier wars, that organizations losing military contracts would hustle to add new kinds of goods and services to their repertoires; the economy might thus get the famous "fallout" of civilian technology which has so long been promised as a byproduct of the work of the military-industrial complex but has so little materialized. The objection that the government is, by definition, responsive to congressional representatives of communities that have come to depend upon war work, and so cannot, or will not, take this step may, of course, also be true.

In effect, these suggested moves at the expense of the existing strategies would merely lift burdens that are now obstructing the normal growth and development processes of cities. In that sense, the reform would be negative. But I think a positive strategy is also desirable and probably necessary. To develop it would take somewhat longer.

The strategy would require a continuous program of data collecting, diagnosis and action, with the data collecting ideally coming first. But realistically, considering the need, diagnosis and action would be desirable at the same time data collecting was getting under way. The whole strategy would be directed at the heart of the matter: city economic creativity.

The relevant data would be economic development rates for cities. These could be determined by first compiling kinds and values of all goods and services, public and private, produced in each given city in a given year. The next compilation, which I would suggest occur five years later, and all succeeding compilations, would sequester kinds of goods and services, and their values, produced in the city only since the preceding compilation; this would be expressed as a percentage of the value of all work shown in the preceding compilation, yielding a development rate of new kinds of goods and services. The second quinquennial compilation, which of course would yield up the first development rate figure, would afford a comparison of a given city's development rate with those of other cities, and so would subsequent compilations. The third quinquennial compilation (and all succeeding ones) would also indicate whether a given city's rate were rising or falling. I am of two minds about a compilation interval as short as five years. The urgency of our situation argues powerfully for it. But a ten-year interval would shake out much ephemera and would give real weight, as the shorter span cannot, to the rapid growth of some innovations after their very early years. Perhaps the wisest course, at first, would be to make both five- and ten-year compilations. Indeed, to compare two successive five-year spans, placing greater weight on ephemera, with a ten-year span that allows greater weight to be given solid achievement, might be exceedingly enlightening. We know too little about these relationships.

In a city with a low or falling development rate, the job would be to diagnose, concretely, what factors were hampering the economic creativity of the city's people. This work should certainly not be approached with rigid preconceptions, but rather with hypotheses and these only because it is necessary to start somewhere. Some possibilities suggest themselves immediately: lack of venture capital; racial and other ethnic discrimination, as far as access to capital is concerned; presence of monopolies (e.g., those imposed by organized crime, by otherwise obsolete franchises and licenses, by shopping center developers in conjunction with zoning laws); unwillingness of local government to purchase experimental and innovative goods and services (e.g., for parks, schools, health services, sanitation work); unwillingness of local government to permit competition to its services (e.g., in public transportation, waste disposal); prevention, by existing enterprises, of breakaways of employees capable of organizing new enterprises; lack of independently produced or supplied input items, available to any potential producers requiring them; lack of incentives to purchase problem-solving goods and services (e.g., noise-combating materials, pollution-catching equipment) such as could be afforded by intelligent performance zoning, for instance.*

This is investigative work from which we would begin to learn, in concrete detail, much we do not now know about the effects of our laws, about the uses and sources of risk capital and, indeed, much about our own natures as city-building (and city-destroying) animals. To learn, and even to publish what has been learned, is by no means also to correct. But it is a beginning, if undertaken in cities where the power structure and the population are honestly concerned about city stagnation. The work could be financed in such cities by using funds now devoted to many unproductive planning studies and other expensive irrelevancies subsumed under city planning. Of course, resistance might defeat any changes required, which is a way, again, of saying it may be too late for reform.

Getting back to development rate data, such figures would continuously be informative and useful for prospering cities as well as for those in desperate trouble. They would indicate when prospering cities were just beginning to stagnate and would signal that preventive diagnosis and action were required. Where development rates were high and rising, they would signal a city's capability for unusual development work on innovative, problem-solving goods and services, vital to the entire economy; if this were not actually coming about, the reasons why should be investigated. Where development rates had been unusually high, but were falling, the movement might represent only the downside of the normal city growth cycle; but the fall,

---

* For more on performance zoning, see "The Real Problem of Cities" in this volume.

if long continued, would be a danger sign. Development rates within varying districts of cities or metropolitan areas could be calculated and these would be extremely useful for diagnosis and action.

To achieve a rather refined portrait of a city's economy and the processes at work there, one would need data on the following: 1. which new goods and services (appearing since the last compilation) represented replacements of imports and, among these, which were transplants of production from elsewhere and which were locally originated; 2. which new goods and services represented new input items; 3. what input items had been lost since the previous compilation; 4. kinds and value of export work lost; 5. kinds and values of work exported and which of these represented new kinds of exports; 6. the genesis of these new exports (that is, whether produced by organizations that had already been exporting, by organizations set up *de novo* for export work, or by organizations formerly producing only for the local market); 7. numbers and types of new organizations created by breakaways from older organizations; 8. kinds and sizes of new organizations being financed locally as distinguished from those financed from outside, and the terms of investment; 9. changes in quantities and kinds of imports since the previous compilation. I have been rather reluctant to enumerate these because the list might suggest that to collect that data is the salient task. But it would be useful only where diagnostic and remedial work were already rather highly developed too. As far as data are concerned, the first need is for the development rates; and I think they are badly needed.

The general strategy would represent, in itself, a problem-solving addition to economic life; that is, work which more than pays for itself, and does so even during its own period of development. There would be no need to begin the service in all cities at once in a multi-city country, nor need it be under the aegis of a single organization; it could be begun independently in various cities. To obtain useful comparative development rates it would, of course, be necessary to employ the same methods of compiling and computing in different cities but even these must at first be somewhat experimental because many difficult questions of judgment must be resolved in ways that will not, in fact, distort the realistic indications of economic innovation and creativity that are needed. The diagnostic and remedial work would be thoroughly experimental at first. Where any experimental work is concerned, an excellent ground rule is to encourage duplication, not monopoly, of effort. This, I should think, applies as surely to development of an effective strategy for helping cities as it does to the other creative efforts that this strategy would be identifying, measuring and—let us hope— liberating and stimulating.

A City Getting Hooked
on the Expressway Drug

THE GLOBE AND MAIL, NOVEMBER 1, 1969

WHEN MY FAMILY AND I SETTLED IN TORONTO ABOUT A year and a half ago, we soon learned the flat we had rented was perched on the putative edge of the Spadina Expressway, variously described to us as elevated, no, depressed; six lanes wide, no, eight; with a subway underneath, no, without; to be built soon, no, not for a long time. Whatever it was, it was not imaginary. Up at Highway 401 we could see what Marshall McLuhan calls the launching pad, a big, confident interchange poised for imminent attack upon a wide swath of raw earth and for the subsequent invasion of still unviolated ravine and pleasant communities to the south.* In the mind's eye, one could see the great trees and jolly Edwardian porches falling before the onslaught.

In the mind's eye, one could see the great trees and jolly Edwardian porches falling before the onslaught.

But surely, we suggested to one another, it would not really

---

*   Marshall McLuhan (1911–80) was the Canadian philosopher and media critic best known for coining the phrases "global village" and "the medium is the message." Jacobs and McLuhan worked together on the campaign to stop the construction of the Spadina Expressway in Toronto. Their collaboration culminated in the script for a documentary film, *The Burning Would,* released in 1969.

happen. Ten years ago, even five, but now? Surely the government in so up-to-date a City Hall must know all about the expressway disaster lands in Boston, Philadelphia, New York, Buffalo, Detroit, Washington—the battles and demonstrations, mounting over the years, by increasingly desperate victims.* They must certainly, we thought, have reflected upon the lesson of Los Angeles, where at rush hour the cars on the great freeways crawl at 10 miles an hour, the same speed the horses and buggies used to achieve, where the poor have no practicable way to reach jobs, where the exhausts have turned the air into a crisis, where expressways, interchanges and parking lots occupy some two-thirds of the drained and vacuous downtown.

But Los Angeles, we soon read in the newspapers, possesses an almost ideal transportation system and affords the model Toronto is aiming at. The speaker quoted was Samuel Cass, director of Metro's traffic department.

Since gaping at his statement, I have learned that the Spadina (no, the Allen) Expressway is but one strand planned, although a most crucial one, in a tight concrete net whose effect, just as Mr. Cass said, will be to Los Angelize Toronto.† Reading and listening to the official and unofficial comment in favor of this policy, I have been struck above all by its innocence. Toronto, it

* These cities were all the scenes of "freeway revolts" in which citizens rose up to stop the construction of highways through their neighborhoods. Jacobs's remark about Toronto's "up-to-date" City Hall, which was inaugurated on September 13, 1965, is a reference to the fact that it was designed in the then-fashionable Brutalist style by Finnish architect Viljo Revell. For a photograph of the building, see the title page of Part Three in this volume (page 157).

† The Spadina Expressway was planned as a downtown connector from an existing ring route, Highway 401. Part of its length would have replaced Spadina Road and Spadina Avenue if it had been completed. Today, the only finished section of the proposed Spadina Expressway is known as Allen Road, after William R. Allen (1919–85), a former "super mayor" of Metropolitan Toronto.

seems, retains illusions about inner-city expressways that have been shattered elsewhere by experience. Let us identify a few of these innocent dreams.

I.

THE ILLUSION THAT THE COST OF AN EXPRESSWAY IS COVERED BY THE CONSTRUCTION APPROPRIATIONS

They are the least of it. As the Spadina Businessmen's Association has accurately pointed out, although few seem to hear, many businesses displaced by city expressways are permanently lost to the city's economy with the jobs they provide.

New quarters for enterprises that do survive, and new dwellings, cost much more on the average than those destroyed, with no net increase in shelter for the increased expenditure.

City streets victimized by increased traffic onto and off expressway ramps must be widened.

Parking space, much of it on valuable inner-city land, must be increased.

Parkland and potential parkland—in Toronto the ravines—must be sacrificed.*

While it is difficult to attach a dollar cost to intensified air pollution and noise, the cost is there.

---

* Thousands of years ago, after the last ice age, retreating glaciers left a thick layer of sand and soil over the entire region surrounding present-day Toronto. Rivers and creeks running to the Great Lakes eroded the soft earth and created a distinctive series of jagged ravines. After Hurricane Hazel in 1954, which caused massive property damage and numerous deaths in these low-lying areas, the newly minted Toronto and Region Conservation Authority expropriated the ravines and preserved them as parkland. They are the inspiration for Toronto's self-conception as "the city within a park."

Similarly, the widespread uprooting of people and disintegration of city neighborhoods exact vast and mounting social costs.

I am only reporting what has been learned from experience in many U.S. cities whose people once thought an appropriation paid for an expressway. These are the bitter realities that recently led Patrick Moynihan, President Richard Nixon's assistant for urban affairs, to sum up a despairing account of fiscal and social havoc with the statement: "More than any other single factor it is the automobile that has wrecked the Twentieth-Century American city, dissipating its strength, destroying its form, fragmenting its life."

I have mentioned only capital costs. Direct and indirect operating costs of expressways have also proved larger than anyone expected.

In some U.S. cities now, repairs and physical maintenance are reaching more than 8 percent of construction costs annually. Put another way, once an expressway begins to age, its cost of construction may have to be duplicated thereafter as often as once every twelve years.

At least one U.S. hospital has noted the interesting fact that its annual deficit is more than equaled by the costs of treating automobile accident patients. Hospital and medical services, ministering to the most dangerous form of city transportation the world has ever known, contribute to the hidden operating costs.

In New York, where the courts are so overcrowded the whole system of administering justice has almost broken down, a huge portion of the load involves traffic violations and traffic accidents, another hidden operating cost.

When land is expropriated for expressways, interchanges and ramps, its cost is not considered a continuing item. Yet in reality there is an annually recurring loss of taxes. One specious means of attempting to compensate for this loss is to zone for high-tax, high-rise apartments beside the expressways. These, too, bear hidden social and economic costs.

The fallacy has been to assume that cost accounting methods which are appropriate for expressways out in the countryside or on the outskirts of cities can be applied also to expressways within cities. The two are simply not comparable. Confusion is compounded when the appropriations for city expressways are compared with costs of public transit. The comparisons are specious.

2.

THE ILLUSION THAT A CITY CAN SIMULTANEOUSLY BUILD AN EXPRESSWAY SYSTEM AND CONTINUE TO DEVELOP PUBLIC TRANSIT

For the reasons just mentioned, no city is rich enough to do so. Public transit inexorably deteriorates when expressways preempt a city's resources. If Toronto goes forward with its present policy, one can safely prophesy that 10 years from now public transit will be much inferior to that of today.*

---

* It's impossible to know whether Jacobs's uncharacteristic prophecy would have come to fruition, since Toronto's "present policy" did not go forward. After years of protests, the Spadina Expressway was finally canceled in 1971, marking a turning point in Toronto's traffic planning. Ontario premier Bill Davis best summarized the spirit of the moment in his June 1971 speech announcing the expressway's demise: "Cities were built for people and not cars. If we are building a transportation system to serve the automobile, the Spadina Expressway

3 ·

THE ILLUSION THAT A CITY CAN
HALT AN EXPRESSWAY PROGRAM
IF IT PROVES INADVISABLE

Unfortunately, there is a point of no return when options have been lost. To understand why this is so, one must realize that what makes an expressway different from an ordinary city street is the expressway's limited access and egress points. You can't leave and enter at every street corner. Limited access, so successful a feature in highways built through open country or at city outskirts, automatically creates traffic jams on city streets leading to and from heavily used ramps. In the case of the Spadina Expressway, for instance, the destination of many drivers will be midtown, the Bloor Street area. The traffic jams will be intolerable unless cars going some distance east and west are sorted out and diverted from the Bloor bottleneck. Therefore, north of Bloor, the longer-distance midtown cars must be diverted into a Crosstown Expressway, linking to Highway 400 on the west and to the Don Valley Expressway on the east. In short, once the Spadina is built, there will be no option to forego the Crosstown. Even Mr. Cass cannot retain that option.

Moreover, as traffic builds up over time, new bottlenecks will result from the Crosstown. Still others will appear south of Bloor in the territory where the Spadina and Highway 400

---

would be a good place to start. But if we are building a transportation system to serve people, the Spadina Expressway is a good place to stop." (Quoted in John Sewell's *The Shape of the City,* 179–80.)

merge and then flow on to the Gardiner. Since the Gardiner is already at capacity, it must be enlarged.*

This dynamic is the reason why a city expressway program is never finished. Loss of the option to halt is built into the system itself. It is rather like getting hooked on an addictive drug.

4 .
THE ILLUSION THAT EXPRESSWAYS
HELP THE SUBURBANITE

This dream seems especially seductive to innocents in North York. Of course, the suburbanites are visualizing a journey to the same downtown they already know, maybe even to an improved version of it. But as the expressways, interchanges and parking lots downtown proliferate, as the local streets grow ever more congested, and the pollution and noise intensify, the quality of the inner city deteriorates. The suburbanite is even cheated of his dream of a swift journey, if he travels during commuting hours.

5 .
THE ILLUSION THAT TRUCKING
IS AIDED BY CITY EXPRESSWAYS

The competition of passenger cars with trucks for street space is the worst handicap to movement of goods in cities, and express-

---

* In fact, not only was the Gardiner Expressway never enlarged, insufficient maintenance funding left it crumbling by the 1990s. By 2011, it cost the city an estimated $12 million a year simply to keep the elevated expressway on life support, and in 2015 controversy flared about whether to tear down or otherwise rework part of the expressway.

ways do nothing but exacerbate this difficulty. The more passengers that can be moved by other means than automobile, the better for movement of goods.

6.

THE ILLUSION THAT THERE IS NO ALTERNATIVE TO CITY EXPRESSWAYS

This, of course, is woefully unimaginative. The illusion is most severe among those who cannot conceive of mankind getting around in cities by means other than feet, automobiles, subways, trolley and bus.

A recent analysis of city transportation problems and solutions undertaken by a firm of California systems analysts at the behest of the U.S. Department of Housing and Urban Development concludes that it is cheaper for a large city (the examples studied were Boston and Houston) to employ new transportation technology than it is to build subways or extend an existing subway system—as well as being cheaper, of course, than instituting or extending an expressway network. The method most favored by the analysts for its economy, convenience and speed is a system of small, public dial-your-destination cars running on their own narrow rights-of-way like trains, joining up together over fast, express segments of the journey, then peeling off to their diverse destinations.*

Unfortunately, virtually all American cities have already lost any option, in the foreseeable future, to use such ideas.

---

* For further analysis of experimental transportation, see "The Real Problem of Cities" in this volume.

They have already bought a system and, bad as it is, buying another is academic. But Toronto is not yet in that position.

No single type of vehicle or service, however, can supply the many complicated public transportation requirements of a large, modern city. A variety of new services and vehicles is required, complementing one another. Hovercraft, already commonplace on the muskeg, have obvious advantages for lake and river cities.* In Toronto they could take part of the commuting load, could provide extremely fast service to Hamilton and, extended thereafter to Rochester, Buffalo and Detroit, the service could take pressure off airports. It might obviate the need for the Harbor Commissioners' proposed inter-city airport off the Beaches. Even sky-cars developed from the types now used for amusement at the CNE and on the Islands, could perform a utilitarian job, swooping people from one part of downtown to another.†

7 ·

THE ILLUSION THAT METRO COUNCIL
HAS ACTUALLY AUTHORIZED THE
SPADINA EXPRESSWAY

To be sure, it has authorized something, but what? It doesn't know. As of Sept. 2, members of Metro's Transportation Committee had not yet seen plans for the expressway and admittedly

---

* *Muskeg* is a Canadian term—derived from Algonquian—for the landscape of peat bogs and other wetlands found in the northern part of the country. Hovercrafts, which use a cushion of air to float above the ground, are well suited to this wet, rough environment.

† At the time Jacobs was writing, the Canadian National Exhibition (CNE) and the Toronto Islands both featured fairgrounds with overhead cable-propelled transportation.

did not know the answer to these and other vital questions: What will happen to traffic at Bloor Street? Where will exit and entrance ramps be and into what local streets will they feed? How will the Gardiner take increased traffic feeding down from the Spadina route?

Presumably Metro Council is still in the dark, as is the city Department of Planning, because the Transportation Committee was told plans would not be available for its information until after the first of next year.

As a relatively recent transplant from New York, I am frequently asked whether I find Toronto sufficiently exciting. I find it almost too exciting. The suspense is scary.

As a relatively recent transplant from New York, I am frequently asked whether I find Toronto sufficiently exciting. I find it almost too exciting. The suspense is scary. Here is the most hopeful and healthy city in North America, still unmangled, still with options. Few of us profit from the mistakes of others, and perhaps Toronto will prove to share this disability. If so, I am grateful at least to have enjoyed this great city before its destruction.

The Real Problem of Cities

——

SPEECH AT THE INAUGURAL EARTH WEEK TEACH-IN,

MILWAUKEE TECHNICAL COLLEGE, 1970

THE SOVIET ENCYCLOPEDIA ALWAYS USED TO BE GOOD FOR a laugh because it claimed that virtually all inventions from the sewing machine to the telephone had been thought up first by this or that obscure nineteenth-century Russian. Perhaps they were. But the ideas were not put to practical use.

The difference between thinking up a useful idea, invention or method and actually incorporating it into everyday economic life is a vital distinction.

The difference between thinking up a useful idea, invention or method and actually incorporating it into everyday economic life is a vital distinction. An economy that cannot or does not put available inventions, methods and services to ordinary use, when they are needed, is a stagnated economy.

A stagnant economy, instead of incorporating the new kinds of goods and services it needs as time passes, concentrates too long and too heavily on production of older goods and services, and depends too long on established organizations and enterprises. The United States now has a stagnated economy. I am not talking about a recession or even a depression but about something much graver, which may possibly even be irreversible.*

Consider, as an illustration, the state of American transportation. Automobiles and trucks are choking cities with pollution. Almost every physical and social amenity in cities is sacrificed to cars, expressways and parking, and the same facilities increasingly debase towns, shorelines and countrysides. Many families are burdened with the cost and upkeep of expensive equipment they can ill afford and yet cannot get along without. The burdens on hospitals and courts are fantastic; automobile travel is the most dangerous form of everyday transportation the world has ever known. And so on. The problems arising from the bloated production of automobiles and gasoline have been endlessly documented, explained and reported. The other form of transportation on which we depend too heavily, the airplane, is rapidly producing its own syndrome of problems and these too are building up to environmental crisis.

Looking at this state of affairs, one might logically suppose that practicable ideas for transportation had been exhausted some sixty to seventy years ago, in the period when the automobile, the airplane and the subway were all radical innovations. But of course that is not true. America now has its own "Soviet encyclopedia," figuratively speaking, of unused ideas for transportation.

---

* In a similar speech for the 1970 Alan B. Plaunt Memorial Lecture, Jacobs expresses her hope that the Canadian tendency toward sober second thought would help avoid what she perceived as stagnation south of the border. Citing philosopher Marshall McLuhan, she observes that America acts as Canada's "built-in Early Warning System" for urban problems of all kinds, a remark she repeats in "Pedaling Together" in this volume.

Earlier this year, for example, *The New York Times* reported that an embarrassment of inventions, some of them American, some foreign, confronts the city's Transportation Authority, which is contemplating 115 different schemes for "people movers" to use on a crosstown subway link. Most of the schemes are already ten, twenty, even thirty years old. Presumably one of them is a system called Carveyor that was fully developed and successfully tested for the 42nd Street shuttle seventeen years ago. It was so rapid and so economical, required so little labor, that it was dropped. It was too upsetting to the status quo.

I would not advise you to hold your breath while the authority makes up its mind which of the 115 possibilities to use and then does something about it, because this particular bureaucracy requires some two years of pondering and a study grant from the federal government to decide whether to ask for another grant to redecorate two subway stations.

For ten years or so I have been reading about another invention, the staRRcar system of small, guided personal capsules into which one slips a fare and dials a destination.* Along express stretches of a route, the capsules link up into exceedingly swift trains, then peel off to their various destinations. Last year a major systems analysis of city transportation, for which the federal government paid, using Boston and Houston as study

* The Carveyor, developed by Goodyear and a conveyor belt company called Stephens-Adamson, would have been a system of conveyor belts carrying a series of ten-person cars. Aside from the 42nd Street route, it was proposed for a variety of other projects, including Victor Gruen's scheme for East Island/Roosevelt Island, which Jacobs takes to task in "Do Not Separate Pedestrians from Automobiles" in this volume, but it never found widespread use. The Alden staRRcar system did, on the other hand, find one permanent incarnation as the Personal Rapid Transit system of Morgantown, West Virginia; it opened in 1975.

examples, came to the conclusion that it would cost less to install this system than to continue building expressways or
subways, that it would provide more rapid and convenient
transportation than either of those other methods, and that a
city deciding to use it could develop it within about five years.
The system requires rights-of-way no wider than a sidewalk to
carry more people, more rapidly, than a six-lane expressway. In
every environmental respect, from pollution to community destruction, it would afford great improvement. All this, of
course, should surprise no one except those who believe that
intelligence reached its climax in Henry Ford and John D.
Rockefeller. Nevertheless, I would not advise anyone to hold
his breath until some American city tries the staRRcar system,
for it has already been available for a long time. It is too upsetting to a status quo that is predicated on inconvenient, deteriorating, obsolete public transit and a very large, reliable market
for automobiles and gasoline.*

---

*   Struck from the final manuscript:

> Everybody is feeling good about the great outpouring of environmental concern during
> Earth Week. I have my doubts. In some ways, it looks to me more like Accepting-and-
> Planning-for-Stagnation Week. Troubles that are the results of stagnation are being ana-
> lyzed all too thoughtlessly as troubles resulting from progress and affluence. But the
> affluence is already vanishing like the progress. Stagnant economies inexorably and
> gradually become poorer as their unsolved problems and undone work pile up and the
> numbers of their idle people grow. This is happening now in the U.S. economy. To be
> sure, stagnant economies have very rich people; the rich even typically grow richer as
> the stagnation deepens, but the numbers of poor increase. Nothing works as well as
> formerly; even the old services perform less well and cost more. And in the profound
> absence of creativity, even money becomes of little avail to improve matters. It operates
> like the vast subsidies that have been poured into our hospital and medical systems
> through Medicare and Medicaid, to little purpose except to inflate the costs of medical
> and hospital care and frighten the wits out of everyone who examines the system to see
> where the money is going.

Let us look a moment into this question of maintaining the status quo. In the seventeen years since the officials responsible for the New York subway system chose not to disturb the status quo with the Carveyor, the system has not remained as it was. It has decayed, in service, equipment and maintenance of equipment, while costs have steadily risen. To maintain the status quo is impossible, in this or in most other things. In most activities, and certainly taking society as a whole, we must be creative or else resigned to decay. This is not simply an imperative of modern economies. It is an imperative of the human condition itself. A stagnant subsistence agriculture finally depletes the land of fertility, especially of trace elements. Economies much simpler than ours that have depended too long and too heavily upon wood for fuel have had disastrous effects on their environments.

We must be creative or else resigned to decay. This is not simply an imperative of modern economies. It is an imperative of the human condition itself.

What maintaining the status quo actually means, in practical terms, is maintaining well established interests, at the expense of a decaying environment. Here is how a pillar of the status

---

The reason I fear this may be Accepting-and-Planning-for-Stagnation Week is that, under the delusion that progress and affluence are causing the rape of the environment, the popular answer is to control the population and reduce its growth. Put bluntly, the argument says that overabundance of automobiles is caused by overabundance of people. Put more abstractly and comprehensively, the argument says that our per capita use and abuse of energy and resources cannot continue unchecked; therefore the answer is reduce the population growth. This is planning for protection of the status quo, and stagnation. Of course, life always becomes cheap in stagnated economies, with their mounting problems, persisting poverty, undone work, and idle angry people. Unless the people are drained off by emigration they become an increasing threat to the established arrangements.

quo, the Chairman of the American Petroleum Institute, was quoted, in 1961, in the magazine of Standard Oil of New Jersey:

> If every car traveled just another hundred miles, the consumption of gasoline would rise almost one per cent. This would mean only three or four more minutes behind the steering wheel each week for each driver, but it would add up to ten million more barrels of gasoline consumed in a year. . . . I most heartily endorse the Institute's new travel program as a stimulant to the greater consumption of gasoline and motor oil.

The destruction of city communities for the sake of expressways and the destruction of beaches by oil slicks in the frantic endeavor to get ever more oil to market are directly linked. The fragile ecology of a city neighborhood and the fragile ecology of the Arctic stand or fall together. Because a mounting problem has gone unsolved in cities, in deference to the status quo, the outermost wilderness is finally threatened.

I have been using transportation as an illustration of our stagnation, and of the ominously evasive response to stagnation supplied by the current powerful and well financed campaign for population control.* But stagnation in transportation, unfortunately, is only one among many instances of failure to solve problems. I am going to mention a few others, not for the purpose of listing a catalog of ills, but to indicate something about the nature of the widespread failure. The pattern I see is

---

* Inspired by the work of Thomas Robert Malthus (1766–1834), strict population stabilization had a popular following among environmentalists of the time, including Gaylord Nelson, the founder of Earth Week, who spoke alongside Jacobs at this event.

that people who are in closest touch with practical problems are rendered powerless to solve them. Decisions are imposed from the top. Development is not permitted to emerge from below, and thus precious little of any real value is emerging anywhere.

Consider, in this light, our long and expensive failures with city housing. One part of the problem, the only one I am going to deal with here, is how to add new dwellings into already built-up cities. Solutions imposed from the top down have the defect of sacrificing much good and reclaimable housing along with bad. This is true whether the new construction is done by private developers or by public agencies or by a combination of both.

The economic effect of both policies of destruction has been wretched. The inexorable result is a net loss of the kind of housing that is most needed and is already in shortest supply—moderate and low cost housing. Often there is an absolute net loss. The result, in other words, is simply to inflate the costs of city housing. Were more money spent on these programs, under these policies, the problem would only be intensified.

To neglect new construction within the built-up parts of cities and to concentrate instead—not just also but instead—on large vacant sites at city outskirts or in satellite suburbs is not an answer. The fact is, built-up parts of cities do need new construction. Old buildings wear out. Fires happen. Vacant lots better not left vacant do exist. And so on. In short, normal attrition of these and many other kinds requires new construction. Furthermore, out there on the outskirts or in the satellite suburbs or New Towns, the same difficulties are only being postponed. The new does not stay new forever; its turn for attrition comes too.

Down on the city streets, the gaps where housing might be inserted without destroying anything useful are very real. They are so real that naturally the thought has occurred in hundreds of neighborhoods, "Fill the gaps." It seems to anyone taking this worm's eye view that it is sane to stretch resources as far as possible by making all new housing construction a net increase in the supply of habitable housing.

I first heard this request for gap-filling about fourteen years ago in a poor black neighborhood in Philadelphia, and I have heard it in many other cities since. Yet as far as I know, only one neighborhood in the whole of this country has a gap-filling scheme under way. The neighborhood is in New York and I know it well; it is the neighborhood where I used to live.

In this case, all the usual objections were made. At first the scheme was condemned outright by the housing and planning bureaucracy. They said it was not economic. This was a curious response, since the cost of the neighborhood plan was less than a third as much as a plan originally proposed by that same bu-reaucracy, while the net increase in housing was almost twice as great as that resulting from the expensive bureaucratic plan. To be sure, the scheme from the top called for large-scale clearance under the rationale that a new, instant, synthetic community would be better than the one that grew organically, so the enormous difference in cost is not surprising. However—and this is more significant—the bureaucracy proposed as an alternative what it called vest-pocket construction. This consisted of buildings which destroyed only such housing and business as was deemed necessary to fill out sites of proper sizes and shapes for economical construction. The neighborhood's gap-filling scheme, which did not destroy anything, also proved more economical than the destructive scheme whose only rationale was its economy.

The neighborhood was very fortunate in the architects it had chosen to work out a solution. The architects did not waste time telling the people they had an insoluble problem and an impractical policy. Instead, they used their brains and made a new departure. They designed a small basic building in three slightly varying proportions. Singly or in combinations, the basic buildings could make use of every fortuitous available site in the neighborhood, on the site's own given terms. In short, advantages of custom building were achieved without its economic disadvantages, along with the advantages of mass production building without its disadvantages.

The buildings are designed to allow extremely flexible use, and easy convertibility from residential to commercial use and vice versa because the neighborhood was looking ahead to the kinds of changes that might well be wanted in the next generation.*

Eventually the bureaucracy cooperated handsomely with the neighborhood, but I would not be honest if I suggested that there is much hope in this story, apart from this one neighbor-

---

* This "gap-filling scheme" is the West Village Houses, originally proposed by Jacobs and her Village neighbors as an alternative to the city's urban renewal plans for their neighborhood. The houses finally opened in 1974, after years of delays and escalating construction costs that eroded the original vision for the 42 five-story walkups. Architecturally undistinguished, the West Village Houses nevertheless remain a source of relatively affordable infill housing in an expensive neighborhood. In the 1970s, the municipal government in Jacobs's adopted home of Toronto initiated a similar infill program to create affordable housing with more success (see "Can Big Plans Solve the Problem of Renewal?" in this volume). Today, this approach has become much more common, as reflected in the increasing popularity of the term *infill*. According to a recent EPA report, "Smart Growth and Economic Development: Investing in Infill Development," in 2014 infill comprised an estimated 21 percent of new home construction in America's 209 largest metropolitan areas.

hood's success. Almost simultaneously with the approval that was finally accorded the scheme, a new provision was added to the city's building code, the effect of which is to make it impossible for any other neighborhood to adapt the scheme or copy the policy.

Meanwhile, in other cities too, people who request gap-filling policies are still being told they are infeasible. In Washington, the elaborate and expensive experimental housing programs sponsored by the Department of Housing and Urban Development are not even posing the right questions.

Why is there such effective resistance to development in a field that so desperately needs it? Perhaps it is too upsetting to the status quo. As one housing commissioner said, seven years ago when the scheme was first worked out, "If we let this neighborhood plan for itself, every neighborhood will want to plan for itself." I think he was seeing the same thing I can see. That gap-filling city housing policies would make most of the vast federal, state and city housing bureaucracies obsolete. Architects could work directly with the people. Maybe the very idea of a radically new approach emerging from below seems, in and of itself, as frightening as a People's Park or as the slogan Power to the People.

Whatever the reason for the suppression of gap-filling, it is too bad because it demands and suggests radically new thinking. The New York scheme is by no means the last word on what could be done. Some architects in Toronto of whom I think highly because of their creativity have told me that, in their view, a basic city gap-filling unit could be as small as 22 feet square, making its multiples, either horizontally or vertically, even more adaptable to fortuitous sites, and that it could be even more flexible than the New York solution in its interior planning and future convertibility and in its exterior cladding and fenestration. Historically, new approaches undertaken for one reason have often provided solutions to quite different problems as well.

In a stagnated economy, the webs of suppression become wonderfully interlocked and pervasive. Wherever one turns, existing arrangements of some kind seem to stand in the way of change.

But in a stagnated economy, the webs of suppression become wonderfully interlocked and pervasive. Wherever one turns, existing arrangements of some kind seem to stand in the way of change. Loose ends become harder and harder to yank out of the web, and when somebody finds one, it is quickly knit back again.

National programs, particularly those with grants attached, are useless in combating stagnation simply because the programs are directed to matters which have already become glaring problems. To be sure, additional theoretical reasons may be given, apart from the existence of mounting problems. For instance, it is sometimes urged that housing is a responsibility of the federal government because housing is a necessity. Clothing is a necessity too. Nobody urges national clothing programs on that account. If the clothing industries performed as badly as the building industries, we might have such programs. No, there is no getting around the fact that national programs with grants attached are associated with problem activities such as housing, transportation, pollution prevention, health care, and so on. And this means the programs are automatically directed to activities that require many new approaches and much development work, not premature prescriptions and standardization.

National programs ensure standardized and premature prescriptions, from the very fact that a problem is being centrally defined. For instance, if a program to combat sewage pollution defines the problem as need for sewage treatment plants, then we may be sure resources are going to be spent on sewage plants. But there may well be other and better ways to combat sewage.

Once a problem has been centrally defined, much standardization of goods and services in its cause then automatically follows. What all this means, in sum, is that each city participating in a given program must respond with goods, services and methods, whether locally produced or imported from other cities, very similar to those of all others participating. The very possibility of creation, and innovation, deliberate or accidental, is being stifled under an impenetrable web of existing arrangements. The surest way to arrange that the status quo is *not* going to be disturbed, that development is *not* going to occur, that a problem with us now is going to be with us indefinitely, is to centralize responsibility for defining it and for administering funds directed to its solutions. The very strategy itself is fatally at odds with a goal of problem-solving.

Indeed, in the case of many current problems there is simply no effective way to get at them from the top, in any event. Development has to emerge from below. An example of this situation is waste recycling, one of the major keys to overcoming pollution of many kinds.

According to a recent report from China summarized in *The New York Times,* some enterprises in Shanghai are turning out building materials from slag, while others are turning out some fifty chemicals, not formerly produced there, from wastes. The policy is described as "reusing wastes instead of allowing them to pile up as garbage or to foul the city's air and water." The report says that waste-recycling work was not handed down from above. It was initiated by workers who handled the wastes. The report then goes on to make a big point of the higher-level ignorance and obstructionism that had to be overcome by the workers. Perhaps this is a flourish of ideology, but the fact is that the point about the importance of workers in direct touch with the wastes checks with much experience in North America.

Many of the rather few advances in waste-recycling here— for instance, conversion of fly ash to cinderblock, return of waste paper to mills for reprocessing, conversion of garbage into light-weight, dehydrated compost, or the now very prosperous industries that reclaim secondhand machinery—were contrived and carried out by people in very lowly positions, people handling wastes.

Back in the early 1960s, a coal-burning electric power plant in Pennsylvania, in cooperation with a large chemical corporation, developed and successfully tested equipment for capturing sulfur dioxide in fuel burning stacks and converting it to sulfuric acid. But left at that stage, which is where it now stands, it is rather like those sewing machines and telephones invented by the nineteenth-century Russians.

To get the idea into effective everyday use is quite beyond the power of the great chemical corporation or the electric company that created the method. Rather, somebody much lowlier—probably a great many somebodies—will have to take the initiative of enlisting customers, installing equipment, servicing it, picking up the acid and channeling it back to wholesalers or re-users. And they will have to find capital for doing this.

Without those people doing that work all the concern in the country about sulfur-dioxide in the air, all the money spent on setting wistful air-quality standards, writing and enacting legislation or paying speakers like me, for that matter, is quite useless. Somebody has to develop the work, and in the course of doing so there will be many failures. There always are when new work is developed.*

Somebody has to develop the work, and in the course of doing so there will be many failures. There always are when new work is developed.

It seems very little understood in this country now, bemused as it is by corporate bigness and by government attempts at big, sweeping solutions, how useless research work by large corporations can be if there are not small and lowly organizations to apply the work. Some years ago, the president of DuPont, reminiscing to a *Fortune* magazine editor about moisture-proof Cellophane, recalled that the product would have failed except for the fact of many very small customers who were willing to take a chance, try out the product in varying ways, and get it to market. Large users adopted it subsequently when they saw how it proved out, but they were neither interested in experimenting with it like the small customers, nor, more significantly, were they even equipped to do this. Their scale of operations, in itself, was wrong for that purpose. I was reminded of this by a *Scientific American* article last year,

* Struck from the final manuscript: "Anyone who imagines that we live in a postindustrial age in which automation is going to take care of most of our production problems has quite forgotten the fact that new kinds of work must be developed, vast numbers of them; or else does not remotely understand how much effort and duplication of effort that development takes, and at best how quite beside the point is automation until methods, goods and services have been devised and have already become well-established."

written by two DuPont researchers, describing materials for overcoming various types of mechanical noise. DuPont makes the materials, but the researchers pointed out that, in a sense, this is the least of the work. The use of the material, as an every-day fact of economic life, helping to cut down noise pollution, depends upon the formation and the work of many, many servicing organizations—I would suppose hundreds and more likely thousands—to prescribe, design and install the materials.

Sulfur-dioxide pollution and noise pollution are only two among many, many types of pollution, all of which require effort and initiative, emerging from below. But in this country now, almost no capital is available to speak of for lowly enterprises, certainly not in the vast numbers and variety needed. Such capital has always been hard to come by, but the situation has gotten worse, not better.

Indeed, will lowly enterprises of the types required even be *allowed* to emerge? As things stand now, I doubt it. Last year, community delegates in a section of Harlem, in New York, tried to include in that vast web of futility called the Model Cities Program something genuinely hopeful and potentially creative: a new, community-run garbage and trash collecting and handling service.* But the proposal was instantly struck from the program by the city officials. I was told by a planner who participated in that decision, and who concurred in it, that the

---

* Passed by Congress in 1966, the Model Cities Program was one element of President Lyndon B. Johnson's War on Poverty. Intended to offset and end the abuses of the urban renewal years, it provided federal funds to underwrite local efforts at residential rehabilitation and programs for social service delivery initiated by community groups. For all their emphasis on citizen participation—and many did provide a road into politics for the disenfranchised—the programs, as Jacobs suggests, often ran afoul of incumbent constituencies in cities. Model Cities was discontinued in 1974.

Sanitationmen's Union would not stand for it, and the city could not afford a conflict with the union over a point so unimportant. It is in the interests of unions, just as much as it is in the interests of oil companies and housing bureaucracies, to maintain the status quo.

Personally, I can think of nothing more important than to encourage and fund, let alone permit, any neighborhood corporation or other enterprise which thinks it could handle wastes better than they are being handled. It would also be worth knowing how those Shanghai workers in touch with wastes managed to overcome higher-level ignorance and obstructionism; current American know-how does not seem to include that know-how.

Intelligence has been defined biologically as "the breakdown of the instinctive fixity, increasing the potential for recombination, both within the organism and the environment."

To be sure, we are not clinging to an "instinctive fixity" because we human beings cannot return, even if we would, to fixed instinctual behavior. The barriers I have been describing, which we are not breaking down, do not serve as well as instinct and certainly not as well as intelligence. We are not breaking down, or breaking through, bureaucratic fixity. Increasingly, bureaucratic fixity has become an attribute of our institutions, private as well as public, labor unions as well as corporations.

Many kinds of bureaucratic fixity have been established as so good and so noble that they have now become almost impervious to assaults by intelligence, and this in spite of the fact that anyone can see that the results of these good and noble fixations are an utter mess. Land-use planning and the zoning that enforces it are illustrations. Anyone who questions land-use planning as a means of dealing with cities and new developments too is automatically supposed to be an enemy of good environment. Yet one need only observe results to know that something is terribly wrong.

To get at the nature of the trouble, let us notice the distinction between performance and land use. An example from the neighborhood where I live in Toronto will illustrate the distinction. In the neighborhood is a fine old house, much appreciated for its idiosyncrasy and attractiveness. A women's club wished to buy it for its quarters. Far from being objectionable, this proposal was welcomed by people on the street, which is zoned for residential land use, and by people in the neighborhood generally, because it ensured the building and grounds would be preserved instead of being bought by a land speculator who would probably demolish the building and use the site for a parking lot or simply leave it vacant while he held it.

But a club is a land use. And a zoning variance granted for this use would automatically make the street vulnerable to variances for clubs no matter how noisy or garish they might be, nor how much automobile parking they might require. Making an exception for the one club would not likely stand up. All right-thinking people know spot-zoning is evil. If it were widely indulged, the very basis of land-use zoning would be destroyed. Land-use zoning must take categories of land use seriously, or it is nothing.

But the trouble, really, is not with exceptions. It goes deeper. The trouble is that the neighborhood is interested in performance, while the bureaucratic fixity is riveted on land use.

Under land-use planning and zoning, as serious problems of noise, fumes and so on, increased in cities, a way was found to evade them by zoning. It did not matter whether or not a facility overcame bad performance, because its performance was not at issue; its category was. This system has done nothing constructive to stimulate better performance. What is more, it does not even work on its own terms of protecting various land uses from harm by unsuitable neighbors. All sorts of truly harmful and destructive things leak through its shield, even without variances, and many a totally harmless and convenient use is gratuitously forbidden. In practice, the chief benefits of this good and noble system accrue mainly to land speculators who often reap fortunes by pushing through land use variances. A philosophy of planning that comes straight from laying out farms—put the orchard here, the feed lot and barn there, the corn fields yonder—and makes sense in agrarian terms, becomes nonsense when it is applied to a different sort of environment.

Go to almost any hearing concerning zoning matters. You will find the experts talking about land use, and the ordinary people talking about performance. To amuse myself the other day, I listed the kinds of performance I had heard ordinary people bring up in conflicts over zoning variances. Here they are, six of them, along with some brief comments of my own concerning relevant types of standards.

1. Noise. Standards could be set according to the number of decibels allowable penetrating from the building. Think what a stimulation this might be to those acoustics services we need.

2. Pollution. In the present stage of the technology, standards could govern the solid particulate matter and sulfur dioxide emitted.

3. Scale. Many streets, especially those intimately scaled, are disintegrated visually by an out-of-scale building. This has little or nothing to do with land use. A street with identical or very similar uses can be rendered visually chaotic by nothing more than incongruities of scale; conversely a street can assimilate an astonishing diversity of building designs and of uses and yet be attractive and harmonious because of the harmonious scale. In practice, disintegration is almost always caused by a building too large, which does not necessarily mean too high. A big one-story building can be disastrous on an intimately scaled street. The relevant standard would be the length of street frontage allowed a building; a small-scale frontage automatically takes care of height in most cases. Differences of one or two stories in height, among buildings of similar width, are not what disintegrate street scale as one can easily see by looking at intimately scaled city streets. Not all streets need to be intimately scaled, but a city lacking such streets is a horrible and inhuman place.

4. Signs. Standards could apply to sizes, beginning with discreet plaques, and to illumination.

5. Traffic generation. Standards could designate the number of parking places permitted. When people seek protection against traffic generators, they seek protection against automobile and truck traffic, not against pedestrians. As it is now, retail uses that go into the same land planning and zoning categories differ enormously in the kind of traffic they draw: automotive or foot.

6. Destruction. As everybody down on the street

knows, what is removed to make way for something is a vital aspect of performance. Standards could designate what cannot be destroyed, and these could include not only the buildings of historic value which occasionally— very occasionally—get such protection now, but whatever the neighborhood considers valuable: say trees over a certain girth, for instance. In times and places of housing shortage, protection could cover all habitable housing.

Under performance zoning, far greater freedom of land use could be permitted than is now the case, with superior results for the environment.* But it is hopeless to suppose that any such radical change in planning and zoning philosophy is going to be initiated by the bureaucracies who have these matters in hand. After all, planners know no more about a kind of zoning code that does not now exist than you do or I do.

Why would a city neighborhood whose people are interested in performance instead of categories of land use not be allowed, if its people wish, to hammer out performance standards, commission an intelligent lawyer to write a performance zoning code, and then be allowed to apply it? No doubt the first homemade codes would have bugs in them, but the present system is all bugs.

If this approach could be used by local neighborhoods within

---

* In chapter 7 of *Dark Age Ahead,* "Unwinding Vicious Spirals," Jacobs provides a slightly updated take on performance zoning. In particular, she adds, "Enforcement should not be ensured by criminal fines but more directly, by civil court orders requiring noncomplying and noncorrecting offenders to halt outlawed performances forthwith or vacate the premises" (p. 156).

cities that wanted to use it, we might expect that the results would eventually have an effect on new development too. Today land-use planning and its accompanying zoning are forcing look-alike, unfunctional, inhuman sprawls around all our cities—the visible evidence, as one critic has put it, of "a society petrified by the accountants who have seized high position." The developers blame the public officials: "They made us do it like this." The public officials blame the developers: "They did it."

Some fifty years ago, the land planning movement called regional planning put forth a line of reasoning purporting to show that cities had become obsolete. The idea was that electric power—which incidentally had arisen in cities of course—made concentrations of industry no longer necessary because electric grids could lace the whole land, and therefore city concentrations of people were no longer necessary. Essentially the same argument has been extended by those today who consider cities obsolete; they add to the original argument the dispersal made possible by air and automotive travel and modern communication.

This line of reasoning has always rested on the unspoken assumption that the salient question is how to locate existing forms of production. In some cases, although not nearly so many as the regional planners and their successors have supposed, it is possible to disperse production out of cities. Indeed, many a company town whose proprietors left cities to find cheaper labor, attests to that fact.

But the argument ignores the question of how new forms of work arise, where they come from, and how. They arise in cities, by a process of adding new kinds of work logically to older kinds. Any settlement in which this happens vigorously becomes a city by virtue of the process itself. To imagine cities have become obsolete is to assume that society can get along well enough with the goods, services, methods and institutions it already has, and the unsolved problems will somehow be solved by dispersal. Of course this is not true. The British, who have put an enormous share of their resources available for development work into New Towns, have solved nothing at all by this means. The winter air over Cumbernauld, out in the country, has exactly the same acrid reek of pollution as the air over Glasgow.* Dispersing populations, instead of solving problems, just disperses problems.

Our trouble is not that our cities, per se, are obsolete, but that they are no longer creative. This is the real problem of cities: to remain creative.

Our trouble is not that our cities, per se, are obsolete, but that they are no longer creative. This is the real problem of cities: to remain creative. When they creatively solve practical problems for themselves and each other, the solutions can then be used in small settlements too. Indeed they are often applied to the countryside or to wilderness directly or indirectly. As an

---

* Cumbernauld is a planned community, or "New Town," outside Glasgow, Scotland, begun in 1956. The term "New Town" is often used to refer to a series of modern, planned communities created in the post–World War II era in the United Kingdom, but the movement began before the war and had parallels and offshoots in the United States, Canada, the Soviet Union, and many other countries. Inspired by Ebenezer Howard's Garden City ideal, reformers all over the world, including Lewis Mumford, pushed their governments to fund the building of dispersed residential communities from scratch outside industrial cities. Most were designed to have carefully delineated zones for residences, workplaces, commercial development, and community amenities all in one development. They were in that sense cities, not suburbs, but their anti–mixed use planning precepts relied on the idea, as Jacobs puts it here, that the traditional industrial city had become "obsolete." As a result, many critics viewed them as essentially anti-urban.

instance of the latter, consider city-contrived plastics. Creative cities prevent the same natural resources from being exploited too heavily and too long. It is stagnant economies that become ruinous to the natural world, as ours is becoming.

My argument is that our mounting problems are owing to undone and undeveloped work, which in turn is owing to the fact that the potential creativity to be found in our cities is being stifled, frustrated, and wasted, and that this is fatal.

Even city governments today are demonstrably too bureaucratized and too centralized to govern creative, problem-solving cities. I have been arguing that one of our most pressing needs is the liberation and funding of communities within cities to govern themselves in most matters and to find and permit solutions of their own. Some would accomplish little, perhaps. But if any were innovative it would be a clear gain, and their solutions could be copied and adapted, as successful solutions always are in creative societies. The present situation is truly hopeless.

The good of the city district or neighborhood corresponds with the good of the whole. The whole, in fact, turns out not to be an abstraction untouched by the fate of the parts.

The usual objection to local self-government within cities is that their people are shortsighted, selfish and either oblivious to the good of the whole or opposed to it. While in some cases this may be true, I am far more impressed by how often the good of the city district or neighborhood corresponds with the good of the whole. The whole, in fact, turns out not to be an abstraction untouched by the fate of the parts.

The stock argument—the clincher—of those who think

power to the people would be impractical or ruinous is to bring up the question of highways and to point out that no community in a city would allow a new highway through it, if it had the effective power to stop it. Precisely. Here we are, back at transportation.

Time has vindicated the selfish, shortsighted city communities that tried so hard to stop expressway programs and failed. Suppose it had been truly necessary for officials to be content with ordinary roadways, when city districts objected to having expressways hurtled through them, their parks cannibalized by parkways, their trees cut, their sidewalks narrowed, their houses destroyed, their air polluted, their streets rezoned for gas stations, and so on. Then it would also have become necessary to employ newer means, in addition to automobiles, for solving city transportation problems.

As it is, increasingly angry talk about banning automobiles entirely is understandable in view of growing desperation. But in practical terms, the bans are gestures; a sort of occupational therapy for protesters; and so they will remain in the absence of the use of new services and vehicles. Just as in the case of waste-recycling and pollution prevention, solutions depend on work now being left undone. Ironically, there is no more dramatic illustration of the need for local autonomy within cities—power to the people—than the stock objection, "They obstruct highways."

I would like to say, since my temperamental preference is to be optimistic, that I see some evidence that intelligence and creativity are breaking through in the United States. I honestly do not think they are.

What I see, instead of relevant change, is a growing acceptance of stagnation, an assumption that we can deal with our mounting problems and undone work not by getting on that work but by reducing population growth.

A population control program is not going to develop a single new waste-recycling enterprise. It is not going to prevent a single oil-slick in the sea because it is not going to develop new transportation services and vehicles. It is not going to clean up the wild and beautiful Abitibi River in northern Ontario, now polluted by the great pulp mills of *The New York Times*. The *Times* frequently editorializes to the effect that protection of the wilderness hinges upon control of population growth. What does this mean? That population control will make sufficient inroads upon the readers of *The New York Times* to clean up the Abitibi? Population control is a cop-out for *The New York Times*. It is a cop-out for the oil companies. Most of all, it is a cop-out for everybody who wants the comfort of a big, sweeping answer to a multitude of complex, hard, perhaps boring realities.

Population control is not only an irrelevant answer for what ails us, it is a dreadfully dangerous answer. There is all the difference in the world between private, voluntary decisions about family size and public programs with public goals. Nothing in America works the same way for blacks and whites, and we may be absolutely sure that population control will not work the same for blacks and whites, either. Many blacks fear it as a plan for genocide. I do not think their fears are unrealistic. I think of how easily and how long white liberals ignored or rationalized away—some still do—the insanities and brutalities of slum clearance, public housing, welfare and urban renewal carried out in the name of abstract societal progress. I wonder therefore how easily and how long genocidal insanities and brutalities could be ignored or rationalized away by white liberals if these were carried out in the name of an abstract—a very abstract—protection of the ecology. The thought is not reassuring. As it now stands, this is demonstrably not a fit society to possess public powers for population control.

Can Big Plans Solve the
Problem of Renewal?

——

SPEECH AT THE RESIDENTIAL AREAS AND
URBAN RENEWAL CONFERENCE, HAMBURG,
WEST GERMANY, OCTOBER 12–14, 1981

SOME PLANS HAVE TO BE BIG, DETAILED, AND STRETCH FOR
years into the future because of their substance. A mundane example is a plan for building a city subway system. Or to take a more romantic illustration, when a trip to Saturn is proposed, the planning has to be very comprehensive, very detailed and very much in control until the whole scheme is complete and the aim is finished. The plan has to be big or it is useless.

It seems to me sometimes that many city and town planners must be frustrated space-travel planners. But pieces of our cities, or for that matter suburbs or even New Towns, are not going to take off for Saturn. They aren't going to take off for anywhere. The substance doesn't mandate big, comprehensive, tightly controlled planning the way either a subway system or a spaceship does. Little plans are more appropriate for city renewal than big plans. First I am going to mention some of the disadvantages of big plans, then suggest how we can treat our cities in ways appropriate for their renewal.

To begin with disadvantages of big plans, let us think for a moment about boredom. Making big plans doesn't bore planners. Indeed, the bigger and more comprehensive the plan, the more it engages all their faculties and so the more it interests and engrosses them. But the results bore everybody else. A scholar who retired some years ago after a lifetime of work in the American Museum of Natural History told me he had been spending a good part of his new leisure exploring post-war housing projects and suburban tracts. What he saw appalled him. Consider, he said, the value that human beings throughout the ages and in all cultures have placed on visual diversity and elaboration. Man is the animal that decorates himself and all manner of things he makes and builds. If we were to find a trait so persistent and widespread in any other species, he went on, we would take it seriously. We would conjecture that so striking and universal a trait had some connection with the success of the animal. His own surmise was that our busy human brains demand a constant flow of extremely diverse impressions and information to develop in the first place, and thereafter must be fed with constant and diverse flows or they are genuinely deprived. In sum, he said, boredom has to be taken seriously, and especially visual boredom. Hatred of boredom may be a healthy revulsion against sense and brain deprivation. Paradoxically, he went on, it is thus probably logical for us to behave illogically, even destructively, if that is what we must do to escape boredom.

Boredom has to be taken seriously, and especially visual boredom.

Whether his analysis is correct or not, his own revulsion against the terrible visual monotony he found in the carefully planned city is not unusual. I myself had assumed the monotony was hard on adults, and perhaps hardest of all on adolescents, and least bothersome to little children. He disputed this.

Little children in genuinely rural or in wilderness surroundings, he pointed out, are inundated with a rich diversity of natural details during their formative years. So are little children brought up amid richly diverse streets of cities and towns where many kinds of activities and sights come to their attention. But in the planned city and suburban precinct, he said, especially those of large scale, small children are being deprived of diverse everyday visual impressions as few children anywhere have ever been deprived before.

Thinking of his words I sometimes wonder whether the hunger for television we see in so many of these little children is a struggle to fill the visual vacuums of their lives. Their homes and playgrounds, so orderly looking, so buffered from the muddled, messy intrusions of the great world, may accidentally be ideally planned for children to concentrate on television, but for too little else their hungry brains require.

Genuine, rich diversity of the built environment is always the product of many, many different minds, and at its richest is also the product of different periods of time with their different aims and fashions.

There is no way of overcoming the visual boredom of big plans. It is built right into them because of the fact that big plans are the product of too few minds. If those minds are artful and caring, they can mitigate the visual boredom a bit; but at the best, only a bit. Genuine, rich diversity of the built environment is always the product of many, many different minds, and at its richest is also the product of different periods of time with their different aims and fashions. Diversity is a small-scale phenomenon. It requires collections of little plans.

Big plans, in theory, are justified as being gifts to the future. Planning is foresight; the future is what it is all about. Yet big plans, in which everything has been foreseen as far as possible, stifle alternative possibilities and new departures. To plan for the future, and at the same time stifle fresh possibilities, is a contradiction in terms.

Where do the fresh ideas about planning itself emerge and prove themselves? In the planned precincts? No, that is the last place to seek them. The fresh planning and architectural ideas of our own time have emerged in unplanned places, or amid collections of many little plans, and we may expect that the same must be true of the future, true of planning ideas we can't foresee today.

Planning has its styles and its changing rationales just as surely as clothing design does, or as any other industry or profession does that is concerned with design and function and the relationship between the two. Nowadays the fashion in planning is to plan for mixed uses. This new fashion didn't arise in the city housing projects, suburban tracts and New Towns that exist today. They were not only the product of a different fashion; they stifled any other fashion in planning thought from incubating there. Thus, ironically, new ideas concerning planning itself had to emerge, if they were to emerge at all, where planning had less influence. Here and there, among muddled collections of little plans in parts of cities that predated modern planning, people found loopholes in zoning and they also found food for imagination. In old industrial buildings, strange new architectural flowers blossomed. Here an abandoned spaghetti factory, there an obsolete chocolate factory, yonder a fine old warehouse took on new life as shelters for skylighted garden restaurants, dance rehearsal halls, little shops, small workshops, all muddled together, sometimes with an office or an apartment sneaked in.* Here and there people began surreptitiously moving themselves and their families into loft buildings, manufacturing spaces, because they liked what they could do with the grand, raw spaces they could transform by grace of their own little plans.

To be sure, in one sense this was nothing new. People in previous generations had converted carriage houses to dwellings, inserted stores into houses, turned former mansions into schoolhouses. But fresh ideas did emerge, especially in former industrial buildings. The architectural adaptations were often stunningly imaginative and humanistic. The very muddles of activities that took to coexisting within buildings, as well as in adjoining buildings, seemed to stimulate architectural imaginations grown weary and stultified under the iron hand of big planning. Finally, after enough of the new little aberrations had emerged, architects a few years ago began talking boldly of planning new buildings, too, for mixed use. The idea of mixed uses, muddled together, has now begun to sink even into the consciousness of big planners and developers.

The principle at work here embraces more than fresh ideas

---

* The places Jacobs references here are, respectively, the Old Spaghetti Factory in San Francisco's North End; Ghirardelli Square, also in San Francisco; and Boston's Faneuil Hall Marketplace. In a similar speech delivered at The Great Cities of the World Conference at Faneuil Hall a year earlier, Jacobs suggests a direct link connecting these three projects, each one elaborating upon a prior little plan until it became a big one. Indeed, Benjamin Thompson, the designer of Quincy Market, had a location of his own store, Design Research, in Ghirardelli Square, and drew upon what he learned there for his "festival marketplace" in Boston.

about planning itself. It embraces ideas about fresh possibilities in general. All new ideas start small and all new ideas, at the time they emerge, flout the accepted ways of doing things. By the time an idea of any sort is risked in big planning, it is already middle-aged or old as an idea. Big plans live intellectually off of little plans. Big plans, precisely because they are big, are not fertile ground for fresh, different possibilities.

The deficiency, like their boredom, is built right into their bigness and coherence. "Renewal" shouldn't imply fossilization. The two are again a contradiction in terms. It is absurd to think of big plans as appropriate tools for city *renewal,* of all things.

All new ideas start small and all new ideas, at the time they emerge, flout the accepted ways of doing things.

My third and final objection to big plans is that once in place, they are so inflexible. The greater the scale of the planning, the more inflexible the result. When change impinges itself on big plans, adaptation to change comes hard. And again the deficiency is built in. It is a price of comprehensiveness and coherence. The United States, for example, has become woefully inflexible with respect to transportation, not accidentally but by plan. The country's great highway program was a twenty-year plan adopted in 1956. It was a big plan both in geographical and in time scale, and into it was dovetailed almost all the country's suburban planning and the cities' master plans too. Now, too late, with alternatives long stifled, the side effects of this grand planning can be seen: exorbitant energy use, pollution, land waste, and costs imposed for personal transportation on people who can no longer afford the costs. But the suburbs built to coordinate with this transportation, and the cities rebuilt to coordinate with it, are unadaptable to alternative ways of moving people and goods, precisely because they were so well planned for the automobile instead.

Big plans make mistakes, and when the plans are very big the mistakes can be very big also. But the objection I am raising when I speak of flexibility and adaptability goes beyond saying that big plans can turn out to be bad plans. In their very nature, big and comprehensive plans are almost doomed to be mistaken. This is because everything we do changes the world a bit. Everything has its side effects and repercussions. Everything others do changes the world a bit too. We can't anticipate all the effects and repercussions of change. Big plans render us unadaptable because we can't adjust to the changes not foreseen in their making; we can hardly even acknowledge the changes as they become evident. We become too committed, in a big way, to our big plans.

Life is an ad hoc affair. It has to be improvised all the time because of the hard fact that everything we do changes what is. This is distressing to people who would like to see things beautifully planned out and settled once and for all. That cannot be.

Life is an ad hoc affair. It has to be improvised all the time because of the hard fact that everything we do changes what is.

Does all this mean that trying to plan is useless? No, of course not. Trying to use foresight, which is what planning is, is obviously so necessary and useful that most of us are practicing it constantly. We plant daffodil bulbs in October and set the alarm clock at night. We can plan for our renewal of cities too, but what I am proposing is that we practice making little plans for that purpose, not big ones. I think we need to relearn the art of doing that, and that there are ways to relearn it.

To explain what I mean, I will tell how the practice of renewal planning has gradually changed in my own city, Toronto. I am using Toronto not because it is necessarily avant-garde or has all the answers. It doesn't. Nobody does, and no place does. But we have been getting a glimmer there of how to plan for little plans, even for large collections of little plans on big sites, and for that reason and because I have watched the change come firsthand, I'll tell a story about Toronto.

The story begins in 1973, when citizens' anger against big planning there boiled over one chilly spring morning before dawn, on a dilapidated street where, the day before, employees of a building wrecking company had erected a high board fence around twenty old houses that were to be demolished, and had begun crashing holes in the roof of the most beautiful house right in the center of the group. These houses, although they were neglected and run down, were interesting and human looking in comparison with what was to go up in their place: six identical apartment towers planned by the province's housing ministry for low income tenants. Actually, the plan for the new housing was not a big plan, as such things go. It occupied not quite half of a single long city block. But it *looked* like a big plan. It shouted monotony, stultification, inflexibility.

The people gathered in the predawn dark that morning to protest what was planned came from neighborhood organizations far and wide across the city. They weren't against low-income housing; they were against big plans and things that looked like big plans which, bit by bit, had been destroying the fabric of the city. They had no plan for how to stop this scheme, except to plead with the wrecking workmen to stay their hands. But as they stood talking together and stamping their feet in the cold waiting for the workmen to come, somebody mentioned that it is illegal to wreck buildings unless a fence has been put up around them. The remark was repeated from person to person, and group to group, and without another word everyone began taking action. You would be amazed at how rapidly and purposefully several hundred men, women and children, with no one directing them, can dismantle a sturdily built fence and turn it back to neatly stacked piles of lumber. When the workmen arrived, just as the last boards were being stacked, they couldn't do anything until they had rebuilt the fence.

The mayor of Toronto, when he learned what had happened, used the few hours of grace the protestors had won to persuade the provincial housing authorities to hold their plan in abeyance while he explored alternatives. The provincial authorities agreed, provided that an alternative cost no more than their scheme and would provide as many housing units. They did not expect those provisions to be met, because big planning had stifled their own imaginations and sense of ingenuity. But over the next few weeks the Mayor, the city's commissioner of housing, and one of the city's most brilliant firms of architects did plan what was supposedly impossible.* Their alternate scheme saved all the old houses and converted their interiors into new flats. The rest of the housing required, which was most of it,

---

* The firm in question is Diamond and Myers, now defunct, though both partners, Jack Diamond (1932–) and Barton Myers (1934–), went on to have laudable careers in their own right. The infill project became known as Dundas-Sherbourne Housing or Sherbourne Lanes.

was put into new buildings inserted in the backyards. The new buildings had to be ingeniously, even a little crazily, worked into the space, and so did lanes and little courtyards. Furthermore, to make the thing fit, the apartments couldn't be more or less duplicates of each other. The scheme, because of the very limitations the site imposed when the old buildings remained, had to embrace a variety of accommodations, from dwellings for families with children on lower floors, to apartments for single people, for elderly couples, and even—in one of the old houses—a boarding house for elderly men. Standardization of any sort wouldn't work on a site so difficult, but variety would.

Getting this alternative accepted was not easy. Even after the provincial authorities agreed to it, there were struggles with federal bureaucracy, the lender of the building funds. The width of every courtyard and lane had to be defended, and even the size and placement of some of the windows. Nevertheless, the city by standing firm won its points. The thing was built. It has now been occupied for almost six years, and it fits so well into the neighborhood, and so much adds to its interest instead of distracting from it, that the old houses across the street, which had also been run down and dilapidated, have now been bought up and rehabilitated privately. No such renewing effect as that occurred on streets bordering the city's big planned projects. The builder of a luxury project in another part of the city so much liked what was being done in this poorer section that he too set his projects behind a row of old buildings, linking the two with lanes. This is the only instance I know of in North America in which an expensive building copied a low-income building.

The success of this first publicly financed infill housing plan led the city to seek out other awkward sites for scattered little plans. Every site was different, with different planning problems. In all cases the old buildings were left, not destroyed, no matter what limitations that imposed. Sometimes the old buildings nearby were incorporated in the new schemes and rehabilitated too; in other cases the new buildings were simply inserted among the old in what had been vacant lots or parking lots. Some of the infill building has been high; most of it is low; but high or low these little plans have all been used to knit together again places of the city fabric that had become frayed or unraveled.

That is one form of city renewal, knitting up the little holes, but what about the very big holes? What about the sites that seem to demand big planning because they are big sites? In Toronto, some of the parts of the city that have needed renewal most are huge areas near the waterfront, which were first blighted by the railroads, then by expressways bordering the railroad, were taken over by industries and then abandoned by industries, leaving them as wastelands of junkyards, parking lots, and weed grown vacant spaces interspersed here and there with an old industrial building, a warehouse, a transformer station.

Just such a great tract was chosen by the city for renewal in 1975, a tract so large that the construction would have to take place in phases, requiring, it was thought, about fifteen years for completion.* Only a few years earlier, the city's planners and

---

* This tract became the St. Lawrence neighborhood, bounded roughly by Front Street to the north, Yonge and Parliament Streets to the west and east, respectively, and the railway tracks to the south. Some accounts claim that Jacobs somehow steered this project, but the parties directly involved in its design contradict this story, according to historian Richard

politicians would have assumed that to do anything here they must first make a comprehensive, detailed plan for the whole thing. But the planners, administrators and politicians who had already previously worked on the infill schemes I have told about had been changed by that experience. Now they respected little plans, ingenuity, opportunism, variety; and from their infill experience they had learned new ways of thinking about planning itself. For this big tract, they did not work out a big, finished plan, but instead a scheme that would be hospitable to many little plans. For this they used five major devices.

First, instead of thinking of the big tract as a place in its own right, to be set apart from the city, they thought of it as just another piece of city fabric, to be knit into the existing city on its north, east and west. They could not knit it in on the south because there it was cut off by the railroad and expressway. So first they planned streets that would attach the tract into existing city streets without a break. They forgot everything they had learned in school about planning cul-de-sacs, and about buffering off residential areas with figurative Do Not Disturb signs, and laid out streets inside the tract that connect every part with every other part. These streets, real city streets, not fake suburban or country streets, together with a long narrow spine of park or commons running through the tract from end to end, are the skeleton of the plan.

Second, apart from providing this skeleton, they did not try

White's article "Jane Jacobs in Toronto, 1968–78." White reports that Jacobs's only formal role was recommending the project's lead planner, an architect at her husband's firm named Alan Littlewood, who notably had no formal training in city planning. That said, the project's masterminds all cited *Death and Life* as a major influence and often chatted casually with Jacobs.

to plan the whole tract from the start. They planned only the first phase to be built, and planned even that loosely. Apart from choosing a location for a combination school and apartment house—a mixed use building—they contented themselves with designating some streets for low buildings and some street locations for high buildings.

Third, they left to developers and their architects how the buildings were to look and what kinds of dwellings they were to contain. The developers include, to be sure, the city's own housing department, but they also include a great variety of independently run housing cooperatives and private developers as well. Some of the housing is for rent to residents, some is for sale. If the developers want to mix stores, restaurants or theaters in with the housing, they can. That is part of leaving room for little plans. There is no shopping center. Shops turn up where other minds than those of the planners think they will be successful.

Fourth, the planners gave thought to other aspects of flexibility. In buildings developed under the city's own supervision, what is today a house for a family can potentially be recycled into flats in the future, and vice versa. What is now housing can potentially be recycled into shops in the future, just as happens in a living, changing city which isn't going to take off for Saturn. Other developers have been encouraged to think in terms of adaptability too.

And fifth, the few old brick industrial buildings scattered about in the site, which had been thought of previously as part and parcel of its blight, were not demolished to create a clean slate. Every one of them is cherished, to be recycled and to help provide a few links with the past and its fashions in building.

The fact that the tract contains so little from the past was not thought of as an asset, but as its chief deficiency. The first of the recycled industrial buildings is now occupied by housing and shops, and a handsome building it is. Significantly enough, even before the site was chosen for renewal, one of the old industrial buildings had already been recycled into a beautiful young people's theater, and of course it remains.

About a third of the tract is now completed and occupied, and its streets are delightful, full of variety with surprises around every corner. It is so popular and successful that the building of the rest is proceeding faster than the planners had at first supposed was feasible.

Recently I asked the architect who had been employed in the city's housing office to lay out the street skeleton and park and choose the school site what he thought would go on a particularly prominent spot, still untouched. "I have no idea," he said. "Nobody knows at this point. All we know is that when the right idea comes along, the city will probably recognize it. We don't have to decide until then, just for the sake of deciding. We don't have any monopoly on ideas for this neighborhood. Why should we?"

Into my mind when he said this flashed a memory from my previous visit to Germany, back in 1966. I remembered a day I had spent with Professor Hillebrecht, the city architect of Hanover.* First he had shown me around the center of the city, and

---

* Rudolph Hillebrecht (1910–99) was, as Jacobs says, the chief planner for Hanover, Germany. He was admired for his attempts to preserve the bomb-damaged historic fabric of the city and do as little clearance as possible. By this point, Hillebrecht had visited Jacobs, in New York in 1964 after reading *Death and Life* and again in 1970 after her move to Toronto. After *Death and Life*'s translation into German, he also helped disseminate its lessons in Germany. Ironically, however, Hillebrecht's Hanover was also regarded by German planners of the time

I was filled with admiration for the skill, sensitivity and imagination with which new buildings had been inserted there to repair the destruction of the city's fabric from the war. Then he took me to the city's outskirts to see a large residential tract, a big plan, as boring as all big plans. Perhaps to cheer me up, the next thing he showed me, also in the city's outskirts, was a romantic looking, vacant and dilapidated, rambling masonry building, which if I remember correctly had once been occupied by a religious order, and which was surrounded by large wooded grounds. "What are you planning to do with this?" I asked. "We don't know," he answered. "The right idea hasn't come along. That doesn't worry me," he went on. "We don't need to decide everything. We have to leave something for the next generation. They'll have ideas too."

With that, my admiration for Professor Hillebrecht, which was already high, really soared. Here was a planner who was really thinking of the future—thinking of it with respect, hope and affection. How different, I thought, from Daniel Burnham. Burnham was an American architect living at the turn of the century. He said something very influential in America. "Make no little plans," he said. "They have no magic to stir men's blood and probably themselves will not be realized. Make big plans, aim high in hope and work, remembering that a noble, logical diagram once recorded will never die, but long after we are gone will be a living thing, asserting itself with ever-growing insistency." Naturally, that sentiment remains to this day a fa-

as a model of car-friendly planning. For more, see Dirk Schubert's article "Jane Jacobs's Perception and Impact on City Planning and Urban Renewal in Germany" in his edited volume *Contemporary Perspectives on Jane Jacobs*.

vorite quotation of American planners. Burnham wanted to control the future.

Planning for all of us is a practical, everyday necessity. No responsible person can get along without trying to apply fore-sight. It is also enjoyable to most of us. Indeed, planning is so enjoyable that the chance to do it in a great big way is one of the seductions of great power: one reason people seek great power. But planning to gratify the impulse to plan, planning done for the sake of planning itself is deadly stuff. If we are going to err in our planning—and we are, because what is perfect?—it is better to err on the side of being loose, minimal, a little too open to im-provisation, rather than the reverse. A good *Make no plan bigger than it must be.* rule of thumb would be to make no plan bigger than it must be, and to project it no farther into the future than we simply have to. Wherever we have the choice between making a big plan or providing instead for collections of little plans, let us choose the collections of little plans and the advantages they bring us with their diversity, fresh ideas, and flexibility.*

* In September 1980, at the Great Cities of the World Conference convened at Faneuil Hall in Boston, Jacobs delivered a version of these remarks in which she celebrated all the "vital little plans" that made the Quincy Market and Faneuil Hall a fresh idea—but she warned that repetition of the "festival marketplace" concept might result in sterility over the long run. It's a fitting way to sum up the core of Jacobs's ideas: To sustain and renew a city's physical, economic, and social vitality efforts must always enable and protect such "vital little plans." That speech can be found in a 1981 issue of *Urban Design International* under the title "Safdie/Rouse/Jacobs: An Exchange."

Jane Jacobs window-shops in front of Book City, a bookstore in the Annex neighborhood of Toronto where she lived, circa 1983–87.

PART FOUR

THE ECOLOGY OF CITIES

1984–2000

THROUGHOUT HER CAREER, JACOBS ENCOUNTERED BEHAVior on the part of politicians and bureaucrats that mystified and frustrated her. Why should New York's government deceive its own people? Why are leaders who excel at military matters so poor at managing their economies? She was baffled at the failure of so many to exercise what seemed to her basic ethical common sense. So after *Cities and the Wealth of Nations,* Jacobs turned her sights on the ethical underpinnings of economic life, which became the subject of her Socratic dialogue *Systems of Survival,* published in 1992. Given her own predilections and past experience, this exploration of morals and ethics became as much a personal exploration as an examination of the behavior of others; it was also a window on a host of related issues, from regulation and equity to governance and privatization.

For fifteen years, Jacobs had been following one of the whims that so often spurred inspiration for her writing. She had been collecting a list of "esteemed behaviors" commonly performed by heroes in literature or attributed to people in their obituaries and biographies. She began to find that many of these virtuous ways were contradictory: honesty and deception, innovation and tradition, dissent and obedience. Finally, when she grouped characteristics that showed up together and eliminated the virtues common to all, she found herself with two lists of mutually exclusive attributes, and the beginnings of an answer to her bafflement. One set of virtues—what she came to call the "guardian moral syndrome"—appeared in writings for and about people in government, military, policing, regulation, preservation, and activism, while the other list—the "commercial moral syndrome"—appeared in writings for and about people in commerce, industry, and science. These two lists formed the basis of Jacobs's *Systems of Survival,* the nuances of which she discusses at length with the conservative journalist David Warren in "Two Ways to Live," included here.

Early in the writing process, Jacobs named those following the commercial moral syndrome "traders" and those following the guardian syndrome "raiders," a negative term that revealed her own initial bias. To her, raiders were those frustrating politicians, planners, and powerbrokers who prized hierarchy, exclusivity, tradition, and obedience, who sometimes used force and deception to get their way. "I'm really a trader and I believe in that," Jacobs admitted in a 1985 interview. She believed first and foremost in honesty, openness, dissent, novelty, and exchange—all traits she said were shunned by the raiders. Nevertheless, she told the interviewer, she would "try and be fair." By the time *Systems of Survival* appeared, she realized that she had been "laggard at recognizing that 'raider' precepts are as morally valid as trader ones, and are grounded in legitimate territorial concerns."[1] Ultimately, Jacobs developed sympathy for guardian ways, understanding that traders like herself rarely trust or understand them and vice versa (as "Market Nurturing Run Amok" succinctly demonstrates).

Jacobs never viewed her work on ethics as simply abstract philosophical musing, and she joined with others to test her theories even as she developed them. From 1981 to 1997, Jacobs served on the board of the Energy Probe Research Foundation, an environmental NGO based in Toronto that challenged the guardian values of both government and the mainstream of environmentalism alike with a distinctly "commercial-minded" alternative.[2] Like Jacobs, Energy Probe considered new goods and services the key to facing our environmental problems and believed that the guardian culture of government was ill equipped to provide them. In 1994, Jacobs co-founded a program of Energy Probe called the Consumer Policy Institute, which, as the "First Letter" in this part explains, made its mission the privatization of government monopolies in mail delivery, transportation, and energy, among other services. Jacobs's support of privatization, however, was not driven by the dogma of indiscriminate "small government" offered by politicians like Ronald Reagan or Margaret Thatcher. The destruction of the social safety net under Thatcher's administration "appalled" Jacobs.[3] In her letter to the Consumer Policy Institute Jacobs explains a clear role she saw for government: regulation—so long as it remains independent from influence, responsive to changing circumstances, and open to creativity. These many nuances of her thought (further elaborated in "Efficiency and the Commons" in Part Five) made Jacobs notoriously difficult to pin down on the conventional political spectrum.

One of Energy Probe's biggest victories was the privatization of Ontario Hydro, the province's electric utility and an example of what Jacobs called a "monstrous moral hybrid" between commercial and guardian work. In 1984, Energy Probe produced a report recommending a clean break between the utility's commercial and guardian roles. The government, it said, should open power generation to the private sector while still maintaining ownership of power distribution and a strong regulatory role. Given the criticism plaguing Ontario Hydro during this period for cost overruns and mismanagement, which Jacobs saw as endemic to commercial organizations operated by guardians, Energy Probe's plan was not seen as a pet project of the political right. In fact, while the ruling right-wing Progressive Conservatives killed the proposal, the two opposition parties, the centrist Liberal Party and the left-leaning New Democratic Party, both endorsed the plan. However, it was not until Premier Mike Harris, a Reagan-style Progressive Conservative, took power in 1995 that privatization began to gain traction. Under the banner of Harris's Common Sense Revolution, the administration passed the Energy Competition Act in 1998, putting many of Energy Probe's recommendations into action.

Meanwhile, in a testament to the complexity of her political beliefs, Jacobs participated in the fight against another arm of the Common Sense Revolution: the amalgamation of Toronto. While working on *Cities and the Wealth of Nations* and puzzling over Québécois separatism, she had come to believe that urban sovereignty was crucial to accountable and nimble governance. As the cradles of technological innovation and the milch cows of nations, cities had to have the power to control their own destinies. As Jacobs said in a speech in Amsterdam in 1984, included here, "the first responsibilities of cities are to themselves." In late 1996, these views became more than merely speculative. Under Premier Harris, the Province of Ontario declared its intent to amalgamate the City of Toronto with its five surrounding municipalities, ostensibly looking to reduce the size and cost of government.⁴ Jacobs joined a group called Citizens for Local Democracy to try to stop the plan, lending her voice to the cause in speeches and testimony (see, for instance, "Against Amalgamation"). However, despite widespread opposition and a referendum in which 76 percent of Metro-area voters rejected the plan, the province forcibly amalgamated the megacity of Toronto on January 1, 1998.

Where some interpreters saw Jacobs's writing on ethics, regulation, and governance as a departure from her previous work on cities, she herself saw continuity. As she suggests in her 1992 foreword to the Modern Library edition of *Death and Life,* included in this section, these new writings complemented her prior insights. Together they can be understood as one unified field of study: "the ecology of cities." Much as an ecosystem is composed of "physical-chemical-biological processes," Jacobs observes, a city is composed of "physical-economic-ethical processes."⁵ In other words, considering economic or city-building matters in isolation from the social norms that drive them ignores an integral piece of the puzzle of city life. After all, how could our great cities harbor so many strangers in such close proximity without a symbiotic ethical system, a "great web of trust" connecting them?

NOTES

1. See endnote in *Systems of Survival,* 218.
2. The Energy Probe Research Foundation is a non-governmental environmental policy organization founded in 1980. Besides its campaign to privatize Ontario Hydro, discussed on 245–46, the organization also took strong stances against nuclear power and foreign aid, and promoted

market-based solutions to environmental problems. In 1997, Jacobs cut ties with the organization, which she believed was becoming more dogmatically associated with the political right.

3.   See Richard Carroll Keeley, "An Interview with Jane Jacobs," *Ethics in Making a Living: The Jane Jacobs Conference* (Atlanta: Scholars Press, 1989) 18.

4.   In *The Shape of the Suburbs,* past Toronto mayor John Sewell argues that the province's hidden agenda was to dilute the power of Toronto City Council, which regularly jousted with the province on various fronts.

5.   Jacobs's second Socratic dialogue, *The Nature of Economies* (2000), offered the most sustained exploration of the analogy of economy as ecology, an idea she'd been pursuing ever since her first forays into the niche economies of Depression-era New York City.

The Responsibilities of Cities

———

SPEECH AT THE ROYAL PALACE,
AMSTERDAM, SEPTEMBER 12, 1984

LIKE OTHERS LUCKY ENOUGH TO VISIT AMSTERDAM, I AM enchanted. It is a joy to be in this splendid city, and in this splendid palace.

Besides enjoying Amsterdam, I revere it because this is one of the European cities of which it was said, "City air makes free."* Amsterdam, like other cities of the Netherlands, played its great part in overcoming feudalism in our ancestral societies, supplanting with its city ways the old social rigidities, economic restrictions and intellectual limitations of feudal life.

I also revere Amsterdam for its workaday innovations through the centuries. By solving its own practical problems of drainage, dredging, canal construction, ship building, manufacturing, marketing, and by seeking supplies near and far, all in its

---

* Jacobs uses this phrase in several of her major works, including *Death and Life* (444). She had long drawn inspiration from Henri Pirenne, a medieval historian who emphasized the role of cities and trade in Europe's economic and cultural revival after the Dark Ages. In the fallout of the Roman Empire, the feudal system overtook Europe, dividing people into strict categories of noble landholders and serfs who tilled the land. The phrase "city air makes free" refers to the fact that after commerce had transformed Europe's forts into the vibrant city-states that Jacobs and Pirenne both celebrate, a rural serf could become a citizen—and thus a free person—simply by living inside the city walls for a year without being reclaimed by his or her master.

own practical ways, Amsterdam continually pioneered equipment, methods and knowledge that have immensely benefited the world at large.

Time and again, warlords and imperialists have coveted this city. Yet here it is, having withstood and outlasted assaults, seizures, tyrannies and alien ambitions. Perhaps even more remarkable, it has survived its own nation's possession of empire, and loss of empire, without losing or diminishing its own function as an important and up-to-date place of work. The city has guarded the ancient, enduring identity and beauty of its core by resisting schemes and visions which, in our time, might very well have terribly debased or obliterated it. Amsterdam is a great survivor, and I revere its vitality with some of the same awe one feels for the integrity and persistence of life itself.

Many years ago, the first time I traveled in Europe, I was given what was, for me, a large check, which I took into a bank entirely foreign to me, and handed over to a stranger to send to a bank in New York. With a receipt in my pocket, I walked out unworried and light-hearted, and then thought how extraordinary this was—that I could feel so secure and protected within a great web of trust, of which my own trust was a tiny part. Without that web of trust and its routine safeguards we couldn't engage in most of the exchanges that make up our economic life and that underpin so many of our other social arrangements as well.* The merchants of Amsterdam, along with those of other Netherlands cities, played major parts in evolving this infinitely

---

* This personal anecdote would later appear in the opening chapter of *Systems of Survival* as the "great web of trust" in economic life, the subject of the book.

precious web of trust and inventing its fundamental instruments and techniques.

I mention these things not to tell you what you already know better than I do. My point, rather, is to remind you of the primacy of cities as creators of technology, trade, arts, markets and cultural practices—creations of city life that, by spreading from cities, become possessions and attributes of national and international life. The nation serves as protector, but cities serve as the creators of so much that a nation protects. In its own small way, this royal palace in which we are gathered symbolizes that very relationship.

Unfortunately, nowadays we need to be reminded of how profoundly we depend on the peculiar energy and creativity of cities. We have been living through a period when it has been intellectually fashionable to trivialize cities as mere conveniences or social luxuries, or even to despise them as social afflictions.

If one knew nothing more about cities than what one could learn from this country's city planning proposals and reports, or from the usual conferences about cities' deficiencies and needs, one would suppose that the chief responsibilities of cities were to move traffic efficiently and provide orderly, regimented housing estates. The internationally influential town planning movement has regarded cities much as if they were empty-headed young la-

The internationally influential town planning movement has regarded cities much as if they were empty-headed young ladies whose main duties were to see that their nails were clean, their curves properly distributed, and their behavior seemly.

dies whose main duties were to see that their nails were clean, their curves properly distributed, and their behavior seemly.

Advocating the dismantling of cities into dispersed New Towns, anti-urbanists argued that modern communications, transportation and electric power generation made cities obsolete and unnecessary. Development economists put their faith not in city economies, but in giant corporations and financial institutions that transcend city economies. The programs undertaken by national and provincial governments have been taken to mean that cities' social problems can be successfully solved by superior governments and that municipalities are relatively trivial as arms of government and instruments of policy.

Reasoning of this sort took hold among experts, and much of the public as well, in spite of the reality that the transportation, communications and electric power had been developed in cities and first put to use in them; in spite of the fact that the great corporations and financial institutions had emerged and established themselves in cities before outgrowing those cradles; and in spite of the circumstances that the very wealth supporting national and provincial social programs continued to be overwhelmingly derived from the taxation of city enterprises and city people.

As we can see in cities that have become alarmingly riddled with crime, purposelessness and idleness, especially among the young, national and provincial programs have not solved the social problems of cities. As we can see, giant corporations are not dependable cornucopias of work and incomes; nor in spite of their immense economic powers are they immensely creative in the face of practical problems of all sorts. For example, when a practical problem, such as acid rain, has become a national and international problem, it means that nobody was coming to effective grips with its causes as they emerged. This is precisely the sort of very complex problem that emerges first in cities. The problems of pollution are now widespread and intractable precisely because cities have for too long neglected to overcome their own practical problems with toxic wastes, in a way that Amsterdam, in the past, did *not* neglect to overcome its practical problems of sewage disposal, water supply or epidemic control. These too would be intractable problems if cities had not undertaken to solve them and then disseminated their solutions. Indeed they remain horrendous problems in many a nation that lacks creative cities.

It is worth remembering that a person of whom nothing more is expected, or indeed really wanted, than dependence and seemly behavior becomes a stunted and unresourceful person, and perhaps frustrated and decadent as well. It is much the same with cities. There is a connection, I suspect, between the fact that as much as ninety percent of a city's public income today can arrive in the form of grants from superior governments, mostly for pre-ordained purposes, and the fact that cities today have been losing inventiveness at overcoming serious public problems.

Historically, it has been the nature and glory of cities to be great laboratories of trial, error, experiment and innovation. Historically, this creativity has emerged from populations of ordinary city people, including the people who are born in a given city and those who have migrated to it because of its jobs or its opportunities for people of imagination and ambition. When I use the terms "a creative city," "an innovative city," or "a problem-solving city," what I am actually speaking of, more concretely, is a city where many, many ordinary people can try out their hopes, insights, ambitions, and skills, and make something of them, often enough something unexpected to others and often enough surprising even to themselves.

When I use the term "a creative city" . . . what I am actually speaking of, more concretely, is a city where many, many ordinary people can try out their hopes, insights, ambitions, and skills, and make something of them.

Since a city's own economy supports life there, as well as giving scope for people's inventiveness, it follows that the most basic responsibility of a city is to be a place where it is natural and possible for ordinary people to engage in economic experiment and innovation.

As a practical matter, this means a place with a continually high birth rate of small, diverse enterprises. Why small and diverse?

Both historically and in our own time, any city where the economy becomes highly specialized is a city doomed to stagnate and decline. All its eggs have been put in too few baskets. Ironically, specialized city economies do not keep even their specialties inventive and up-to-date, for lack of new ideas and practices.

All truly new kinds of goods and services tend to start out in a small way. So do many kinds of work that are merely improvements of goods and services that already exist. Historically, and in our own time too, small enterprises have been more fertile at innovating than already large enterprises. Also, small enterprises, collectively, account for more new jobs than already large enterprises.

Small enterprises inherently depend on one another for everyday needs. They live by symbiosis, not by relative self-sufficiency. For this reason, to thrive and prosper, small city enterprises must be both numerous and diverse.

Cities are forever losing their older work. Once an enterprise grows large and well-established, it can successfully move out, or else channel its further expansion into branch plants or branch offices. Indeed, this is one of the great services of cities: to cast up industrial transplants for towns and villages whose people need jobs and incomes and yet can't generate them as cities can. Cities lose older work for other reasons too, such as obsolescence and competition. It is pointless to repine over losses of older work or to suppose they represent extraordinary misfortune. The losses inexorably happen. In an economically fertile city, young and newer work compensates for losses.

It is short-sighted to suppose that a city's exporting enterprises are more important than enterprises producing only goods or services for the city itself. Strictly local enterprises are especially valuable if what they are producing replaces former city imports, or if they are innovative. These frequently become a city's exporters of the future. There is no way to know in advance how and where valuable economic mutations may arise in a city's local "gene pools" of work.* All we can be sure of is that the greater the numbers of enterprises in a city, and the greater their diversity, the likelier the chances for innovations.

A city enjoying a high birth rate of diverse small enterprises

---

* This became one of Jacobs's favored analogies to express the value of diverse, local kinds of work. See, for instance, her foreword to the Modern Library edition of *Death and Life* in this volume. It also foreshadows the biological and ecological analogies of *The Nature of Economies*.

needs cheap, versatile and diverse working spaces, and not only where they are least visible, as if small, experimental forms of work or struggling enterprises are somehow disreputable or should be decently hidden, like undergar-

A city enjoying a high birth rate of diverse small enterprises needs cheap, versatile and diverse working spaces.

ments. After all, the more the people of a city are aware of its economic life, and the more that they can see it is normal and natural for small things to take root in it, the more the economy which exists can serve as an example of what more might be done. City zoning needs rethinking. It has been developed, on the whole, without regard for promoting economic creativity. It seems to me that the actual performances of specific enterprises with respect to such things as noise, generation of traffic and pollution are to the point. Performance standards, rather than zoning categories of uses, would provide incentives for enterprises to overcome noxious problems in order to achieve greater freedom of location.

Any unnecessary international, national, provincial or city mandated standardizations of goods or services, other than the relatively few really needed for health or safety, are destructive. Many such standardizations merely serve special interests, or have been adopted for the convenience of bureaucracies, or have been short-sightedly invoked in the name of efficiency.* They need rethinking. How can city producers undertake differentiations for their local markets if deviations from standards are discouraged or forbidden? And who knows what further rami-

---

* For an in-depth discussion of "the cult of efficiency," see "Efficiency and the Commons" in this volume.

fications in methods of production, materials or purposes are being doomed?

Cities can learn from one another about conditions that serve or encourage economic fertility. A number of economic observers have recently been much impressed by the proliferation of symbiotic small firms in the city clusters of northeastern Italy, and by the high quality, inventive, technically sophisticated work they are doing. If I were a city official attempting to promote economic fertility in my own city, I would examine this Italian phenomenon. It might even be worthwhile to promote visits by small entrepreneurs from other European cities to see what ideas they could pick up from the northeastern Italian experience.

Any type of sales tax on producers' goods and services discriminates against symbiotic city enterprises. In symbiotic production, the burden of paperwork becomes horrendous, and the sales taxes must be disproportionately financed as a cost during production, in comparison with the same taxes falling on large enterprises capable of supplying many of their everyday needs internally. However, it is impossible for city governments to overcome this form of discrimination against symbiotic city production, as long as municipal governments are helpless with respect to such taxation policies.

Poor districts of a city that persistently fail to generate enterprises of their own, originated by their own people, remain interminably stunted economically, and socially stunted as well.

Although ethnic or immigrant economic ghettos often seem hopeless, they are not inherently devoid of economic opportunities. Their own cultural peculiarities provide some opportunities, the most obvious being ethnic food stores and restaurants.

Clothing, decorative, and entertainment preferences of their own people present other ready-made opportunities for ethnic entrepreneurs. So does preservation, production and promotion of ethnic crafts, whether locally made or imported from the home country, and like ethnic restaurants and entertainment, these can appeal to the city at large. Ethnic communities often contain skilled people, women as well as men, whose skills find no market among large employers but could in the ghetto itself.

Here let us stop and think a moment about underground economies. Even in advanced nations it is becoming hard to tell just how large an economy is, statistically, because the official figures omit so many barter arrangements and underground enterprises. And in some Third World cities, such as Lima for instance, the underground economy is now believed to account for as much as sixty percent of production and two out of three jobs.

Underground economies are by definition illegal, but for the most part not because their production is harmful. On the contrary, it fills real and pressing needs for goods and services on the one hand, and for jobs and incomes on the other. The illegalities are evasions of taxes, and avoidance of licenses and the demands of bureaucracies. It is all very well to say these illegalities are wrong, but the hard fact is that if firms in the underground economy were not operating illegally, many would not be operating at all. They get by only by cutting corners. The result of effectively clamping down on them is not necessarily larger tax yields, but rather greater poverty and more idleness.

I am not advocating that we should turn a blind eye to tax evasion or other illegalities. The notion that operating outside the law is ethically acceptable is a terribly dangerous notion.

But what I would suggest is that we seriously consider exempting young and small enterprises from the usual burdens of taxation, and perhaps their workers as well, which would lower their wages without lowering their incomes commensurately, and hence lower costs. By analogy, we do not expect our babies and young children to take on the household chores they will assume when they are older, stronger and more experienced. We realize that their first job is to develop, learn, and get a good foothold in life; if they accomplish that, they can pull their weight later.

This might be a desirable way of regarding young and small city enterprises generally, at the time they are getting a start. In persistently poor and stunted economic ghettos, I suggest that such a policy would not only be desirable, but may be absolutely necessary. These ghettos, in a way, are like little pieces of Third World cities lodged within more advanced economies.

However, it is of course impossible for cities to experiment with such policies, as long as municipalities have so little control over the taxation that affects their own economies. Perhaps it is worth remembering that medieval cities, which had so little in comparison with modern cities, and yet were astonishingly fertile and creative, had at least one thing our modern cities have typically all but lost. They had a right called "farming their own taxes."* That right was so important to them that it was usually

---

*   In *Dark Age Ahead,* Jacobs explains the origins of this saying through the etymology of the word *farmer*: "The *Oxford English Dictionary* gives, as the first meaning of *farmer,* 'one who undertakes the collection of taxes, revenues, etc.' The word comes from medieval French for a fixed fee. It came to mean, in English, an agriculturalist, because farmers were subject to paying landlords fixed fees. The charter allowing a city to farm its own taxes meant that the city could appoint its own tax collectors, responsible to the city rather than to the royal treasury, the church, or a regional warlord. Cities with these powers sometimes overtook what

part and parcel of a city charter, hard-won from feudal authorities. Maybe it is almost as important for modern cities as well.

To get back to ethnic economic ghettos, of course their economic deficiencies are intertwined with social problems. I have no easy answers to difficulties associated with discrimination, segregation, and cultural conflicts. However, the experience of my own city, Toronto, may be suggestive.

For historic reasons, Canada never adopted the ideal of the melting pot for immigrants. This is one of many ways in which Canada differs profoundly from the United States. The Canadian ideal is expressed metaphorically as the mosaic, the idea being that each piece of the mosaic helps compose the overall picture, but each piece nevertheless has an identity of its own.[*]

As a city, Toronto has worked hard and ingeniously to give substance to this concept, as torrents of migrants from Asia, the Middle East, the Caribbean and Europe—especially, of course, the poorer parts of Europe—have poured in during the past generation. The city government, and many other city institutions, continually celebrate the ethnic differences among the citizens, and tirelessly emphasize that this diversity is a source of social and economic richness. Many of the ingenious ways of

---

became major regional or national improvements. For instance, the merchants of London, financing a campaign against piracy, laid the foundations of the English navy" (199–200).

[*] According to Jacobs the mosaic narrative is mostly a result of the longstanding tension between English and French Canada. The federal government used the mosaic narrative to balance the need for national unity with the desire of the Quebecois for independence and cultural distinction. When asked whether she would like Quebec to separate from Canada in a 1970 interview with the *Toronto Star,* Jacobs replied, "If I were a Quebecoise, I would probably be a separatist. But since I am an Ontarian, I hope Quebec stays with us. I believe many of Canada's best national qualities are the direct result of Quebec's presence and prickliness: e.g., the rein on centralized powers in favor of provincial powers; the image of the mosaic instead of melting pot."

doing this have been thought up by immigrants themselves, and then have been supported and encouraged. The provincial government, which has its capital in Toronto, has followed suit through its Ministry of Multiculturalism. In the schools, special efforts are made—all of them experimental and some controversial—to assure children who are immigrants themselves, or whose parents are immigrants, that their identities are valued and the languages and ways of their parents are respected. When I became a Canadian citizen, the immigration judge who examined me, and who had been an immigrant herself, told me that she always speaks seriously to the children of immigrant families obtaining citizenship, about how brave their parents were to come to a new country, and how valuable the language, the memories, and the customs are that they brought along with them.

As far as I can see, assimilation of immigrants into Toronto's life and its ways occurs at much the same rate as assimilation into the American melting pot, if anything faster, but without the institutionalized assaults on individual and group self-respect or on children's respect for their parents that the ideal of the melting pot so often imposes. I am convinced that in Toronto we have a much happier city than we would without our ingenuity at celebrating cultural differences, and that bigotry, resentments, feelings of mutual fear, feelings of inferiority, and conflict, have been greatly minimized. I am also convinced that this is no small thing.

As cities have grown in population, scale and complexity, central municipal governments have been expanded to cope with changes. Along with this has gone increasing national centralization of governments, removing powers and responsibilities into still remoter and higher realms. No wonder so many city people feel—or act as if they feel—powerless to affect their environments. Those who protect policies or try to shape governmental decisions through popular movements have to claim that they speak for people who, in fact, have never given them a mandate to do so. There is no way to give such mandates. That is a great weakness and handicap of popular action groups, and it can be a great danger as well if self-appointed leaders use their powers unscrupulously or have devious reasons for building their power. Yet a vacuum of caring is even worse. The rise and proliferation of informal action groups, and sometimes their desperation as well, tell us of serious institutional failure. We get the same message, delivered in a different way, when city people are discouraged about the problems of their neighborhoods, to the point of apathy.

Enormous fields of political, social and governmental invention and evolution lie unexplored, untried and waiting, right within cities themselves.

I suggest that we need to experiment with decentralization of government within cities.* That task is not the same as merely copying small town or village governments within a city. The potential pitfalls are different. The relationships of city districts with the municipality as a whole, and with each other, are inherently complex. Which responsibilities are suitable for district or neighborhood control, and which are not, cannot be worked out abstractly but only through experiment and experience. Thus enormous fields of political, social and governmen-

---

* Her remarks here provide one solution to the unanswered questions put forth by "Metropolitan Government" in this volume. Jacobs also argues for a similar decentralization of municipal government in chapter 21 of *Death and Life,* "Governing and Planning Districts."

tal invention and evolution lie unexplored, untried and waiting, right within cities themselves. Modern cities, I think, need to be fully as inventive in their own fashions as the little medieval cities were in theirs when they accomplished the amazing and creative feat of substituting city ways for feudal ways.

Logically, it might seem that the best way to go about experimental decentralization would be to decentralize this and that specific municipal government function, starting with those that have been major targets of popular dissatisfaction, and then keep adding still more decentralized functions. For example, when planning decisions became the major issues rounding citizen protest and anger, my own city, Toronto, proceeded to decentralize parts of its Department of Planning into neighborhood offices, more responsible to localities than they previously had been, and more responsive to local needs and wishes. This has been working for about a decade and has proved to be a good move, both from the viewpoint of localities and the viewpoint of the central municipality.

Indeed, that decentralization worked so well, that portions of the buildings department were decentralized so that householders planning structural, electrical, plumbing or other renovations, or those wishing to build small additions to their homes, could deal with an office geographically more convenient to them than the central office, and at times more convenient to them, in the evenings. The officials in these offices, rather than concentrating merely on approvals or disapprovals of plans, and on inspection of finished work, also became very helpful at explaining what corrections were needed and why, and suggesting how they could be made. In sum, the task was carried out in a fashion more direct, swift and convenient than previously and from what people using this service have told me, they genuinely feel the government is working as their servant.

So far so good, but observe, also, what has gone wrong here. The buildings department service does not correspond geographically at all with the decentralized planning department services. This is what always seems to happen when decentralization occurs by functions. Each function, or department, adopts its own decentralization rationale, different from that of other departments. The sum total is a very confused, fragmented and makeshift form of decentralization. Perhaps this is simply because municipal governments lack a true and serious commitment to decentralization. But perhaps it may be true, as one Canadian philosopher has said, that you can't decentralize centrally.* Whatever the reason, this functional approach to decentralization has customarily petered out in confusion. While I am not suggesting that it is worthless, I think we must be suspicious of it in the absence of some other framework leading to decentralization.

Such a possible framework would be formal district governments, with formal elected procedures. How many city district governments would ultimately be necessary would depend upon the size of a given city itself, and also upon the number of popularly understood, natural communities within the city. Since we must assume that a central city government would also continue to be necessary, with its own election machinery, there is no reason why city districts should all be artificially made the same size geographically, nor is there any reason why

---

*   The Canadian philosopher in question is Jacobs's friend and collaborator Marshall McLuhan. Jacobs was fond of this saying; it pops up three times in this volume.

all district governments should be instituted at one and the same time. Indeed, there would be advantages in a municipality feeling its way and starting experimentally with a first few.

Sooner or later, a municipality experimenting seriously and successfully with decentralized government will have to decentralize control over some of its taxation powers, and over many of the discretionary uses to which public money can be put. If that thought sounds alarming, it is only because we have become so deplorably accustomed to regarding the ordinary people of cities as if they were too ignorant to know what is good for them, or too irresponsible as not to be trustworthy. We have placed such exaggerated confidence in centralized expertise on housing, social work, education, economic development and many other matters that we have come to make less and less use of ordinary city people's knowledge about life, common sense, imaginations and financial responsibility. This is not social progress, but the reverse. The pendulum has swung too far.

Centralized expertise means standardized solutions to city problems. Standardized solutions, and the programs that result from them, are seldom or never really the best that could be done in any specific location. They are very cumbersome, as well, and inherently sluggish at responding to changing conditions or to newly emerging needs or newly emerging possibilities. Worst of all, standardized answers and programs stifle localized ingenuities, and forestall diverse innovation and inventiveness.

We have placed such exaggerated confidence in centralized expertise on housing, social work, education, economic development and many other matters that we have come to make less and less use of ordinary city people's knowledge.

In sum, what I have been saying is that the first responsibilities of cities are to themselves. A city has to be responsible for keeping its own economy inventive and prospering. No other entity but the city itself can generate the high birth rate of diverse and small enterprises a healthy city economy endlessly requires. A city has to be responsible for keeping its own society endlessly involved with maintaining a city its own people can feel at home in and proud of. No other entity can do that job. If a city itself fails at solving reasonably well these economic and social problems of its own, the result is bound to be economic and social deterioration of the city.

In other words, the less that cities use their own people's economic and social capacities for experimenting and inventing, the more decadent and stunted cities become; also, the more surely, in that case, widespread national and international practical problems must pile up, unsolved.

But for that pessimistic side of the coin, there is an optimistic obverse. The more that cities can make of their own ordinary people's capacities for economic and social invention and experiment, the more useful and valuable cities become—not only for their own people but also for their nations.

Pedaling Together

SPEECH AT SPOKESPEOPLE: ENERGY PROBE'S
CONFERENCE ON BICYCLE ADVOCACY, CITY HALL,
TORONTO, APRIL 26–27, 1985

PROBABLY ALL OF US HERE THINK THAT CYCLING SAFETY IS important and do a certain amount of worrying about it. I know I do. Without minimizing that problem, however, I would like to remind you that accidents also happen with stationary bicycles on which people merely pedal around and around for exercise without going anywhere.

In the United States in 1983—the last year for which figures are available—people using mechanical exercising equipment such as stationary bicycles and rowing machines, and treadmills with elastic and pulley stretchers, suffered 18,000 accidents severe enough to require hospital emergency treatment. That was a 75 percent increase over 1981.

Many of those accidents were very severe, and some involve such tragedies as loss of eyes and paralysis from the neck down. One woman in San Antonio was so severely hurt on a stationary bicycle that the manufacturers gave her $900,000 in an out-of-court settlement.

The article in which I read about all this, in *The Wall Street Journal* earlier this month, went on to describe another phenomenon. To pedal an indoor bicycle becomes so boring as to drive many people to their wits' ends, it seems. One couple in Houston whom the reporter interviewed were planning to watch television while exercising on their new stationary bike—a bicycle for which, by the way, they were laying out $1,500. If that seems like a lot of money for a bike that doesn't go anywhere, consider that some stationary bikes can cost as much as $3,448. They have built-in computers to assure you that what you are doing is having an effect apart from just making the wheels go around. People have also taken to fighting the boredom by buying videocassettes that unroll scenery for them on the walls of their rooms.

Before we snicker at these extravagances or snort at these artificialities, think about the fact that many of these poor souls literally have no feasible place where they can ride actual bicycles and go anywhere. They live in expressway cities like Houston, Dallas, Los Angeles or Detroit, and even smaller places as well, like Needville, Texas, or Kalamazoo, Michigan. For them, it's as if to get anywhere much, you'd have to take your bike on the Gardiner or the 401.*

This is what Metro would be like too, if its highway and traffic department's plans had not been stopped by citizen action. Sam Cass, the department's chief, boasted back in 1970 that when his plans were carried out, no spot in this city was to be farther away from a major expressway than three quarters of a mile. Ramps and interchanges were to abound. What was to be left of the city would amount, in effect, to the clover in the clover

---

* Jacobs here names two prominent expressways in Toronto. In the next sentence, "Metro" refers to the now-defunct metropolitan level of government in Toronto, including York, East York, North York, Etobicoke, Scarborough, and the old city itself. In 1998, the Government of Ontario forcefully amalgamated these municipalities into one "megacity."

leaves.* That is no environment for biking, nor for public transit either. In such an environment, of course sane people would take their bicycles indoors and run the scenery on the walls.

This is what Metro could just possibly still become, as schemes afoot right now warn us. I am thinking of such things as the proposed Leslie Street Extension, now under serious and expensive study with the apparent support of the City of Toronto's own planning department, over the objection of North York neighborhoods that would be damaged. I am thinking of the recently proposed widening of Spadina below Bloor, which, if I have been correctly informed, has already tentatively been put into the next capital budget by Mr. Cass. This too, alas, seems to have the support of the City of Toronto's own planning department. That scheme happens to be precisely what was originally planned by Mr. Cass for the lower end of the Spadina Expressway. It amounts to building the Expressway from its southern end northward, an old trick I am familiar with in the United States: if opposition stops an expressway at one end, then you start building it from the other end.

Marshall McLuhan once said that Canada enjoys an early warning system, if it had the sense to heed what has happened in the United States. What has happened in the United States is that the expressway system of attempting to deal with transportation between suburbs and downtowns has now succeeded in making suburbs themselves the very worst scenes of traffic jams and backups in the nation.

---

* Patterns of expressway interchanges often take the form of four interlocked loops, which resemble a four-leaf clover. To say that only "the clover in the clover leaves" would remain is to say that only the unused and mostly unusable scraps of grass inside the looping on-ramps would remain.

An article about this phenomenon, also from *The Wall Street Journal* earlier this month, begins:

> Fairfax County, VA. Every weekday morning Gretchen Davis drives down Fairfax Farms Road on the way to work at the Ayr Hill Country Store in nearby Vienna. Sounds pastoral, doesn't it?
>
> But a short way down the road, Mrs. Davis reaches Route 50, a major arterial highway. . . . There a river of cars roars through the suburban calm. . . . What used to be a pleasant 20 minute commute [stretches] into a nerve-wracking hour.

Can you imagine Mrs. Davis choosing to negotiate this on a bicycle? Or sending her children, if she has them, on bicycles to what is their suburb's own downtown?

What has happened in this suburb is, if anything, becoming all too typical, the report goes on to tell us, with nuggets like these: Millions of suburbanites now share Mrs. Davis's frustration. Urban planners now say traffic tie-ups are becoming the major problem of the suburbs. Buildings at the business nodes are too far apart for walking, so any movement between them must be by car. The morning traffic is horrendous, but lunchtime only brings more traffic jams as people flood out of office buildings, jump into cars and head for restaurants. As suburban highways choke, they spill into small roads, disturbing the tranquility of residential neighborhoods. The Dallas and Houston metropolitan areas now suffer bumper-to-bumper traffic on many highways twelve or more hours a day. Snarled traffic in the suburbs of San Francisco now regularly adds up to a total backup of some 170 miles, and so on.

In sum, warnings from the U.S. tell us that suburbs, which it was long supposed were benefiting from the expressway system of trying to handle transportation between suburbs and downtowns, have themselves inexorably become victims of the system—a lesson that people in North York, for one, are just now starting to grasp, although their politicians haven't.

I have been dwelling at length on expressway folly, in part to emphasize that this way of trying to meet a city's transportation needs leads to a wretched environment for cyclists. But let us look at this in a broader context too. In many respects, the interests of cyclists are identical with the interests of other groups who are deeply concerned about the quality of life in cities and suburbs.

I am thinking, for instance, of

- People who care about cities and suburbs as safe and pleasant places to bring up children;
- People who care about the tranquility of residential areas and the dangers to them of environmental degradation;
- People who value ravines and other city oases of nature, and care about protecting them from paving, traffic and noise;
- People who care about the quality, convenience, and financial resources and soundness of mass transit;
- People who care about the mobility of children, the elderly, and those too poor to own a car or—as may be the case—*two* cars;
- People who care about combating emissions that help cause acid rain and other pollutants;

- People concerned about profligate wastes of energy, and the consequences of that waste for ourselves and the planet.

People with concerns like these are natural allies of cyclists, whether sports cyclists, touring and other recreational cyclists, or utilitarian cyclists. Intrinsically, these people's battles are also the cyclists' battles, and cyclists' battles are their battles, because all these superficially different interests converge. They all amount to trying to keep city and suburbs as high-quality places for people—not just people who are spending part of their day in cars, but people walking, strolling, running, pedaling, playing, gardening—or for that matter, listening for bullfrogs.

About those bullfrogs: last year I was flabbergasted to hear an official of a cycling organization say his organization and its membership were simply uninterested in the sorts of interests and allies I have just mentioned, and that his organization would in all likelihood support a proposed new traffic artery or a widened road which was opposed by the neighborhood it would damage, if the scheme would save a few minutes for cyclists. Same for a highway through a formerly wild ravine. I fear he thought I was slightly balmy, or anyhow impractical, when I told him that somebody who cared deeply about preserving a habitat for bullfrogs was more of a natural ally for him than an expressway builder or a road widener or an automobile traffic planner. Only last week I happened to read a remark by another cycling official, to the effect that whatever is good for cars is good for bicycles too, apparently on the premise that both kinds of vehicles roll on pavements.

The logical end result of short-sighted or wishful policies like those is, of course, stationary bicycles going around and around indoors. Literally pedaling alone, with videocassette scenery for comfort, becomes all too logical a sequel when cyclists figuratively pedal alone without empathy or regard for other people interested in the quality of city life, for their own or other reasons.

At present, cyclists don't have much clout in pushing for the facilities and city qualities they need and want. I think they would have more clout if they pedaled along with their many, many potential allies, getting aid from those allies in support of cyclists' needs, and in return helping their natural allies in *their* battles for better quality of city life: working in mutual support with people who care about bullfrogs, or about traffic lights where the schoolchildren cross, or about threats of expropriation to their working places or their homes, understanding that the specific needs and desires of city cyclists can be furthered only within a broader context of the city as a decent place for people to live and get around in.

As a practical matter, how do loose but effective alliances among city groups come about? I will mention a bit of history as an illustration, because it occurred at a time when the very notion of such diverse alliances had to be invented or stumbled into. Back in 1956, I happened to be one of a group defending a community park in New York, where I lived at the time—defending it against being bisected by a proposed expressway.*

We weren't making much headway at first. As Robert Moses, New York's chief highway planner and vandal of the time, said at one public hearing, we were "nothing but a bunch of mothers." We had no clout.

---

* The park in question is Washington Square Park, and Jacobs's passionate and witty defense of the park can be found in "Reason, Emotion, Pressure: There Is No Other Recipe," in this volume.

All the established organizations in the community had their own important concerns on which they focused. Most of them should logically have been our natural allies, but even those that recognized this tended to be too bureaucratized to be effective allies. Of course they didn't think of themselves so, but like most organizations they were automatically little bureaucracies with executive committees, or boards of directors, or the like. They had to go through time-taking procedures, more often than not at infrequent meetings, to debate and pass resolutions endorsing support of this action, so much the worse. If there wasn't time for it at the end of the agenda, it got short shrift. And if some members of the executive disagreed with the object of stopping the expressway, as sometimes was the case, so much the worse still.

We felt as if we were stuck in flypaper, unable to mobilize effectively the really big support that actually was out there in the community—and elsewhere in the city too—as we knew from petitions, letters to editors, talk with neighbors, and other evidence.

At this point, a public-spirited man with considerable experience in citizens' organizations suggested we ought to start what he called an umbrella movement on the issue, a rallying organization for embracing natural allies in either an informal or a formal way, an organization whose members would simultaneously help natural allies in their battles which were congenial to our cause.* That is what we did, calling our outfit The Committee to Save Washington Square from All But Emergency

* The "public-spirited man" in question is Raymond "Ray" Rubinow (1905–96), a lifelong administrator of charitable organizations, preservationist, and activist who also helped save Carnegie Hall.

Traffic. The method worked. Not only did we find our allies and defeat the expressway and close off even the existing narrow roadway through the park for all except fire engines, ambulances and the like, but in the process we got other natural alliances going, alliances that worked for many other constructive mutual purposes.

A city good for cycling is also a city good for walking, strolling, running, playing, window-shopping, and listening for bullfrogs if listening for bullfrogs is your thing.

Something much like this happened in Toronto also during the early 1970s, when many neighborhoods were engaged in crisis battles to preserve themselves from outrageous schemes by developers and traffic promoters. Neighborhood groups took to working together under an umbrella confederation, supporting one another. The Stop Spadina Save Our City Coordinating Committee played a key role in initiating the alliances, although of course not the only role.

It seems to me that cyclists need to get analogous support from natural allies, and give analogous support to them. Otherwise cyclists are unlikely to get very far in improving this city for cycling and, in the process, helping to improve it for all those others who care, for their own reasons, about the city's quality of life.

Whether effective mutual support will develop, I don't know. Certainly it won't develop without effort, or without understanding that a city good for cycling is also a city good for walking, strolling, running, playing, window-shopping, and listening for bullfrogs if listening for bullfrogs is your thing.

Foreword to *The Death and Life of Great American Cities*

——

MODERN LIBRARY EDITION,

OCTOBER 1992

WHEN I BEGAN WORK ON THIS BOOK IN 1958, I EXPECTED merely to describe the civilizing and enjoyable services that good city street life casually provides—and to deplore planning fads and architectural fashions that were expunging these necessities and charms instead of helping to strengthen them. Some of Part One of this book: that's all I intended.

But learning and thinking about city streets and the trickiness of city parks launched me into an unexpected treasure hunt. I quickly found that the valuables in plain sight—streets and parks—were intimately mingled with clues and keys to other peculiarities of cities. Thus one discovery led to another, then another. . . . Some of the findings from the hunt fill the rest of this book. Others, as they turned up, have gone into four further books. Obviously, this book exerted an influence on me, and lured me into my subsequent life's work. But has it been influential otherwise? My own appraisal is yes and no.

Some people prefer doing their workaday errands on foot, or feel they would like to if they lived in a place where they could. Other people prefer hopping into the car to do errands,

or would like to if they had a car. In the old days, before automobiles, some people liked ordering up carriages or sedan chairs
and many wished they could. But as we know from novels, biographies, and legends, some people whose social positions required them to ride—except for
rural rambles—wistfully peered
out at passing street scenes and
longed to participate in their ca-
maraderie, bustle, and promises of
surprise and adventure.

*It is not easy for uncredentialed
people to stand up to the
credentialed, even when the
so-called expertise is grounded
in ignorance and folly.*

In a kind of shorthand, we can
speak of foot people and car people. This book was instantly
understood by foot people, both actual and wishful. They recognized that what it said jibed with their own enjoyment, concerns, and experiences, which is hardly surprising, since much
of the book's information came from observing and listening to
foot people. They were collaborators in the research. Then, re-
ciprocally, the book collaborated with foot people by giving
legitimacy to what they already knew for themselves. Experts
of the time did not respect what foot people knew and valued.
They were deemed old-fashioned and selfish—troublesome
sand in the wheels of progress. It is not easy for uncredentialed
people to stand up to the credentialed, even when the so-called
expertise is grounded in ignorance and folly. This book turned
out to be helpful ammunition against such experts. But it is less
accurate to call this effect "influence" than to see it as corrobora-
tion and collaboration. Conversely, the book neither collaborated with car people nor had an influence on them. It still does
not, as far as I can see.

The case of students of city planning and architecture is similarly mixed, but with special oddities. At the time of the book's publication, no matter whether the students were foot or car people by experience and temperament, they were being rigorously trained as anticity and antistreet designers and planners: trained as if they were fanatic car people and so was everybody else. Their teachers had been trained or indoctrinated that way too. So in effect, the whole establishment concerned with the physical form of cities (including bankers, developers, and politicians who had assimilated the planning and architectural visions and theories) acted as gatekeepers protecting forms and visions inimical to city life. However, among architectural students especially, and to some extent among planning students, there were foot people. To them, the book made sense. Their teachers (though not all) tended to consider it trash or "bitter, coffee-house rambling" as one planner put it.* Yet the book, curiously enough, found its way onto required or optional reading lists—sometimes, I suspect, to arm students with awareness of the benighted ideas they would be up against as practitioners. Indeed, one university teacher told me just that. But for foot people among students, the book was subversive. Of course their subversion was by no means all my doing. Other authors and researchers—notably William H. Whyte—were also ex-

* Edward J. Logue (1921–2000), a planner and urban renewal official in Boston, New Haven, and New York, opens his review of *Death and Life* with the line, "Jane Jacobs has produced 448 pages of bitter, rambling coffeehouse talk mostly attacking urban renewal, public housing and city planning." Ironically, Jacobs thanks Logue in the acknowledgments of the book, since she interviewed him about his work in New Haven, Connecticut. When asked about this contradiction in a 1985 interview with Richard Carroll Keeley, Jacobs responded, "Ed Logue always horrified me. . . . But I learned from him."

posing the unworkability and joylessness of anticity visions. In London, editors and writers of *The Architectural Review* were already up to the same thing in the mid-1950s.*

Nowadays, many architects, and some among the younger generation of planners, have excellent ideas—beautiful, ingenious ideas—for strengthening city life. They also have the skills to carry out their plans. These people are a far cry from the ruthless, heedless city manipulators I have castigated.

But here we come to something sad. Although the numbers of arrogant old gatekeepers have dwindled with time, the gates themselves are another matter. Anticity planning remains amazingly sturdy in American cities. It is still embodied in thousands of regulations, bylaws, and codes, also in bureaucratic timidities owing to accepted practices, and in unexamined public attitudes hardened by time. Thus, one may be sure that there have been enormous and dedicated efforts in the face of these obstacles wherever one sees stretches of old city buildings that have been usefully recycled for new and different purposes; wherever sidewalks have been widened and

> *Although the numbers of arrogant old gatekeepers have dwindled with time, the gates themselves are another matter. Anticity planning remains amazingly sturdy in American cities.*

---

* William H. Whyte (1917–99), well-known journalist, editor, and author of *The Organization Man,* an influential 1957 study of white-collar life, was an editor at *Fortune* in the 1950s when Jacobs was at *Architectural Forum*. Both magazines were part of Henry Luce's Time-Life empire. Whyte included Jacobs's article "Downtown Is for People," also reproduced here, in his influential *Fortune* series "The Exploding Metropolis." Later, inspired in part by Jacobs, he began his own investigation of urban life, in particular a series of books, articles, and a film on "the social life of small urban spaces."

vehicular roadways narrowed precisely where they should be—
on streets in which pedestrian traffic is bustling and plentiful;
wherever downtowns are not deserted after their offices close;
wherever new, fine-grained mixtures of street uses have been
fostered successfully; wherever new buildings have been sensi-
tively inserted among old ones to knit up holes and tatters in a
city neighborhood so that the mending is all but invisible. Some
foreign cities have become pretty good at these feats. But to try
to accomplish such sensible things in America is a daunting or-
deal at best, and often enough heartbreaking.

In Chapter Twenty of this book I proposed that the ground
levels of self-isolating projects within cities could be radically
erased and reconstituted with two objects in view: linking the
projects into the normal city by fitting them out with plentiful,
new, connecting streets; and converting the projects themselves
into urban places at the same time, by adding diverse new facilities along those added streets. The catch here, of course, is that
new commercial facilities would need to work out economically, as a measure of their genuine and not fake usefulness.

It is disappointing that this sort of radical replanning has not
been tried—as far as I know—in the more than thirty years
since this book was published.* To be sure, with every decade
that passes, the task of carrying out the proposal would seem to
be more difficult. That is because anticity projects, especially
massive public housing projects, tend to cause their city sur-

---

* The City of Toronto began a pilot "tower renewal" initiative in 2009, which has since
become a permanent program. The program aims to help tower owners make their buildings
more environmentally friendly, while also improving the built environment of the surrounding neighborhoods, including new mixed-use zoning and infill, much as Jacobs suggests in *Death and Life*.

roundings to deteriorate, so that as time passes, less and less healthy adjoining city is available to tie into.

Even so, good opportunities still exist for converting city projects into city. Easy ones ought to be tried first on the premise that this is a learning challenge, and it is good policy for all learning to start with easy cases and work up to more difficult ones. The time is coming when we will sorely need to apply this learning to suburban sprawls since it is unlikely we can continue extending them without limit. The costs in energy waste, infrastructure waste, and land waste are too high. Yet if already existing sprawls are intensified, in favor of thriftier use of resources, we need to have learned how to make the intensifications and linkages attractive, enjoyable, safe, and sustainable—for foot people as well as car people.

Occasionally this book has been credited with having helped halt urban renewal and slum-clearance programs. I would be delighted to take credit if this were true. It isn't. Urban renewal and slum clearance succumbed to their own failures and fiascos, after continuing with their extravagant outrages for many years after this book was published. Even now they pop up when wishful thinking and forgetfulness set in, abetted by sufficient cataclysmic money lent to developers and sufficient political hubris and public subsidies. A recent example, for instance, is the grandiose but bankrupt Canary Wharf project set in isolation in what were London's dilapidated docklands and the demolished, modest Isle of Dogs community, beloved by its inhabitants.*

---

* The Canary Wharf project, which redeveloped the old West India Docks on the Isle of Dogs into an office district, began in the 1980s and continues today. With over 14 million square feet of office and retail space already built and more residential and commercial space planned, its cluster of high-rises has altered the skyline of London, created a new financial

To return to the treasure hunt that began with the streets and one thing leading to another and another: at some point along the trail I realized I was engaged in studying the ecology of cities. Offhand, this sounds like taking note that raccoons nourish themselves from city backyard gardens and garbage bags (in my own city they do, sometimes even downtown), that hawks can possibly reduce pigeon populations among skyscrapers, and so on. But by city ecology I mean something different from, yet similar to, natural ecology as students of wilderness address the subject. A natural ecosystem is defined as "composed of physical-chemical-biological processes active within a space-time unit of any magnitude." A city ecosystem is composed of physical-economic-ethical processes active at a given time within a city and its close dependencies. I've made up this definition, by analogy.*

The two sorts of ecosystems—one created by nature, the other by human beings—have fundamental principles in common. For instance, both types of ecosystems—assuming they are not barren—require much diversity to sustain themselves. In both cases, the diversity develops organically over time, and the varied components are interdependent in complex ways. The more niches for diversity of life and livelihoods in either kind of ecosystem, the greater its carrying capacity for life. In both types of ecosystems, many small and obscure components— easily overlooked by superficial observation—can be vital to the

---

district in the city, and, as Jacobs notes, sparked no end of controversy over the gentrification of the Isle of Dogs and other nearby working-class communities.

* Jacobs explores this connection between urban and natural systems more fully in *The Nature of Economies*. Her definition of ecology seems to come from "The Trophic-Dynamic Aspect of Ecology," a 1942 article by the seminal ecologist Raymond L. Lindeman.

whole, far out of proportion to their own tininess of scale or aggregate quantities. In natural ecosystems, gene pools are fundamental treasures. In city ecosystems, kinds of work are fundamental treasures; furthermore, forms of work not only reproduce themselves in newly created proliferating organizations, they also hybridize, and even mutate into unprecedented kinds of work. And because of their complex interdependencies of components, both kinds of ecosystems are vulnerable and fragile, easily disrupted or destroyed.

If not fatally disrupted, however, they are tough and resilient. And when their processes are working well, ecosystems appear stable. But in a profound sense, the stability is an illusion. As a Greek philosopher, Heraclitus, observed long ago, everything in the natural world is in flux. When we suppose we see static situations, we actually see processes of beginning and processes of ending occurring simultaneously. Nothing is static. It is the same with cities. Thus, to investigate either natural or city ecosystems demands the same kind of thinking. It does not do to focus on "things" and expect them to explain much in themselves. Processes are always of the essence; things have significances as participants in processes, for better or worse.

This way of seeing is fairly young and new, which is perhaps why the hunt for knowledge to understand either natural or city ecology seems so inexhaustible. Little is known; so much yet to know.

We human beings are the only city-building creatures in the world. The hives of social insects are funda-

It does not do to focus on "things" and expect them to explain much in themselves. Processes are always of the essence; things have significances as participants in processes, for better or worse.

mentally different in how they develop, what they do, and their potentialities. Cities are in a sense natural ecosystems too—for us. They are not disposable. Whenever and wherever societies have flourished and prospered rather than stagnated and decayed, creative and workable cities have been at the core of the phenomenon; they have pulled their weight and more. It is the same still. Decaying cities, declining economies, and mounting social troubles travel together. The combination is not coincidental.

It is urgent that human beings understand as much as we can about city ecology—starting at any point in city processes. The humble, vital services performed by grace of good city streets and neighborhoods are probably as good a starting point as any. So I find it heartening that The Modern Library is issuing this beautiful new edition for a new generation of readers who, I hope, will become interested in city ecology, respect its marvels, discover more.

Two Ways to Live

——

INTERVIEW WITH DAVID WARREN,
THE IDLER, SUMMER 1993[*]

THINGS THAT RUN TOGETHER

DAVID WARREN: As early as 1985 you were using the words "Trader" and "Raider" to describe two ways of making a living, and the two "moral syndromes" that go with them. What started you down this forked road?

JANE JACOBS: When I was researching *The Economy of Cities,* I thought how extraordinary it was that even in early medieval times, in primitive circumstances, ships met to trade and primitive fairs were held in England and the Baltic and other places too. How extraordinary that they would exchange goods instead of grabbing things from each other.

Independently of this, I began noticing what kind of behavior was approved and esteemed, and what was not. I made lists of esteemed behavior and found many of the items contradictory, all kinds of things mutually exclusive. So I kept on making these lists and, much like Kate, my character in the book, I

---

[*]   David Warren is a conservative Canadian journalist known for his roles as the editor of *The Idler* and as a controversial columnist for the *Ottawa Citizen.*

began combing them out—this is esteemed for *this* purpose but not for *that* purpose.* Near the end of *Cities and the Wealth of Nations,* I have a remark about very successful military people—Castro and Mao and many others—who are just dreadful flops when they try to run an economy. They have expectations, intuitions, assumptions that are different from people who build up economic institutions. By that time, I had gotten the two syndromes separated.

WARREN: The characters in your book discover and expound what you call the "Guardian syndrome" and the "Commercial syndrome." The impulse to trade comes later in the evolutionary order, so I suppose in this sense the Guardian syndrome is prior, and we could discuss it first.

JACOBS: Well, I started with the Commercial one.

I don't think that the Guardian syndrome is more basic to *us.* What is uniquely human is more basic for us than what is generalized. Think how important language is. If we are going to say something, we can growl and clutch and do various things, but speaking comes more naturally. The word *syndrome,* which comes from the Greek, means "things that run together." We use it to denote a bunch of symptoms that characterize a condition. These collections of precepts and morals and values characterize certain conditions, functional conditions.

---

* "Kate" is one of the characters in Jacobs's essay in the form of Socratic dialogue, *Systems of Survival.* According to Robert Kanigel's biography *Eyes on the Street,* Jacobs imagined the character as an amalgam of her daughter, Burgin, and two of her nieces, all bound up in the guise of an aspiring animal behaviorist.

WARREN: Didn't the word "syndrome" make your skin crawl?

JACOBS: No. I think it is the only jargon word I use and it is so common by now. The items in a syndrome are not separate; they are interrelated. It would be a mistake to think of them standing independently.

WARREN: Then we'll start with the Commercial syndrome. "Shun force," "come to voluntary agreements," "be honest," "collaborate easily with strangers and aliens," "compete," "respect contracts," "use initiative and enterprise," "be open to inventiveness and novelty," "be efficient," "promote comfort and convenience," "dissent for the sake of the task," "invest for productive purposes," "be industrious," "be thrifty," "be optimistic"—all of this smacks to me of Tawney and Weber and the Protestant work ethic.*

JACOBS: But these precepts existed before Christianity, let alone Protestantism. They are incorporated in what we call the Protestant work ethic, but they existed before there was any such thing, in places where Protestantism was unheard of, and they exist today where Protestantism has no sway. The reason for them is that they work for the function of trade and production for trade.

WARREN: Where do you first spy these qualities?

---

*   Both Richard H. Tawney (1880–1962) and Max Weber (1864–1920) discussed the idea— originated by Weber—of the "Protestant work ethic," a theory suggesting that the Calvinist morality of thrift and productivity contributed to the rise of capitalism.

288 || VITAL LITTLE PLANS

JACOBS: Phoenicians, among the oldest traders we know of—
actually there were bound to be earlier ones—traveled from port
to port. They were enterprising. They had invested for productive purposes or they wouldn't have had those ships and those
jars of oil. For their times they were probably efficient. As for
"shunning force," they hated pirates. All ancient traders hated
pirates. Roman and Greek commercial law, and in fact Hammu-
rabi's laws, had respect for contracts in them. Oh, you can find all
of these qualities in the Phoenicians. I don't know about "be optimistic," you certainly must have expectations, and nowadays,
as in ancient times, the traders and producers are extolled for
their optimism, for the cheery way they think they can manage.

WARREN: There is a human tendency to take sides, to say Syndrome A is people like us, and Syndrome B is people like them.
Were you tempted by this?

JACOBS: No. Well, to begin with perhaps, but not for long.

WARREN: In the book you seem especially to relish manifestations of the Commercial syndrome.

JACOBS: No, I don't.

WARREN: That is not your disposition?

JACOBS: My disposition probably, but no, it's not that one is
good and one is bad. Each syndrome is good for its functions,
and if you mix them up—if you try, for instance, to run a government as if it were a business—it is a disaster. Or if you try to

run a business as if it were a government, it is equally a disaster. You must have both syndromes. Each is bad in the wrong place, but each is necessary and good for its suitable function.

WARREN: The Guardian Syndrome: "shun trading," "exert prowess," "be obedient and disciplined," "adhere to tradition," "respect hierarchy"—my Tory heart is already glowing—"be loyal," "take vengeance"—ah! vengeance may be wrong but it is so sweet. . . .

JACOBS: Well, vengeance is at the root of justice. We all believe in justice, and we believe that the authorities ought to see justice done.

WARREN: "Deceive for the sake of the task," which I take as opposed to "dissent for the sake of the task" . . .

JACOBS: They are not really opposites there. "Deceive for the sake of the task" is opposed to "be honest." "Dissent for the sake of the task" is opposed to "be obedient" and "adhere to tradition."

WARREN: "Make rich use of leisure": I think of art and poetry.

JACOBS: And sports.

WARREN: And then, "be ostentatious," "dispense largesse," "be exclusive," "show fortitude," "be fatalistic," "treasure honor." You apply these qualities not only to civil servants but to the police, the army, to every sort of protection racket.

JACOBS: To the courts, too. They don't all emphasize the same qualities to the same degree, but all are infused with them. The Guardian syndrome also applies to people outside of government. That's one reason I called it that, instead of the Governing syndrome or the Territorial syndrome. Our civil life is full of self-appointed Guardians and we find them indispensable—the free press, people who start movements. Environmentalists are self-appointed Guardians. We take lots of these things for granted—a museum and its board, a library, the many public agencies that are staffed by volunteers.

WARREN: Volunteers who shun trading.

JACOBS: That's right; you must shun trading by not regarding income as the bottom line when you are doing public service. And if you don't shun trading you will mess it all up. Consider the opportunity a museum board has, and must resist, to sell off acquisitions under the pretense that they're worthless when really somebody on the board or a friend wants to get them. You see, a museum board consists of self-appointed Guardians. Even if it receives no public money, just endowments, members must stick to the Guardian code.

WARREN: While Canadian public life more and more imitates that of the United States, we retain more pomp and circumstance. We have always been more comfortable with that Guardian code, and therefore perhaps inclined to be a little less corrupt.

JACOBS: Yes, ostentation is a way of getting respect for government and the authorities. It is perfectly all right for the court to erect an unusually ostentatious building, but Ontario Hydro is doing commercial work and it regards itself as somehow above that. And see what a mess it has gotten into.

WARREN: The evils come from hybridizing these syndromes.

JACOBS: From using each for the wrong functions, or from mixing them up. An obvious example is the Mafia. With a couple of exceptions, it operates under the Guardian syndrome. The exceptions are that it trades, but not the way the Commercial syndrome tells you to trade. It doesn't shun force, it doesn't respect voluntary agreements, it isn't honest, though it values enterprise.

WARREN: And since the collapse of the Soviet Union, it has become possible for everyone to see that Communists work much like Mafiosi.

JACOBS: They try to run commerce with the Guardian syndrome. Structurally, they are like the Mafia. The motives are different, the history is different, but structurally they are very similar.

WARREN: One reason for their collapse was that they could not keep up with the military spending and technological development of a trading nation, when the United States pursued the Cold War. And they failed even though the whole Soviet economy was built around the military.

JACOBS: They didn't have the commercial success to support the military spending. The United States may not either. This is very insidious—most empires end up poor from a combination of reasons—but the Soviet Union was so extreme in disdaining the Commercial syndrome that it came a cropper pretty fast.

WARREN: Among wealthy families, there is a tendency over time to switch from Commercial to Guardian mores. I think of an Italian who once boasted, to the scion of a titled English family, "My ancestors went homosexual a century before yours even made their money."

JACOBS: Such families come to disdain trade, to be ashamed if their money came originally from trade.

WARREN: But why only two syndromes? Can't we think of a third?

JACOBS: We have two basic ways of making a living, and everybody has the natural capacity for both. You can rack your brains—I did anyway—trying to find ways other than taking and trading. You can live on gifts, inheritances, patronage, whatever, but that only means somebody else worked up the wherewithal. People recoil against this, they would like to think that there is something besides taking or trading. They invent utopias where everything just magically falls into the right mouths, but these don't hold up.

ON PLATO'S SHOULDERS

WARREN: I wonder if the syndromes offer complementary versions of the Fall of Man.

JACOBS: What did man fall from? I don't know. That's very metaphysical and I'm trying to deal in the functions of the real world.

WARREN: I'm not referring to something abstract, but to man's fundamental propensity to do harm, to screw up, to put the gooper in, no matter which the syndrome.

JACOBS: That's true, and I wish you wouldn't just say "man" all the time. This is a human thing and it applies to women as much as men.

WARREN: Believe me, I know it applies to women. I use the word "man" in the traditional inclusive way.

JACOBS: Yes, and I don't like it, because we get a distorted view of who has been doing all these things. Women have been doing them too and they're just as important. In the commercial system, they may be more important.[*]

But back to your question: We have the capacities both to take and to trade, and there are times when it is appropriate to

---

[*] For more on Jacobs's views on the connection between so-called women's work and the commercial moral syndrome, see "Women as Natural Entrepreneurs" in this section.

use one or the other. If we do them inappropriately, yes, then we're bad and things are going to turn out badly. You're being immoral when you force people, under the pretext of trade, without their voluntary agreement, or if you are dishonest about what you are trading. If you take bribes in the Guardian syndrome, that's immoral. Sure, people have infinite capacities for making a mess and being cruel, for using industriousness in warfare or murder, but they also have capacities for doing and being good. And the world wouldn't work at all if they didn't. We emphasize sin, and violence; but we should also emphasize the marvels of the arts, of altruism, the wonderful things people create and are. So you can call that the Rise of Man.

Sure, people have infinite capacities for making a mess and being cruel, for using industriousness in warfare or murder, but they also have capacities for doing and being good. And the world wouldn't work at all if they didn't.

WARREN: The natural law tradition is singular: it is good to go with nature and bad to go against it. Now you discern two natures. This is breathtaking. But there can be nothing new under the sun. Whose shoulders did you climb on?

JACOBS: Well, Plato's. He separated all the activities into two great classes. I could have saved myself a lot of work if I had read Plato before I started trying to make sense of my precepts. Afterwards, reading Plato, I thought, "Hey, hey. He got here first!" I pay tribute to him, incidentally, by using the terms "Guardian" and "Commercial." But Plato doesn't entirely agree with my precepts.

WARREN: Where do you differ?

JACOBS: Plato doesn't allow for self-appointed Guardians. His system is sometimes called fascistic. It's really a paradigm of the whole idea of caste. And some castes have been very Platonic; old Japan's was. He thought you could only be in the Guardian class by birth, you couldn't switch back and forth. He is a precedent because he said all injustice and the worst harm to the State came from mingling the two kinds of work. He seems to have thought that no one human was capable of doing both kinds well. I certainly disagree with him there. People have often done both kinds of work well and been moral in each kind. Benjamin Franklin is a marvelous example.

WARREN: Yet it is possible to read the *Republic* and *Laws* in another way: to take the State as a metaphor of the human soul.

JACOBS: Yes, but I think Plato fell into a trap—and this is very arrogant of me to talk this way, I know—but he did. He fell into the trap of trying to unify everything, so he had to warp and ignore things to make them fit. Taking and trading cannot be unified. They can be symbiotic.

I think philosophers in general have emphasized two things: what virtuous ruling is and what the virtuous private life is. They have tried to reconcile these, and to some extent you can. But the philosophic tradition has been to ignore commerce and its system of morals. I think that is because philosophers are self-appointed Guardians. When they have not ignored the whole Commercial syndrome, they have regarded it as ignoble or secondary. That's why I bridled when you wanted to put Guardians first and Commercial second. You're very Guardian-minded. Political scientists too. They beat their brains about government and other Guardian affairs—and trade as an aspect of government policy. But they are neither much interested in commerce nor respectful of it in its own right.

WARREN: And yet Adam Smith was a philosopher.

JACOBS: Adam Smith was extraordinary. A great many economists since Adam Smith—and Smith had a tincture of this himself, but less than many who came after—have actually identified with the Guardian syndrome because they advised rulers. Advisors to commerce are what we call microeconomists, advisors to Guardians tend to be macroeconomists. And these latter think that Guardians can manage an economy.

The macro-picture isn't more important than the micro-picture. The macro-picture is made up from the micro-picture.

WARREN: You have yourself "worked up the ranks" from microeconomics.

JACOBS: It isn't a matter of rank, of intellectual hierarchy. The macro-picture isn't more important than the micro-picture. The macro-picture is made up from the micro-picture.

I think Plato had hold of a great truth in distinguishing Guardian people from Commercial people, if he had only carried further his analyses of the reasons for distinctions between Guardian and Commercial *functions*. But you can't expect one man to do everything, when there was no one before him to lay the ground. What I find amazing is that nobody took up those insights of Plato's and pursued them to their logical conclusions.

HOW GUARDIANS GROW

WARREN: It strikes me that open-mindedness is not a quality of either syndrome; that a person may be open-minded from whichever vantage.

JACOBS: Well, you can look at this in another way and say, isn't it sad that you have to regard someone as open-minded who can see things from both these vantage points? Every normal person is capable of taking and trading. And so, if we want to talk about what is natural, it is natural not only to do both things, but both things correctly. The fact that some people cannot see the other syndrome at all, or see it only as evil, or that they can't work correctly within the other syndrome, or within either, means that a natural capacity of human beings has been warped or suppressed by indoctrination and education. And this is a terrible indictment of our system of education. Little children are capable of taking—they grab things from each other, they play cops and robbers, they love Robin Hood, they can identify empathetically and sympathetically with the whole taking side. They make heroes of takers like Robin Hood.

WARREN: They are naturally conservative.

JACOBS: To some extent, but they also love novelty. They are also capable of exchanging and trading. When I was a child, we played pirates and made people walk the plank from an old stump and that sort of thing. But we also did things like trading cards. Ours were election cards with the candidates' pictures on them. We would trade them. Children naturally trade from a very early age. They love lawn sales and lemonade stands. They are capable of both ways of getting a living, unless one is stamped out of them before they can even try.

WARREN: You said once that there are two kinds of education: apprenticeship, in which the teacher is a role model; and the old aristocratic form where the teacher is the social inferior of the student: Aristotle teaching the young Alexander, or the poor English governess with her privileged charges.

JACOBS: You can also be an apprentice to a commercial system. But our schools for the most part are Guardian institutions. They want obedience, they want loyalty, they want hierarchy among their own functionaries; they're bureaucracies, and the larger they get, the more bureaucratic they become. Children in elementary school are being apprenticed to the teacher. The children who do best there are quite commonly little girls who want to be teachers too when they grow up. By the time they are in high school, they're being apprenticed to bureaucrats, and the ones who do best are fitted to become bureaucrats. That's what we apprentice promising children for—and that's what universities traditionally have done, trained students to be Guardians, either for the Church (which founded most of the universities) or for the State.

I think it significant that science came into universities very late, as did technological vocations. The old universities, like Oxford and Cambridge, taught classics and the things that would make people suitable members of Parliament and the bench and bar. Science was beneath them. The first scientific schools arose out of separate schools of technology. Only recently have universities begun to assimilate them. Science became intellectually respectable and unignorable, and so you got things like the Cavendish Laboratories, the physics departments in American universities, and natural history—which was first called natural philosophy.*

A great evil of our school system is again derived from Guardian principles, and that is the separation of junior high— the students of the seventh, eighth, and ninth grades—from the rest. This is a hierarchical, an army point of view. Junior highs are awful places. Children are troublesome at that age. The idea was to isolate them, but that didn't civilize them. During adolescence, you want all the civilizing influences possible. You want to cultivate in adolescents care for the younger children, and expose them to aspirations that can be imparted by the older ones. I think the terrible decline of the public education system dates from that separation. By the time they get into high school, the kids have been through a bad experience in junior high.

WARREN: What about the old aristocratic education?

JACOBS: I got that idea from Ivan Illich, though it's right in front of everyone's nose.† Talking one day, he said that the great

---

*   Cavendish Laboratories is the Department of Physics at the University of Cambridge, founded in 1874.

†   Ivan Illich (1926–2002) was a philosopher, perhaps best known for his 1971 book *Deschooling Society,* a radical critique of institutionalized, universal education. Aside from her firsthand experience as a parent, Jacobs certainly learned about the challenges of public schools, as well as potential alternatives, during her time as the editor of schools for *Architectural Forum.* For instance, an unbylined June 1956 article titled "Tomorrow's High School"

educators of modern times are not only in service to students, they are in awe of the students' capacities and originality and charm. They even regard themselves as inferiors in that sense. He thought that was why they were such inspired teachers.

WARREN: Why has education gotten this way? Is it through neglect of the principles of "education through art," as expounded from Plato through Sir Herbert Read?*

JACOBS: I would say because the school is a Guardian institution, making the mistake that everybody should follow its principles. Now, what is right for a school system is not necessarily right for students. Art, to my mind, didn't arise from an educational system at all, it has been appropriated. It's been so much appropriated that it has come to be thought basic to education. But if you follow that to its logical extreme, schools and learning and work become play. And maybe you never learned to read because it was work, or you didn't do math, which is hard for many people. I'm convinced that art came from leisure. Hunters have a great deal of leisure time, as do women gatherers, at least in groups that exist today, and we may assume that this was true in the past. It was necessary for them to take time off, for otherwise they would overexploit their territories to no economic purpose. They would exterminate their prey.

(*Architectural Forum* 104) discusses the experimental "Random Falls" model for high school education, which incorporates learning spaces into the fabric of the town and citizens of the surrounding community into the classroom experience. In its practical, open-ended, community-based approach, this proposal foreshadows Jacobs's commentary here and the more radically decentralized peer learning networks proposed by Illich.

* Sir Herbert Read (1893–1968) was a poet and critic whose life work was advocating arts-based education for youth.

So what do you do with leisure time? You can lie around, and your capabilities will deteriorate and it's unpleasant and dull. Or you can pursue things that are demanding and interesting but have no economic purpose. And that is what sports and games are, and also what a great deal of art is. You find art in the most primitive groups (by our terms) of hunters and gatherers; also storytelling, religious rituals, dancing, and making music, making beautiful things that are neither sold nor supported by patronage, really art for art's sake. In Guardian organizations throughout history you find jesters and troubadours, cathedrals and costumes and tournaments; the aristocratic tradition of the amateur. The aristocrats didn't patronize technology and technologists, the people who made the windmills and so on. A lot of science, probably most of it, comes out of questions raised by technology. If that had been left up to Guardians, science would still be narrowly metaphysical.

OF RABBIS AND RESTAURANTS

WARREN: Baudelaire said that no economy has yet been invented that makes room for poets.

JACOBS: He has gotten hold of a sad but important truth there. Of course, places have to be made for them. But art and sports, if I am correct, arose neither from taking nor trading, they are outside. They were a form of not taking, specifically, and to this day artists have a hard time finding ways to support themselves. From the beginning, artists didn't support themselves by art, they supported themselves by the hunting or whatever else.

WARREN: For centuries rabbis had to have a trade.

JACOBS: Yes, and many artists today find the same necessity. They work in the post office and write poetry or music outside. Actors commonly work in restaurants. Often art brings only part of an artist's living: it is a catch-as-catch-can thing. Patronage has been extremely important to artists, and also to governments, to rulers in general, for patronage often commands loyalty to a territory and a regime. All kinds of arts—music, dance, drama, novels, poetry, sculpture—give human meaning to a territory, and a territory or a regime without art, if you can imagine such a thing, would command very little loyalty. People wouldn't feel much attachment to it.

WARREN: The amount of largesse poured by the province of Ontario into the SkyDome, for instance, makes sense in your scheme.*

JACOBS: It is a perfectly natural thing, and it is also perfectly natural that the province, city, and Metro contribute to the Toronto Arts Council. All civilized regimes support the arts, and the fact that they have gone from feudalism and various kinds of autocracies to democracies doesn't make any difference.

WARREN: I think of a remark in one of Baudelaire's Salons. He sees a policeman beating an anarchist in the street, and says in his heart: "Thump on, thump harder, thump again. O beloved

* A stadium in downtown Toronto named for its distinctive retractable roof, the Sky-Dome opened in 1989. Though rechristened the Rogers Centre in 2005, many Torontonians still call it by its old name.

constable! The man you have in your hands is an enemy of literature and fine art!" Through the Thatcher-and-Reagan years I noticed how artists adhered to the State, how they ran in horror from business and the specter of "privatization." Afraid of being orphaned, they clung to the devil they knew.

JACOBS: Of course there is a great danger here. The State can, as the Soviet Union did, show great disrespect for artists by demanding obedience. But artists are really outside both syndromes and when *Artists must look after* they are forced to be instruments of the *themselves to preserve* State it is bad for art, and bad for artists, *their freedom.* quite as bad as when they are forced to commercialize art or debase it for the sake of commercial income. In Canada we've been very good about dispensing government funds to artists at arm's length.

Artists must look after themselves to preserve their freedom. They have to care about it, they have to be more devoted to their art than they are to anybody's politics or attempt to use them in service. Much commercial support of the arts is really commercial advertising.

WARREN: And that is also a kind of corruption, is it not? I've seen so many talented but unassertive people wasted in some form of commercial advertising.

JACOBS: I don't mean in advertising itself. I mean when you see on public television this oil or that pharmaceutical company is supporting this particular edition of *Masterpiece Theatre*—that's a form of commercial advertising. It's institutional advertising and it can be done at arm's length too. Sometimes it's surprising to see what they have paid for. Take the cigarette companies that sponsor sports and art events: when it is suggested that it is not appropriate for a cigarette company to be extolled, that they should continue giving to these events but that the company's name should be omitted—Whoosh! All that funding is going to disappear. This is what terrifies a lot of arts groups here who depend to quite an extent on tobacco. Now if it were real charity, if it was really done for love of the sport or the art, the company would say, sure you don't need to use our name. No, no, no, if their name isn't advertised, they aren't going to fund it.

WARREN: But I was thinking of the patronage that consists of actually employing people: industrial designers, packaging experts, ad illustrators, etc. It is in the nature of the Commercial syndrome to be industrious, to put things to practical use; to get people painting chocolate boxes instead of chapel ceilings.

JACOBS: Don't be scornful of all this. For a long time, high-minded people were scornful of the movies because they were commercial. It took time for them to go back and look at early films and see how marvelous some of them were as works of art; to see what an artist Charlie Chaplin was, or Buster Keaton. Art appears where it appears and there is no use being snobbish about it.

WARREN: Artists themselves often say that they have been prostituted.

JACOBS: Some do and some don't, and you are being snobbish without reason, without looking at the particular case.

WARREN: But you're leaving us Guardians with the army and the police and precious little else. Now you're trying to take art away from us.

JACOBS: It never did belong to Guardians economically. It was *not* taking, that's the difficulty of the whole thing. That's why artists have to get by as best they can, and it is no more demeaning per se to take money from a businessman than from another kind of patron. It's what the artist does with his time and his opportunity that is, or is not, debased.

WARREN: What about the preservative function of art, for even when it appears most original and revolutionary, great art embodies and develops a tradition.

JACOBS: Certainly. Someone as highly original as Shakespeare was working within a tradition; the Dutch painters of domestic scenes, streets and markets, were very radical in their day, but they too worked within a tradition, and the same artists also did classical and religious paintings. Art works usually within traditional contexts, and great artists are apt to be people who have discerned new possibilities within the traditions. There is a kind of originality which deliberately wants to jettison all tradition, and it is quite evident in our times, although not as much is jettisoned as is often thought. I think of Virginia Woolf, who was radical in her idea of the novel. At the time this didn't appeal to many people. But she was working within the tradition of fine literature which she greatly respected and loved, and as time has gone by people have more and more appreciated what she did. So artists can be ahead of their time as we say, yet also within the greater or encompassing tradition.

Now when tradition is jettisoned in anger or vainglory by any of the forms of art, an ironic thing happens—it tends to become dated very quickly. When modern architecture eschewed ornament and put itself on stilts and made itself into boxes and dropped all recognized symbolism, it dated very quickly.

BUYING CIVILIZATION

WARREN: Then put this another way. Coleridge, that penetrating conservative, defended institutions, including apparently pointless ones, that symbolize important things. Take the Canadian Senate. Perhaps it is worth two hundred million a year simply as symbol for the idea of "sober second thought," even if its meetings are confined to ritual.*

JACOBS: Let's stop there a minute. The Senate has another very practical function. There are people who work at politics very hard, or have done so in the past, yet they aren't in elected jobs.

---

* The Senate is Canada's upper house of Parliament. Much like in the American Congress, Canada's senators are intended to equally represent the regions of the country, counterbalancing the lower level (the House of Commons), in which Members of Parliament are popularly elected. However, in Canada, senators are appointed by the governor general on the advice of the prime minister, making the office an ideal—and controversial—tool of both partisanship and patronage. As of 2016, the debate over Senate reform is ongoing.

What kind of jobs do you find for such people? They have to make a living. You need institutions to support such people. On a lesser scale, in New York there used to be "pothole inspectors." They were ward political leaders, they were important and they worked hard, pulled their weight in the political system, sometimes for good and sometimes for ill. How were they going to be supported? They were supported, in that case, by phony jobs. Well, you can't just leave such people adrift. If you don't have a Senate, you might make them judges, and that would be worse.

WARREN: Yet we have a long tradition of government monopolies, and monopoly franchises. Are there no natural monopolies? What about railways?

JACOBS: The really important, vital government monopoly is over the use of force. All civilized governments must strive constantly to monopolize vengeance and force. To the extent that they don't succeed—private murders or extortions, robberies, organized crime, terrorist groups, vigilantes, lynching mobs, or the like—civilization and its securities have broken down. Of course governments can be uncivilized themselves in use of force—that's all too clear—but that doesn't negate the need for government monopoly over force in civilized regimes.

But to extend monopoly powers to things like railways or the mail service, which are basically commercial, is pretty ridiculous. You see, it is perfectly clear that the railway competes with airlines, with buses, and with private cars. And so why not with other railways? There is no natural monopoly in transportation.

WARREN: In Thatcher, and Reagan, we had the paradox of politicians coming to power on the promise of less government, more commerce. Yet when you study Thatcher, especially, you realize what a Guardian type she was—"Attila the Hen" they called her. Given this paradox, is it possible for privatization to succeed?

JACOBS: Yes. Privatization doesn't inevitably fail.

WARREN: Or if it works practically, must it fail politically?

JACOBS: It all depends. You have to think what is being privatized and how. For example, if Ontario Hydro were to stick to distributing electric power, and let go of generating, that would be privatizing the generation of power, and where that distinction has been made, between distribution and generation, it has worked rather well. But you have to know what it is you are privatizing and how you're doing it.

The Canadian government used to disallow competition to the mail service, but this became impossible to enforce because the mail service became so lousy. Private couriers sprang up, and the government itself was embarrassed at using them when it had urgent things to deliver. It gave up on the monopoly, so you might say the mail service has been partially privatized. Now, you can call making the old Post Office a crown corporation a kind of halfway house of privatization but that is a different thing.

WARREN: And seldom a satisfactory thing. It still isn't a business, trying to maximize profits. Yet it has lost that spirit which

Herodotus attributed to the Persian post-riders: "Neither snow nor rain nor heat nor gloom of night stays these couriers from the swift completion of their appointed rounds."

JACOBS: And when they had morale and were younger and didn't have as much business, the mail services used to be extremely honest. Part of the breakdown of morale, the inefficiency, the lackadaisicalness, is that you can't trust postal systems anymore; things get stolen all the time.

WARREN: I spoke recently with a retired customs officer who made the same point: that customs officers now routinely bill the government for things that used to come out of their pockets, such as cab fares. They no longer dream of saving taxpayers' money. He said that the old ethic was conveyed by heredity—the son of a customs officer often became a customs officer. The tradition of public service was bred in the son from childhood.

JACOBS: Well, there are societies where it is customary to give bribes and people bred to public service take in that tradition from childhood. They've traditionally breached the Guardian precept to shun trading.

WARREN: But ours wasn't one of them. Another example came up the other day: a Jamaican lady I know owns a roti shop. She had to pay a bribe to get a liquor license. She thought that sort of thing didn't happen in Canada.

JACOBS: This is specifically a corruption of the precepts on trading, because a bribe is a trade.

By the way, the catch in that hereditary thing, the customs officer's son becoming a customs officer, is if you get people doing jobs because it is expected, you get a lot of square pegs in round holes. You get artists who are forced into business.

WARREN: So how do we revive that Guardian code, that sense of honor, when it has fallen through cynicism into disuse?

JACOBS: That is one reason I wrote the book. I think people have gotten very confused about what is proper to do in association with different functions and they need to be un-confused about these things. For heaven's sake, they need to *know* when they are doing wrong.

WARREN: Have we not been systematically corrupted by excessive taxation?

JACOBS: Parkinson went into that.* In fact, he went so far as to tell what percentages of taxes are small enough that people will pay them as a matter of course. The old feudal authorities that used to tax the commerce that went through their territories normally kept it low enough, he said, to prevent evasion or rebellion. Then it got higher.

WARREN: One imagines a sociology of taxation.

---

* The Parkinson in question is probably C. Northcote Parkinson (1909–93), a humorist and critic of bureaucracy and taxation best known for Parkinson's Law: "Work expands so as to fill the time available for its completion." Jacobs is likely citing one of his less-known books, *The Law and the Profits* (1960), which revolved around another law: "Expenditure rises to meet income."

JACOBS: I don't. Sociology had a subject, supposedly, which is the science of society. That's how it justified itself, how it got the *-ology* on its name. Sociologists never have made a science of their subject, they just do busy work. I'm afraid this will sound conceited, but our present discussion has more to do with the science of society than sociology does.*

WARREN: Agreed. Sociology is death. So back to taxes.

JACOBS: Parkinson says that when they reach a certain percentage—I forget what—then a lot of people begin cheating. This is, of course, very bad for the general moral tone of a country. And when they get still higher practically everyone cheats or finds loopholes. Oliver Wendell Holmes said that he positively liked paying taxes because he thought he was buying civilization and that is a nice feeling.† I *used* to have that feeling. When Holmes was writing, taxes were relatively low. Who feels that any more? And yet a good part of our taxes do go to buying civilization. But what about all these government-supported

---

* Jacobs often mentioned her frustrations with sociology, which date back at least to her days in the late 1930s at Columbia University, where she took an unimpressive class on the subject. Also sociology, particularly at midcentury, the heyday of the social sciences, tends toward the deductive—analyzing people and society through theoretical categories—rather than Jacobs's preferred inductive method, in which she argues up the scale, so to speak, from individual clues to overarching conclusions. Ironically, the book she would be most remembered for, *Death and Life,* often carried a subject recommendation for stores to shelve it in the sociology section.

† Oliver Wendell Holmes (1841–1935) was a Justice of the U.S. Supreme Court and continues to be one of the most cited jurists and legal writers in history. His particular brand of realism and his knack for aphorisms must have spoken to Jacobs, since she chose his words for the epigraph of *Death and Life,* summed up in the phrase: "Life is an end in itself, and the only question as to whether it is worth living is whether you have enough of it."

commercial megaprojects? They're pork barrels. I think that the government cons itself into believing that they are productive. And now billions are going into these things and other types of subsidies to commerce.

WARREN: There was a headline in the *Star* the other day: "NDP's $1 Billion Job Creation Project Nets 670 Jobs."

JACOBS: So you aren't buying civilization, you're buying nothing but waste and demoralization, which are certainly anticivilization.

WARREN: But only right-wing governments seem to understand that excessive taxation is demoralizing, in the full sense of that word: that it not only discourages citizens, but undermines their sense of right and wrong.

JACOBS: You were speaking about the Fall of Man earlier. There are certain levels of temptation that hardly anybody can resist, and it is well recognized that to entrap people by putting a temptation in their way is an immoral thing to do. You can look at taxes in that way: they reach a level where you are, in effect, tempting people so badly you are entrapping. And since the Guardians are supposed to look out for the moral and spiritual well-being of the people in their territories, this is an outrageous thing.

WARREN: And once corruption enters the soul it spreads like cancer.

JACOBS: Yes! And this theological notion—that when corruption enters in one place it soon gets into others—is that dynamic I tried to explain in mingling syndromes. Other precepts are automatically corrupted, and still others fall by the wayside in expedience.

WARREN: Economists sometimes argue that one kind of taxation is more progressive than another. Do you have preferences?

JACOBS: In general, taxes levied on the principle of ability to pay based upon size of income are progressive. You certainly don't want to charge very poor people as much for support of the schools, or whatever the taxes are going to, as you do people who have higher incomes. But taxes have been so manipulated for trying to accomplish so many other purposes than just giving support to public facilities and needs that they are in a terrible mess and have all kinds of injustices attached to them. But that is partly inevitable if the sheer level of taxation increases too much: because then the loopholes come, then the injustices come, then the cheating comes.

WARREN: Any government that wants to reduce taxes will run into the problems Reagan had with Congress. The president thought: If I deny them tax increases, they'll have to curb their spending. But Congress spent more anyway, then blamed Reagan for the deficit.

JACOBS: Well, it becomes a vicious circle because when the taxes become insupportable you get a point where the yield goes down partly from cheating and partly from practical reasons.

WARREN: Sounds supply-side to me.

JACOBS: Obviously. I was reading the other day about the miners in Siberia. The State takes four-fifths of their output, but the rest they are now free to export. This, it was thought, would increase their production and incomes so that the State would not have to pay so much. But what the mines there have to pay in taxes, in various duties on the portion they export for hard currency, exceeds the amount they can get in hard currency. This is an extreme and ridiculous case of taxes reaching a point of utter insupportability. In Sweden, taxes have gotten so high that one of the great worries of the government is the tremendous amount of barter. People find their own loopholes if the State does not create them.

People find their own loopholes if the State does not create them.

SUCCESS THROUGH FAILURE

WARREN: But you still haven't told me if there is any form of taxation that you find intrinsically wicked.

JACOBS: A family business may be very small or middle or large size. Unless it is very small, death duties can compel sale of the business to pay the tax. Then the business is likely to pass to a conglomerate or to a very large organization. Thus, those death duties help lead to centralization of economic power. Now, that was probably not the intent at first; by now maybe it is the intent. There are groups that have a vested interest in that happening, in being able to pick up companies in a distressed buyer's market.

Another thing of this kind: if you contribute money to a registered charity you can take it off your tax. That pretty much compels giving contributions to organizations that have this imprimatur, yet there are lots of organizations that don't have it; this is a way of centralizing charitable power. Why should just approved charitable organizations have the power to give donors a tax break? Yet if government doesn't vet the groups, we may be sure charlatans and rascals would make a racket of these tax breaks. This is an example of the complexities, discriminations, and unsalutary side effects, inevitably built into all attempts to use taxation methods for social engineering purposes as distinguished from raising revenue. Guardians have plenty of leeway for social engineering in their use of largesse, the *yield* from revenues.

WARREN: Toronto has recently had a storm over property taxes, an attempt by the suburban boroughs to impose "Market Value Assessment" over the dead bodies of inner city ratepayers. What's wrong with it?

JACOBS: Well, certain forms of taxation are inimical to cities, and that is serious because cities are the most fertile ground for new businesses, innovations, all the things you must have if you are not going to stagnate. And the little businesses depend a lot upon each other or they can't function. This is the great commercial value of cities, that there are places where this can happen. This makes city land valuable, these concentrations and these opportunities, not only the land but the buildings. As soon as you attempt to base a tax on that kind of value, you are doing social engineering so counterproductive that it undercuts the whole advantage of cities.

WARREN: The glib argument in Metro Council was, "We are only adopting a system that many American cities have tried," and of course any intelligent person who happened to be watching would flinch to think what happened in those cities.

JACOBS: Value-added taxes are also very bad for cities and for innovations. Value-added taxes are a sales tax on every transaction of a business. Now, a large company with many of its services and supplies self-contained doesn't have to pay its value-added tax until the end of that process. A firm that depends on a lot of outside suppliers has to keep paying the value-added tax at each stage of the transaction. It particularly strikes at the advantages and the necessities of city commerce and production. I think the people who make up these taxation systems don't understand this at all.

WARREN: I take it this argument applies to the federal government's much-admired Goods and Services Tax.

JACOBS: Small city businesses are often held in contempt— they aren't megaprojects, you see—and they're called "mom-and-pop" stores. A city's business does not exist on mom-and-pop stores; it floats on a lot of other work underneath.

WARREN: Large organizations like to deal with other large organizations, such as governments. Whereas small businessmen are not equipped for the demands of large bureaucracies. In this case the large bureaucracy expects the mom-and-pop store to meet the same reporting requirements as a multinational.

JACOBS: And that's an added cost for them. And even if they can meet these bureaucratic demands, the fact that it has to be done so many times over is a great added cost.

WARREN: So what should we do? Have a tax revolt?

JACOBS: In the end I think we have to depend on more understanding of how these Guardian measures work and, in this case, don't work. And here we have so many economists and lawyers who ought to understand these things and obviously don't. Again, you might say that their education has been bad.

A STATE OF FINE CONFUSION

WARREN: Has the way you work changed over the years?

JACOBS: No, it hasn't changed, and that is one reason why I'm slow. When I start a book I have an idea, but it is not well developed. I don't know what I'm looking for, and by the end I find that I haven't written the book I expected because my ideas have changed. If I had known what I was getting into I would never have gotten in. There are so many more ramifications and clues and keys to things that you can't anticipate. Since I don't really know what I'm doing when I start, I read as omnivorously as I can, and listen to people, and look at things. It is a state of great confusion. But I've learned to trust myself about what is interesting, because so often I'd be interested in something but would consider it beside the point. I would say to myself, "Come on, get back to work," and throw this thing away, try to put it out of my mind. And then I would find later that I needed exactly that thing. It was germane. I've learned to trust myself—if I'm interested in something, to regard it as of potential value.

I read as omnivorously as I can, and listen to people, and look at things. It is a state of great confusion.

I just keep on, despite confusion, and I often try writing at an early stage because writing is, for me, a rigorous form of thinking. When you put things down on those blank sheets of paper you find the holes in what you suppose. I do a lot of drafts, and a lot of discarding, and often realize that my organization is wrong, that very important things must be told *before* what I thought I could begin with. In *The Economy of Cities* I was going to begin with what turned out to be the fifth chapter. Every time I wrote I would start digressing, and when you digress so much, something is wrong with your organization. What was wrong was that my digressions were essential, but bad initial organization forced their displacement.

WARREN: This is what every original thinker must do. Flounder.

JACOBS: The one thing I haven't told you is that in the midst of this confusion I am always tempted to throw everything I have into one of those green garbage bags and get rid of it. I get in such despair sometimes. It is so uncomfortable to be in this confusion, but there are two reasons why I don't throw it all away. What else would I do then? Also, I'll always be in this confusion if I don't work it out. So I don't throw it away. I just keep on.*

WARREN: Sheer Guardian will.

JACOBS: Well, it's worse to stop than to keep on. Certain patterns begin to announce themselves. It's not that I think them up; I'm not consciously thinking about them. Whish! There they are, and that's exciting.

WARREN: But it was you who spotted them.

JACOBS: They were there all the time, but I didn't spot them until a certain point. I'm very slow and full of trial and error and plodding and I wish I knew some faster, more efficient way to work, but experience hasn't taught me any.

WARREN: Would it be fair to say that you have participated in a late twentieth century rethinking of "scientific method": a resurgence of teleological reasoning, if I may be so bold?

JACOBS: Actually, I think that what is called the scientific method often works the way I do. You don't know. By the time you know

---

* Although Jacobs never threw away her writing entirely, she did make a habit of throwing out entire drafts of her books and starting from scratch. According to her son Jim, she used writing as a way to think through her subject matter, so when she found an error in reasoning while editing her work, she took it as a sign that she needed to think it through again.

what you are looking for, you've already found it. You can't know ahead of time what you are going to discover. How can you find out, except by fiddling around?

WARREN: Yet the one universal feature of the scientific method, no matter where you start, is that you end at: Eureka!

JACOBS: Yeah, that's right. You know the man who discovered penicillin. He was propagating various bacteria in Petri dishes and molds got into some of them and killed the bacteria. And that was not what he was looking for. He regarded the ones that were contaminated as worthless. And he put this away for about eighteen years, and then suddenly it struck him—*Eureka!* The molds are killing bacteria. *Hey!*

WARREN: Why do you use the dialogue form in *Systems of Survival*?

JACOBS: I started to write the book like my other ones, in essay form, and got bored with that. And I always am carrying on dialogues in my own head. All my life I have had a couple of imaginary companions: Thomas Jefferson and Benjamin Franklin. Since I was a little girl I've been carrying on dialogues with them in my head just to keep from being bored, so it was natural for me to think of the dialogue form when I got bored with writing a long, long essay. At first I dismissed it as ridiculous, because I didn't know anything about writing dialogue and so on.

This is another example where you have to trust yourself when you are interested. More and more I thought: If something is going to rescue us it will be people talking to each other about moral questions, and not shoving them under the rug, or thinking that if they are told to do something wrong the choice is either to exit, or to shut up and do it. I don't think that is satisfactory. People should talk about these things.

If something is going to rescue us it will be people talking to each other about moral questions, and not shoving them under the rug.

Dialogue is the natural form for this subject, because people have to struggle with it: they have second thoughts; there are qualifications; wisdom comes out of experience. It is no accident that writing on moral questions has often been in the form of dialogue. It is suited to the subject matter. I'm not an artist but I like to have my form agree with the content, and I like it to conceal the labor that went into it.

WARREN: And why was the dialogue set in New York?

JACOBS: I began by imagining it here in Toronto. The characters were not much formed in my mind, and as Canadians they didn't work. Canadians are so polite. I like this politeness and, in comparison, New York is much less gentle and even cruel. I had to have characters who would raise their objections right then and there, and not try to paper them over or change the subject. So I converted them to New York characters and, like the characters in a novel, they then began to take on a life of their own.

WARREN: Perhaps the dialogue form is inevitable for philosophy. You sense this reading even the *Critique of Pure Reason*. Each idea, or interest, assumes a dramatic personality. Not even Kant can quite suppress it, though he tries to be impregnably dull.

They have their entrances and their exits, and between they squabble like players on a stage.

JACOBS: So they could be characters. I don't think I was successful at changing prose rhythms for my different speakers. Although many readers of prose don't realize it, if prose has a rhythm it carries you along and if it doesn't, it's obnoxious. An author has a rhythm that is unconscious, it is a component of style even when the style is as transparent as Edmund Wilson's.* He has a wonderful transparent style! You are not conscious of it, but it has a rhythm. It is Wilson's voice. I tried to differentiate my characters' speech, but I was unable to do it in the fundamental way I would have liked to. It would have been better to give each character his own idiosyncratic prose rhythm. That is what masters of dialogue do.

WARREN: A good writer reads better to others than to herself. Often your dialogue continues for pages without a character being identified, and I, for one, never lost track of who was speaking.

JACOBS: I'm glad to hear that.

WARREN: "Morals" is the word in your title—Moral Foundations, not Ethical. Why?

---

* Edmund Wilson (1895–1972) was an influential American writer, literary critic, and cultural commentator. He was at various points an editor at *Vanity Fair* and *The New Republic* and the chief book critic for *The New Yorker*. He wrote more than twenty books, including *Axel's Castle* (1931), *To the Finland Station* (1940), and *Patriotic Gore* (1962).

JACOBS: I think it is more embracing than the word *ethics*. Ethics has taken on a meaning of such little pettifogging things in many instances, like classes on ethics—journalistic ethics, medical ethics. . . .

WARREN: Ethics are for people who lack morals, morals for people who lack love.

JACOBS: No, love goes against both syndromes. It's untamed.

WARREN: It is "above" both syndromes.

JACOBS: I don't say it is above them, I say outside them. Again I'm being down-to-earth. I'm not trying to be hierarchical. You keep wanting to put all these things in a hierarchy. I don't see it that way. I see them all as components of life and who's to say that one is superior to the other, or under what circumstances? Love is outside the syndromes, not above.

WARREN: Nevertheless, we grasp truth through love. This is something you've touched on in each of your books, though usually indirectly.

JACOBS: I think it is a big mistake for people to try to reform something they hate, because their destructive feeling will ooze into what they prescribe. That was one of the great troubles with city planning; it was formed by people who really hated cities and they couldn't help but be destructive to them. People who love cities ought to be doing the planning for them. Marx detested the Commercial syndrome, yet tried to prescribe for commerce, production, and trade. You wouldn't want a doctor who doesn't like human beings—well, women sometimes run across doctors like that. You want people who value the objects of their ministrations. So love, or respect, whichever is appropriate, is extremely important. I don't deny that.

I think it is a big mistake for people to try to reform something they hate, because their destructive feeling will ooze into what they prescribe.

WARREN: Perhaps I can ask what lies ahead. You have followed what in retrospect seems a very clear path; does it begin to seem clear in prospect?

JACOBS: It was not obvious at all. I wish it had been.

WARREN: There is a wonderful consistency of direction in your writings, from the earliest journalism on parks and city corners through the organism of cities to the principles of public life: the vantage rises and rises. . . .

JACOBS: Not so much up but outward.

WARREN: Okay, "outward," I give up. What lies further out?

JACOBS: You're asking what my next book is going to be about, if I do one? I'm not really sure. I have a couple of ideas, but it would be premature to bring them up. I'm not a prophet about anything in the world, and I'm not a prophet about myself.

WARREN: All your life you have asserted the value of youth, of a generational change. You have tried to see old things in a new light. Now, what are the advantages of age over youth?

JACOBS: One of the advantages of age is that so many loose ends get tied up. You see things that happened earlier and how they turned out, and you see things that

One of the advantages of age is that so many loose ends get tied up.

mystified you and then later developments that helped demystify them. And just the experience of living a long time dumps into your lap and your head a whole lot of interesting information that, by the nature of things, you can't get in a short life. My knees are creaky and my eyes aren't as good, but on the whole, I don't resist getting older because I want to see how things turn out. And eventually, of course, I'm going to die, and my great regret is that I won't see how so many things next happened.

First Letter to the
Consumer Policy Institute

ENERGY PROBE RESEARCH
FOUNDATION NEWSLETTER, 1994

Dear Probe Supporter,

Affordable, convenient public transit is vital, yet Canadian cities
are plagued with costly, inadequate systems. Time and again,
transit managements and politicians with public funds at their
disposal embrace foolish, extravagant policies while ignoring
common-sense alternatives and neglecting innovative thinking.
Those decisions are paid for in higher fares, lost customers, rotten
service, tax subsidies and lost opportunities. The environment
pays in over-use of automobiles, pollution, energy waste and
exorbitant urban sprawl.

It used to be reasoned that public service monopolies would
benefit from lack of "wasteful" competition and economies of
scale. They don't. The post office is a notorious example. Only
when that monopoly began to break down did many badly needed
innovations from independent businesses become available. Or
consider long-distance passenger rail services: they are a disgrace,
forever deteriorating yet becoming more costly.

To govern well, governments must neither monopolize commercial services themselves nor foster monopolies by others. Government needs to be independent of business to avoid conflicts of

interest that prevent honest regulation or invite corruption.* Good service delivery must be responsive to customers' ever-changing needs, not protected from customers by limiting their choices or evading failure by winning government favors. Hopping the gravy train is no way to run a railroad or any other successful commercial service.

Yet more and more we hear of government-industry projects and "partnerships" that cloud what should be arm's-length relationships between businesses and regulator. Little wonder that our federal and provincial capitals swarm with lobbyists for corporate interests that find it more profitable to court politicians than customers. Little wonder that the environment is victimized or that we become triple victims as consumers, taxpayers and citizens.

That's why the Energy Probe Research Foundation, of which I have been a director since its inception, has decided to establish a new division, the Consumer Policy Institute. Other groups within our Foundation deal primarily with environmental and resource policies. The Consumer Policy Institute will work for consumers with the aim of increasing fairness, choice, safety, reliability and affordability.

If you believe Canada needs an alert, research-oriented consumer watchdog and advocacy organization to take on powerful corporate interests and government monopolies, please join me in being a co-founder of this much-needed new agency.

Sincerely,
Jane Jacobs

---

* In *Systems of Survival,* Jacobs explores the mechanics of how the mingling of "commercial" and "guardian" values causes such "systemic moral corruption." See also "Two Ways to Live" in this volume.

Women as Natural Entrepreneurs

———

SPEECH AT THE CANADIAN WOMAN ENTREPRENEUR OF
THE YEAR AWARDS, METRO TORONTO CONVENTION
CENTRE, TORONTO, OCTOBER 29, 1994

I WANT TO BEGIN BY TOUCHING BRIEFLY ON THE PHENOMENON
of the glass ceiling—the ceiling that, as we all know, seems to
obstruct women from reaching our gender's share of top positions in business. Objectively speaking, that share ought to be
somewhere around fifty percent. It is closer to only a tenth of
that.

These wretched statistics are connected with entrepreneurship. Any entrepreneur who establishes an enterprise is, at least
for the time being, its proprietor. And by definition, proprietors
of businesses occupy top positions there. No glass ceiling there,
for them.

Most existing businesses in our country are run by males, no
matter what the enterprise's origins or its industry's early history may be.

Women are not the only people frustrated by glass ceilings.
Historically in North America, there have been obdurate glass
ceilings for people who belonged to religious minorities, like
Jews, or to Asian, Middle Eastern, Native American or African
races, or to some other ethnic groups such as Italians, Catholic
Irish or, in Canada, French Canadians.

For some groups the glass barrier has now dissolved, at least very appreciably; for some it has begun dissolving; and for some the ceiling remains paralyzingly obdurate.

When the ceiling does dissolve it does not do so because of wishing. It does not do so because legislation says it must. It does not do so because writers like me say it doesn't make sense. No; it dissolves because members of this or that group which couldn't breach the glass ceiling have taken to becoming proprietors of their own businesses, made successes of them, and continued to run them as they developed and grew. This is the significant avenue by which people in former out-groups are recognized as people of ability and merit, and are promoted as a matter-of-course on qualifications and merit. If no successful entrepreneurs and proprietors emerge in a given group, or very few—for whatever reason—members of that whole group remain stuck in middle management at best. Often enough, although they may resent it, they even accept that that is where they belong.

It is the same with members of our group, our gender. Few women both founded their own businesses and then saw to it that women continued to run them as they grew and developed, whether modestly or spectacularly.

This is odd because great numbers of women are natural entrepreneurs and probably always have been. Commercial cards and announcements that business people used in sixteenth and seventeenth [century] England included surprising numbers and varieties issued by businesswomen. They were proprietors in occupations such as importing and supplying other enterprises with fuel, let alone the more expectable dressmaking and purveying house furnishings.

Look at a market in an under-developed economy and notice how many of the stalls are presided over by women. Less visible, but just as real, are African and Caribbean women who are resourceful long-distance merchants in their economies, overwhelmingly more so than the men in their societies.

In Latin America, bankers who make micro-loans to small business enterprises have consistently found that well over half their borrowers are businesswomen, and that the proportion is growing.

A public service advertisement that repeatedly appears in *The Globe and Mail* encourages help from Canadian business people to foreign micro-entrepreneurs by making surplus and obsolete equipment available to them. The ad is adorned with an enthusiastic Latino man who is saying, "Give us the tools and we'll finish the job." I do not mean to carp at such admirable endeavors, but if *The Globe and Mail* were reflecting what is really happening out there, it would instead be running the picture of a woman saying, "Give us the tools and we'll finish the job." But then, after all, *The Globe and Mail* is directing its appeal to Canadian business executives and for that purpose it has probably chosen the right gender, both to make this program believable to them, and to avoid its ad becoming a target of snide double-entendres. Alas on both counts.

The larger and more successful today's micro-lending programs are, the greater the proportion, as well as the absolute number, of women entrepreneurs they serve. In Canada this has been happening with Native American programs.

The Grameen Bank in Bangladesh began lending to male micro-entrepreneurs without even contemplating that it would serve women. But in about fifteen years, during which

that bank proliferated into some 900 branches, providing business credit to about 900,000 borrowers, the proportion of
women borrowers swelled to 90 percent. That was two years
ago. Now, I hear, the percentage of women borrowers hovers
around 95 and 96 percent. All the more amazing because Bangladesh is a Muslim country in which the first women borrowers had to be extraordinarily brave and daring. The bank does
not discriminate against men. It is just that poor women have
been taking more naturally and swiftly to entrepreneurship
than men there.

To understand how that could be, one thing to ponder is
that the human race has typically organized itself so that women
have had certain traditional duties and men have had others.
Women's traditional work, from away back, not only included
feeding and other care of small children, but also most food
preparation and serving; spinning, weaving, dyeing, and sewing
cloth garments; leather tanning and making leather garments;
contriving bedding and other home comforts; laundering,
cleaning and improvising necessary equipment for that work;
midwifery and nursing the sick; fire tending and fuel gathering;
basket making; water carrying; preparing cosmetics . . . the list
could go on and on.

The nursery rhyme says:

> *Curly locks, curly locks, wilt thou be mine;*
> *Thou shalt not wash the dishes nor yet feed the swine.*
>   (obviously both women's work)
> *But sit on a cushion and sew a fine seam*
>   (more women's work)
> *And feed upon strawberries, sugar and cream.*

The cushion was a product of women's work, the cream was handled by a dairy-maid, and the strawberries were likely picked and hulled by women and children. The sugar may have been produced by slaves, both men and women.

In sum, most kinds of material production for everyday life was traditionally women's work. The greatest ranges of work, and therefore the greatest variety of skills, were in women's hands.

Men's traditional work included hunting, along with skinning and butchering or fleecing animals, herding relatively large animals such as cattle and sheep, waging war and conducting other military work, collecting taxes, making and enforcing laws, supervising religions, sea-faring, quarrying stone, constructing with stone and heavy wood, and mining and metal work.*

Although the work of collecting taxes and legislating burgeoned and warfare is obviously still much with us, much of the traditional male work has dwindled wherever economies have developed significantly. This is especially true as far as the traditional male economic contributions to everyday life are concerned. Hunting has become of little economic importance, taken in the whole. Animal herding uses few workers, taken in

---

*   Though she never says so explicitly, the way that Jacobs has divided up different kinds of work between women and men here mirrors the moral division she proposes in *Systems of Survival* between "commercial" and "guardian" work, respectively. In that book, Jacobs argues that the activities she associates with men in this speech—war, governing, hunting, and exploring—are guided by a set of moral precepts emphasizing loyalty, exclusiveness, and tradition, while material production and trade, which she associates with women, are guided by an opposing set of precepts favoring honesty, inclusiveness, and novelty. Jacobs here is suggesting that much of that commercial way of life originates in devalued domestic labor, which by her estimate has in most places for most of human history been the purview of women.

the whole. Stone, heavy wood and even metals count for smaller proportions of the materials we draw on now than they used to. In the meantime commercial derivatives and offshoots of traditional women's work have proliferated.

When Willie Sutton was asked why he robbed banks, he said, "Because that's where the money is." When we ask why so many micro-entrepreneurs in Bangladesh or Bolivia are women, it's because that's where the work is.

An economy like our own includes, by now, almost incomprehensibly vast amounts and varieties of traditional women's work and its derivatives, such as commercial food processing, preserving and preparation; textile and apparel industries; manufactured soap and all other appurtenances of laundering and cleaning; cosmetic industries; pharmaceutical corporations which are the direct derivatives of patent medicine companies which were direct offshoots from women's herbal concoctions initially put into commerce by women. Etcetera. Etcetera.

Suppose, hypothetically, that all the men in economically advanced societies like ours were suddenly to be deprived of everything but traditional men's work and its offshoots. No work for men making advertisements for cold remedies. No more work for lawyers who depend on corporate clients doing baking, cheese-making, canning, detergents. No French chefs and Savile Row tailors. No salesmen of sewing machines, refrigerators, hospital sterilizers. Even no work for manufacturers of metal or high-tech fiber cables, because cables of all kinds derived from strings, then rope, and strings, like baskets and straw mats, were traditionally women's products.

We can be glad that traditional women's work and its modern offshoots have assimilated so many men because otherwise such vast numbers of men would be economically redundant—just like so many men in badly underdeveloped economies who don't pull their weight economically while, at the same time, women there are busy, busy, busy.

I am not being far-fetched when I point out that instances of women's work emerging into commercial life speak loudly and insistently to us of businesswomen. Men typically shun women's work until it has shown it can be commercially lucrative, hence respectable. So in the nature of things women, not men, have had to initiate the process. To put the matter symbolically, few men anywhere go in for washing baby diapers by hand at home, and if they do they don't bruit it about. But men don't draw back from making pick-ups and deliveries for a commercial diaper service, or taking employment in a firm manufacturing disposable diapers. These jobs derive distantly from the work of women who long ago began earning money by taking in dirty laundry from the public.

Men typically shun women's work until it has shown it can be commercially lucrative, hence respectable.

If women naturally and readily take to entrepreneurship, and also have taken initiatives in converting unpaid household work into commercial life, we must ask: How come men have so often replaced those women as commercial proprietors? How did a glass ceiling in economic life ever manage to form and frustrate our gender?

The first men to be assimilated into women's microenterprises tend to be family members. To take one illustrative example, a poor woman in La Paz, Bolivia, took to making metal window and door frames that other people could afford.

She sold them part-time in a market stall. The first males assimilated were her two sons. Thanks to her membership in a women's borrowing circle, she was able to purchase increasingly large quantities of material, rent a store and workshop, plan machinery purchases, and contemplate hiring an employee. At this point her husband, who was working hundreds of miles away on a construction project, returned home to join the enterprise too.

Similarly, the first Italian restaurants in Rochester, New York, typically began like this. A wife and mother started earning money in her own kitchen by feeding Italian men who were unmarried or whose wives had not yet emigrated to join them. Typically, the point when the husband was assimilated into that work was when he was laid off his job. Rochester happens to have had a historian who was interested in how the early restaurants there evolved, and looked into their origins. No doubt much the same sequence happened repeatedly in many cities. A different example of this common initial male assimilation process is the Maidenform Brassiere Company, which was founded by two women in their dressmaking shop. After they got the company established and it looked to be successful, their husbands quit their jobs to join the business as sales and production executives.

I am not arguing—and I emphasize this—that men should not be assimilated into companies founded by women, but just that when they are it doesn't necessarily follow that women should lose proprietorship.

Nor am I arguing that entrepreneurial women should be so narrow as to cleave to sources within traditional women's work.

That needs emphasizing too. In our society by now all manner of occupations have become appropriate, whether derived from women's work, from men's, or are new under the sun.

The point to which I have been leading is this: It is weird that men should acquire monopolies or near-monopolies of proprietorship, even over businesses established by women.

In former days, when people tended regularly to call companies after themselves, names like Joseph Brown & Son or Wilson Bros. were common. Josephine Brown and Daughter, or Wilson Sisters, are quite as logical, and symbolically speaking, absolutely necessary now.

It isn't enough for businesswomen to establish successful companies, vital though that is. Still another step is needed. Women entrepreneurs can consciously seek, test and encourage daughters, sisters or unrelated women able to share top responsibilities with them as the enterprise develops and grows, whether the growth is modest or spectacular.

Otherwise, it means that when women take one step forward in economic life, they partially cancel it with one step back, in spite of all the natural advantages women possess for commercial life. Historically there have been all kinds of good reasons, along with bad reasons, for such a limping sort of economic progress. But today there are no good reasons for it—certainly not in our place nor in our time.

It will still take a while to dissolve the glass ceilings. But I have seen how rapidly you and other women like you have ridden a new wave of proprietorship by women. It is one of the great changes that have occurred in my lifetime. If you don't give away the shop once you've started it, in your lifetimes you will see how rapidly the glass ceiling dissolves.

Market Nurturing Run Amok

———

OPENAIR-MARKET NET (website),

1995

HERE'S A SMALL, TRUE STORY. A FEW YEARS AGO THE VIET-namese in an immigrant area of Dallas asked permission to hold a weekly market in a large vacant lot there owned by the city. If the market succeeded and grew, it could add to the hours or days it operated. City Hall was sympathetic to the scheme; its planners made studies of what the market should be like, how regulated, how prettified, and so on; meantime they applied for a government grant to cover such costs.

The city proceeded as fast as it could but all this paperwork and thought naturally took time, and when the grant and plans were in place more than a year had elapsed. By then the Vietnamese merchants had all given up and moved away, out of Dallas. The entire exercise was pointless. Merchants or craftsmen with a living to make can't put their plans and lives on hold the way a vacant lot can be put on hold.

This fiasco was especially silly because people from Southeast Asia are among the world's greatest experts on how to organize, set up and run stall markets. All the city needed to do was recognize and respect this reality and grant permission to use the lot with two provisos: that it be open to all merchants (of legal goods) in the community and that the market take re-sponsibility for satisfactorily cleaning up after itself. Even al-lowing for meetings and a hearing this shouldn't have taken more than a month at the outside.

Moral: Watch out for the inclination of civil servants to make big deals out of what naturally comes economically and speedily.

Against Amalgamation

———

TESTIMONY BEFORE COMMITTEE OF
ONTARIO LEGISLATURE, QUEEN'S PARK,
TORONTO, FEBRUARY 3, 1997

I OPPOSE AMALGAMATION OF TORONTO, NORTH YORK, ETOBICOKE, Scarborough, York and East York for many of the same reasons others oppose it, but will use my ten minutes to emphasize that cities do not thrive from central planning—including megacity planning.

A city of social and economic vitality contains and nourishes details and differences in mind-boggling quantities. Respect for details and differences is of the essence.

For instance, a small town can be economically pretty much all of a piece— that is, flourishing or declining as a unit. But in a city some places are apt to be in social or economic trouble at the same time other parts are prospering or maintaining an even keel. Thus a city's govern-

A city of social and economic vitality contains and nourishes details and differences in mind-boggling quantities.

ment ought to be flexible enough to respond to radically different needs and opportunities at the same given time. For example, last year at the initiative of the Mayor and Council, the City of Toronto introduced a new planning philosophy into two small, specific downtown areas in serious trouble. Not incidentally, the change was made with patient and complete democratic procedures and safeguards.*

Megacity bureaucracies do not employ this sort of pinpointed awareness and responsiveness. They can't, because their jurisdictions are too big and complex. I would judge that the City of Toronto is probably close to the limit at which true, flexible responsiveness of the kind mentioned is feasible.

Appointed neighborhood citizens' bodies, like New York City's community planning boards, are not remedies for the shortcomings of megacities. I served on one of those community boards for many years and I assure you, though we tried hard and though our board was one of the more conscientious and fair, the system was a flop compared with the human-scale, elected local governments we are lucky enough to have.

All bureaucracies make mistakes, but megacity bureaucracies tend to make big, big mistakes—like the elevated Gardiner Expressway for example. What is worse, they tend thereafter to be paralyzed with respect to correcting their mistakes or learning from them. For instance, when the City of Toronto was granted autonomous control over its social housing under Mayor Crombie about twenty-five years ago, it promptly switched away from housing projects in favor of socially and economically superior infill-housing and also created the St. Lawrence neighborhood, deliberately modeling it on city strengths rather than project weaknesses. Contrast this with the brain-dead and oth-

---

* "The Two Kings," as the initiative dubbed them, were two underused industrial areas centered on the intersections of King Street and Spadina Avenue and of King and Parliament streets, on either side of downtown Toronto. Under the guidance of Mayor Barbara Hall and Chief Planner Paul Bedford, land-use zoning was liberalized in these areas, allowing residential and nonindustrial workplaces to move in alongside existing industrial uses. The one caveat was that existing buildings could not be torn down.

erwise notorious record to this day of the Metro housing authority, the third largest landlord in North America.

Apparently the Ontario government wants to amalgamate our city governments for the purpose of cutting out confusions and duplications, improving services and reducing waste. Good aims; but depend upon it, in real life the side effects of amalgamation would contradict those aims. It defies common sense to afflict the businesses and residents of six cities with government that will be less responsive than what they have now, more prone to costly error because less on top of detailed realities, more inert and very likely more vulnerable to favoritism and hidden agendas at the expense of taxpayers and the public treasury.

We all recognize, I think, that these are times of rapid change when we need to welcome innovative, better ways of doing things. Many traditionally monopolistic public services need to be opened up to entrepreneurs and others with good ideas— also with good jobs if their initiatives pan out. Great ranges of activities from transportation and sewage treatment to recycling services, products and technology invite innovative development. But governments can and too often do discourage experimenting, and prevent or delay privately undertaken initiatives that trespass into their traditional preserves. All central planning is at odds with multiple and diverse experimenting. To be sure, small bureaucracies can be as brain-dead as big ones, but at least if they are multiple, when one says, "No," or just doesn't get it, the old saying applies: not all the eggs are in that basket.

Whatever Metro's virtues were at the start, it now behaves like a dysfunctional family. Its members are suspicious of one another, they gang up on each other. The wrangles concern activities that are already amalgamated. The few Metro coordinating services really necessary are now geographically irrelevant.

Anyone who supposes harmony will prevail and efficiency reign after whole-hog amalgamation has taken leave of common sense. These six cities really are different, and the differences won't be erased by dint of everybody trying to mind everybody else's business and beat down every local vision different from their own. The Golden Report had it right: strengthen the local city governments by doing away with Metro.* Coordinate fewer and more carefully selected responsibilities at scales which are actually rational for their functions.

The ugly conflicts in Metro over methods of property taxation arise, ultimately, because over the years large and inappropriate burdens have been piled upon property taxes, the only way Ontario cities have of levying taxes. Property taxes hit poor renters and struggling businesses disproportionately heavily compared with their means. That's why welfare costs in property tax bills are unjust as well as impractical. The same applies to support of public schools, essentially another type of social transfer payment. Both belong on income tax.

Provincial governments, no matter whether Conservative, Liberal, or New Democratic, have one and all been frightened of biting that bullet. But the injustices and makeshifts of the property tax mess are now intractable. To place still further inappropriate burdens on that tax will make what is now intractable, intolerable, no matter how the take is pooled.

---

*   Jacobs is referring to the 1996 document "Greater Toronto: Report of the GTA Task Force," chaired by Anne Golden, a colleague of hers. The report recommended not only strengthening local governments but also amalgamating the five *regional* governments in the Greater Toronto Area and clarifying their role in planning and coordination.

There are ways out of relationships if and when they become intolerably destructive. One possible escape could be to create a new province, South Ontario. In that event, South Ontario and North Ontario could each set its own preferred tax and other provincial policies. North Ontario of course would still depend heavily on subsidies from South Ontario's economy, but only indirectly through Ottawa, much as if North Ontario were an Atlantic province. However, it would be much, much more sensible to avoid an intolerable future leading to deterioration and disruption by intelligently and courageously facing realities in the fine province of Ontario we do have.

A recursive portrait of Jane Jacobs taken by her daughter, 1996. The effect mimics the self-similar nature of fractal geometry—a theme Jacobs explored in The Nature of Economies *and* Uncovering the Economy *in this volume. The smallest photo in the series appears to show Jane Jacobs in front of her home at 69 Albany Avenue in Toronto.*

PART FIVE

SOME PATTERNS OF
FUTURE DEVELOPMENT,

2000–2006

IN A RETROSPECTIVE MOOD AT THE END OF HER LIFE, JACOBS found herself returning to ideas she had pondered for years in search of fresh perspectives on contemporary problems. Relatively famous in her old age, she was sought out for her opinions on topics large and small—even by those she had criticized in the past. In a conversation with World Bank officials, she took on the pressing problem of globalization and the foreign aid and trade policies that promote it. She likened debt-based strategies of development to the old modernizing impulses underlying urban renewal, arguing that they may simply be reinstating the abuses of imperialism. Elsewhere, as in the interview included here, "Efficiency and the Commons," Jacobs returned to the standoff between commerce and regulation she had explored in *Systems of Survival*. At a moment when privatization was all the rage, she worried that it was undermining public life. The disrupted balance between guardians and traders had infected public education, science, criminal justice, medicine, and other professions—a concern she would take up in her final book, *Dark Age Ahead* (2004).

Meanwhile, her calls for devolution of powers in *The Question of Separatism* and *Cities and the Wealth of Nations* returned too, during the continued fight for urban sovereignty in Canada. Despite the earlier failure to stop Toronto's amalgamation, in

2001 she joined businessman and philanthropist Alan Broadbent and the mayors of five of Canada's largest metro areas—Toronto, Montreal, Vancouver, Calgary and Winnipeg—under the banner of a group called the Charter 5, or C5, which hoped to secure a charter for cities equivalent to that reserved for provinces (see "Canada's Hub Cities"). After meeting only three times, however, the C5 had the wind taken out of its sails when the federal government upped funding for cities—without fundamentally altering their place within the political order.

Perhaps Jacobs's most consequential look back came in the realm of economics. Reviewing her work, she felt that her economic thinking had failed to coalesce into one overarching theory. She started a new book, to be called *Uncovering the Economy,* that aimed to rectify that problem by putting her ideas about urban growth, innovation, and macroeconomics into logical order, rather than the shape they assumed as she had discovered each piece of the puzzle years before. In the process, she found opportunities to embellish or clarify earlier concepts as well. Some of these updates she discussed only with her son, Jim Jacobs, who was, at this late stage of her life, helping her with typing tasks. In the latter cases, we have included these additions as annotations to our excerpt from the book, which she never finished.

Alongside these retrospective reflections, Jacobs also set out to write a book that would interpret the trajectory of civilization from its deepest past into its incomplete future. She aimed, she said, to write nothing less than a short biography of the human race. Jacobs had long been interested in how societies rise and fall, and by the turn of the millennium she had begun to worry that North American society was headed for trouble.

Her last published book, *Dark Age Ahead,* was a prelude to this final work. It offered a pessimistic look at the present and future. Published in 2004, two years before her death in 2006, it examined failures in five institutions of North American life: family and community, accessible and effective education, the scientific mindset, accountable government and taxation, and the self-policing of professions. Without the stabilizing influences of these cultural mores, Jacobs felt, very little stood in the way of North America falling into a new Dark Age, an era where we literally forget what it means to be American or Canadian through generation after generation of mounting problems, deepening poverty, and desperation. Forever hesitant to foreclose on the future, however, she concluded *Dark Age Ahead* on an ambiguous note: "At a given time it is hard to tell whether forces of cultural life or death are in the ascendancy."

The last piece in this collection, "The End of the Plantation Age," is the only known fragment of her second unfinished book, tentatively called "A Short Biography of the Human Race." In this speech she ranges across a host of different topics, from skyscrapers to memorials to Lewis Mumford, but at its core is Jacobs's hope that the forces of life are indeed in the ascendancy. It expands upon her theory, briefly explored in the final chapter of *Dark Age Ahead,* that since the first cities began to emerge from the Dark Ages of Europe a thousand years ago, society in the West has been undergoing a long transformation from one great era of human history to another. The Plantation Age reigned supreme for centuries, but has for some time now slowly been giving way to a post-agrarian age in which a minuscule portion of the population is engaged in food production. Drawing on biologist Jared Diamond's popular history *Guns,*

Germs, and Steel, which found that, over the long term, the cultures that reorganized themselves around agriculture ascended while their hunting and gathering counterparts declined, Jacobs proposes that, so too, the first cultures to truly embrace what she calls the "Age of Human Capital" will be the new "cultural winners." In this still-emerging era, the capacity for exchange and new work will drive growth, while imperial expansion and control over resources will wither as a means of holding power. Societies that harness their tremendous collective capacity for ingenuity and embrace the organized complexity of city life will free their citizens from industrial and agricultural peonage and thrive.

If this possible emancipation of human potential sounds uncharacteristically utopian, Jacobs is careful to show that this new age will upend and reorganize human conflict, not end it. If history during the Plantation Age was mainly a contest over land and resources, reaching its bloody depths in European imperialism or the Nazi pursuit of *lebensraum,* in the Age of Human Capital this may no longer be the primary way to secure prosperity. Land and resources "can be held exclusively," Jacobs remarks. "Ingenuity cannot be." This deceptively simple observation suggests new understandings of her earlier insights into cities and economies. Wherever the urban-focused values of the Age of Human Capital have found a way to germinate, new patterns of prosperity take hold. In this light, it makes sense that a tiny, resource-poor island like Japan can thrive on the creativity of its cities, as she argues in *The Economy of Cities.* Or, as she recounts in both *The Question of Separatism* and *Cities and the Wealth of Nations,* that the people of a kingdom like turn-of-the-century Sweden actually could benefit from losing a large portion of their territory to a secessionist faction like Norway, since both Stockholm and Oslo then each had their own national governments and currencies responding to their own economies, and the hinterlands had two creative, empowered cities instead of one. Or, as she says in this final speech, that the great rural breadbaskets of the world, once necessities of vast empires, now require massive subsidies and protections to stay viable. They burden as much as they propel a nation. In short, if the Plantation Age was a zero-sum game in which mastery over land, labor, and resources guaranteed power, the Age of Human Capital is a non-zero-sum game with a more complex, unpredictable, and—one hopes—equitable set of rules.

As she neared the end of her life, she was hesitant to favor one future over another. "Maybe this is wishful thinking," she remarks in "Plantation Age," "and the only definitive thing to be said echoes Charles Dickens's introductory comment to *A Tale of Two Cities*: 'It was the worst of times and the best of times.'" Her ambivalence raises questions for all of us. Will we overcome the intertwined challenges of climate change, inequality, and stagnation or succumb to a new Dark Age? Will the "vital little plans" Jacobs celebrates multiply or simply evolve into more ingenious and insidious forms of the plantation? The answer, as always for Jacobs, rests with everyone, working singly and together for an open-ended future. "As we negotiate the difficult transition out of the dead, but not buried, Plantation Age," she says, "we need unlimited independent thinkers with unlimited skepticism and curiosity."

Time and Change as
Neighborhood Allies

VINCENT SCULLY PRIZE LECTURE,
NATIONAL BUILDING MUSEUM, WASHINGTON, D.C.,
NOVEMBER 11, 2000 *

WE TAKE IT FOR GRANTED THAT SOME THINGS IMPROVE OR are enhanced by time and the changes it brings. Trees grow larger; hedges grow thicker; fine old buildings, put to uses not originally anticipated, as this building has been, are increasingly appreciated as time passes.† But some other things are too seldom enhanced or improved by the workings of time. On the whole city and suburban neighborhoods have very chancy records of dealing well with time and change. I'm going to discuss briefly four common kinds of failure for city neighborhoods and make a few suggestions.

My first suggestion concerns immigrants. Right now, in locations extending from the Virginia metropolitan fringes of Washington and the Jersey metropolitan fringes of New York to

---

* The Vincent Scully Prize is awarded by the National Building Museum to recognize excellence in scholarship, criticism, and practice in architecture, preservation, and urban design. Scully (1920–) is a famed historian of architecture who taught at Yale University from 1947 to 2009. Jacobs was the first recipient of the Vincent Scully Prize after Scully himself.

† The National Building Museum is housed in the 1887 headquarters of the U.S. Pension Bureau designed by architect Montgomery Meigs.

the Los Angeles fringes of Los Angeles, striving immigrants from Pakistan, Bangladesh, India, China, the Philippines, Latin America, the Caribbean and Africa, are settling in woebegone city suburbs to which time has been unkind. Right now newcomers are enlivening dull and dreary streets with tiny grocery and clothing stores, second-hand shops, little importing and craft enterprises, skimpy offices and modest but exotic restaurants.

Either of two fates can befall these newly minted immigrant neighborhoods. On the one hand, if members of the new populations and their children melt away as they find their feet, the sequel for the bottom of the ladder is probably followed by yet another population. Ample experience informs us that neighborhoods serving only as immigrant launching pads repeatedly take a step or two forward, followed by two or three steps backward, while dilapidation inexorably deepens with time.

In contrast, as many a Little Italy and Chinatown attest, along with less celebrated examples, immigrant neighborhoods that succeed in holding on to their striving populations are neighborhoods that improve with time, becoming civic assets in every respect: social, physical and economic.* Progress on the part of the population is reflected in the neighborhood. Increasing diversity of incomes, occupations, ambitions, education, skills and connections are all reflected in the increasingly diversified neighborhood. Time becomes the ally, not the enemy, of such a neighborhood.

---

* See chapter 15 of *Death and Life,* "Slumming and Unslumming," where Jacobs describes how neighborhood revitalization is best achieved by the retention of residents as they improve their lot in life. Jacobs's thoughts about steadily "unslumming" neighborhoods dated back to her earliest experiences in New York. She considered Greenwich Village between the 1930s and '50s a great example of the phenomenon.

Self-respecting people, no matter what their ethnic origins, abandon a place if it becomes fixed in their minds that it is an undignified or insulting place to be. Here's my suggestion: smart municipalities ought to contradict those perceptions before they take firm hold—no time to lose—by making sure that newly minted immigrant neighborhoods receive really good municipal housekeeping, public maintenance, and community policing and justice services, along with some respectful amenities. Traffic-taming and street trees come to mind, and especially quick, hassle-free permissions for people to organize open-air markets if they ask to, or run jitney services, or make whatever other life-improving adaptations they want to provide for themselves.

Simple, straightforward municipal investments of the kind just mentioned, and sensitive, flexible bureaucratic adjustments are minor in comparison with costs and adjustments demanded by city megaprojects. But if those minor costs and adjustments attach newcomers to neighborhoods in which they can feel pride and proprietorship as they are finding their feet, and afterwards, they carry a potential of huge civic payoffs. Time and change will then have been enlisted as allies of these neighborhoods.

My second suggestion has to do with communities' needs for hearts or centers and with a related problem: damage done to neighborhoods by commercial incursions where they are inappropriate. The desirability of community hearts is well recognized nowadays. Much thought goes into designing them for new communities, and inserting them into neighborhoods that have lost community hearts or never had them. The object is to nurture locales where people on foot will naturally encounter one another in the course of shopping, doing other errands, promoting their causes, airing their grievances, catching up on gossip, and perhaps enjoying a coffee or beer under pretty colored umbrellas.

Let's think a minute about the natural anatomy of community hearts. Wherever they develop spontaneously, they are almost invariably consequences of two or more intersecting streets, well used by pedestrians. On the most meager scale, we have the cliché of the corner store or the corner pub that is recognized as a local hangout. In this cliché, "corner" is a significant adjective. Corner implies two streets intersecting in the shape of an X or a T. In traditional towns, the spot recognized as the center of things surprisingly often contains a triangular piece of ground. This is because it is where three main routes converge in the shape of a Y. In communities where historically much traffic was waterborne, a heart often located itself at the intersection of a main waterfront street with the exit from a busy dock where passengers disembarked; when water travel declined, the heart moved elsewhere. Large cities of course have typically developed not only localized neighborhood or district hearts, but one or several major hearts, and these also have almost invariably located themselves at busy pedestrian street intersections. All but the very smallest hearts—the corner store—typically provided splendid sites for landmark buildings, public squares, or small parks.

The converse logic doesn't work. Living, beating community hearts can't be arbitrarily located, as if they were suburban shopping centers for which the supporting anatomy is a parking lot and perhaps a transit stop.* But given the anatomy of well-used pedestrian main streets, hearts locate themselves; in fact

Living, beating community hearts can't be arbitrarily located . . . but given the anatomy of well-used pedestrian main streets, hearts locate themselves.

they can't be prevented from locating themselves. Of course good design can greatly enhance or reinforce them, as I implied with my remark about landmark buildings and public squares.

Now for the related problem of commercial or institutional facilities intruding into inappropriate places. From time to time I glance at plans and artists' renderings for charmingly designed residences with their yards, and I wonder where future overflow of commerce can be pleasantly accommodated. Perhaps this consideration doesn't matter in a village which is destined to remain a village. But it matters very much in a city neighborhood or in a town or village which becomes engulfed by a city. In cities, successful hearts attract users from outside the neighborhood, and they also attract entrepreneurs who want to be where the action is. These things happen. In fact, if these things didn't happen cities would be little more advantageous economically and socially than villages; they wouldn't generate urban surprise, pizzazz and diversity.

So with time and change, originally unforeseen commercial and institutional overflows can occur in city neighborhoods. Where do they go? They may have to find and convert make-

---

* In a 2001 interview with Bill Steigerwald in *Reason* magazine, Jacobs specifically calls out the New Urbanist architects and planners on this mistake: "The New Urbanists want to have lively centers in the places that they develop, where people run into each other doing errands and that sort of thing. And yet, from what I've seen of their plans and the places they have built, they don't seem to have a sense of the anatomy of these hearts, these centers."

shift quarters. Occasionally the makeshifts are delightful, but most commonly they register as ugly, jarring, intrusive smears into residential streets where they were never meant to intrude. Watching this happen, people think, "The neighborhood is going to the dogs." So it is visually—and soon, as a sequel, perhaps socially; in the end, perhaps economically as well. So much is this form of deterioration disliked and feared, that one of the chief purposes of zoning regulations is to prevent it. Even if the regulations succeed at holding time and change at bay, as enemies, any success they have comes at the cost of squelching city potentialities, meaning convenience and innovations.

Here is where the anatomy of natural neighborhood hearts can come to the rescue. One important adaptive advantage of open-ended main pedestrian streets forming intersections is that these streets are logical places to locate convertible buildings before there is a need to convert them. They can be a designed form of neighborhood insurance, so to speak. For example, row houses can be designed to convert easily and pleasantly to shops, small offices, studios, restaurants, all kinds of things. Several joined together even convert well to small schools and other institutions. And of course many buildings originally put up for work, especially loft buildings, convert pleasantly to apartments or living-and-working combinations. In sum, I am suggesting that urban designers and municipalities should not think about the street anatomy without also providing or encouraging easily convertible buildings on those streets as opportunity to do that arises. This is a practical strategy for dealing with time and change as allies, not enemies.

My third suggestion concerns gentrification of low-cost neighborhoods to which time has not been kind but which have valuable assets. Typically, the first outsiders to notice those assets are artists and artisans. They are joined by young professionals or other middle-class people whose eyes have been opened by the artists' discoveries. For a time, gentrification brings heartening renovations and other physical improvements into a neighborhood that needs improvements, along with new people whose connections, life-skills and spending money can be socially useful to the neighborhood's existing inhabitants, and often are. As long as gentrification proceeds gently, with moderation, it tends to continue to be beneficial, and diversifying.*

Nowadays especially, a neighborhood's period of what might be called its golden age of gentrification can be surprisingly short. . . . It explodes into a feeding frenzy of real-estate speculation and evictions.

But nowadays especially, a neighborhood's period of what might be called its golden age of gentrification can be surprisingly short. Suddenly, so many, many new people want in on a place now generally perceived as interesting and fashionable that gentrification turns socially and economically vicious. It explodes into a feeding frenzy of real-estate speculation and evictions. Former inhabitants are evicted wholesale, priced out by what Chester Hartman, urban planner and author, aptly calls "the financial bulldozer."† Even the artists, who began the process, are priced out.

---

* This distinction can be found in *Death and Life* as well. As we've seen, Jacobs calls such gentle, diversifying, internally driven gentrification "unslumming," while in chapter 13, "The Self-Destruction of Diversity," she describes the more common contemporary understanding of gentrification: rapid upscaling, homogenization, and displacement.

† Chester Hartman (1936–) is a planner, writer, and activist. Jacobs wrote the introduction to his collection of writings, *Between Eminence and Notoriety: Four Decades of Radical Urban Planning* (2002).

The eventual ironic result is that even the rich, the people being priced in, are cheated by this turn of events. They were attracted by what they perceived as a lively, interesting, diverse and urbane city neighborhood—in short, by the results of gentle and moderate gentrification. This kind of urbanity is killed as the place becomes an exclusive preserve for high-income people.

Time is not kind to high-income preserves in cities, unless they are small and cheek-by-jowl with livelier and more diverse neighborhoods. One need only notice that many a poor and dilapidated neighborhood contains once-beautiful, proud and ambitious dwellings to see evidence that exclusive preserves of the rich do not necessarily hold up well in cities. The rich, it seems, grow bored with undiverse, dull city neighborhoods, or their children or heirs do. This is not surprising because such places are boring.

When gentrification turns vicious and excessive, it tells us, first, that demand for moderately gentrified neighborhoods has outrun supply. By now, experience has revealed the basic attributes of such places—attributes artists discover: the streets have human scale, buildings are various and interesting, streets are safe for pedestrian use and many ordinary conveniences are within pedestrian reach and neighbors are tolerant of differing lifestyles. It is pitiful that so many city neighborhoods with these excellent basic attributes have been destroyed for highway construction, slum clearance, urban renewal and housing projects. Nevertheless, some currently bypassed civic treasures do remain, and where they do, moderate gentrification—I emphasize moderate—could be deliberately encouraged to help take the heat off other places being excessively gentrified. Another way of adding to supply could be by encouraging judicious in-filling of housing in neighborhoods with human scale but not excessive compactness or density.

However, more than increased supply of desirable city neighborhoods is needed to combat socially vicious evictions of existing inhabitants. Artscape, a Toronto organization concerned specifically with protecting and promoting the interests of artists, has come to the conclusion that the only sure way of preventing artists from being priced out of their quarters is ownership—in this case, ownership by nonprofit organizations. The same is probably true for many other existing inhabitants—ownership by cooperatives, community development corporations, land trusts, nonprofit organizations—whatever ingenuities can be directed to the aim of retaining neighborhood diversity of population.

My final suggestion concerns the hazards of a somewhat different form of popularity. As I mentioned earlier, some community hearts and their associated street anatomies attract many outsiders and are widely enjoyed. This is not a bad thing; on the contrary. The hazard is this: as leases for commercial or institutional spaces expire, tenants are apt to be faced with shockingly increased rents. Property taxes on the popular premises can soar too, instigating even further increases. If zoning prevents commercial overflow, so much the worse. The upshot is that many facilities are priced out of the mix. The hardware store goes, the bookstore closes,

As diversity diminishes, into its place comes a kind of monoculture: incredible repetitions of whatever happens to be most profitable on that street at that time.

the place that repairs small appliances moves away, the butcher shops and bakeries disappear.

As diversity diminishes, into its place comes a kind of mono-culture: incredible repetitions of whatever happens to be most profitable on that street at that time. Of course these optimists don't all succeed. Six of the seventeen new restaurants, say, die off rather rapidly, and five of the seven gift shops don't make it through the next Christmas. Into their places come other opti-mists who hope something will be left in the till after the debt costs on renovations and the incredible rents are paid. But start-ing gradually while times are good, and rapidly when they aren't, the street becomes dotted with vacancies. The old conve-niences don't return to fill them. They can't afford to. All this is not owing to competition from malls or big boxes—but because success has priced out diversity.

A popular main pedestrian street running through my own neighborhood is now afflicted by this dynamic. However, for-tunately the hardware store remains, so does the bookstore, one butcher shop with its associated European grocery, and a large general bargain and outlet store.* Not only do these remain, they flourish; one—the hardware—has doubled its space. The secret of their stability is that they own the buildings where they do business, so were not vulnerable to being priced out by soaring rents. The banks also remain; they own their buildings.

---

* The street Jacobs describes here is Bloor Street in Toronto's Annex neighborhood, down the street from her house at 69 Albany Avenue. The businesses she lists are likely Wiener's Home Hardware, Book City or BMV Books, the Elizabeth Deli, and Honest Ed's, respec-tively. As of 2015, one bookstore and the deli have closed, and Honest Ed's plans to close by the end of 2016, to be replaced by a new mixed-use development.

This has caused me to think about home ownership. When it became public policy in the United States to encourage home ownership, financial devices such as long-term mortgages, small down payments, and mortgage acceptance agencies, primarily the Federal Housing Administration (FHA), proved successful at promoting the policy. Tract housing sold to homeowners under these arrangements was sprawling and otherwise ill-conceived for fostering much sense of community, but that is another matter. At least, fostering ownership worked. Today some 65 percent of American households own their own houses or apartments, the highest percentage in the world.

This has made me wonder whether similar techniques would enable or encourage small businesses—especially those whose success depends heavily on location—to own their own premises. Of course not all would want to, and among those that did, all would not be able to; but that is also true of households. Why shouldn't it become public policy to foster business stability, and stability of city streets and neighborhoods, by enabling enterprises to protect themselves, through ownership, against abruptly rising rents? In other words, I've arrived at much the same conclusion as Artscape: that ownership is the surest protection against being priced out of a place of work.

These four suggestions may seem trivial compared with other municipal concerns such as racism, poor schools, traffic, unemployment, illegal drugs, inadequate tax revenues, crime, persistent poverty, what to do with garbage, how to lure tourists, whether to build another stadium or a convention center, and so on. Nevertheless, neighborhoods that decline are pretty serious too. Two steps forward, followed by three steps back, is no way for a city to progress, and it doesn't help solve other municipal problems either; the pattern makes them more intractable.

The pattern isn't new. It has practical causes and unless these forms of civic ineptitude are faced and overcome, North American city neighborhoods are as unlikely to deal well with time and change in the future as they have been in the past. The suggestions I've made may not be politically possible. There may be better, or at any rate different, means of accomplishing similar aims. My purpose is to help stir up some creative thinking, now lacking, about effects of time and change on city neighborhoods; above all to stir up thinking about how to enlist time and change as practical allies—not enemies that must be regulated out and fended off on the one hand, or messily surrendered to on the other. We might as well learn how to make constructive alliances with the workings of time because time is going to continue happening; that's for sure.

Canada's Hub Cities

———

SPEECH AT THE C5 CONFERENCE,
WINNIPEG, MAY 24, 2001

FIVE CITIES AND THEIR ADJOINING CITY REGIONS ARE BY FAR Canada's major economic assets. Without Vancouver, Calgary, Winnipeg, Toronto and Montreal, Canada would be so poor that it would qualify as part of the Third World.

Income and consumption taxes from businesses and residents in these cities and their regions are what make the programs of provincial and federal government financially possible.

Foreign immigrants and their children rely overwhelmingly on these five cities and their regions for work, income and educational and other opportunities. So do domestic migrants from rural Canada.

Many a little city or company town throughout the country depends on transplanted industries or offices that were generated in these five cities. Many also depend heavily or entirely on sales in these five cities and their regions.

Our host, Mayor Glen Murray, calls them "hub cities." It's a good description, more succinct than "economically diverse," "economically creative," "economically innovative," or "economically synergistic." Those labels speak of underlying causes for the extraordinary economic and social power of those cities. The label "hub cities" speaks of results of those causes, more suggestively than simply saying "big cities." In today's world, these are Canada's primary economic engines.

But in spite of the fact that these five cities exist, many other facts inform us that Canada is a poor environment for hub cities.

For one thing, large regions of the country have no hub cities to pull them out of relative poverty. The Atlantic provinces, for instance, have none. Saskatchewan has none. Neither do large but relatively poor regions of Ontario, Quebec, Manitoba, Alberta and British Columbia. It isn't that they lack cities *per se*. Like the Atlantic provinces, most do have cities, including promising ones with many admirable and interesting attributes. But these remain arrested in a sort of economic adolescence. With luck, one in half a century might grow up and take off, as Calgary has done.

That isn't enough, considering the need. For a country the geographical size of Canada, and for a population as striving and capable as Canada's, five hub cities are few.

Even the five can't be taken for granted. Suppose, hypothetically, that Winnipeg were to stagnate and gradually thin out and dwindle, leaving the vast geographical gap between Toronto and Calgary as an economic gap. Actually, this is not so hypothetical. Winnipeg has come perilously close to stagnating.

The well-being of the other four can't be taken for granted either. I suspect that all of you mayors have wish lists of services and infrastructures your cities need—in some cases urgently need. Perhaps you have ideas about how some of these could be filled in new or better ways than are now conventional. But possibilities must be postponed or even abandoned because you lack resources to invest in them. So Canada is already falling behind in fields such as waste recycling, public transportation, sewage treatment, energy conservation, assisted housing, products and methods for preventing toxic pollution. Social nets are becoming so fragile.

Another thing: to flourish, a hub city needs strong and many-faceted trading, information and other relationships with other hub cities. These everyday, working relationships among hub cities within Canada are not strengthening as time passes. On the contrary. If this slackening continues, Canada will become a country only in name, if that.

All these are symptoms that Canada provides a poor environment for the emergence of vigorous hub cities, and inadequate environments for maintaining those it does have.

Although the symptoms show up locally, they occur country-wide. They are not temporary, either. Changes of government don't correct them. In other words, Canada's poor environment for cities is clearly systemic, by which I mean that it is embedded in the country's political and financial arrangements. The damaging effects run wide and run deep.

At their roots is a systemic flaw. It's such a silly flaw, really. Its origins go back to the time when most of the country's population lived and worked in small market towns, narrowly based company towns, and agricultural, fishing, mining, logging or other rural-resource villages and hamlets. Even the largest, even those that included garrisons or seats of administration, were economically and socially simple with limited ranges of expertise.

And so logically enough, municipalities of the time were bracketed with asylums and taverns as provincial responsibilities.

As wards of provinces, municipalities were permitted to

levy only property taxes—probably not a bad idea when usual municipal capabilities were limited to maintaining roads, fighting fires, making water and sewers available—in short directly servicing properties. The somewhat more sophisticated provincial governments took care of most other management.

Times, of course, have changed beyond recognition. Canadian municipalities are no longer country bumpkin villages. But the antiquated arrangements failed to change with the times. They still haven't changed. They've only been tinkered with, adapted superficially, as little basically as has been possible.

One adaptation has been to load up property taxes with municipal costs that have nothing to do with servicing property. This has had side effects of making property taxes regressive and inequitable and skewing them into destructive unintended consequences.

The other type of adaptation consists of patchwork grants from provinces and sporadic acts of largesse from the federal government, makeshifts that are circuitous and inefficient. They are also crippling. They demean city governments, forcing them into the demoralizing position of being assumed to be too incompetent to assess and deal with internal affairs except at the discretion of superior governments. Provincial and federal grants, permissions and largesse can't help but reflect those governments' priorities. They certainly can't and don't reflect each city's own circumstances at a given time—for instance, just when this city or that one needs to undertake innovative infrastructure or services and can feasibly do so.

It is no wonder that so few hub cities emerge from this cumbersome and happenstance mess. And it is little wonder that the well-being of the few that have emerged is so precarious.

That said, the practical question is how the outdated and crippling system can be disposed of. Historically, cities themselves have had to take the initiative for the reforms they require.

If the five hub cities of Canada, the C5, don't take initiative for reform, I can't imagine who will. You are in a position to make a case for greater responsibility and greater resources that must be seriously heeded by the federal government. You have allies in your regions who realize that they share your difficulties and frustrations. You have potential allies among stunted cities elsewhere who need you to break a trail that would benefit them too.

Most important, you have a wealth of human capital—people with intelligence, talent and experience that equips them to deal with city needs and opportunities; or you can get them. Your citizens are anything but stupid. Many are fed up with paying generous income and consumption taxes, and then watching how the government closest to their daily lives must plead and wheedle to receive a share of that very same money in round-about ways. Many are already dissatisfied, even contemptuous of the childish roles their cities are forced to play in deference to an outgrown, arbitrary system.

Possibly the hardest part of winning reform will be resisting old, ingrained habits of accepting municipal dependence and practicing opportunistic beggary.

In contrast to that, you have an opportunity here to think out of the box. It is unprecedented for the elected leaders of the country's hub cities to discuss together what powers and resources they would like their cities to have, as of well-earned right. For instance, why shouldn't the federal government shift its allocations of income-tax points and consumption-tax yields: shift them so that the shares municipalities require for responsibilities they are capable of assuming would go directly to them instead of by inefficient, round-about and crippling routes? This is also an unprecedented opportunity to organize yourselves with the object of winning reform.

If you can do this sort of thinking and self-organizing—and I see no reason why you can't if you choose to—you could well achieve something as constructive and significant for Canada in our time as the Fathers of Confederation achieved in their time.

Efficiency and the Commons

———

CONVERSATION WITH JANICE GROSS STEIN,*

GRAZING ON THE COMMONS CONFERENCE,

TORONTO, NOVEMBER 15, 2001

JANE JACOBS: As you already said cogently in your Massey Lecture, efficiency harms medical care, public schooling, accountability and choice. It invites stupid police and slapdash justice. It undermines wholesome communities. It cheats the interests of posterity and toys very dangerously with all types of security—from water to airports. Your question, "Efficiency for what?" is the right question, with its emphasis on effective results. But here's the rub: Effective health care, schooling, accountability and so on are not the bottom lines that register political effectiveness. Rather, the bottom line for political organizations is success at winning or retaining power to govern. In Canada, this means winning elections.

No matter how specious the cult of efficiency is, if enough voters fall for it, we get it. So, your brilliant analysis of the cult's fraudulence is important civic education. But what about the many, many well-educated experts who help the voters fall for this because they, themselves, have?

*   Janice Gross Stein (1943–) is a Canadian political scientist and the founder of the University of Toronto's Munk School of Global Affairs. Her Massey Lecture, which this conversation addresses, was published as *The Cult of Efficiency*.

Do you think miseducation helps lead civil servants, elected officials, the media and institutional administrators as well as voters astray? Do universities, schools, governments, businesses and departments of economics and political science have an important part to play in unmasking the fraudulence of this cult? Is information from the new science of complexity developed by physicists, biologists and ecologists needed by social scientists and civil servants? Do you think university communities are listening to you? I would value your thoughts about any concrete means for putting government efficiency on a saner intellectual setting.

JANICE GROSS STEIN: I agree with every word you said, Jane. We just assume that efficiency is an end, not a means. So pushing that one step further, and asking people, "Efficient at what?" should enable us to get beyond this myth of efficiency that drives our public policy and harms our public good. The rub is that politicians run a four-year cycle; their goals are short term. I think the real place this discussion has to happen is among citizens. And it's a tough conversation to have.

I had an email today from two high school principals in British Columbia who said they were dissatisfied with the accountability measures in schools because the timelines are too short. What is really the measure of an effective school? It's how well that school equips the students to be citizens; how well the school equips people to be productive members of society.

In my book, I ask one of the vice presidents of one of our hospitals, "If it were up to us as citizens, what criteria should we use to judge a community hospital? What is reasonable?" The answer was, "Well, we measure work, we can't be held accountable." I bet that wouldn't be good enough for you, Jane. And I think Michael Adams, who does all this work on citizens and their attitudes, would say, "It's not good enough for most citizens."[*]

Where's the bottom-up conversation coming from citizens? How do we get parents and schools to really engage and say, "You know, I don't really like this standardized test. My kid is more than the ability to answer a multiple choice question."

JACOBS: Well, we do need accountability, obviously. One reason that this nutty cult of efficiency got power is that it became clear that throwing money at problems didn't solve them. That doesn't mean that nothing works but I think we've got to look at what is sneeringly called "anecdotal evidence."[†] It's good to have statistics but I think anecdotal evidence is often sharper and truer.

It's good to have statistics but I think anecdotal evidence is often sharper and truer.

It's like novels. If you want to find out about a part of the world you haven't personally experienced, you probably will get a better idea from a good novel than you will from any nonfiction. Novels are like collections of anecdotal evidence. We should take them seriously and look much more at what happens with many indi-

---

* Michael Adams (1946–) is a Canadian cultural commentator and co-founder of Environics, an opinion poll company often cited in the Canadian media. He has published several books on Canadian attitudes.

† As Jacobs observes in a 2005 interview with John Sewell, whereas statistics can only capture correlation, not causation, stories keep intact the intricate connections between factors and the chains of cause and effect, a virtue particularly important in studying multivariable complex systems like cities.

viduals, not as statistics but as stories, and use that as an important ingredient of accountability. Does that make sense to you?

STEIN: It does make sense to me. One of the things I was asking these two high school principals was, "What about following individual students when they're at school and when they leave? What about following high school students when they graduate? A year later, do the students feel they have learned what they needed? Can they tell us what they wished they had learned?" Let's make the measure of effectiveness the stories of the people involved.

People can identify gaps in the public institutions that I call "gluey" because they stick to citizens. Those institutions haven't done a great job in working with citizens to be accountable. So, the guardian culture comes in and says, in Jane's words, "We're going to do it this way and we're going to impose these measures, whether you like it or not."* My big problem is, where are the levers to start this? I see individual citizens doing it. I see some communities doing it, but how do we scale this up from small groups so we get some critical mass?

JACOBS: I'm always amazed at how many people don't trust their own experience. They don't think that what happened to them can be important.

STEIN: Are you saying selfishness can serve the public good?

---

* The "guardian culture" refers to one of Jacobs's two "moral syndromes" in *Systems of Survival*. For an in-depth explanation of this ethical system and its counterpoint, the commercial moral syndrome, see "Two Ways to Live," in this volume.

JACOBS: Yes, indeed it can. There are many kinds of selfishness and unfortunately greed is what pops into most people's heads when they hear the word *selfish*. But selfishness can mean concern for your family and your neighborhood. It can mean concern for what touches you, and many things touch you besides material things.

STEIN: I was working on school choice. When I listened to parents talking about why choice mattered to them, I was struck with how strong support for school choice is in minority communities where their culture, their language and their community matters to them. Those parents feel their kids aren't well served in the larger public school system. They want to be able to choose their kid's school but still stay within the public school system. They might be called selfish, but they were telling a story that was very important to them.

JACOBS: That's the kind of selfishness that is so important.

STEIN: That's right. And when I asked, "Are you worried that if you set up a school just for your community, your kids won't have the chance to get to know kids from other communities?" their answer was, "We need to provide a safe environment where our kids can learn and become more self-confident, more secure; then they will be able to go out and meet kids from other communities."

This is tough for me because, as somebody who works in international politics, I know what happens when people stay only within their own communities. They develop stereotypes about others and opinion polarizes. But if we don't listen to what these parents are saying matters to them, we're not going to fix anything.

JACOBS: I think it is absolutely wrong to sacrifice your children to any ideology or affinity that you have. You absolutely have to change it if it's not working for your children. That's your first responsibility when you've had children. Any child is more important than any idea.

> *I think it is absolutely wrong to sacrifice your children to any ideology or affinity that you have. . . . Any child is more important than any idea.*

When parents want their children to be educated in their own community because they're safer, there's something very wrong. One thing I have admired about Toronto is that there are not ghettos in the sense that there are in American cities. The nearest thing we have to ghettos in Toronto are the misguided public housing projects but we're finally learning how to do it right.

We also need to look at specific things that make parents feel unsafe. Bullying is very bad. And it's amazing how prevalent it is, generation after generation. My husband went to a nice suburban public school and he had many stories to tell me about bullying and how frightened he was to walk home at night. I went to a nice suburban public school and I had no such trouble. But I remember my brothers did. So anecdotal evidence suggests it's a male problem.

STEIN: Safety is one of the biggest issues that concern parents. The strongest support for school choice is among African Americans who are moving to charter schools; the communities come together, set up and run their own schools. These parents feel passionately that these exclusive community schools are their highest priority.

JACOBS: I think it's very important that such schools should be publicly funded because in real life one size doesn't fit all. Every individual is different. We know that. Every town. Every city is different. Every chain store isn't different and that's getting very boring.

STEIN: If one size doesn't fit all, why is "choice" a right-wing word? When did choice become a right-wing word?

JACOBS: It's a right-wing word but it's not a right-wing deed. And it leads to the second question I have for you.

Within hierarchies, differing arrangements are possible. That's choice. One available choice is called subsidiarity, meaning that higher governments can delegate various responsibilities and resources downward to governments that are in closer touch with local needs and possibilities.* Under this principle, the federal government hands many functions and resources to the provinces. All federalism is built on this idea. Under the same principle, provinces and the federal government should be able to yield to municipalities many responsibilities and resources they badly need but now lack; they can handle these much better than the provinces because one size doesn't fit all municipalities.

---

* In chapter 5 of *Dark Age Ahead*, "Dumbed-Down Taxes," Jacobs uses the principle of subsidiarity to critique the paternalistic relationship between governments at the so-called senior (state/provincial and federal) and junior (municipal) levels. She favors, wherever it is possible and prudent, devolving the powers of government to the local level.

But here's the rub. For historical reasons that are now long out of date, municipalities must consistently resort to begging from higher levels of government. They're also forced to embrace the cult of efficiency. It seems that Marshall McLuhan was right when he observed that you can't decentralize centrally.

STEIN: You can't decentralize centrally. But I think we're on the edge of meeting some of the concerns that you've addressed in your work, Jane. The big missing voice in our politics is cities and communities. We can't make that voice heard. What stops us is that cities and communities have no political home in our structures. I think we're on the edge of seeing a change because I think hierarchy is diminishing. Our culture isn't as supportive of hierarchy today as it was fifteen years ago. So, even the state, which is, after all, the ultimate hierarchy, is changing on us.

Government today has to reach out. It has to pull in advice from outside. It has to find partners because it doesn't have the resources or the knowledge to do it all. The old top-down hierarchical state that we had all through the last century is beginning to transform itself. And that's the one big positive of efficiency. In a sense we've bought the argument that old top-down hierarchical structure isn't very efficient and so it's changing. But here's where citizens are going to have to weigh in.

I think citizens are correctly distrustful of hierarchies. They're skeptical about markets, too. It's that skepticism among citizens—the lack of deference to authority—that I'm counting on to change the way we as citizens relate to these institutions. It's confounding to me that we have a guardian culture with values. And we have a commercial culture with a set of values. But where's the citizen culture? How do you fit the citizen culture into your picture?

JACOBS: The hierarchy, I agree, is changing. I think we live in a time of what you might call "dying priesthoods" of all kinds. You can't believe how intimidated women used to be by doctors not so long ago and how intimidated everyone was by lawyers. And, of course, if you read novels, you will see that people were kept in line by clergy.*

We're also probably living in the last days of feudalism. It's been a long-term, thousand-year thing, but change is happening rapidly lately. So, we are digging away at hierarchy. And I think that's reason for optimism. On the other hand, and there is another hand about this, if we get too starry-eyed about the market and what it can do, we get really monstrous things like prisons run by profit-making organizations. That is an abomination to my way of looking at it. And yet right here in Canada we have it. And we're threatened all the time with having our health system destroyed by the American-type system and that's an abomination to my mind.

We have to be very clear about what we dare make the responsibility of the market and what we must keep as the responsibility of the public service and the public good.

We have to be very clear about what we dare make the responsibility of the

---

* In chapter 6 of *Dark Age Ahead*, "Self-Policing Subverted," Jacobs compares contemporary professions to ancient priesthoods, which preserved the right to regulate their own affairs. Unfortunately, police, architects, and Catholic priests alike, she writes, have been failing to fulfill the duties that traditionally afforded them that right, hence "dying" priesthoods.

market and what we must keep as the responsibility of the public service and the public good. When they get too mixed up—and this cult of efficiency is exactly such a mix-up, taken without understanding from commercial life and applied idiotically to government—it hurts the common good. There are lots of things that are not subject to being judged by financial success.

STEIN: I think we need to think about citizenship not just as voting in an election. We need to start thinking about citizenship as a part-time job that we all have. And then we ask ourselves, "Okay, which job am I going to take on? Am I going to go work in my local school? Am I going to go help out in the local clinic? Am I going to help out with a community issue?" Because it seems to me that's what crosses that bridge that we built between states and markets.

We know states do some things and markets do others—how do we fit this part-time citizen into our economy?

JACOBS: I think what you are describing has a great deal in common with art, which has always been a big question mark. Art done for art's sake is outside economic life. Artists do need, somehow or other, to eat but that's not why they do art. They do it because they're driven to it. And it's a gift. And I think that community things are done not for livelihood and not for power. That's where that work belongs.

In the past, all major empires have gradually become stagnant when they were unable to maintain themselves. In hindsight, we can see that the course of this melancholy pattern is marked by warfare that might be described as "continually sporadic," which sounds like an oxymoron, in order to combat insurrections, safeguard resources, strengthen unstable borders, bring client states into line, and oppose rival and would-be powers. Beginning with the Korean War, the U.S. seems to have fallen or been pushed into this pattern of continually sporadic warfare. The anticipated peace with the end of the Cold War has not materialized. What do you make of this, Janice? Is this an inevitable pattern for empires until they disintegrate or is there plausible reason to believe the U.S. could be an exception?

STEIN: That's a short question I could spend the rest of my life answering. My instinctive response is we don't know. I think the U.S. may be the exception and why do I think that?

I think that warfare was highly organized, and I think that's now in our past. We'll see some of it—just like people dueled even after dueling was outlawed. But I think that large-scale, mass movement, command and control warfare, which not only defined empires but which made states, is coming to a close. The modern state, as we know it, grew out of the capacity to make war. So did empires. War was the handmaid. Bureaucracies grew around war making. I think that idea is coming to a close. I really do. And we're moving to a different kind of network: knowledge-based world will. There will be lots of struggle. Power will still matter. It's naïve to think it won't. Work will still matter. Economics will still matter, but we may have passed through the death of empires through continuous warfare.

JACOBS: Good. I certainly hope you're right. That's what I would like to believe, too.

The Sparrow Principle

EXCERPT FROM "URBAN ECONOMY AND DEVELOPMENT,"
INTERVIEW WITH ROBERTO CHAVEZ, TIA DUER,
AND KE FANG OF THE WORLD BANK,
TORONTO, FEBRUARY 4, 2002

OPENING

JANE JACOBS: First I would like to mention some points that I think are basic, going through the list of questions you have given to me. The significance of cities for developing countries, and also for developed countries, is their economic behavior and their indispensability for a prospering economic life and everything associated with that, which is a lot of things that we call noneconomic.

This is a new idea to many people, and also to the World Bank. The last time I talked with the World Bank in 1984, it was assuming rural life with its agriculture and raw materials resources supported an economic life, and cities were a frill.

TIA DUER: I think it's changed a lot.

JACOBS: And for a long time, the Bank ran on those premises, and it was one reason I was reluctant to get involved again until you explained to me that they had learned better, because it was a waste of time.

DEVELOPING ON EACH OTHER'S SHOULDERS

JACOBS: Important as livability infrastructure is in cities, I don't think it is as basic as infrastructure that connects cities which are in about the same stage of development as one another. The conventional supposition in developed countries, which have often been imperialist, of course, has been to concentrate on infrastructure between very developed cities and poorer, undeveloped economies. That's okay to provide a kick-start for an undeveloped economy, but if that remains the only significant connection between a developing city and the rest of the world, what you get is something like Argentina or Uruguay. Their cities had strong connections with European and American developed cities, and for a while this seemed very successful. But they had little connection with each other or with other cities of Latin America. Yet economic connections between cities in initiative stages of development are vital; they can sell to each other, copy each other, and feasibly replace their imports from each other. And they can develop much of their economic life on each other's shoulders, which they can't do only on the shoulders of a highly developed economy because the gap in capabilities is too large.

ROBERTO CHAVEZ: The metropolis.

JACOBS: They can be given transplanted companies, but that doesn't provide them with the process for their own development. An infrastructure connecting cities in more or less the same stage of development must be safe, and to be waylaid by bandits is very bad, or to have thugs extorting tolls. The infrastructure, whether it is for pack animals, or for people on foot, bicycle, train, truck, water transport, or plane, whatever it consists of, it must be safe, and extortion-free.

SPECIALIZATION IS NO ANSWER TO LOCAL ECONOMIC DEVELOPMENT

JACOBS: Here's something that the World Bank didn't understand in the past and I am not sure it does now. Specialization of economic activity in a city can be a starter, a transitory starting point. If the city doesn't diversify rapidly, specializing is a dead end. No specialty is safe. All become either obsolete or outgrown. That's true whether in Detroit or Uzbekistan. So forget it as an economic strategy, except as a very transitory phase. The world is littered with little cities that once had a successful specialty. A city can even have once been successfully diversified—this was true of Detroit—and then decline, often specializing, as Detroit did, in favor of an activity that became particularly successful. As a strategy for cities, specialization is never good.

CHAVEZ: In connection with that, could I ask a question? We have something of a debate in the Bank about promoting the competition or the competitiveness of cities, and the assumption underlying that is that some cities will be better suited to develop certain areas or specialization. We're suggesting that we should encourage competitiveness, by finding out what makes a city "special" in order to build upon that. This seems to be in contradiction with what you're saying.

JACOBS: Yes, it's very much in contradiction. For example, Halifax in Nova Scotia was a great port and shipbuilding site in the early nineteenth century, the days of wooden ships and sail. Nova Scotia stagnated economically. It never progressed to building iron and steel ships, powered by steam. In contrast, Norway, which had been much like Nova Scotia in the days of wooden ships and sail, not only progressed in shipbuilding but diversified into navigation instruments which it could export everywhere and proceeded to diversify much further, with many kinds of design, technology and products, one kind of skill building on another. The notion that some cities are best suited for this or that kind of work is a carryover from Adam Smith's notion of regional division of labor.

Of course, geography and weather give Smith's idea some grounding. Gruyere cheese made in Switzerland is better than imitations elsewhere. You can grow apricots in some places and not in others. But there are very few things that one city is naturally equipped to do better than other cities.

DUER: One thing you're pointing to is how to support, not stand in the way of but hopefully also support, people's inherent creativity and looking for opportunities.

JACOBS: Yes, but when something is successful in a city, it can be a danger, if almost everything else is given up and starved of capital and encouragement.

DUER: It's like monoculture in agriculture. It's not sustainable.

JACOBS: Yes, exactly.

DIRECTLY LEND TO CITIES

JACOBS: But it is also destructive to try to make all the cities of a nation alike by putting them into a comprehensive development framework. This ignores the particularity of cities. The minute you begin to prescribe for cities' infrastructure or programs comprehensively, you try to make one size fit all. Actually, different cities, if they're working properly, are not behaving the same way at the same time. Some may be doing well on exporting but aren't replacing imports much. Others are doing just the opposite. Some, at a given time, may be receiving many immigrants. Others are not. If they're behaving properly, each has its own kinds of work emerging. Creative cities have even more individuality than nations. Cities are much older economic entities than nations. I think it's important that whoever is working on aiding cities doesn't work on bunches of cities through a centralized intermediary government.

DUER: Not through an intermediary, but one city at a time?

JACOBS: One city at a time, focusing on each individually and on its own situation at that time. So I wonder whether the

Bank's negotiations and loans always need to be with national governments.

DUER: This is a big, big issue for us with regard to supporting cities.

JACOBS: If you really are serious about supporting cities, you should be able to lend directly to cities and negotiate directly with them. After all, you've got a big clout—the money that you have gives you a big clout. If you are intimidated into dealing only with national governments, your intended help for cities will be inefficient at best and perhaps self-defeating.

CHAVEZ: That certainly doesn't have the city's best interest at heart.

JACOBS: National governments often don't. They often are afraid of cities. For one thing, economic development always upsets the status quo, and it does this first in cities. You have to face the fact that what you want to do for cities is not going to make everybody happy.

The main thing for livability is to outlaw crime, extortion, fraud, whatever is victimizing people; facilitate ownership and facilitate entrepreneurship. You probably know Hernando de Soto's book about registering property.

CHAVEZ: *The Mystery of Capitalism,* yes.*

---

* The Peruvian economist Hernando de Soto's book is actually called *The Mystery of Capital: Why Capitalism Triumphs in the West and Fails Everywhere Else*. In this and other writings, de Soto (1941–) argues that the solution to the spread of informal settlements in the cities of

JACOBS: And getting rid of all the nonsense that means it takes years to establish a tailor shop or anything productive.

DUER: Could I just pick up on the last point before we even go into anything else? You raised this point about facilitating ownership and entrepreneurship, and in many of the really profoundly poor slums in the cities in developing countries, people don't have secure tenure. It's the worst possible insecurity for them. They can be rousted out of there anytime and the whole area razed to the ground.

JACOBS: Yes. It's what makes gentrification so dangerous.

DUER: Are there ways in which the thinking that you've been doing about this question of supporting local entrepreneurship can support working directly with the communities in those slums—you know, dealing with the slum dwellers in terms of their own self-organization and getting the services in that they want and so on? What are the key things you think that we should bring to bear?

JACOBS: I think it goes without saying, almost, that the authorities ought to pay real attention to what the people in an area say they want. I have mentioned tree planting because I

---

the Global South will be found in giving squatters the right to own the land they are occupying. Formalizing informal settlements (and informal economies) will give those currently outside the political and social system a stake in maintaining that system and a role in promoting developing market economies. Critics suggest this silver bullet approach is a narrow version of more radical land reform visions and will simply increase inequality by giving some already more powerful settlers advantages over others who are less fortunate.

388 || VITAL LITTLE PLANS

love trees, but everybody doesn't love trees. And there may be other things that they want more, like a market.

Who can say what they care about the most?

CHAVEZ: Only they can.

JACOBS: Only they can. And that should be listened to very carefully and, above all, not disregarded on grounds that the authorities intend to do away with that district eventually, or give it a big makeover. No, small responsive evolutionary things are the ones that matter, and of course ensuring security of tenure.

COMMUNITY-BASED
ORGANIZATIONS

KE FANG: Jane, I have a question following up on this topic. In terms of better understanding what those dwellers and the residents need, what do you think about the role of community-based organizations?

JACOBS: You have to be careful that nobody is playing that old imperialist game of naming the organizations that authorities will recognize. Puppet organizations.*

We had a genuine citizens' organization that very success-

---

* This comment was likely inspired by Jacobs's experience battling urban renewal in 1960s Greenwich Village. There she found that before the public announcement of the project, New York officials had already approached carefully selected community organizations and even cultivated new "tenant" organizations for the cause. Elsewhere, she calls these groups "cuckoo committees," after the birds that co-opt the nests of other birds.

fully fought a dreadful urban renewal project in New York. Anybody who lived or worked in the neighborhood could belong to this organization. There were no dues, and no other qualifications. You only had to be there. Anybody who saw some need could start working on it, and anybody who wanted to join with them could do so. Totally permissive except for one hard and fast rule: Nothing that was done in connection with the community association could displace any person or business in the area. That was like a rule against murder.

We're used to the idea that you can do all kinds of things, but you can't murder somebody in the course of doing it. We called it the sparrow principle: not a sparrow shall be moved. Now, almost 45 years later, it's still a very vigorous organization, and it still has that rule and it still has that looseness of organization.

How is it supported with no dues? It needs money for quite a lot of things, including the newsletter, which I still get, and various other things. It has fundraising events. That's good because they're fun and bring people together. People can give small donations if they like, and specify their purposes.

But inclusiveness is what's important, and so is recognition that do no harm is basic to doing good. First, do no harm.

When authorities want an organization that they can co-opt and handle, they approach it very differently. It's not inclusive. There are various qualifications. They get very formal about *Robert's Rules of Order*.[*] In our organization, we never voted on anything. We depended on consensus.

At the annual meeting, anybody could get up and say what

---

[*]   *Robert's Rules of Order* (1876) is a book on parliamentary procedure, adherence to which would likely create a barrier to entry for the uninitiated.

they thought should be done, like the playground at such and such a place needed supervision, or there was a terrible plan afoot to do something or other to the neighborhood. There are always terrible plans afoot in New York. So as anybody mentioned something to be done, or the need to carry on with something already under way, it would be written on the blackboard and given a number. At the end of the meeting, everyone interested in number one would be told to go over beside the piano, anybody interested in number two go near the door, and so on. Maybe nobody would respond to a number except the person who had said it. Maybe many members would respond to other numbers.

Whoever showed up as wanting to work on a given task—cared about fundraising or whatever—would elect their own chairman out of their groups of volunteers. This was self-organization. Regular meet was held once a month. If there was a squabble about something, or an emergency arose, the system was flexible enough so that members could add or subtract what was being done. If there was dissension about any proposal or program, we wouldn't continue it or start it in the first place. What was done was always what people agreed should be done or at least had no persuasive objection to.

DUER: That is a really important lesson, actually, the—I mean, I know it has to be reinvented with every group, but in a sense, you know, the experience of this is really, really instructive. And helping groups that are starting to organize by having them meet and talk with people who have lived through this, gone through this, could be really helpful.

What's the name of this particular one?

JACOBS: This was the West Village Committee. They still have a newsletter. And as far as I know, they are the only neighborhood in New York that succeeded in getting a plan for housing built: the West Village Houses. It was hard to get. The city planning department lost the plans and there were other delays of seven years. Somebody at one of the planning department meetings said if we let this neighborhood plan for itself, every neighborhood will want to plan for itself.

DUER: What a great idea.

JACOBS: And it would have saved the city so much money because we worked out a plan that didn't require anything to be demolished. The new houses could go into vacant places. We had good architects who worked out three different plans that could, in combinations or alone, fit in any site. You could have the advantages of scale in design and construction without needing a big clean slate. And those houses remain very popular. They were an early example of infill.

COMMUNITY PARTICIPATION

JACOBS: Community participation was a great danger to us, too. It was mandated in the national urban renewal law but the way the city planning commission and other city agencies interpreted it was that if any community organization discussed with the officials or their staff what they thought would be good for the community, no matter whether they were going to get it or not, the participation provision in the law was fulfilled.

DUER: Oh, my God.

JACOBS: We would have been caught, trapped.

CHAVEZ: Just by talking.

JACOBS: Just by talking. Fortunately, somebody in our neighborhood, by pure luck, knew the federal official who was in charge of the New York and New England office of urban renewal. She got him to tour the neighborhood and see if he thought it was a slum. He didn't; he thought it was a wonderful neighborhood. But he told us about community participation, and said that if we wanted to save this neighborhood, the one thing we must never do was to speak of what we would like. This was the single most important thing we learned. We were called names for this: selfish and negative. What a bunch of negative people! But everybody in the neighborhood understood and was careful never to talk to anybody in government about what we would like.

We knew what we would like. Those houses I told you that we finally got? We were discussing those among ourselves. We were getting up a booklet about them. But we said never a word about them to the city until after we got the urban renewal designation officially removed. Absolutely, the only thing we would tell the government we wanted was to remove this designation.

We went to hearings where we proved that according to law the neighborhood wasn't a slum. That made no difference to the city. We were a slum; we were designated. But always they were trying to get us by one trick and another to say what we would like. Everybody in the neighborhood knew why but we never could get the newspapers to print this information. *The New York Times* wouldn't print it, although many of its reporters knew why we seemed so negative. We told them, and they could look at the law. Their editors wouldn't allow it to be printed. This information was such ammunition for the public that the establishment just didn't want the public to be armed with it. We were so lucky we had it.

DUER: And all because someone knew someone on the inside, basically.

JACOBS: That's right. I'm sure that this kind of thing happens in cities the Bank works with, and I wouldn't think you would want to cooperate with that kind of chicanery.

DUER: No, no, no.

JACOBS: I see over and over your emphasis on the importance of community participation, and I want to make sure you understand what traps can be arranged under its name. The Bank should not be a party to these traps, even if people are not warned and fall into them and are victimized by them, maybe especially then. People will know what happened to them. They will know who to hate, and the Bank will be among those.

This is vicious stuff, and under such nice names: community participation, power of the people, and so on. You always have to look for the substance of these things, not how nice they sound.

CHAVEZ: I think that's extraordinarily important for ourselves, for our work. I'm thinking back to a point you made earlier which had to do with doing for the people rather than the people doing for themselves. Somehow that ties into what you're saying here now. The true community action is where you're not substituting for the people or using that label to push your own agenda, but rather, to really allow the people to do for themselves.

JACOBS: Yes, that's very well put. I don't like the conception of economic trade-offs, meaning you sacrifice this in order to get that. Or social trade-offs either. It implies belief in a zero sum of social good or a zero sum economy instead of an expanding economy in which nobody needs to be worse off.

Also, communities that want a certain thing are derided for saying "not in my backyard." If you listen to "not in my backyard" people, their objection is often to something that shouldn't be in anybody's backyard. What has been proposed should be done differently. One example in America was low-income housing projects, awful projects, which shouldn't have been done that way. People were quite right not to want them. But they were called selfish and told they must accept a trade-off for the sake of the housing.

When enough people said no, either of two things happened: low-income housing was dropped, which is bad because it is needed, or planners learned how to do it better than just doing projects.

Housing projects weren't a necessary way to build affordable housing. Sewage treatment shouldn't be done in a way that stinks up a neighborhood. Those are just examples. But trade-offs, and the notion that people have to make them, always need examination.

ON GLOBALIZATION

JACOBS: Your material comments that globalization can be a political opportunity for redistribution policies that favor the poor. Redistribution policies are stopgaps but not cures for poverty. You want to help the poor be able to support themselves. If cities' economies are working, they keep manufacturing a middle class. There probably will always be some poor, but they needn't be the same poor and there needn't always be so many. In fact, good economies and good policies can reduce the poor to almost none.

In the Netherlands, there are almost no poor. In Switzerland, there are almost no poor. It can be done, but it isn't accomplished by redistribution. I'm not saying there shouldn't be redistribution, which is vital for some people, but it's no cure for poverty.

Globalization does involve shifts in economic power, and these shifts do not always favor the already powerful. In fact, the shifts never favor the already powerful. It wouldn't be a shift.

CHAVEZ: That's right.

JACOBS: Development, whether it's globalized or not, always involves shifts in power. If development occurs in a feudal economy and feudal society, it undercuts the power of the feudal authorities. In a capitalist society, development undercuts the

Development, whether it's globalized or not, always involves shifts in power. . . . It doesn't mean absolute losses in prosperity for people who formerly were well off. But it does mean losses of ability to control other people.

power of old money, older capitalists, enterprises and fortunes. Bound to happen. You might as well recognize this. It doesn't mean absolute losses in prosperity for people who formerly were well off. But it does mean losses of ability to control other people, which is a different thing.

DUER: Because there's more power sharing in real development.

JACOBS: Yes, sure. And so that's going to happen. I find it hard to put myself in the place of people who want to control other people, and to whom that's important to their own identity. But there are people like that, and they are in an unavoidable conflict with development. Better that such people should become dissolute playboys.

I don't think that's so bad as becoming tyrants.

Your material mentions that global growth often threatens the environment. But so does stagnation, lack of development, because the same resources are exploited too long and monotonously. Parts of the world have been devastatingly deforested where wood was used too long for fuel.

It's only in developing and growing economies that you find shifts to alternative resources, and ways of repairing what was done in the past. That's where hope lies.

Global warming is quite rightly emphasized in your material, also pollution by fossil fuels. Notice what kind of stagnation goes along with that: stagnation of transportation in

America and Canada. It's not because there's been progress in the sense of development of transportation. In fact, we need development to combat this pollution.

DUER: Yes, get past it. Diversification, types of transport.

JACOBS: I thought this material about the different waves of globalization is very interesting. The period from 1870 to 1914 was notable in the United States for inventions and innovations of all kinds, and also for globalization of trade. The gains in transportation were only part of a much larger, very complicated collection of technical changes and also shifts in power. The country went through a period of growth of monopolies and trusts, but then embarked on trust busting and breakup of monopolies, which was important to allow development to continue.

I'm old enough to be very aware of what an extraordinary period that was because my parents were born in the 1870s. I loved hearing about their childhood when I was a child in the 1920s. It was like another world, things had changed so much. When my mother was eight years old, she was chosen to push the button that turned on the first electric lights in her town.

Imagine no electricity there before. This is so close to me, it makes modern history seem very short.

In the period from the First World War until after the Second World War there was much less invention and innovation. I marvel at that too. For instance, my family had a dishwasher in the 1920s. And yet there were no further advances in dishwashers for decades and few more people had them. My parents weren't rich, but they liked to try practical improvements.

My father, who was a doctor, had an automobile so he could use it to call on patients before the First World War. They had a telephone, again, because that was important for a doctor. At the same time, the building where he had his office had an elevator. I even flew in an airplane as a child. Then came the long period of not much change except in fashions. Now we have the Internet and another wave of globalization. So I think I was fascinated to read this about these waves.

One thing very different in the two—I hope it's different—is that the first wave of globalization coincided with imperialism. Back in 1905, there were only fifty sovereignties in the whole world.

DUER: That's amazing when you think of it.

JACOBS: Yes. Now there are about 187. The reason there were only fifty was the fact of empires. Think how much of the world came under the sovereignty of the British and how many new sovereignties have broken from that empire. There were the Austro-Hungarian and the Ottoman Empires and Russian, German, French and Dutch Empires. Why settle on 1905 as the high point of empires? Because in 1905 a new sovereignty, the first one for a long time, came into being. That was Norway, which broke away from Sweden. Once, of course, Sweden had been a great empire but about its only possession left at the time was Norway.

The reason I said I hope globalization is different this time is that there is a danger that the current globalization wave can be a kind of new imperialism. This is what frightens many people. It's very common to call America an empire. This is not only because of the World Bank and the IMF, but these institutions are reasons for people fearing a new empire, especially if your policies are like imperial policies.* For instance, economic specializations in conquered possessions were so often imposed by imperial governments. It's another reason for you to be so wary of specializations.

DUER: What role do you think multinational corporations have in pushing this kind of imperialism in the sense that they have much more power than a lot of countries have, they're trans-jurisdiction, they can move from place to place at will. And they have, as all corporations have, much more economic power than the dispersed consumers who are doing the purchasing. It's that much greater a disparity when you're talking about the people in fully organized societies.

JACOBS: Yes. Multinational corporations may not be monopolies, but they have a lot in common with monopolies. The reason why they're menaces and why they remain disproportionately powerful is that there is not a good birth rate of other enterprises in their field. There have long been these multinational corporations. Under imperialism, they were the East India Company and so on.

---

* The International Monetary Fund is an organization founded in 1944 (along with the World Bank) to promote international trade and global economic growth through lending to member countries. In *Cities and the Wealth of Nations,* Jacobs sharply criticizes the economic policies and practices of the World Bank and the IMF. Like many other critics, Jacobs objects to the power the IMF and the World Bank have in determining and overseeing local economies from the outside through debt-based lending and administrative rules determined in Washington.

400 VITAL LITTLE PLANS

DUER: Big tool of imperialism.

JACOBS: The opium dealers who started opium sales in China—

CHAVEZ: Were English.

JACOBS: They were a combination of what now we would call a drug cartel and a monopoly, and ruinous in many ways. That's why there were the Opium Wars. President Roosevelt's ancestors made their money selling opium in China.[*] It was a big Yankee thing. Turning Chinese into junkies, that was awful.

These are not new. Whether they're drug cartels, which are another kind of multinational corporation, or whether they're McDonald's or Walmart, they aren't new. And the only way to keep them from concentrating power is for competitions to keep emerging. Walmart itself is an example which rose up from some little town in Arkansas and did a better marketing and assembling job than old department stores, which were very powerful in their day, but stagnated and have been disappearing, along with Woolworth and Sears. Walmart really did do a better job for consumers than they did. But it will probably stagnate. Even if it doesn't, we can presume others will arise, and this is not so bad.

The worst multinational corporations are not ones that go after customers in that way; they're very vulnerable. Consumers are flighty. Somebody else will take their fancy, just as

---

[*]   Indeed, Warren Delano (1809–98), the grandfather of Franklin Delano Roosevelt, made his fortune selling opium in China, widely recognized as an immoral trade, even by Delano himself.

Walmart won them away from Woolworth's or Penney's or other stores. The really dangerous ones are corporations that are big buyers. They are the ones that use pressure on forestry companies to clear-cut. They use pressure on all kinds of companies to trim costs at the expense of their workers and at the expense of the environment.

DUER: You're talking about ones that are mining companies and manufacturing—

CHAVEZ: Gas trading companies.

JACOBS: Right. And it's useful to distinguish between those two kinds because Walmart is not really hurting the environment. It might even turn into an Ikea.

DUER: Well, you could make arguments that stores like Walmart really undermine local economies because they come in at such scale, and they also don't care about the environmental impact where, in fact, they're developing. But I can see what you're saying. It's a different scale of impact overall. It's on the locality in which they operate.

CHAVEZ: It's not global.

JACOBS: That's right, and the reason they undermine local economies—I look at this also from the viewpoint of a consumer—is that in so many places there isn't a decent general store. There could be, like the good local bookstore I told you about on my shopping street, or our hardware store, which have flourished in spite of big chains.* Even though they own their buildings, if they weren't good stores, too, they would succumb.

So for anything that's in direct contact with consumers it's true that to a great extent the consumers are their bosses. In some places consumers may be prisoners of stores; there may be only one grocery store. When my father finished medical school, the first place he worked as a doctor, as part of his apprenticeship, was for a mining company, as a company doctor, in West Virginia. The people there had no choice of anything. The mining company controlled the entire local economy.

DUER: It was a company town, basically.

JACOBS: I'm full of admiration for lots of things in your globalization paper. It mentions that developing a sound investment climate is primarily a national and local responsibility and should focus particularly on the problems facing small firms. It points out that employment in small- and medium-sized firms in towns and rural areas will be central to raising living standards of the rural poor. It's also even more true that in cities employment in small- and medium-sized firms is central to improvement. Plenty of such firms represent the best chance for development, and this will also indirectly help rural economies.

---

* Although it is omitted from this interview, Jacobs describes her shopping street, Toronto's Bloor Street, in "Time and Change as Neighborhood Allies," in this volume.

Your material about the high returns from education is very good, and how important this is to poor people.

I'm glad to see that empowerment with respect to organizing property rights and government in a way that involves poor people is mentioned.

Debt relief is mentioned. Yes, there must be debt relief for unrealistic, unpayable debts, the same as in any bankruptcy. Think of debt relief in the context of pseudo-imperialism; that is, how did these bad debts to rich countries arise? What were the assumptions behind them? Who did the loans benefit?

Canada is culpable in this respect. For instance, much of Canada's foreign aid is not really for the benefit of people who are getting the aid. These are actually subsidies to Canadian companies, called foreign aid to make them more palatable. They go especially to Quebec companies because of domestic Canadian problems.* At least in these cases Canadians, not poor countries, pay. But all tied aids need to be looked at suspiciously, as economically imperialistic.

CLOSING

DUER: It would be, I think, really important if you could reflect on what you think would be the most important advice to give urban staff working in the Bank in terms of the role that

---

* The primary "domestic problem" to which Jacobs is referring is Quebec's separatist movement, which she defended in her 1980 book *The Question of Separatism*. In *Cities and the Wealth of Nations,* she would go on to investigate the various measures that nations take to keep their constituencies loyal, including such foreign aid contracts.

the Bank should play in urban development. What's the most important type of contribution that should be made?

JACOBS: Maybe the Bank isn't the right instrument for urban development if it must deal with superior governments all the time.

DUER: In some countries it can lend through subsidiary loan agreements down to city governments.

FANG: The Bank is proposing to establish a new fund through which the Bank may directly give some funds to cities, because it is, as you mentioned, very important for supporting urban development.

JACOBS: If you have a means of doing it, it should be done in preference, whenever you're dealing with cities. In preference to going through a central government, it's better to deal directly with the city and the city government. If you can't do that, it's questionable whether you ought to be doing anything.

DUER: Well, you raise something that's a real challenge for us, actually. It's something we're trying to come to terms with, but it's a real problem. It's also a problem because when you operate through central ministries, it will often be a certain sector, like the Ministry of Construction, that actually is the conduit for the funds. And then you don't, in fact, get a whole city government with all its departments interacting around solving the problems.

JACOBS: That's absolutely right, it undercuts city autonomy as well as particularity. It is serving the agenda of another government, which may not even recognize what is actually needed in the city. I was serious when I said maybe not do anything. Remember, do no harm. You may just be adding to future unpayable debt. Which is harm.*

---

*　On the cover page of the original transcript of this interview, Jacobs offered this commentary: "The three staff members of the Bank were bright and mean well, but the Bank is sure to louse up their efforts."

Uncovering the Economy:
A New Hypothesis

——

EXCERPT FROM UNPUBLISHED BOOK, 2004

PART I: THE TRIPLE PROCESS

INTRODUCTION

THIS IS AN ECONOMICS TEXTBOOK. IT SETS FORTH A NEW WAY of understanding macroeconomic behavior: how it organizes itself and operates at urban, national, continental, imperial and global levels, sustains—or fails to sustain—itself. Macroeconomic life is also large-scale in the sense of time.

I urge readers to retain prudent skepticism and to remain protective of their individual judgments and experiences, a caution that applies, or should apply, to alert reading of any work on economics to avoid being misled by authorial enthusiasm. This book is no different in that respect, of course. If anything, it is more demanding than other economic texts because both its substance and form are unconventional.

My points of departure and frequent touchstones are three commonplace economic phenomena. One of these, the first I shall describe, is a peculiar pattern of sporadic city growth that is absent in villages and towns. The pattern was conventionally taken to be *inexplicable* in olden times. Since the eighteenth-century Enlightenment, the Age of Reason and Science—a period we still inhabit—the sporadic growth pattern has been deemed *irrational*.

The second commonplace, city import replacement, has conventionally been thought to be both too irrational and too trivial to account for anything of much importance.*

The third phenomenon, city import shifting, is an automatic response to city import replacement. It has conventionally been ignored, although if I am correct, it is a phenomenon largely responsible for economic expansion.

After studying these three seemingly separate phenomena, I have concluded that they are actually three different aspects of one and the same phenomenon. Acting together, they organize self-sustaining macroeconomic activity and its smaller-scale derivatives (in real life, everything connects with everything else; nothing is isolated).

The three phenomena (actually one) together exert such force and power that they are spookily more in charge of our macroeconomic fates than the human beings who assume they are directing what happens and determining what is to be expected from *their* activities.

The body of this text consists largely of extracts drawn from previous books of my own. I have arranged the extracts in a new sequence, aimed at improving their coherence and clarity. Also, I have rigorously stripped them down. Originally this ma-

---

* By "import replacement," Jacobs simply means the replacement of products or services that a city once imported with improvised local versions. See "Strategies for Helping Cities" in this volume for a more detailed description of the process, and its connection to innovation.

terial was interlarded with many examples and substantiations, taken as I found them by following promising clues. Shorn of these and other embellishments of context, the lean and sequentially rearranged material appears here as straightforward statements of fact. Readers curious about omitted sources, justifications or other contextual information are referred to citations of my original material at the close of each extract or condensation. The reader can readily flesh out the citation by referring to notes following texts of chapters. These give sources of my information, frequently with other bits of germane and auxiliary information. Here is a sample citation:

"The most truthful information that statistics give us is that for some reason researchers have become interested in what they're counting," commented Armbruster.*

The negative correlation is that things not interesting to investigators don't get counted.

In sum, my stripped-down extracts and condensations are a self-selected anthology of my germane findings over a period of almost fifty years. During much of that time, I myself wasn't sure what I was doing, nor what I was looking for, until the clues I followed revealed their relationships and meaning of their own accord. What I was doing was learning. This is not an

---

* This sample is drawn from *The Nature of Economies,* p. 60. Armbruster was a character in this book and in *Systems of Survival.* He is a retired publisher—perhaps a nod to her long and close friendship with famed publisher Jason Epstein (1928–)—and in both cases the instigator of the social gathering that is the occasion for the book.

efficient way to learn, or to guide others. But it is the only way when one must start from scratch.

Having inefficiently learned, finally, what I was doing—revising economics, the better to understand what economies are doing on their own terms—I am now able to explain it to myself in a textbook which aims to explain it to others.

POWERFUL YET HELPLESS

Economic life that was surprisingly highly developed and admirably expanded is much older than our attempts to explain it to ourselves. Prehistoric achievements still serve as foundations for many economic activities today, the world over. Think about weaving, pottery, the wheel; think about river and ocean navigation; metals and alloyed metals such as bronze; stringed bows to twirl as fire-makers; hearths, smoke holes, roof-carrying carved timber columns, brick and stone construction with roof-carrying walls and arches; cooking, vegetable-oil pressing, fermentation; bartering and trade customs for acquiring valuable amber and pigments from far-distant sources, and superior cutting edges from distant, cooled volcanic glass flows; local weights, measures and (probably) local markets for local crafts; spears, nets and traps for hunting, raiding and warfare; awe-rousing tombs, embalming, corpse clothing, burial furnishings; painting; sculptures of wood, stone and clay; jewelry; percussion, stringed and wind instruments for making music; horticulture, grain agriculture, and domesticated animals for meat; transportation and by-products such as skins, feathers, leather, fur, fibers, horn sinews and teeth . . . all this and more, including specialized tools and tools to make tools.

Prehistoric means, of course, "before written documentation." Knowing this, the alert and skeptical reader will in a flash offer an alternative proposal to the unbelievable antiquity of foundation goods, services and skills; their prehistoric ancestry may merely testify instead that, amid the complex and diverse abundance and complicated interrelationships of skills, the craft of converting spoken language and the art of recording quantities with numeracy (which probably preceded writing) may have been very late bloomers.

In our Eurocentric way, many of us tend to think of foundation goods and services such as those I've just mentioned as having been contributed to general or world economic life from parts of Europe now popularly known as "the West." Some evidently were, especially from portions of the continent touching the Mediterranean and Black Seas, or territory close by, now known as Mesopotamia and the Middle East. But North Africa was a notable originator and contributor, and also Asia, especially what are now India and China and their offshoots.

What is now known as the West began its modern development and expansion just about a thousand years ago in postclassical and pre–Late Medieval times in what is now Spain, Portugal, Italy, France, Switzerland, the Netherlands, Greece and what is now Turkish Anatolia. Apart from some regions that have long outlived their formerly prospering heydays, the West currently contains the world's most prosperous, strongest and most influential economies. But it is curiously helpless too.

Alone, and working together through larger economic organs such as the World Bank, the International Monetary Fund, and World Trade blocs, nations sharing this rich and powerful economy have lavished great wealth and efforts to overcome poverty and economic backwardness in poor countries, often to little or no avail. Often the objects of this rich largesse are left burdened with debts so large and economic schemes and plans so unrealistic that the debts are unpayable; even interest payments to keep the unfortunate beneficiaries technically out of loan default must be borrowed, often from the banks that advanced the original loans, to keep them technically solvent.

More tellingly still, rich and powerful nations of the West have even less success attempting to overcome causes of poverty and economic backwardness in persistently poor pockets (and whole large regions!) of their own home territories, to transform these into places capable of developing self-sustaining economies.

Important pieces of economic understanding must clearly be missing or misleading.

PUZZLING BURSTS

My formal education in the conventional economics of the day, Columbia University (at the dawn of Keynesianism), was scanty and superficial, and then and for years afterwards I thought the subject bored me.* What engaged my attention eventually was a

* As Jacobs writes in the first chapter of *Cities and the Wealth of Nations,* John Maynard Keynes (1883–1946) was "the most influential economist of this [the twentieth] century" (16). According to her summary, Keynes argued that oversaving could lead to reduced demand and thus economic slowdowns and rising unemployment. To counteract this, he reasoned that governments could use deficit spending to catalyze private spending and thus economic growth.

peculiar, sporadic growth pattern—a commonplace for cities, but not for villages and towns. A puzzle.

Embryonic cities (except for those originating as planned ceremonial centers) have few obvious differences to distinguish them from other small and budding settlements; gradually and tamely the city-to-be enlarges its economy as its initial export work grows and earns imports from both domestic and foreign producers. The embryonic city's exports, like its imports, include goods and services in both domestic and foreign trade.

However, after an indeterminate period—which may be as short as only a year or two—the embryonic city abandons its tame and gradual mode of growth and experiences a burst of unaccountable growth and economic diversification. After another indeterminate period, the growth burst runs its course and disappears as abruptly and unaccountably as it appeared; it returns to slow and gradual import-earning export growth again, lasting until and unless another sporadic burst recurs. If it does, the repeat burst is usually larger than the first, and the next one—if there is a next one—is still larger, and so on.*

We hardly recognize a little city to have become a city until

---

* According to her son Jim, in *Uncovering the Economy* Jacobs hoped to further explain the conditions that prompt these explosive bursts of import replacement. First, she surmised that a city must be in the midst of a period of high unemployment. While painful, this downturn acts as a catalyst, increasing the number of people who are available and motivated to undertake new work and test out new ideas. Second, these unemployed entrepreneurs must also have access to enough unrestricted capital, whether through their own savings, family loans, or similar informal mechanisms, to invest in their untested business. Finally, and perhaps most importantly, the city must still retain a healthy network of small, diverse producers for these new businesses to draw upon and creatively recombine. For this reason, a city only has a short window after an economic downturn for this self-organizing process to take place. Otherwise, the network of producers begins to break down, and savings dry up. By Jacobs's reckoning, the rarity of these three conditions appearing together accounts for the similar rarity of explosive city growth.

it has had a first growth burst and in the process rounded itself out with the usual goods and services common to other little cities of its time and place. Even small cities that have grown only briefly and then stagnated decisively have had at least one period of extraordinarily abrupt and astonishing development and expansion. Often we can tell just when it happened by observing the architectural period of the little city's buildings; so much was built during a single swift interval. Villages and towns do not grow this way, but then they do not become cities either. The alert, skeptical reader will probably say at this point, in a flash, "Hey, maybe this peculiar growth pattern is not an innate attribute of cities; maybe it demonstrates that any settlement behaving that way *becomes* a city, as a consequence."

The alert reader may be right. It is an arguable point, much like interminable debates whether nature or nurture or both form human personality and character traits. Whether the pattern makes the city or the city makes the pattern, the result demonstrates an oddity unique to cities. The weight of evidence, for reasons I will explain later, indicates that the city makes the pattern. Odder still, with rare exceptions, all large cities have experienced many sporadic bursts, and all great cities, without exception as far as I know, have experienced such enormous bursts that these are more aptly described as growth explosions.

This pattern, by the way, is both notably stubborn and ancient. When Rome, at the start of the fourth century B.C. experienced an explosive episode (surely not its first) sufficiently powerful to alarm the city fathers, they adopted a policy to thwart it by forbidding further immigration into Rome and encouraging Roman residents to leave the city. Like many attempts to defeat growth explosions since, the civic policy instead was defeated by the explosion, which proved invincible. This episode has long puzzled historians because Rome's exports were not growing at the time, nor can the economic surge be explained by conquest. Rome conquered the Italian peninsula, beyond Latium, the city's immediate hinterland, *following* this growth explosion.

Now I am going to break my own self-imposed rule, mandating austerity of contextual prolixity, because to omit a few examples and some substantiation while communicating the enormous power and force exerted by city growth explosions would be as artificial as discussing big animals without mention of elephants and whales.

Ordinarily when a city is host or hostess to a growth explosion, it still retains some of its important older import-earning exports; the imports they customarily earn for the city's economy can thus remain at much the same value and volume as previously, or else expand gradually. However, sometimes the development and expansion owed to a growth explosion is unequivocal, and clearly responsible for overcoming a period of decline. In Los Angeles a situation of just this kind occurred as World War II was coming to a close. During the war, in spite of wartime shortages, the city economy had soared in the value and volume of its export work and the imports it had earned.

Companies manufacturing aircraft, the city's largest industry, laid off about three-quarters of their workers from the end of 1944 to the end of 1945, reducing employment in the industry from 210,000 to 18,000. Shipbuilding, the second largest industry, reduced its workforce a bit more slowly, with a decline in jobs from 60,000 to 18,000 between 1945 and 1949. The Hollywood motion picture industry was embarked on a long-term decline. Petroleum, once the city's largest import-earning export and still an important one until 1946, was thereafter lost to the city's import-earning export economy because the city's people and enterprises took to consuming so much gasoline that the city economy ran a petroleum deficit and became a petroleum importer. One type of old and formerly stable export work had been depot service associated with nationwide distribution of citrus fruits, walnuts and avocados grown in the hinterland. The depot service, and much of the arboricultural produce as well, were lost as import-earning exports because the groves were uprooted to clear land for low-density housing tracts, shopping malls, highways, expressways and parking lots in the city's immediate suburban hinterland. Farther out, in lower density exurbs, the groves were sacrificed to track farms supplying the city and its growing numbers of restaurants, gourmets, inspired amateur chefs and ethnic food enthusiasts with produce and novel dining ingredients.

During almost a decade the fortunes of Los Angeles's economy sank until they were lower than at any time except the depths of the Great Depression of the 1930s. Yet as the 1950s dawned, prosperity returned; the city in 1949 had generated more jobs than it ever had previously. The necessary imports poured in, yet export-earning imports had not poured out, one more case to confuse economists and other experts who *knew* that growing imports ought to mandate growing exports, and were in the presence, instead, of economic growth seemingly detached from an export-import part of a relevant economy.

It wasn't "seemingly" detached, it really was detached from the city's import-export economy. The Los Angeles economy had unpredictably and suddenly taken to earning imports by a different method. It was engaging in a torrent of replacements of the city's funds of previously earned imports: an explosion of import replacements with local production for local markets.

The enterprises adopting the "unconventional" tactic were always small to begin with, much smaller than the old, shrinking exporting firms. They were also improvising. They consisted of very few proprietors and workers, anywhere from two or three to forty-something. They started in corners of old loft buildings with cheap rents, in Quonset huts and backyard garages, in basements and living rooms. They poured forth sliding doors, china, mechanical saws, shoes, bathing suits, underwear, futons, sleeping bags and other frugal furnishings, cameras, hand tools, hospital equipment, scientific instruments, engineering services and hundreds of other things. One-eighth of all the new businesses started in the United States during the latter half of the 1940s were started in Los Angeles. Not all were replacing former imports, but most were. Not all were successful, but many were—some stunningly. For example, a company making sliding doors for local house builders was started in 1948 by a young engineer who had left his previous job in the materials laboratory of Douglas Aircraft to manufacture a furnace that soon was obsolete. He then started the door business in a Quonset hut with a young architect as partner. They succeeded locally, and by 1955 were exporting doors far and wide. It had become the biggest exporter of glass doors in the United States.*

---

* This account, Jacobs notes, was condensed from *The Economy of Cities*, pp. 151–53.

A DISTINCTLY CITY PHENOMENON

We are concerned here with a force of enormous social power and economic might. Los Angeles's experience of its unequivocal force was not singular. Allowing for cultural and other differences separating sixteenth-century England and twentieth-century America, the enigma of Los Angeles seems to have occurred in London at a time when both the foreign and domestic imports of that city were shrinking drastically from differing causes. Nobody knows when London experienced its first growth burst, but it was before London was granted a royal charter to collect its own taxes. Starting, nevertheless, in the late sixteenth century and pushing into the seventeenth, London experienced a notable growth explosion. A case could be made that the golden age of Elizabethan England and the initial voyages of its great explorers depended on the growth explosion. How poor London would have been without it.

Or consider the growth pattern of Paris. In the twelfth century Paris had been no more important than half a dozen other French commercial and manufacturing cities. But during the thirteenth century Paris unpredictably became five or six times the size of the next largest city in the realm. Again, growth of exports doesn't account for that episode, nor does royal favor account for it. The city's promotion to France's major city and, after that to the permanent royal or capital city, followed the growth explosion that bestowed urban dominance.

New York's growth explosions followed so rapidly upon one another that from 1820 to 1930 it was either entering, experiencing or ending (with much disorder and anxiety) a growth explosion. Early in that period, it supplanted older and richer Boston and Philadelphia as the preeminent U.S. city.

In classical times, a comment by Herodotus implied that he recognized this mighty sporadic force, saw it as a distinctly city phenomenon, but took it for granted.* Until the eighteenth-century Enlightenment, which idealized Reason and Science as the human talents that legitimized mankind's lordship over the earth and all its fruits and creatures, most earthly phenomena were considered either inexplicable or projections of inscrutable super-natural decisions. Catherine the Great was an early disciple of the Enlightenment (Voltaire himself was her mentor) and a fan of Reason, at least in the abstract. An exasperated Catherine looked at the distribution of work in the world she knew, and wrote:

> Most of our factories are in Moscow, probably the least advantageous spot in all Russia. It is dreadfully overpopulated and the workers become lazy and disso-lute. . . . On the other hand, hundreds of small towns are crumbling in ruins. . . . Why not transport a factory to each of them, according to the produce of the district and the quality of the water? The workmen would be more industrious and the towns would flourish.†

Catherine was not asking the hard questions: Where did the factories that bloated Moscow come from? And what if there weren't enough for all those crumbling towns?

---

* Jacobs is likely referring to the passage by Herodotus that she uses as the epigraph to *The Economy of Cities*: "I will [tell] the story as I go along of small cities no less than of great. Most of those which were great once are small today; and those which in my own lifetime have grown to greatness, were small enough in the old days."

† This passage comes from *Cities and the Wealth of Nations,* pp. 103–4.

REASON AND PROGRESS TAKE ON THE CITY

Growth bursts and explosions have seldom been welcomed by people taking serious responsibility for city livability and finances. City boosters without responsibility for public affairs or, to use a fine old term, the common good, are another matter. It is easy to understand the hostility of responsible people. Unplanned and unpredictable, the bursts and explosions heedlessly ruin good agricultural land and ecological treasures at city outskirts. They obliterate previously established city amenities and convenience. They overwhelm the capacities of existing infrastructures and those that have been planned for future needs, from schools and sewer systems to adequate transportation systems and tidily operating institutions of government. They drive up land prices, drive out facilities that no longer have expansion room on which they had counted, drive away residents who no longer recognize their home communities nor feel at home in them. As a final outrage, at just about the time when compromises and makeshifts start to corral chaos, the growth rate

City growth patterns . . . are messy and leave messes in their wake. They insult trust in order and offend authority of all kinds.

can plummet as suddenly and unpredictably as it appeared, leaving forecasts embarrassingly deflated. City growth patterns, in sum, are messy and leave messes in their wake. They insult trust in order and offend authority of all kinds; perhaps that is their most unpardonable perversity.

In modern times, I firmly believed, many experts with better educations than mine, and sharper or quicker minds, must have become aware of such striking and commonplace phenomena as city growth bursts and explosions. How could they not have become aware? And some among these savants must have asked themselves the same questions for which I sought simple, direct answers: What starts a growth explosion? What terminates it? What is going on during its frenetic activity? (And one more generalized question: why is this a *city* pattern of growth?) So I airily supposed I could pick up, ready-made, the information I sought. Good. I wouldn't have to reinvent the wheel.

I was wrong.

Because of my job at the time, as a writer and a sub-editor for an architectural and planning magazine, I was able to speak readily with highly respected city experts in the United States to see how Reason and Progress were doing in North America. No matter what their nationalities, they all agreed on their aim of defeating the nasty way cities grow. Their ideas of how to accomplish this were sometimes far out. Some advocated forcing cities to take the form of long, narrow, densely settled strings. Others preferred cookie-cutter (meaning standardized) configurations located at major expressway intersections. That was a favorite of my own editor. Of course, eccentricities like these went nowhere except as fads to spice up international conferences and journalists' feature stories. My program of learning about the peculiar but commonplace city growth pattern went nowhere too.

Whether in person or in print, the experts I consulted were much too reasonable and too pressed by their ongoing important tasks to waste time investigating what they already knew was irrational. I heard a lot from them about city growth, but only from the viewpoint of beating Reason and Science into cities. They generously and patiently instructed me in what they were doing: in sum, they were creating, refining and touting ways and means of putting work where they reasoned that it belonged and squelching it where they reasoned it didn't. Catherine would have been proud of them all. The experts were laboring at the hard and absorbing work of preventing city growth explosions from happening, or thwarting them if they started.

The experts and their colleagues and graduate students worked out elaborate master plans for cities and their regions, and nation and continent-wide transportation plans, and worked even harder at getting these accepted and funded. They contrived for cities and suburbs anti-city zoning codes, outlawing high densities and high ground coverages and mandating segregated land uses such as shopping in controllable malls, and housing tracts so uncontaminated by any other land uses that cars became necessities merely to get on with life. To get all this worked out effectively, financed and enforced was a big, big task; it amounted to means of creating sprawl, no trivial achievement.

If it seemed to the tidy-minded experts that more was needed, including injections of charm, New Towns and Garden Cities were planned and some were built to try and attract factories or other work places. Greenbelts were mapped as barriers to city growth bursts and explosions.

I believe in Reason and Progress too. We still dwell in the period of the Enlightenment, and as a human being I appreciate deeply the benefits Reason and Science have given to beneficiaries fortunate enough to receive them. But it did not seem plausible to me that a growth pattern so stubborn, evident over such long periods, responding to some mysterious clock of its own, could occur for No Reason. Surely, the operation of Cause and Effect had not been abolished, and that was all I was seeking—causes and effects of a commonplace phenomenon.

I believe in Reason and Progress too. . . . It did not seem plausible to me that a growth pattern so stubborn, evident over such long periods, responding to some mysterious clock of its own, could occur for No Reason.

I was already suspicious of the quality of Reason being applied to cities. From my experience of daily living and raising children in a large city (New York) I was not convinced that the diagnoses and prescriptions of the experts whom I consulted and whose advice and its consequences were being demonstrated were giving cities, their people and their businesses the help and improvements they needed; on the contrary, they were being harmed.[*]

Another thing: the experts I consulted or read were united in assuming that the growth explosions they were battling were a pushover. This is not true. Every now and again, the magazine on which I worked carried inspirational essays, the purpose of which was that given sufficient (but not exorbitant) public funding plus society's determination and enough political guts, the willful ways of cities could handily be suppressed. Come on guys! We can do it! It's not that hard! People who kid themselves are not trustworthy guides through the complicated mazes of reality.

From early childhood I had liked cities; they contained so many surprising and interesting people and things to see and think about. It was no treat, then, seeing them described as car-

---

[*] Jacobs here notes that the reader should see *Death and Life,* "which in its entirety was devoted to this subject."

riers of a disease called Blight and, later on, as *being* a disease, Cancer, requiring radical surgery:

> You are in effect suggesting that an old surgeon give public judgment on the work of a confident but sloppy novice, operating to remove an imaginary tumor to which the youngster has erroneously attributed the patient's affliction, whilst over-looking major impairments in the actual organs. Surgery has no useful contribution to make in such a situation, except to sew up the patient and dismiss the bungler. . . . *

LUCKY FRACTALS

With my progress stalled, in spite of several years of diligent interviews and reading, I turned to other interests and shoved my paltry findings into a dead-storage bin for abandoned puzzles in the back of my mind, drawn wistfully forth now and again to scan for another clue. There the discard would probably have stayed permanently had I not, entirely by chance, bumped into a revivifying fractal in the marvelous pre-computer card catalogue in the New York Public Library's main reading room. . . .

"I keep coming across references to fractals," said Hortense, "but what are they? And why should we care about them?"

---

* Lewis Mumford, letter, October 18, 1961, to a Mr. Wensberg, looking for comment on an article by Jacobs. Reprinted in Max Allen's edited volume *Ideas That Matter: The Worlds of Jane Jacobs*, 96.

"They're complicated-looking patterns that are actually made up of the same motif repeated on different scales," said Kate. "For instance, a muscle is a twisted bundle of fibers. Dissect out any one of those fiber bundles, and you find that it, too, is a twisted bundle of fibers. And so on. When you get down to the irreducibly smallest fiber, which you need an electron microscope to see, you find that it's a twisted strand of molecules. That's a real-life fractal. Mathematicians make computer-generated fractals, fascinating in their complexity and seeming variety, yet each fractal is made of repetitions."

"We should care about fractals," said Hiram, "because lots of things that seem impossible to comprehend become more understandable if we identify the basic pattern and watch what it produces through repetition. It's a way of dealing with some complexities that otherwise are impenetrable—the way development as we've described it was impenetrable to Aristotle."*

Although fractals were new to me too, I felt that I had always known about them because of a nursery ditty for English-speaking toddlers:

> *Little drops of water,*
> *Little grains of sand*
> *Make the mighty ocean*
> *And the pleasant land.*

---

* An excerpt from Jacobs's second essay in dialogue form, *The Nature of Economies*, 22–23. Kate, Hortense, and Hiram are, like Armbruster, characters in her imagined dialogue.

Maybe all we need to put this macroeconomic puzzle together is the fact of repetition at different scales.

My lucky fractal, which revived my interest in the city growth puzzle, had been published in 1925. It told that in the late nineteenth century Japan's economy had been suffering severely from cheap Western imports with which Japan could not compete or could not make at all. Among the imports were bicycles. They had become enormously popular in big Japanese cities, where shops to repair them had sprung up. In Tokyo the repairs were done in large numbers of one- and two-man shops. Imported spare parts were expensive and broken bicycles were too valuable to cannibalize for parts.

Many repair shops thus found it worthwhile, themselves, to make repair parts—not too difficult if its mechanics specialized on one kind of part, as many did. In this way, groups of shops were almost doing the work of making whole bicycles.

That step was taken by bicycle assemblers who bought parts on contract from repairmen. Far from being costly to develop, bicycle manufacturing in Japan paid its way right through the development stages. The Tokyo-assembled bicycles were even more popular than the foreign imports had been because they cost less. They were financially feasible. Moreover, most of the work of making production equipment was added too, gradually and as rising sales warranted.

The Japanese got much more than a bicycle industry, the report pointed out. They had acquired a pattern for breaking complex manufacturing work into relatively simple fragments in autonomous shops. The method was rapidly used to produce other popular imported products, such as sewing machines, and was still being used in 1925, said the report.

This fractal did not electrify me because it was about bicycles but because it was about a process, the commonplace phenomenon I call city import replacement. It appeared to be the launching point of a quite complex process that organizes macroeconomies, guides how they operate, and shapes smaller microeconomies that are creatures of the great macroeconomies. I was already familiar with the plot line of this import-replacement story because I had already encountered it repeatedly in American and European cities, but the narrative in this case was less sketchy; it told me so much. It told why the replacement of an import had been financially so feasible.

What does financial feasibility mean in import replacement? It means that the replacements are not so expensive (nor so ineptly made) that they cost as much or more than the imported versions. Complete bicycle manufacturing in Tokyo might have proved to be infeasible had its entrepreneurs attempted to copy the model presented, say, by the contemporary plant of the large American bicycle trust in Hartford, Connecticut. It was financially successful, too, and a tempting model, but it would have required the Japanese to import many expensive machines to begin with, and also required them either to pay for imported management services or to send Japanese managers abroad for training.

However, by using manufacturing methods tailored to Tokyo's already existing capacities—a creative thing to do—the assemblers and their suppliers made the work economically feasible.

The new work's location itself gave it two major assets: The first asset was the existing pool of customers right at hand to form a worthwhile market. The second was the existence of germane skills capable of undertaking the work. Moreover, the possessors of these skills did not need to search each other out;

they already formed a known community, a network. These two assets were a basic existing foundation for the financially viable new departure. That is why I call this commonplace phenomenon *city* import replacement.

At this point the alert and skeptical reader becomes impatient. "This is just a long-winded way of saying that import-substitution benefits a country financially. Everybody knows that already. Besides it doesn't work. Back in the 1970s import-substitution bankrupted Uruguay. It's all about supplies, right? Well that substitution program was devised and supervised by the best teams of supply-side economists in America, and they took into consideration a lot more things than I've just heard from you."*

Yes, I'll get around to that fiasco in due course. The many things it took into account were beside the point. What its sponsors did not take into account were the long-winded explanations of necessary basic assets found in cities.

What other assets does financial viability include? Savings could be made in transportation costs which had to be absorbed by customers, and were partly eliminated by city import replacements. It also means that local costs had to leave enough margin to pay for extra bicycle supplies now needed by Tokyo assemblers; say, steel for framework, rubber for tires, leather for

---

* This line of argument refers to a now-obscure economic development scheme initiated by the Uruguayan government after it fell on hard times in the 1950s, which Jacobs recounts in *Cities and the Wealth of Nations*. As its specialized export-based economy of animal products stagnated, Uruguay could no longer afford the imported goods it relied heavily upon, so the government embarked on a program to substitute those imports with local production. However, without "the ranges of skills, the symbiotic nests of producers' goods and services, and the practice at improvising and adapting" generated by active urban economies—the heart of Jacobs's version of import-replacement—the scheme failed.

seats, and who knows what finicky items for production machinery when it became justified by growing sales.

"This undermines global trade," fumes the alert and skeptical reader, who is now more skeptical than alert. "When Tokyo began making its own bicycles, former exporters to Tokyo lost business, and global trade must have shrunk."

No. Here is where import-shifting, the third commonplace phenomenon I mentioned, comes into the equation. Tokyo did not import less in value than it otherwise would or could as a result of its city import replacement. It shifted some of its purchases from elsewhere. This was, in part, automatic and unavoidable. As already mentioned, the bike assemblers needed extra imports like steel, rubber and leather they hadn't required before. As bicycle sales increased, growing numbers of workers automatically required more food, clothing, shelter and other consumer goods and services for themselves and their dependents than the Tokyo economy previously needed. Look at it this way. After the Tokyo economy began making its own bicycles, the city had everything it possessed before the event: as many or more bicycles and the basic assets that made the bicycles' success possible, *plus* the city's extra shifted imports. The source of the shifted import purchases differed, also their composition, but because they were an add-on the world's trade and the world's economy, taken as a whole, had not shrunk; it had expanded a little.*

Let's return to unaccountable growth bursts and explosions. One of my main questions had answered itself of its own accord: Why is the peculiar city growth pattern a city phenome-

---

* Jacobs notes that this discussion of the Japanese bicycle industry is drawn from *The Economy of Cities*, 63–65, 145–50.

non? Answer: because smaller and simpler settlements lack both existing pools of customers and existing production capability to replace those same imports. But another mysterious question remained: why do the bursts always eventually subside?

THE DIS-ANTHROPOMORPHISM
OF THE ECONOMY

Here is my hypothesis for a city growth burst or explosion: The settlement begins like any other; it finds an export successful enough to earn the imports it needs. It grows gradually and slowly, but sooner or later it generates a few more exports, and, therefore, also more imports. Eventually it acquires an import it can make for itself, and it does so.

The embryonic city grows until it contains enough potential customers, and at the same time a large enough collection of people with skills and experience to make another, or several more, of the settlement's imports for itself using the same basic principles as the bicycle assemblers in the fractal.

In place of the goods and services they used to import for their customers, the growing city's import-replacing industries are now importing much less. The city economy is shifting its imports to the raw materials, semi-finished goods, and auxiliary services that the import-replacing industries need, and also to the food and other necessities, luxuries and services that the much larger number of workers and their dependents now earn or need.

For hundreds of years economists and proto-economists have seen that settlements, towns, villages, and cities have sold exports to earn imports. They have believed and taught that cities and their economies are export-led, and most of the public has accepted this too. But here is a way of earning imports *without* gaining exports. The new imports that the city economy is earning are the shifted imports. This is the explanation sought by mystified historians who could not understand how great cities were growing vigorously at times when their exports were not increasing.

The initial process of replacing city imports with local production continues to use up the imported goods and services available for replacement until this phase comes to an end from shifts to products not suitable for replacement. This can be because they require rural production, because the economy is not yet technically advanced enough, because the city lacks a large enough pool of potential customers, or for other reasons. Having used up its fuel, the little city now must gradually develop new imports plus the capabilities and the capacity to once again ignite a complex chain reaction of import replacing and shifting, made evident by another burst of explosive growth.

To sum up: The most radical idea here is that once it gets going the macroeconomy continues by itself, self-organizing like a biological process. A new macroeconomy starts when fractals of an existing economy continue to replace imports, thereby earning imports for the economy. The result is a rapid burst of growth that incrementally expands the world economy as well. When, for a combination of reasons, the fractals of the macroeconomy run out of grist for the import-replacing mill, the import shifting decreases and the macroeconomy settles down to another period of gradual growth. This continues until and unless it piles up another collection of imports and the other conditions necessary to set off another burst of import replacing and shifting. The triple process—followed by quiescent periods of indeterminable length—can repeat indefinitely.

Each time a burst or growth explosion occurs the city experiencing it is much changed. Among the most stunning changes are that it becomes a much larger city and the portion of its economy which is devoted to production for its own people—including its own exporters—becomes enormous in proportion to its import and export economy. It has grown room in its economy for goods and services it never previously had—neither imported nor homemade.

With each of its enlargements by this method of growth, such a city becomes a sea of activities unique in the world. No other city reproduces its arts, learning, points of view, styles of life and the like. Its influence on its own region and on other cities can be profound; yet paradoxically, it has become a very local economy. Throughout the peculiar growth process that has made this possible, from beginning to end runs a theme of human creativity and human improvisation. The economy responds automatically, according to the intensity of the stimulation and its timing. This is what I mean by the dis-anthropomorphism of the economy.*

---

* The cover letter accompanying this excerpt that Jane Jacobs sent to her editor, David Ebershoff at Random House, included a table of contents that gives us a glimpse of what else she hoped to accomplish in *Uncovering the Economy*. Although the project was still in flux, after this opening chapter she imagined eight additional parts to the book, each addressing a different aspect of the "Triple Process" she describes here: a chapter each on the effects of "the Process" on individual cities, groups of cities, and rural places, plus four more on faking, blocking, killing, and living with the Process. The book would end with a reflection on "the Process's roots in modest attempts by ordinary people to make do with what they have and of improvisation as an integral part of innovation."

The End of the Plantation Age

———

LEWIS MUMFORD LECTURE,

CITY COLLEGE, NEW YORK,

MAY 6, 2004

PROFESSOR SORKIN, LADIES AND GENTLEMEN, MY OSTENSI-
ble subject tonight is the past, present, and future of office skyscrapers.* But my real subject is the troubles induced from false
perceptions of what is actually past, present or future. I've
pinned these ruminations to skyscraper offices—in part to attach them to the tangible, everyday world, and in part because
clusters of skyscraper offices and their gorgeous skylines in midtown and lower Manhattan are so central to New Yorkers' sense
of the city's identity.

Past, present, and future is an enormous swath. Future is the
tense most easily disposed of because nobody can know what it
is until it has already happened.

It has already happened that skyscrapers are no longer the
preferred habitats for headquarters of all self-respecting corporations, nor for the legions of workers in administrative, finan-

---

* Michael Sorkin (1948–) is an American architect and urbanist. His own interpretations
of Jacobs's work can be found in *Twenty Minutes in Manhattan* and the foreword to *What We
See: Advancing the Observations of Jane Jacobs*.

cial, research, design, engineering and marketing jobs associated with corporate headquarters. In the Toronto area, much of this work has decamped to converted factory buildings in the suburbs, and in the United States to suburban office parks. In neither variation is the trend from towers to the suburbs a reaction to the terrorist attack on the World Trade Center towers. In the Toronto area, the new trend began two decades ago and was very well established by the late 1980s.

In New York the trend began still earlier although the city tried to block it, and sometimes did, by offering corporations, especially those with high public profiles, inducements to stay in the city. So timing tells us that causes other than fears of terrorism must have driven this change.

The movements of headquarters to the suburbs became possible, of course, and had the cachet of being up-to-date because electronic communications release executives and associated jobs from proximity to other corporations with which they do business and from the law firms, advertising agencies, insurance firms, banks, and employment agencies that serve many enterprises jointly. For face-to-face meetings, a centrally located pied-à-terre is sufficient. This need not even be under corporate ownership or lease. A city restaurant or a hotel or convention meeting room suffices. This has already happened too.

Economy was another driving force, although it does not explain as much as is commonly supposed. Suburban economy conceals many hidden or denied expenses. Many costs are downloaded on car-dependent workers and their families. Many others, including direct and indirect costs of suburban land use and its redundant infrastructures, fall on taxpayers at large, including tax-paying corporations that move to the suburbs to reduce expenses. The major suburban economy that indisputably remains after all disregarded and denied costs are stripped away is the amplitude and cheapness of suburban car parking, with which downtown offices can never compete.

Because of reduced demand for space in downtown towers, it has become harder than it was a generation or two ago for developers to land big or rapidly expanding office tenants. This is also why some existing tower space has become available for hotels, residence, studios, and live-work space.

Simultaneously, suburban offices have been changing. Many are now deliberately designed to maximize contact and understanding among people and departments *within* the organization. They have become self-involved to the point of becoming introverted. They have also become attractive and interesting to the point of becoming narcissistic, if buildings can be said to be narcissistic. I think they can. Suburban offices can make traditional office cubicles and desk pools in towers look dull and deprived. Maximizing an organization's self-regard and self-involvement risks minimizing contacts among people with different experiences, knowledge and ambitions. Introversion reduces the number and varieties of unplanned, indeed unplannable encounters.

Organizational introversion is commonly a precursor to stultification and eventual failure. We say, in retrospect, that the organization got out of touch. All sorts of organizations can get out of touch: royal courts, a manufacturer of men's shoes or cameras; a department store, a philanthropy. Entire cities can get "out of touch," usually by fixing too long on an outstanding past success; Akron, Ohio, is sometimes cited as a classic example.* Even nations can get out of touch, and often have; usually—but not always—deliberately.

A designer, engineer or skilled craftsman who works in an attractive suburban office ideally gets speedily and eagerly to the office, parks the car, becomes engrossed in the organization, lunches with colleagues behaving similarly, loads the briefcase into the car for the drive home, having seen or heard nothing the entire day to pique his or her curiosity or jolt an old ambition or new daydream into life.

Economic developments, and social or cultural developments too, do not arise out of thin air. They are always built upon prior developments, often on a combination of two, three, or more, and upon a society's capability of building on these, meaning ability to adapt, produce and sustain the new development. But the outcome, particularly if the development is an innovation, is always unpredictable, even to its own originator and the pioneers who believed in it and launched it. The first financially successful railroad in the world was an amusement ride in London.† Many of us remember when plastics were useful for little except toys, kitchen gadgets, and decorative touches that tastemakers derided for their vulgarity. That was before

---

* Akron, known as the "rubber city" because it was home to Firestone and other automobile tire manufacturing concerns, boomed in the first half of the twentieth century, but like many other industrial cities dependent on one industry fell on hard times in the postwar era.

† It's likely that Jacobs is here referencing the "steam circus" that the British inventor and steam rail pioneer Richard Trevithick (1771–1833) exhibited for a few weeks in London in the summer of 1808. A small engine called "Catch Me Who Can" went around a circular track in Bloomsbury to the delight of spectators. Whether it was the first "financially successful" rail operation or not, it was not the first railroad. Earlier horse-drawn and steam railroads had been used in mining and other industrial operations.

strong, lightweight plastics, reinforced with fibers of glass, boron or carbon, replaced metals in some kinds of springs, joints and construction components. These plastics transformed serious spectacle frames like mine. At last I have frames that never hurt my nose and ears, and that last for years without weakened joints. These plastics were originated by makers of tennis rackets and rods for surf and sport fishing. Wonderful!

I don't know whether the string of encounters that led from a fishing rod to my spectacle frames included an eavesdropper excited and indiscreet enough to blurt out, "I know somebody you ought to talk to!" It is the kind of thing that happens in a society whose people commonly believe the business of the whole world is their business. That seems to be what developers of the boastful old towers thought: they invited the public in to gape at their grand lobbies, buy newspapers and candy bars, use telephones and ride in their elevators to the roof to share the stunning views.

Like people who want to become recluses, organizations that genuinely want to be in touch chiefly with themselves will find ways to do so; then costs, distances and locational freedoms are beside the point. We must wonder whether the rapid increases in suburban offices, along with their changing social attitudes, mean that New York's clusters of office towers are now destined to gradually become faded and thinning remnants of a vanished sensibility and outworn economy.

Apparently that is to be expected in the short run, but not necessarily in the long run. Less opulent, more diverse and more experimental sorts of tenants than traditionally filled the towers might theoretically save them. After enough oddities wiggle into vacant tower spaces, and into buildings and streets among them and alongside them, New York's old office districts might become notable economic and cultural incubators. Much as I would like to predict that future, the sooner the better, I can't do it in good conscience because, as far as I can see, such a change shows no signs of having already happened.

What I do see—don't laugh—is cities reinventing agriculture—something so unlikely and counterintuitive that when signs of it are suddenly glimpsed in many cities in a number of countries, it begs to be noticed.

Don't try to predict what will come of it, if anything. It's too early. Maybe gardeners on flat-topped city buildings are merely having fun showing off how they can conserve water and energy while creating beauty. Maybe they are only well-off customers for removable greenhouses and new roofing materials, and well-off suppliers of the freshest vegetables and herbs to in-house restaurants. But maybe it's actually time for a rerun of the hanging gardens of Babylon, this time omitting the hubris and tower that followed the success of the gardens. Towers are not really the right shape for either sun-catching or sun-shunning agriculture.

Now I will leave the future and digress a long way into the past. But I promise to return to skyscrapers, and physical planning, and think out loud about Lewis Mumford.

Beginning with the emergence of agriculture and animal husbandry some ten or twelve thousand years ago, the Agrarian Age got under way. Those of you who have read Jared Diamond's Pulitzer Prize–winning book, *Guns, Germs, and Steel,* will recall Diamond's brilliant analyses of why the large and dense populations of successful agrarians defeated older hunting and gathering societies and also why agrarians more successful at producing food consistently won military victories over societies less successful at doing so. But even if you have not read Diamond, you are surely aware that foragers have lost out so universally to agrarians that foraging cultures are now almost extinct.

Greeting card publishers, illustrators of children's books, buyers of the cards and books, and many others enjoy sentimentalizing agrarian life with jolly portrayals of snug family farms. But in most times and most places, family farms have seldom been able to provide a decent subsistence living even for their proprietary families. And even when they have produced cash crops, the yields have usually been marginal additions to the wealth and power of conquering agrarians.

Although Diamond does not say so, the powerhouses of agrarian supremacy were plantations. In the Middle East, early plantations supported the earliest empires: Sumer, Babylon, Assyria. In classical Rome and its conquered and annexed territories, large estates owned by large-scale importers and exporters were outproducing Rome's family farms, which were traditionally lands granted as pensions to military veterans. Family farms were vanishing even before the republic vanished.

Successful plantations and less successful family farms all but disappeared during the Dark Age that followed Rome's imperial collapse. When Western Europe emerged from its famous Dark Age about a thousand years ago, it was as territories and cultures organized by warlords and abbots into feudal estates, some of which became agrarian cores of successor European empires.

Wherever imperial agrarian powers conquered, they took along with them the arts of plantation organization. Practices perfected in the vineyards and grain, flax, olive and almond plantations of the old world were transferred to other climates, as plantations for sugar, cotton, indigo, tea, coffee, cocoa, tobacco, coconuts, pineapples, rubber, opium poppies, peanuts, bananas, spices, soybeans, and much else, along with herds, some with summer and winter pasturage as large as small nations. Vestiges of that ancient dynamic continue still. Numbers of North American family farms continue dwindling, year after year, while numbers and sizes of the modern plantations we call agribusinesses and factory farms continue to increase. Even cranberry bogs have become efficient plantations. Musician friends tell me that the reeds used worldwide for oboes and other wind instruments come from plantations in southern France where canes grow thickly to heights of forty feet. Papyrus plantations, now long extinct in Egypt, may once have presented scenes similar to these modern cane plantations.

A century ago Americans were not as sentimental about agrarian life as we are and as we teach children to be.

When I was a schoolchild in the 1920s, textbook anthologies of English literature typically included a poem entitled "The Man with the Hoe," by Edwin Markham. On the facing page was a depressing reproduction of a painting called "Man with Hoe" by Jean Francois Millet. Markham, an Oregon educator, was inspired to write the poem in 1899 by the painting made forty-six years previously.

A century ago Americans were not as sentimental about agrarian life as we are and as we teach children to be.

Millet was a peasant himself. As a child he worked on wheat plantations of a French estate. As a mature painter he made a record of that life. A critic remarked that he neither softened nor exaggerated his scenes. Millet was a documentary maker ahead of his time, using memory and canvas instead of camera and film. Markham neither softened nor exaggerated what the painting documented. I will read you a few lines from his long, indignant poem:

> Bowed by the weight of centuries he leans
> Upon his hoe and gazes on the ground . . .
> The emptiness of ages in his face . . .
> Who made him dead to rapture and despair,
> Stolid and stunted, a brother to the ox? . . .
> Whose breath blew out the light within this brain? . . .
> Who loosened and let down this brutal jaw? . . .
> There is no shape more terrible than this . . .
> More packed with danger to the universe . . .

Both the poem and painting are almost forgotten now, scorned as moralistic preaching.

The Plantation Age is no longer supreme. It has become the turn of agrarian cultures to be defeated by warriors using ingenuities of the Age of Human Capital.

Some people call the young post-agrarian age the Knowledge Age, implying that we now know everything needful. Of course we don't. Every age has used whatever information and misinformation its people have acquired, for better or worse. Trying to make out what post-agrarian life portends for the future by noticing what has already happened, many people pessimistically expect ever more cruel and dangerous ingenuities punctuated by uncontrollable epidemics, irreversible climate changes, interminable civil wars and other catastrophes. Other people optimistically expect an unprecedentedly creative age, grounded in the emerging science of complexity which recognizes that everything is connected inexorably to everything else, whether we like that or not, and recognizes also that we cannot understand biology or social sciences, or for that matter physics, by means of the old and inadequate science of bivariant simplicity and the statistics of disorganized complexity. The optimists looking at what has already happened still manage to find plausible portents that constructive creativity is in ascendancy and will win out. Maybe this is wishful thinking, and the only definitive thing to be said echoes Charles Dickens's introductory comment to *A Tale of Two Cities:* "It was the worst of times and the best of times."*

Despite the Plantation Age's many remaining ugly residues, such as racism, that age was slowly but inexorably undermined by skills, observations and cultural changes that gradually accrued during the past thousand years.

For one thing, breadbaskets that formerly fed much of the world are no longer economic assets to their nations, but have become, instead, serious drags on national economies: for instance, rural Sicily, rural Argentina, Uruguay and Ukraine. In their time, the great North American prairies rendered many smaller breadbaskets redundant, such as New England, upstate New York and the Ottawa Valley and Atlantic provinces of

---

★   Perhaps to emphasize hope rather than doom and gloom or perhaps by mistake, Jacobs has reversed Dickens's own phrasing, mirroring the title of *The Death and Life of Great American Cities.*

Canada. Now redundancy threatens even the prairies; already they soak up such huge protectionist subsidies that these led to complete breakdown of the latest attempted round of world trade negotiations.

Of course we still need to eat and clothe ourselves, and millions are not well fed or well clad, but attempts to solve or even to understand that enigma as a simplistic flaw in distribution are no longer credible in poor countries receiving foreign aid, nor to increasing numbers of aid-givers either. If nothing succeeds like success, it is equally true that nothing fails like failure.

For another indication of the Plantation Age's demise, an exorbitant share of a population is no longer needed to produce food and fiber for itself and others. In advanced economies like America's and Canada's, only about four percent of the working population actually farms or herds, and even some of those only part-time. In poorer economies, where traditionally as much as eighty or eighty-five percent of the population was destined to work with crops or pastures, as soon as tractors and irrigation pumps and pipes become available, abundant farm work decreases drastically.

Land can be held exclusively. So can other natural resources like oil wells, fisheries, and gold ores be held. Ingenuity cannot be.

Thus wars of expansion or colonization can no longer be won in the same sense as in the Plantation Age. In the past, victors could and did consign losers to plantations, ordering them to do as they were told and shut up. But because of agrarian redundancies—an unimaginable luxury in the Plantation Age—plantation making has lost its point for conquerors. It doesn't pay. Furthermore, some military losers have adopted or created horrible ingenuities of their own. Land can be held exclusively. So can other natural resources like oil wells, fisheries, and gold ores be held. Ingenuity cannot be.

The great achievement of the Plantation Age was the stupendous multiplication of members of our species. The good-growing successes on unprecedentedly large scales may have saved our species from early extinction that could have followed extinctions of wild crops and food animals.

The Plantation Age did not generate many economic ideas valid for our times and economies. Those taken for granted were based only on what worked for agrarian imperialists. The biggest idea came directly out of agrarian experiences of poor harvests. This idea is that relationships exist among supply, demand and prices. What is abundant is cheap and can be disposed of with little or no regret, in distinction from rarities. Forests were seen to be abundant. Also, ominously, soil, water, and fresh air were abundant, therefore cheap and disposable. Many people still think this way.

Abundant human life could be construed as cheap and disposable. Otherwise ordinary patriotic citizens came to accept and even to glorify prodigious slaughters such as trench warfare, mustard gas attacks, contrived famines, blitzkrieg, kamikaze and napalm attacks, genocide, ethnic cleansing, jihad, suicide terrorism, land mines and wholesale lethal dislocation of people from their homes when their presences had become inconvenient to crazed visions of crazed but persuasive super-patriots.

The attempt to escape difficulties by invoking death, instead of by calling up the powers and resources of life, was the great shame of the Plantation Age during its own dying throes.

The Plantation Age was a lengthy and durable epoch. I've harped on its chief social and economic prop. Generations of plantation workers were bound in place by peonage of some sort, and kept in place by force and threat of force. They fell into these miserable situations as prisoners of war or conquest; as foundlings, orphans, and kidnapped young people sold into slavery; as serfs, feudal tenants, indentured servants; children born into slavery or into families of sharecroppers shackled by discrimination, forced ignorance, fear and debt.

Peons are seldom enthusiastic workers. Three master plantation precepts made peons productive.

First, a successful plantation was organized as a monocultural enterprise specializing in one product.

Second, a monoculture was made still more efficient by enlarging its scale.

Third, an expert planned the end result in advance. The object was to anticipate everything needed, and thus avoid unexpected adaptations, alterations and improvisations.

Plantations adhering to these three precepts: specialization, large scale, and anticipated end results—could succeed. Those that flouted them failed.

When something succeeds for time out of mind it is not much questioned, except by such imagined options as utopias. Thus the plantation model guided much of the infancy of the Industrial Revolution. In England, Manchester and its large conurbation of industrial towns turned out flabbergasting quantities of thread, yarn and cloth. The industrial experts who shaped these mass-production monocultures used their improved power sources—running water, coal-powered steam—

merely to increase the scale of operations, not to alter the vision itself. They were actually shaping a dead-end industrial economy. But it took a couple of centuries for England to recognize that disaster, and though many a demand-side and supply-side nostrum has been applied in the century since, a cure for the abused industrial economy of northern England has still to be found.

The first American efficiency expert, F. W. Taylor, was in total thrall to plantation mentality. He showed his large industrial clients how to break down work into such simple and repetitive bits that workers could be used as if they were cogs in production machinery or peons on a plantation. Taylor and his many imitators called the method "scientific management."* Workers could be trained in a trice and were as quickly disposable and replaceable. Charlie Chaplin memorably satirized such workplaces in his film *Modern Times*.

However, because American steel, automotive, meat-packing, coal-mining, garment-stitching and other industrial workers were not actually bound as peons, "scientific managers" and rebellious workers pitted themselves against each other.

Probably the earliest industrial mass producers to abandon plantation mentality were the thousands of printers who rap-

* One of the first management consultants, Frederick Winslow Taylor (1856–1915) was a mechanical engineer best known for the system of workplace efficiency he designed for the new assembly line factories of the early twentieth century. Among other things, "scientific management" sought to control the way workers worked, as Jacobs suggests, by breaking down the process of a given task into individual, repeatable units of movement and time. He thought his time and motion studies would encourage workers to be more efficient, but "Taylorism" became a feared system for many workers and unions, because employers used it as a speed-up technique to extract more work from employees, regiment their workday, restrict their autonomy, and reduce their control over their own work process.

idly proliferated in sixteenth-century European cities. They could not predict what would fall into their hands, and therefore what they might be printing a year or even a month in the future. So they had no choice but to abandon monoculture. Along with tried and true products—books of sermons, translations of scripture, translations of learned works of philosophy and science, they took on travel reports, scripts of plays, pamphlets of invective, scandal, doggerel, and political attacks smuggled past government censors, and in due course periodicals, news reports and novels.

Publishers, who developed from printers, also broke loose from the precept that favored larger scales of production to grasp larger profits. Publishers noticed that enlarged production scales could be ruinous. To be sure, a larger printing of an edition would predictably bring down the cost of each item in the edition, but it was more economical for publishers to estimate the limited demand for each edition and second-guess themselves, if necessary, by heeding feedback on sales, as publishers, and for that matter manufacturers of hay balers, do to this day. This was a radically new and original model of mass production, owing as much or more to craft practices as to plantation precepts. For those using this model the remaining third plantation precept was meaningless. There could be no finished end result. Instead, at every stage of production, what was needed was nimble current knowledge of markets and, for publishers, of writers and illustrators.

Manufacturers of mass-production skirts, blouses and dresses and of cut and printed tissue-paper patterns for home dressmakers also realized that they could use mass production but not monoculture.* By hindsight the new model would seem to be inevitable for fashion industries, but in a world of custom couturiers and tailors for the haves, and rags for the have-nots, it was not adopted for fashions until almost three centuries after the printers had shown the way. This time the insight came to fashion and women's-interest journalists in mid-nineteenth-century New York. Foreigners marveled at how fashionably New York shopgirls dressed.

Makers of home furnishings and household appliances learned the new model from the example of the New York fashion industries. In only a few more decades, industrialists in New England and Chicago and other Midwestern cities began to catch on. Instead of resting indefinitely on their mechanical harvesters, they mass-produced additional rural labor-saving devices. Automobile makers were slow at learning to use the new model as a key to industrial evolution. Henry Ford's development of the tractor, and General Motors' invention of the acceptance corporation, a powerful financing and marketing tool, were the American automotive industry's last world-altering innovations, both created at about the time of the First World War. This is remarkable, considering the opportunities open to the industry in more than three-quarters of a century since.

Land planners and suburban real estate developers have been

---

* Jacobs recounts this shift from mass production to "differentiated production" more fully in the final chapter of *The Economy of Cities*, "Some Patterns of Future Development," from which the title of this section takes its name. In unused notes for the book, she describes this new approach to work as "the Age of Differentiated Production," perhaps foreshadowing the ideas she presents here.

even slower than automobile manufacturers to shed plantation mentality. Modern suburbs are caricatures of plantations. Look at them: monocultural housing tracts, erected on ever-larger scales, like so many endless fields of cabbages. Standardized shopping centers multiplying like so many flocks of sheep. All of this framed in imitation of plantation-to-seaport limited access rail corridors inappropriately adapted for trucks, commuters, in-city and intercity travelers needing *un*limited access to countless micro-destinations—not limited access to relatively few macro-destinations. Never before, except on plantations, have normal human beings been consigned to planned environments dominated by such poverty of imagination.

Some land planners who predetermine these perfect end results have come to despise the consequence of their own work. But they are caught in a time warp from which they, and their profession, and their teachers seem unable to extricate themselves. Modern land planners' tool kits consist of prescriptions based on anti-urban assumptions—that high densities, high ground coverages and mixed uses are bad.

The two World Trade Center towers looked futuristic, but they were caught in a suburbanized time warp too. Their heights and volumes proclaimed infatuation with supposed efficiency of great scale. The intention of filling them with enterprises engaged in global trading was a gimmick that shrieked of faith in monoculture. The empty plaza forming a tower platform, so alien to the interesting and unpredictably detailed hurly-burly of adaptable small business on New York's streets, announced confidence in perfect, predetermined end results.

During the political maneuvering that cleared the way for the planning, some developers and rental agents warned against the disorder that the millions of square feet of rentable office space would bring to limited demand in the city for additional offices. They were correct. Nor did cumbersome size make the buildings economical to operate. The monocultural plan for tenanting them floundered too. The perfect plaza remained bleak and purposeless instead of impressive and popular. New York City, to its credit, is not a congenial context for plantations or plantation mentalities. These towers got by at all only by grace of decades of public subsidies and spin-doctored information.

Among the hundreds of small businesses whose presence was inconvenient to the planners of these towers was the largest cluster of electronic enterprises in the city at the time. It was called Radio Row. The businesses of Radio Row were regarded as pathetically small and their protests about what was to happen to them were jokes to city, state, and federal power brokers and their experts. No one can say whether the ruined Radio Row might or might not have evolved into a major asset in the city's and region's economy. All we can know is that it was a sort of prehistoric Silicon Valley for a time. No more can ever be known because the cluster was not permitted to live and develop in an unpredictable, open-ended New York way.

The planning profession currently showing most promise of liberating itself from plantation mentality seems to be landscape architecture. Perhaps this is because many urban landscape architects and theorists of the behavior of city public spaces have been influenced by the study of ecosystems.

Although the purpose of plantations is crop growing, they could not be more different from ecosystems.

Ecosystems are absolutely never monocultural. Monoculturalism is death to them. Their ideal is size capable of sustaining populations of greatly diverse natural inhabitants that carry direct or indirect benefits for one another. Ecosystems take successions of form from successions of adaptations. Their mature forms are potentially unpredictable. Who could have predicted redwood forests? Ecosystems need protection from specific harms and situations that threaten them from time to time. Identical harms do not threaten all ecosystems at the same time. However, picking ecosystems off, one at a time, weakens the planet's ecosystems as a whole. Everything connects with everything else. In their modes of connecting, their deep organizational principles, ecosystems are much like cities and not at all like plantations.*

Part of the dead and unburied, putrefying Plantation Age is the fantasy that cities and their people are unproductive parasites, idly battening on wealth bestowed upon rural and wild places. Some people still believe this, including some ecologists whose breezy diagnosis of all troubles are "too many people."†

It follows from simple bivariant misanthropy—bad city guys, good rural and wilderness guys—that rural places must be morally finer and more nurturing spiritually than urban environments. Thomas Jefferson, for one, believed this, although perhaps more in theory than in practice. Although he was cer-

---

* For more on the similarities between ecosystems and cities, see the foreword to the Modern Library edition of *Death and Life* in this volume, as well as *The Nature of Economies*.

† For Jacobs's critique of the Malthusian fear of overpopulation, see "The Real Problem of Cities" in this volume.

tainly able and intelligent, he was incompetent as a plantation proprietor; but he lavished loving and attentive pride successfully on his architecture and landscaping for the city of Richmond and on his remarkably urbane campus for the University of Virginia.

Many a smidgen of rural pasture, minus the grazing sheep, horses, mules, cattle, or swine, has been inserted into cities with the deliberate intention of combating urban decadence. Some people still have faith in the moral superiority of an upbringing attended by well-sprayed and well-trimmed lawns.

Now I AM GETTING into the subject of memorials. At the time of one of the anniversaries of the September 11th terrorist attack, I was astonished to read in *The New York Times* that New York possesses no great memorial. Nonsense. The Statue of Liberty is surely the world's most widely known modern memorial and perhaps its best loved. It memorializes "the huddled masses yearning to breathe free" who pursued their dream to America, often enduring much woe and hardship before taking passage, during passage, and after landing. Liberty does not rise on a symbolically uplifting pasture. She rises from the harbor waters like Venus herself arriving on her seashell. As a memorial, Liberty owes nothing, in either form or substance, to plantation mentality.

It's a rare American city park, whether it bears a memorial or not, that bids users enjoy contact with fellow citizens and city culture. New York has splendid examples in tiny Paley Park, larger and older, redesigned Bryant Park, and some portions, particularly along or near its Fifth Avenue border, of large Central Park. Notable examples in other cities include Rittenhouse Square in Philadelphia, Paul Revere Park in Boston's North End, and the Music Garden in Toronto, a magnificent gift to the city from a great cellist, Yo-Yo Ma. Washington's memorial to America's dead in the Vietnam War departs, in its own way, from plantation mentality. The fifty-eight thousand names, each distinct and dignified on its black granite, semi-buried background, speak of the irreplaceable worth of each individual's lost life.

One of the difficult design problems associated with the sixteen-acre site at Ground Zero is that there is so much to memorialize; so much, that it has placed the public and the planning committees in the sort of super-dilemmas called quandaries.

Many want to memorialize the martyred buildings themselves: their heights, by means of towering gee-whiz illumination, or their depths, by revealing the engineering triumph that defeated incursions of an innocent bystander, the Hudson River, into the towers' foundations. Some citizens want one or the other of these building mementos to memorialize Ground Zero. Other people want both.

Many people prefer memorializing the human victims and the sorrow of their survivors, or want to make sure that the heroic firemen and police who lost their lives in rescue work will never be forgotten. Some who emphasize the sad premature deaths in what should have been the victims' fullness of life, want Ground Zero to remain perpetually sacred burying ground. Still others view a memorial as an opportunity to refurbish lower Manhattan. Ideas of how that can be done are unlimited. Among them are a museum explaining what happened at this site, perhaps also serving as a magnet for tourists; fine new recreational facilities and other amenities for residents of the district, perhaps restoration of anchorages for the coastal steamers that used to ply the waters between New York and Boston, Providence, Philadelphia, Wilmington, Washington and Richmond, on their delightful little overnight summer ocean voyages. Almost nobody wants something incoherent or too crassly commercial that will be an embarrassment to posterity. Everybody hopes that the memorial, whatever it is, can be experienced as art.

But art is not tamely dutiful. It is subverted when it is pressured into shouldering too many meanings, however noble. It is never timely in the slogging way that newspaper reports and headlines are, or public opinion polls. At its best, art is timeless, communicating with generations of viewers. It

Art is not tamely dutiful. . . . It is never timely in the slogging way that newspaper reports and headlines are, or public opinion polls. At its best, art is timeless, communicating with generations of viewers.

works this magic by paring itself down to an emotional essence. To discern and express such an essence, and to appreciate it too, often requires perspective developed after a lapse of time. That is no disgrace. Some important things cannot be rushed.

Ground Zero will probably require two memorials: an interim design, followed in the fullness of time by a permanent memorial. One way to deal with a quandary is to get tired or bored with it and let it slide. Not a good policy, if for no other reason than neglected quandaries can backtrack and torment the slothful.

A much better policy is to fall back on truth. As of now, the truth about Ground Zero is still simple: It is a very significant site, but agreement is lacking on what its significance is and how to express it.

Professor Sorkin, you may be surprised at how seriously I take your solution, arrived at so swiftly, as an interim solution. I think the version I saw must have been from the Protetch Gallery exhibition, but I'm not sure where it was shown or published.* For those who have not seen it, the design is a large circular earth berm, a literal zero, occupying the whole Ground Zero site. I admire it because it is bold, handsome, unfussy and dignified, because it tells the truth as of now, and because it does not foreclose consideration of most other permanent possibilities.

The berm and its generous circumference resonate with the distant past, specifically with the beautiful circular forts the Irish built from small slabs of stone piled up as walls without mortar. The example in Donegal I'm thinking of may have been the seat of an Iron Age Celtic king, according to a tourist leaflet picked up miles away. No interpretive material or other clutter is necessary at this site. It speaks for itself, unforgettably, telling of the timeless human longing for security, and the equally timeless human impulse to venture daring peaks and make sorties into the great world.

In any case, an interim solution is necessary because the site, it seems, will not be ready for a permanent memorial for some fifteen to twenty years of repair and reconstruction work at the

---

* Michael Sorkin's proposed memorial was exhibited in the show "New World Trade Center: Design Proposals" at the Max Protetch Gallery in New York. All the designs in the show were later published as a book, *A New World Trade Center: Design Proposals from Leading Architects Worldwide* (New York: HarperDesign, 2002) and acquired by the Library of Congress.

site and in its close vicinity. With or without an allowance for lapse of time to grant perspective, an interim solution should not look or be makeshift or banal. Its design quality will surely influence quality of the permanent solution.

BELATEDLY, I COME TO Lewis Mumford.* My belatedness is not meant ungraciously. It is splendid that the State University of New York is memorializing Mr. Mumford with annual lectures on subjects he cared about. I'm grateful and honored to have been chosen to deliver the first talk in the series.

Mr. Mumford would have disagreed with much I have said tonight. The one thing he might applaud is my expectation of a problematic future for office skyscrapers.

He did not like skyscrapers. He did not like big cities either. He did not value them for having peculiar economic traits and unique social characteristics. He would have liked big cities to be replaced by collections of carefully planned, suburban-like towns, misnamed Garden Cities. He placed his hopes for city decentralization in the powers of centralized regional planning such as were exercised by New York's Regional Plan Association. Marshall McLuhan put his finger on one among many failures of this vision when he commented years later that "you can't decentralize centrally."

---

* As the architectural critic for *The New Yorker* for over three decades and the author of numerous books, Lewis Mumford (1895–1990) was America's foremost public writer on cities and city life in the first half of the twentieth century—a title Jacobs arguably inherited. In fact, as Peter L. Laurence relates in his book *Becoming Jane Jacobs,* when the Rockefeller Foundation provided funding for Jacobs to write *Death and Life,* it was through the foundation's urban design research initiative, which as its administrator put it, sought to answer the question of "where there were to be found other Lewis Mumfords" (p. 246).

But Mr. Mumford was a disciple of the British planner, Sir Patrick Geddes.* Sir Patrick correctly surmised that far-flung electricity grids were to be expected later in the twentieth century. He thought that they would make possible such unprecedented freedom of industrial location that factories, and hence settlements for workers and their families, could be placed wherever rational human beings such as planners judged them to be desirable. Neither Mr. Mumford nor other planners sharing this world view saw any reason why "obsolete" big cities should continue to encumber the earth. This supposition was highly popular in the 1930s among people with allegiance to all shades of political opinion, from conservative right to radical left.

Nevertheless, Mr. Mumford recoiled against the ruthlessness with which limited-access expressways were being bashed through cities, suburbs and countrysides, largely by Robert Moses in the New York area, in the 1940s, 1950s and 1960s. Mumford had been among the very first Americans to scent the threat to all community values by what he called "the insolent chariots." He stimulated many citizens to wonder, for the first time, whether the kind of transportation they were getting really did constitute progress. He became surprisingly protective of cities, perhaps surprising even himself. He sent an effective statement to the Board of Estimate, the New York City governing body at the time, urging its members not to approve the state-planned and federally financed Manhattan Expressway, which would have bisected the city a little north of Canal Street

---

* Sir Patrick Geddes (1854–1932) was a Scottish city planner. He pioneered the regional planning movement whose latterday proponents Jacobs criticized harshly in *Death and Life*.

to make a slightly faster route between Brooklyn and New Jersey. The members of the Board of Estimate—the Mayor, Comptroller, and borough presidents—followed Mr. Mumford's advice. Their vote, and hence his statement, helped delay the expressway another year, an interval during which public understanding grew of the proposal's destructive consequences for the city at large. That growing realization eventually defeated the scheme for good.*

Those of us who prefer Chinatown, Little Italy and Soho to a wide expressway with its apparatus of ramps, parking lots and uplifting garnishes of chain-link-fenced pasture bits owe Mr. Mumford's memory a large debt of gratitude. I sometimes wonder what he would think of Soho. I suspect he would think it decadent. But he generously helped to give it a chance to live and develop in an unpredictable, open-ended New York way.

I first met Mr. Mumford in 1956 at an academic symposium. He was friendly, kind, and encouraging to me then and on the few occasions when we encountered each other during the following five years. But upon publication of my first book, *The Death and Life of Great American Cities,* he was outraged by it and by me.† His Lower Manhattan Expressway statement about a year later briefly made us allies, but with that exception his bitterness against me lasted until his death, as far as I know.

I didn't take his disappointment with me personally. We are

---

* It was Jacobs who asked Mumford to write his letter to the Board of Estimate, even after *The New Yorker* published his scathing review of *Death and Life,* described below.

† Mumford wrote a critical thirty-page review of *Death and Life* for *The New Yorker*. The title of the article, "Mother Jacobs' Home Remedies," captures the veiled condescension of his critique, which concluded by comparing her piecemeal approach to reviving the city to giving a cancer patient "a homemade poultice," when of course, it's implied, he needs surgery.

all much molded by our dates of birth, and even more by the extra decades we may be granted at the other end of our life span. Mr. Mumford, as a kind paternalist, was a man of his time. He was half a generation older than I, and he did not get the extra decades later, during which he might have become used to the fact that women didn't necessarily aspire to being patronized. He seemed to think of women as a sort of ladies' auxiliary of the human race. This attitude is evident in his planning philosophy and the kinds of projects he approved of. The point is that I was a person of my time, and our times and minds were different.

He was correct that he and I didn't think alike, especially about cities. Another way we differed is that I don't want disciples. My knowledge and talents are much too skimpy. The very last thing I would want is to inadvertently limit other people with minds of their own. As we negotiate the difficult transition out of the dead, but not buried, Plantation Age, we need unlimited independent thinkers with unlimited skepticism and curiosity.

Our adaptability seems to be magnificent when we keep our wits about us.

I haven't touched tonight on values and influences from the past that it is necessary to retain in the present and carry into the future. While I am serious about not wanting disciples, I hope that my most recent book, *Dark Age Ahead,* which went on sale in bookstores yesterday, will help stir up some of the independent thinking urgently needed as a wake-up call for America. Some of my new book's content overlaps with what I've said tonight, but mostly it goes into other subjects. I've been giving you here a partial preview of a future book I hope to write, under the optimistic assumption that we have not reached a point of no return in loss and corruption of our culture.* Not yet. But we could.

I appreciate your patience, Professor Sorkin and ladies and gentlemen, as I struggle, like all of us, to find sane footing in the pervading insanity and insecurity of our shaky present tense.

One reason for taking comfort from history is to learn that transitions from one epoch to another are always difficult at best. Our culture is not more stupid or ugly than others, and our adaptability seems to be magnificent when we keep our wits about us.

---

* The future book, to be titled "A Short Biography of the Human Race," would have traced the trajectory of humanity from its "infancy," some two hundred thousand years ago, to our forthcoming maturity in the Age of Human Capital. The final chapter of *Dark Age Ahead*, "Dark Age Patterns," outlines a similar hypothesis of a postagrarian age, but it relies more heavily on Jared Diamond's *Guns, Germs, and Steel* and Karen Armstrong's *Islam* and omits elements of this speech, like the specific tenets of the Plantation Age and the history of agriculture and industry.

Acknowledgments

———

Thank you first of all to the estate of Jane Jacobs, and particularly Jim Jacobs, for his enthusiasm, generosity, memory, and sharp mind.

Thanks to Max Allen, Peter Laurence, and Robert Kanigel for their indispensable research on Jane Jacobs, without which this volume would be far poorer, and for their generosity with their time. Thanks also to the staff of the New York Public Library; to Shelley Barber and Andrew Isidoro of Boston College's Burns Library, where the Jane Jacobs Papers live; and to Ben Tyler at Brown University's Rockefeller Library.

For the images that illustrate this volume, thank you to Peter C. Holt, Mary Engel of the Ruth Orkin Photo Archive, Jim Jacobs, John Sewell, Maggie Steber, and Charlotte Sykes. And for making this book possible, thanks to Caitlin McKenna, Amanda Lewis, Anne Collins, and the staffs of Random House and Random House Canada. Zoë Pagnamenta, with Alison Lewis, worked to make this book a reality too, shepherding a thoroughly cooperative North American publishing endeavor to a successful conclusion.

We're grateful to Christina Bevilacqua, who gave us our first chance to think and talk about Jane Jacobs together; in many ways, this book began that evening at the Providence Athenaeum in 2014. Thanks also to Tim Mennel, Max Page, Suzanne Wasserman, and Mike Wallace at the Gotham Center for New York History, the Municipal Art Society, Sam Franklin, and Dan Platt for various opportunities to debate Jacobs, cities, and economies over the years. Tara Nummedal, Tim Harris, and Gary De Krey helped us sort through some knotty problems in the history of early London.

Nate would like to thank Max Allen, who first plunged him headlong into the worlds of Jane Jacobs, as well as Heather Ann Kaldeway, Gillian Mason, Mary Rowe, and Margie Zeidler, fellow travelers who greatly deepened his understanding of her ideas. He would also like to thank the many engaging and challenging professors he had at the Ontario College of Art and Design who taught him how to see, think, and write, especially Esther Choi, Caroline Langill, Michael Prokopow, Charles Reeve, Jennifer Rudder, Dot Tuer, and Jessica Wyman, as well as his advisors at Brown University, Steven Lubar and Anne Valk.

Finally, Nate would like to thank his ever-supportive family: Dwight, Kathy, and Nick Storring, Mark and Paul Sarconi, and Claire Johnson, as well as his wife, Emma Sarconi, for her nearly bottomless encouragement, advice, and occasional reminders to stop working and live a little. Sandy thanks Ilona Miko for her discerning eye and her many years of lively, loving counsel.

Selected Bibliography

─────

WORKS BY JANE JACOBS

Butzner, Jane, ed. *Constitutional Chaff: Rejected Suggestions of the Constitutional Convention of 1787, with Explanatory Argument*. New York: Columbia University Press, 1941.

Jacobs, Jane. *The Death and Life of Great American Cities*. New York: Random House, 1961.

———. *The Economy of Cities*. New York: Random House, 1969.

———. *The Question of Separatism: Quebec and the Struggle over Sovereignty*. New York: Random House, 1980.

———. *Cities and the Wealth of Nations*. New York: Random House, 1984.

———. *Systems of Survival*. New York: Random House, 1992.

———, ed. *A Schoolteacher in Old Alaska: The Story of Hannah Breece*. New York: Random House, 1995.

———. *The Nature of Economies*. New York: Random House, 2000.

———. "Random Comments." *Boston College Environmental Affairs Law Review,* vol. 28, no. 4 (2001): 537–45.

———. "Introduction: Dickens as Seer." *Hard Times* by Charles Dickens. New York: Modern Library, 2002.

———. "Introduction." *The Jungle* by Upton Sinclair. New York: Modern Library, 2002.

———. "Introduction." *The Innocents Abroad* by Mark Twain. New York: Modern Library, 2003.

———. *Dark Age Ahead*. New York: Random House, 2004.

WORKS BY OTHERS

Alexiou, Alice Sparberg. *Jane Jacobs: Urban Visionary*. New Brunswick, N.J.: Rutgers University Press, 2007.

Allen, Max, ed. *Ideas That Matter*. Owen Sound, Ont.: Ginger Press, 1997, rev. ed. Washington, D.C.: Island Press, 2011.

Ascher, Kate. *The Works: Anatomy of a City*. New York: Penguin Books, 2007.

Ballon, Hilary, and Kenneth Jackson, eds. *Robert Moses and the Modern City: The Transformation of New York*. New York: Norton, 2007.

Banfield, Edward. *The Unheavenly City*. New York: Little, Brown, 1970.

Broadbent, Alan. *Urban Nation*. Toronto: Harper Perennial, 2009.

Caro, Robert. *The Power Broker: Robert Moses and the Fall of New York*. New York: Knopf, 1974.

De Landa, Manuel. *A Thousand Years of Nonlinear History*. Brooklyn, N.Y.: Zone Books, 1997.

De Soto, Hernando. *The Mystery of Capital: Why Capitalism Triumphs in the West and Fails Everywhere Else*. New York: Basic Books, 2000.

Desrochers, Pierre, and Gert-Jan Hospers. "Cities and the Economic Development of Nations: An Essay on Jane Jacobs' Contribution to Economic Theory." *Canadian Journal of Regional Science,* vol. 30, no. 1 (Spring 2007): 115–30.

Diamond, Jared. *Guns, Germs, and Steel: The Fates of Human Societies*. New York: Norton, 1997.

Flint, Anthony. *Wrestling with Moses: How Jane Jacobs Took on New York's Master Builder and Transformed the American City*. New York: Random House, 2009.

Gans, Herbert J. *People, Plans, and Policies: Essays on Poverty, Racism, and Other National Urban Policies*. New York: Columbia University Press, 1991.

Glaeser, Edward. *Triumph of the City: How Our Greatest Invention Makes Us Richer, Smarter, Greener, Healthier, and Happier*. New York: Penguin Press, 2011.

Glaeser, Edward et al. "Growth in Cities." *Journal of Political Economy*, vol. 100, no. 6 (1992): 1126–52.

Goldsmith, Stephen A., and Lynne Elizabeth, eds. *What We See: Advancing the Observations of Jane Jacobs*. Oakland: New Village Press, 2010.

Gratz, Roberta Brandes. "A Conversation with Jane Jacobs." *Tikkun,* vol. 16, no. 1 (May 2001): 27–31.

———. *The Battle for Gotham: New York in the Shadow of Robert Moses and Jane Jacobs*. New York: Nation Books, 2010.

Greenberg, Ken. *Walking Home: The Life and Lessons of a City Builder.* Toronto: Random House Canada, 2011.

Harris, Blake. "Cities and Web Economies: Interview with Jane Jacobs." *New Colonist,* 2002. Available at www.sustainablecitynews.com/jane_jacobs-html/.

———. "Jane Jacobs: Unraveling the True Nature of Economics." *Government Technology,* vol. 13, no. 11 (November 2003): 18–25.

Hartman, Chester. *Between Eminence and Notoriety: Four Decades of Radical Urban Planning*. New Brunswick, N.J.: Transaction Books, 2002.

Kanigel, Robert. *Eyes on the Street: A Life of Jane Jacobs*. New York: Knopf, 2016.

Klemek, Christopher. "From Political Outsider to Power Broker in Two 'Great American Cities.'" *Journal of Urban History,* vol. 34, no. 2 (January 2008): 309–32.

———. *The Transatlantic Collapse of Urban Renewal: Postwar Urbanism from New York to Berlin*. Chicago: University of Chicago Press, 2011.

Kunstler, James H. "Godmother of the American City." *Metropolis,* vol. 20, no. 7 (March 2001): 130–87.

Laurence, Peter L. *Becoming Jane Jacobs*. Philadelphia: Penn Press, 2016.

Lawrence, Fred. *Ethics in Making a Living: The Jane Jacobs Conference*. Atlanta: Scholars Press, 1989.

Lucas, Jr., Robert E. "On the Mechanics of Economic Growth." *Journal of Monetary Economics,* vol. 22, no. 1 (1988): 3–42.

Lynch, Kevin. *The Image of the City*. Cambridge, Mass.: MIT Press, 1960.

Nowlan, David. "Jane Jacobs Among the Economists." In *Ideas That Matter,* ed. Max Allen. Owen Sound, Ont.: Ginger Press, 1997.

O'Connor, Ryan. *The First Green Wave: Pollution Probe and the Origins of Environmental Activism in Ontario*. Vancouver, B.C.: University of British Columbia Press, 2015.

Page, Max, and Timothy Mennel. *Reconsidering Jane Jacobs*. Chicago: Planners Press, 2011.

Parkinson, C. Northcote. *The Law and the Profits*. New York: Random House, 1960.

Pirenne, Henri. *Medieval Cities: Their Origins and the Revival of Trade*. Princeton, N.J.: Princeton University Press, 1925, rev. ed. 2014.

Rowe, Mary, ed. *Toronto: Considering Self-Government*. Owen Sound, Ont.: Ginger Press, 2000.

Sabel, Charles F., and Michael J. Piore. *The Second Industrial Divide*. New York: Basic Books, 1984.

"Safdie/Rouse/Jacobs: An Exchange." *Urban Design International,* vol. 2, no. 2 (1981): 26–29, 38.

Schubert, Dirk, ed. *Contemporary Perspectives on Jane Jacobs: Reassessing the Impact of an Urban Visionary*. London: Ashgate, 2014.

Sewell, John. *The Shape of the City*. Toronto, Ont.: University of Toronto Press, 1993.

———. "Jane Jacobs in Conversation." *Ideas That Matter,* vol. 3, no. 3 (2005): 31–33.

Solnit, Rebecca. "Three Who Made a Revolution." *The Nation* (March 16, 2006). Available at thenation.com/article/three-who-made-revolution/.

Sorkin, Michael. *Twenty Minutes in Manhattan*. London: Reaktion Books, 2009.

Steigerwald, Bill. "City Views," *Reason*, June 2001. Available at reason.com/archives/2001/06/01/city-views.

Stein, Janice Gross. *The Cult of Efficiency*. Toronto: House of Anansi Press, 2002.

Taylor, Peter J. *Extraordinary Cities: Millennia of Moral Syndromes, World-Systems, and City/State Relations*. Cheltenham, U.K.: Edward Elgar, 2013.

White, Richard. "Jane Jacobs in Toronto, 1968–78." *Journal of Planning History,* vol. 10, no. 2 (2011).

Whyte, William H., Jr., ed. *The Exploding Metropolis*. Garden City, N.Y.: Doubleday, 1958.

Zipp, Samuel. *Manhattan Projects: The Rise and Fall of Urban Renewal in Cold War New York*. New York: Oxford University Press, 2010.

Image and Text Credits

——

Frontispiece: Jane Jacobs and Ned Jacobs, 1961,
by Ruth Orkin, courtesy Photo Archive Ruth Orkin

Part Three: City Hall Belongs to the People,
by Charlotte Sykes, courtesy of Charlotte Sykes.

Part Four: Jane Jacobs on Bloor St., by Maggie Steber,
courtesy of Maggie Steber

"Reason, Emotion, Pressure: There Is No Other Recipe."
The Village Voice (May 22, 1957): 4, 12. Copyright © 1957.
Reprinted by permission of *The Village Voice*.

"Downtown Is for People." *Fortune* (1958), copyright © 1958
Time Inc. All rights reserved. Reproduction in any manner
in any language in whole or in part without written

Index

Page numbers in *italics* refer to illustrations.

JANE JACOBS (1916–2006) was a writer who for more than forty years championed innovative, community-based approaches to urban planning. Her 1961 treatise, *The Death and Life of Great American Cities,* became perhaps the most influential text about the inner workings and failings of cities, inspiring generations of planners and activists.

ABOUT THE EDITORS

SAMUEL ZIPP is a writer and historian. He is the author of *Manhattan Projects: The Rise and Fall of Urban Renewal in Cold War New York,* which tells the larger history of the battles over urban renewal that propelled Jane Jacobs to national fame. He has written articles and reviews on urbanism and culture for *The New York Times, The Washington Post,* and *The Nation,* as well as other magazines and journals. He is associate professor of American studies and urban studies at Brown University.

NATHAN STORRING is a writer, curator, and designer who specializes in making contemporary urban design, planning, and policy accessible to the general public. He has served as acting curator of Urbanspace Gallery in Toronto (founded by colleagues of Jane Jacobs) and worked on permanent exhibits at the Chicago Architecture Foundation and the Boston Society of Architects. He has written for various outlets, including *Canadian Architect, Next City,* and the Metropolitan Revolution blog, and is a regular contributor to the Project for Public Spaces blog.

ABOUT THE TYPE

This book was set in Bembo, a typeface based on an old-style Roman face that was used for Cardinal Pietro Bembo's tract *De Aetna* in 1495. Bembo was cut by Francesco Griffo (1450–1518) in the early sixteenth century for Italian Renaissance printer and publisher Aldus Manutius (1449–1515). The Lanston Monotype Company of Philadelphia brought the well-proportioned letterforms of Bembo to the United States in the 1930s.